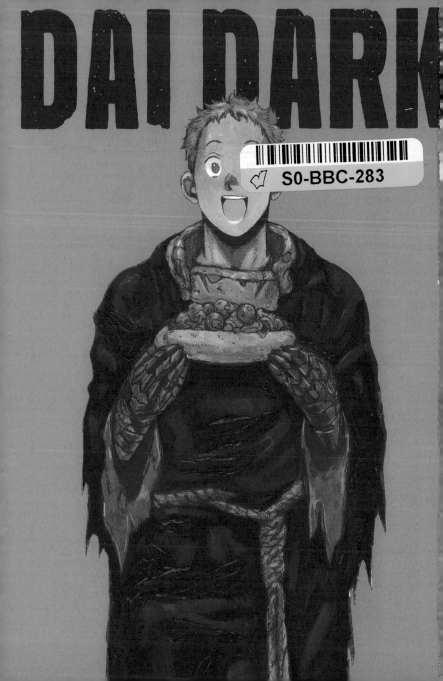

DAI DARK

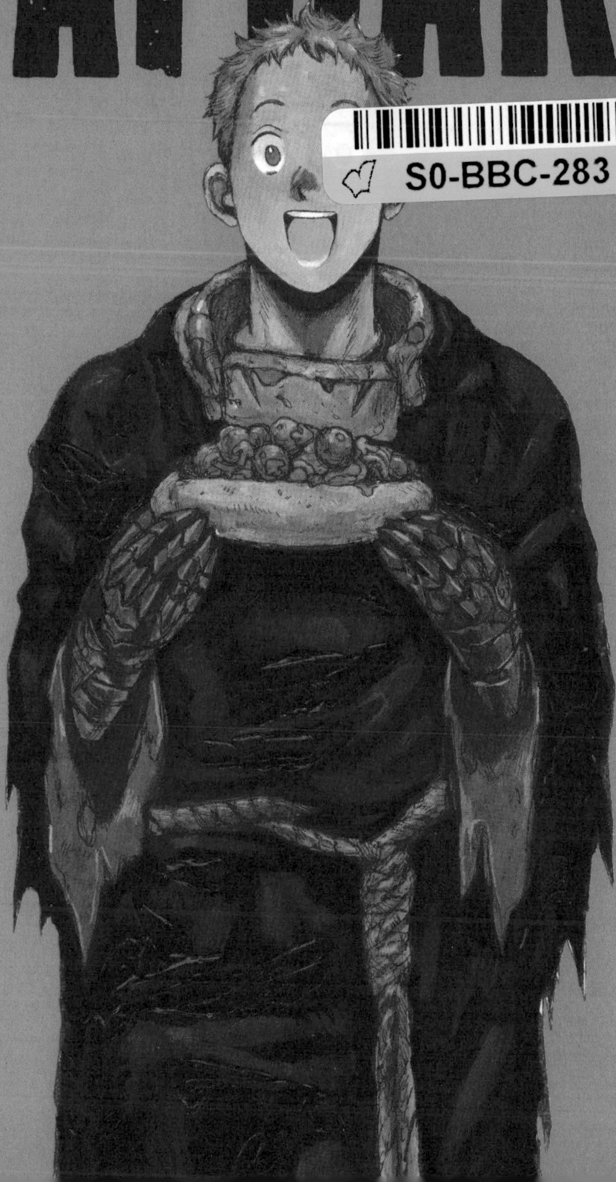

DAI DARK

DAI DARK ①

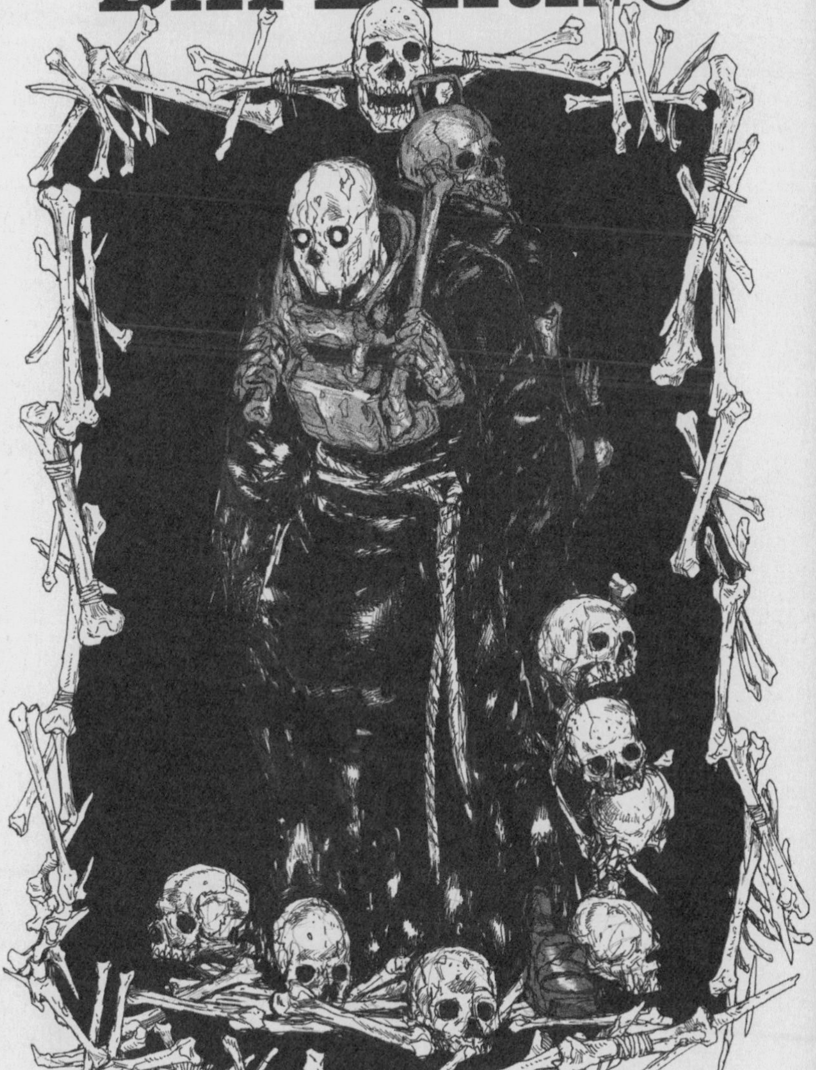

Q HAYASHIDA

Dai Dark, vol. 1

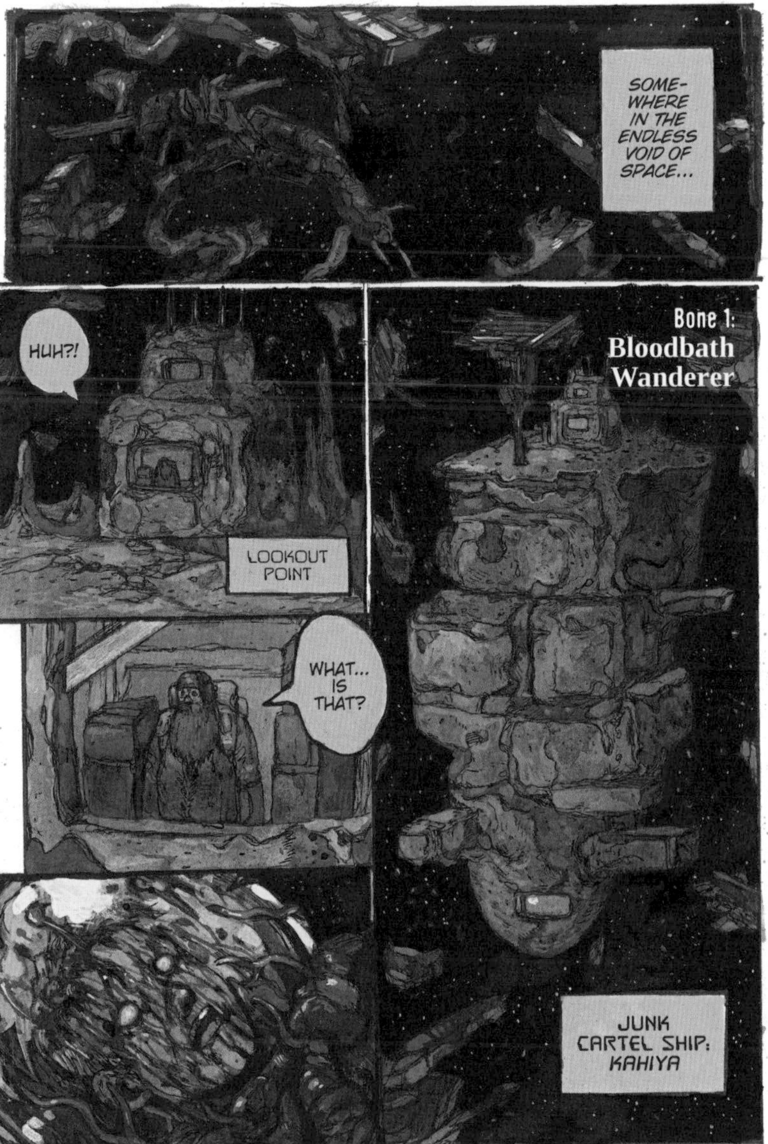
SOME-WHERE IN THE ENDLESS VOID OF SPACE...
Bone 1: Bloodbath Wanderer
JUNK CARTEL SHIP: KAHIYA
HUH?!
LOOKOUT POINT
WHAT... IS THAT?

Bone 1: Bloodbath Wanderer

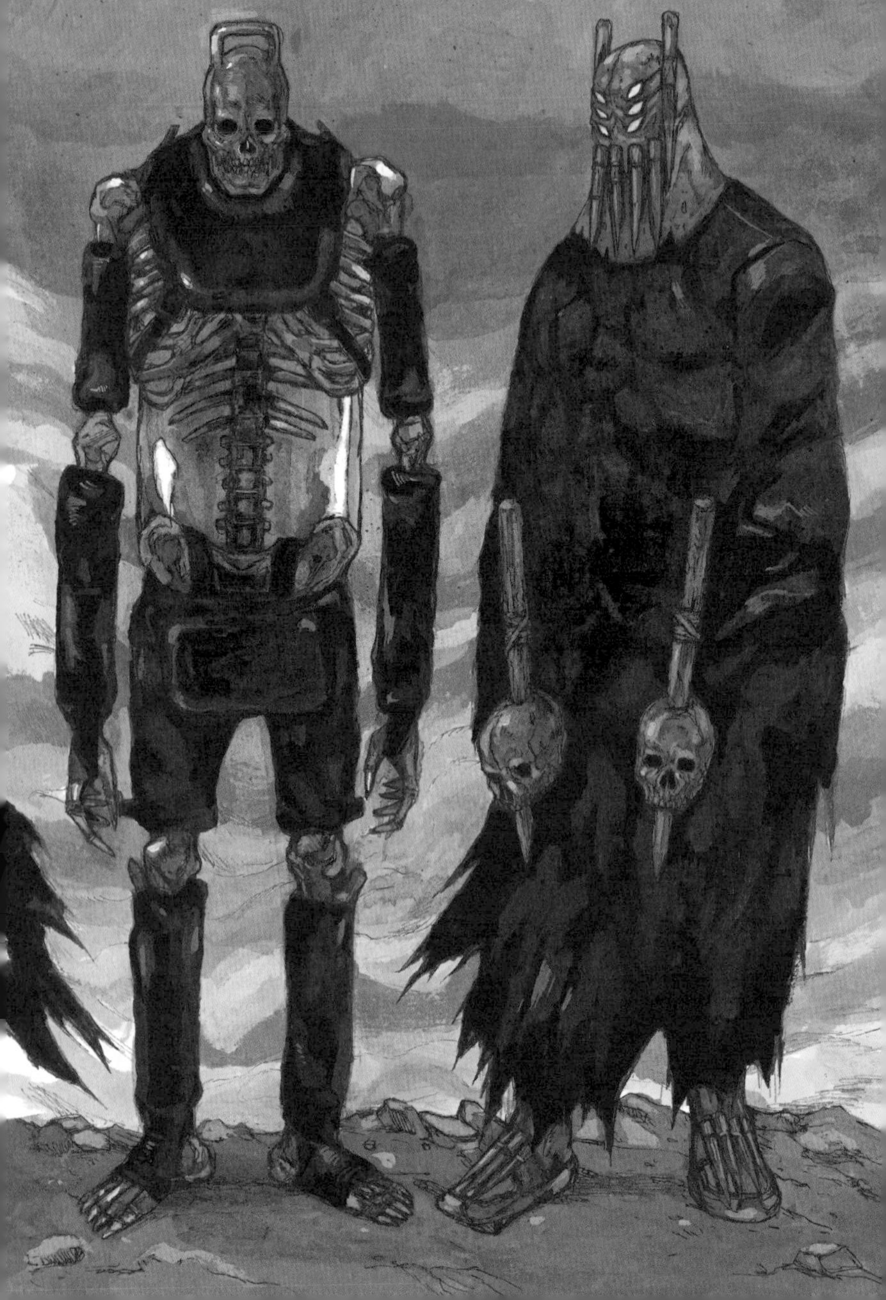

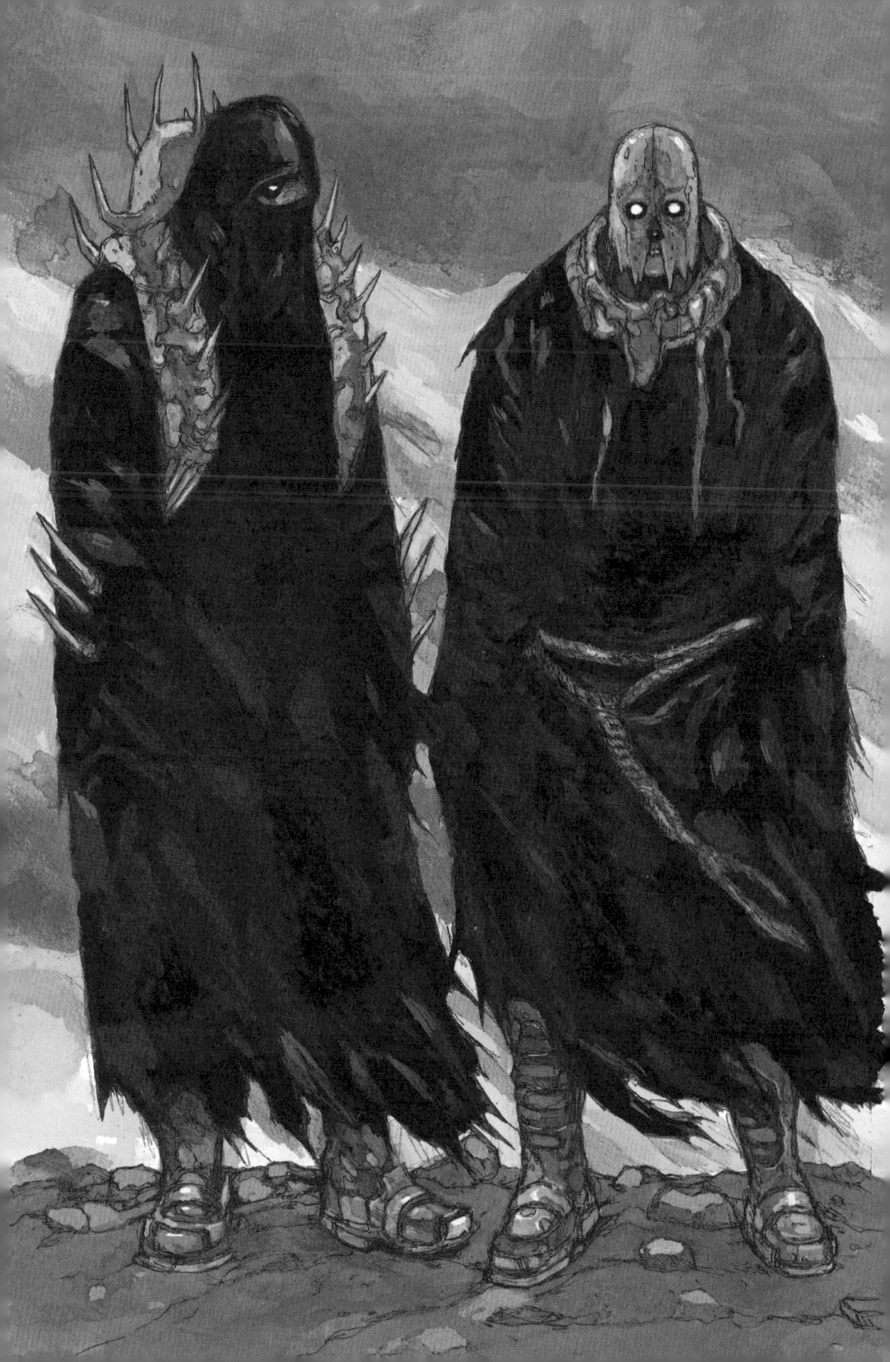

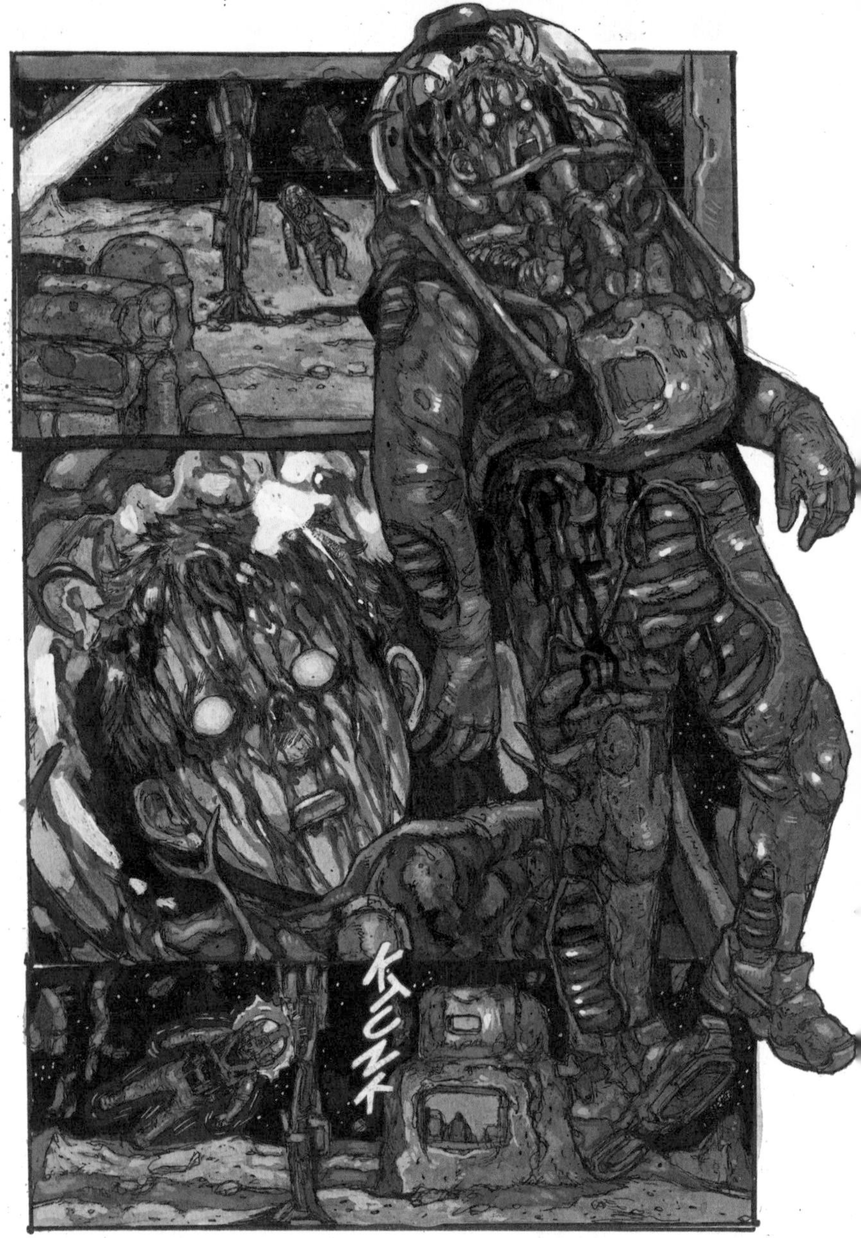
KTUNK

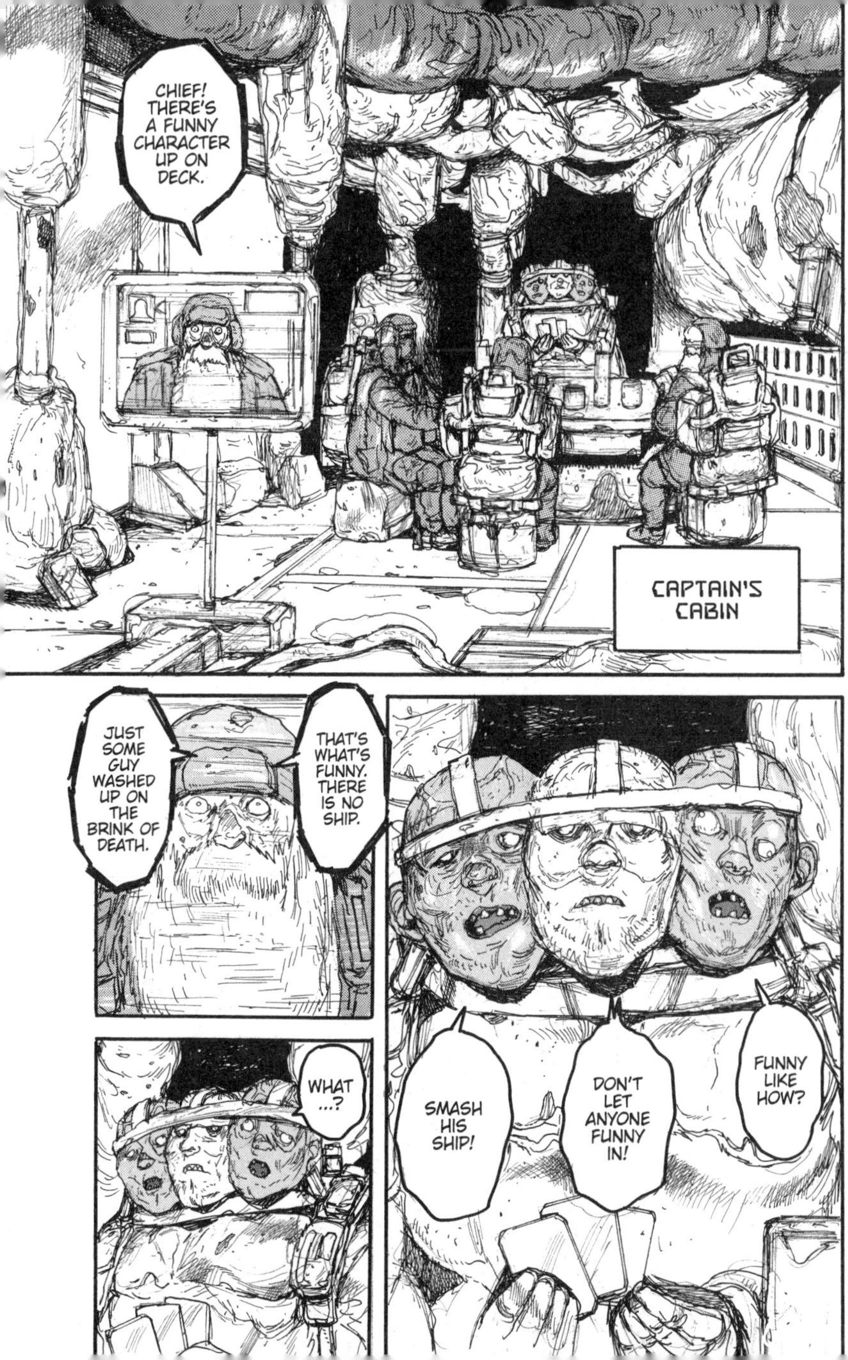
CHIEF! THERE'S A FUNNY CHARACTER UP ON DECK.
CAPTAIN'S CABIN
FUNNY LIKE HOW?
DON'T LET ANYONE FUNNY IN!
SMASH HIS SHIP!
THAT'S WHAT'S FUNNY. THERE IS NO SHIP.
JUST SOME GUY WASHED UP ON THE BRINK OF DEATH.
WHAT ...?

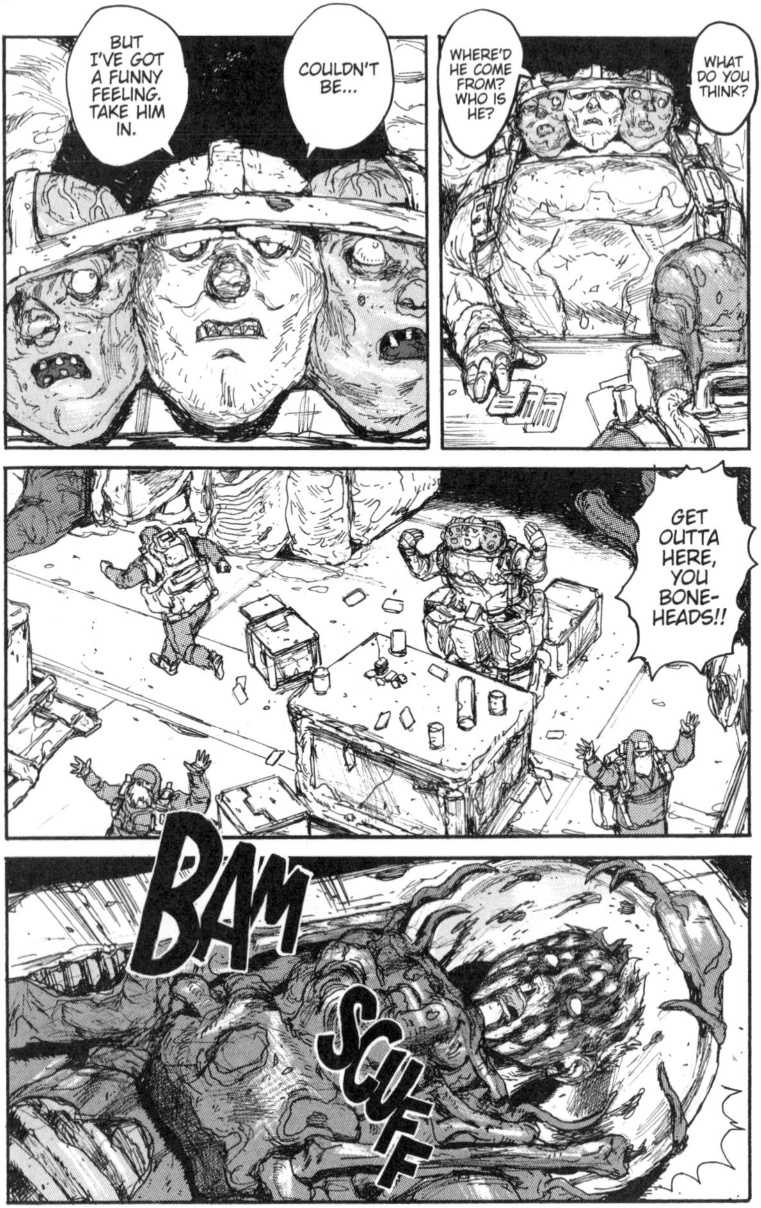
WHAT DO YOU THINK?
WHERE'D HE COME FROM? WHO IS HE?
COULDN'T BE...
BUT I'VE GOT A FUNNY FEELING. TAKE HIM IN.
GET OUTTA HERE, YOU BONE-HEADS!!
BAM
SCUFF

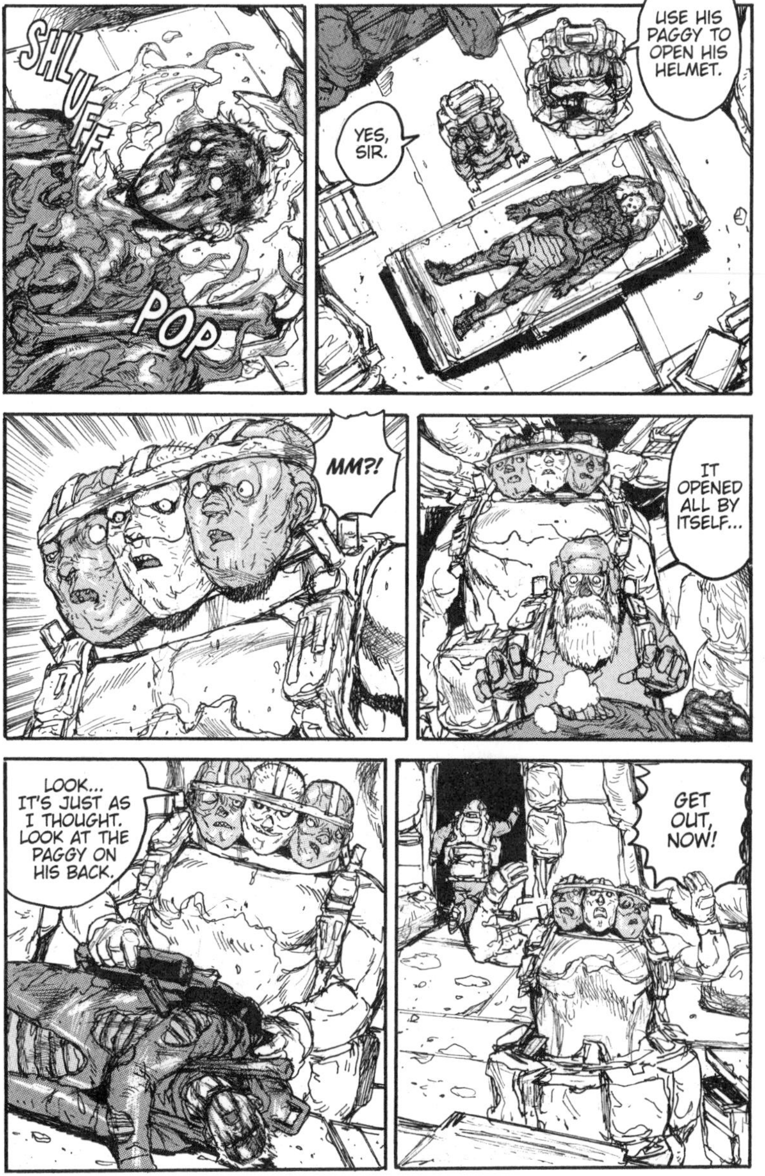
USE HIS PAGGY TO OPEN HIS HELMET.
YES, SIR.
SHLUFF
POP
IT OPENED ALL BY ITSELF...
MM?!
GET OUT, NOW!
LOOK... IT'S JUST AS I THOUGHT. LOOK AT THE PAGGY ON HIS BACK.

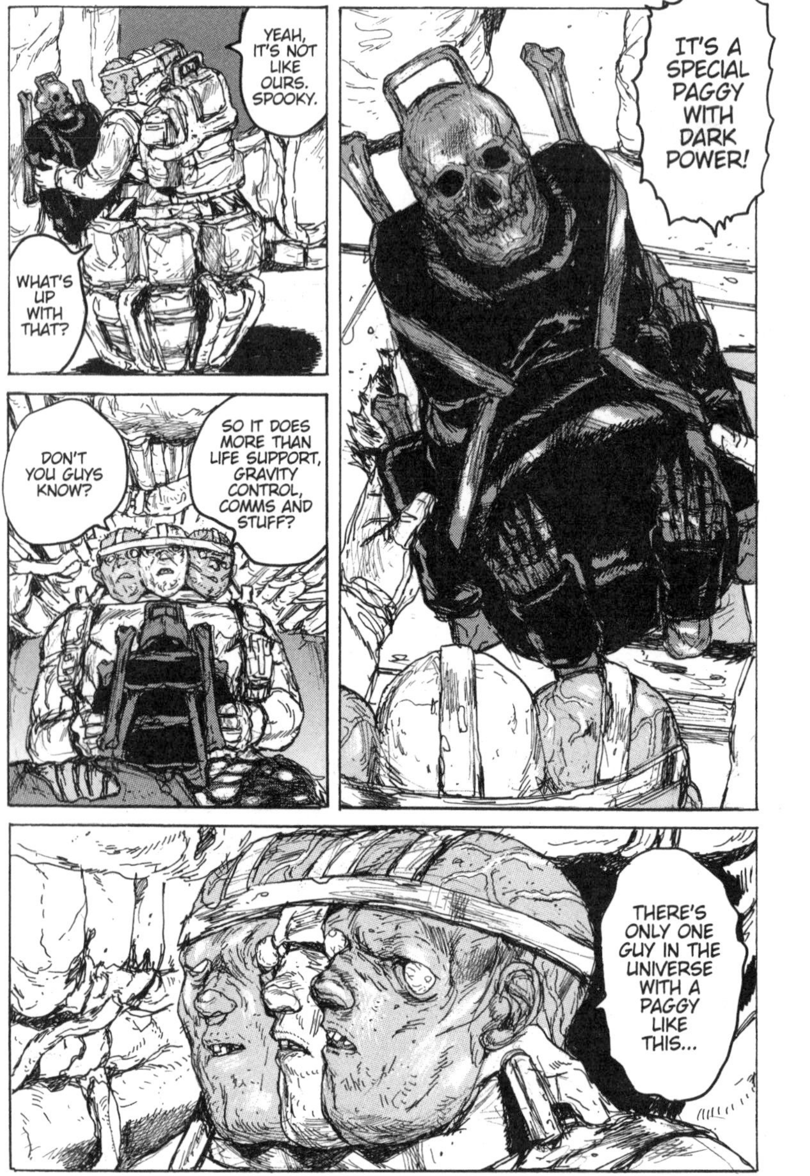
IT'S A SPECIAL PAGGY WITH DARK POWER!
YEAH, IT'S NOT LIKE OURS. SPOOKY.
WHAT'S UP WITH THAT?
SO IT DOES MORE THAN LIFE SUPPORT, GRAVITY CONTROL, COMMS AND STUFF?
DON'T YOU GUYS KNOW?
THERE'S ONLY ONE GUY IN THE UNIVERSE WITH A PAGGY LIKE THIS...

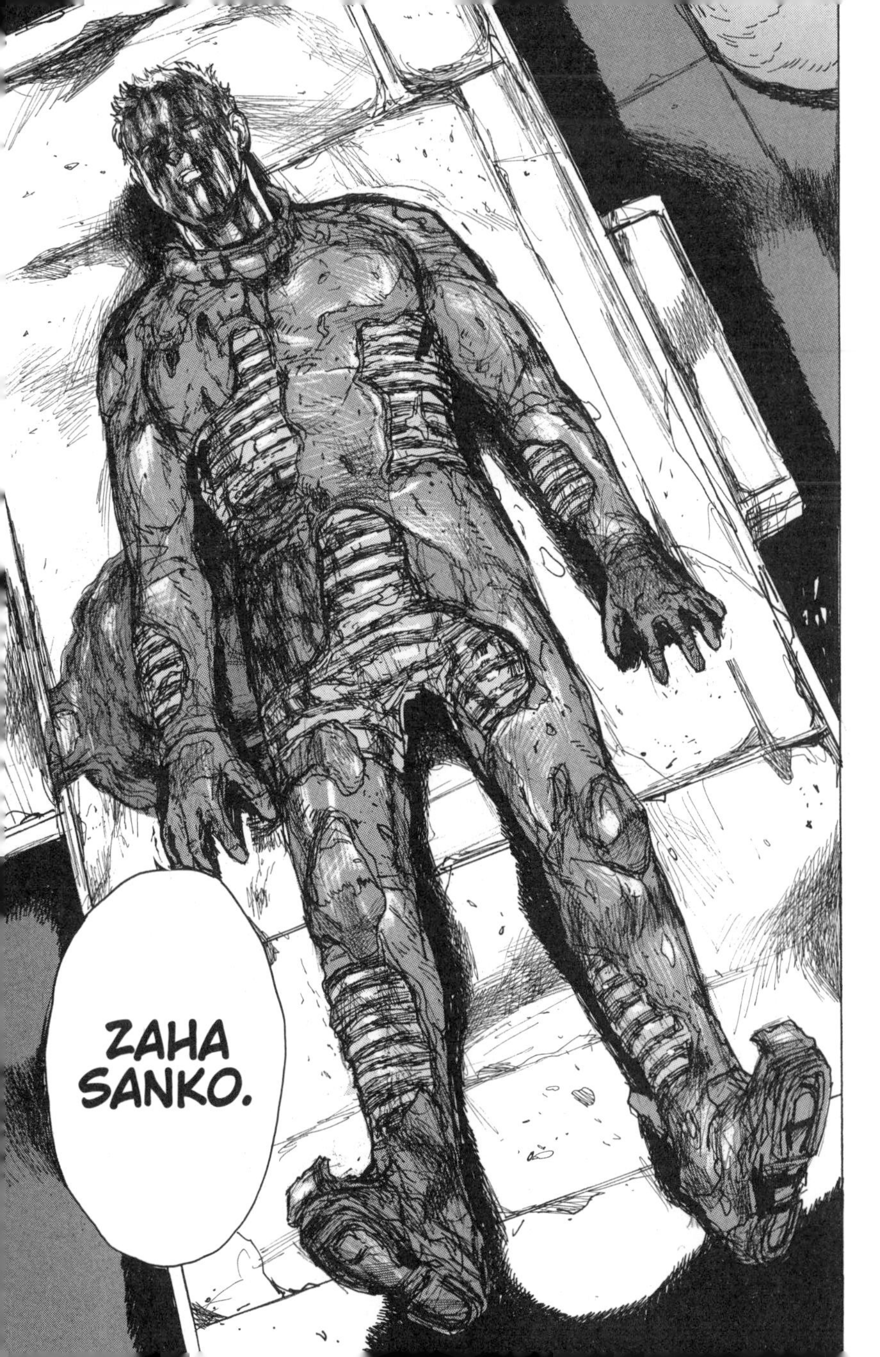
ZAHA SANKO.

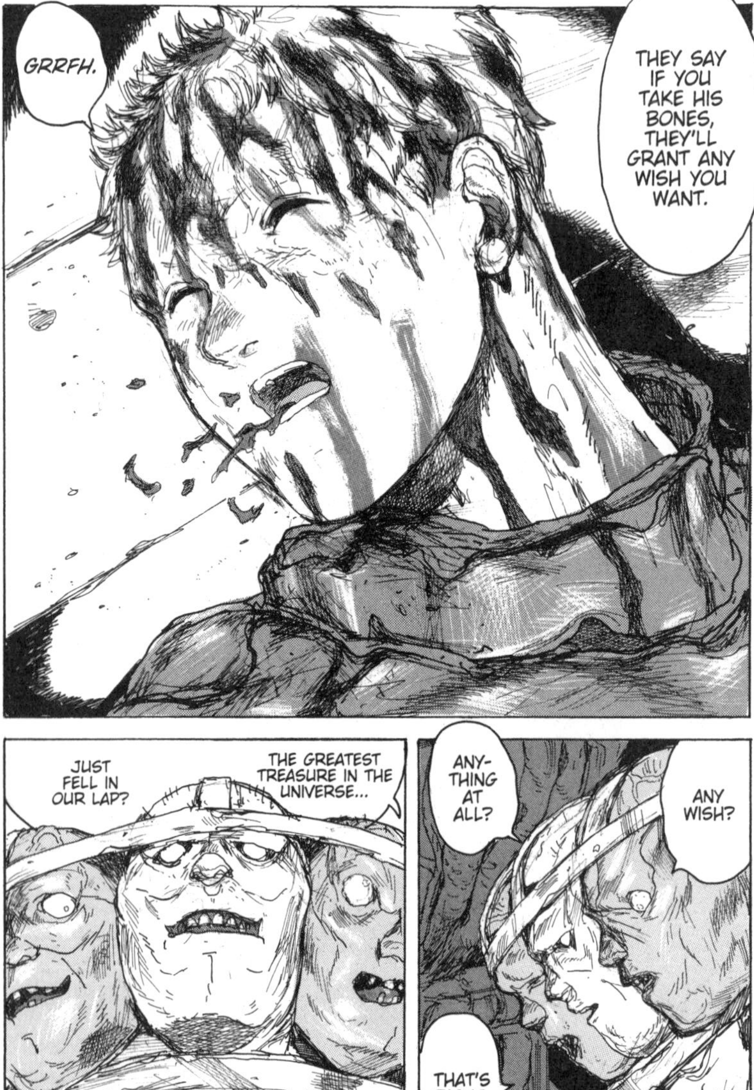
THEY SAY IF YOU TAKE HIS BONES, THEY'LL GRANT ANY WISH YOU WANT.
GRRFH.
ANY WISH?
ANY-THING AT ALL?
THAT'S RIGHT.
THE GREATEST TREASURE IN THE UNIVERSE...
JUST FELL IN OUR LAP?

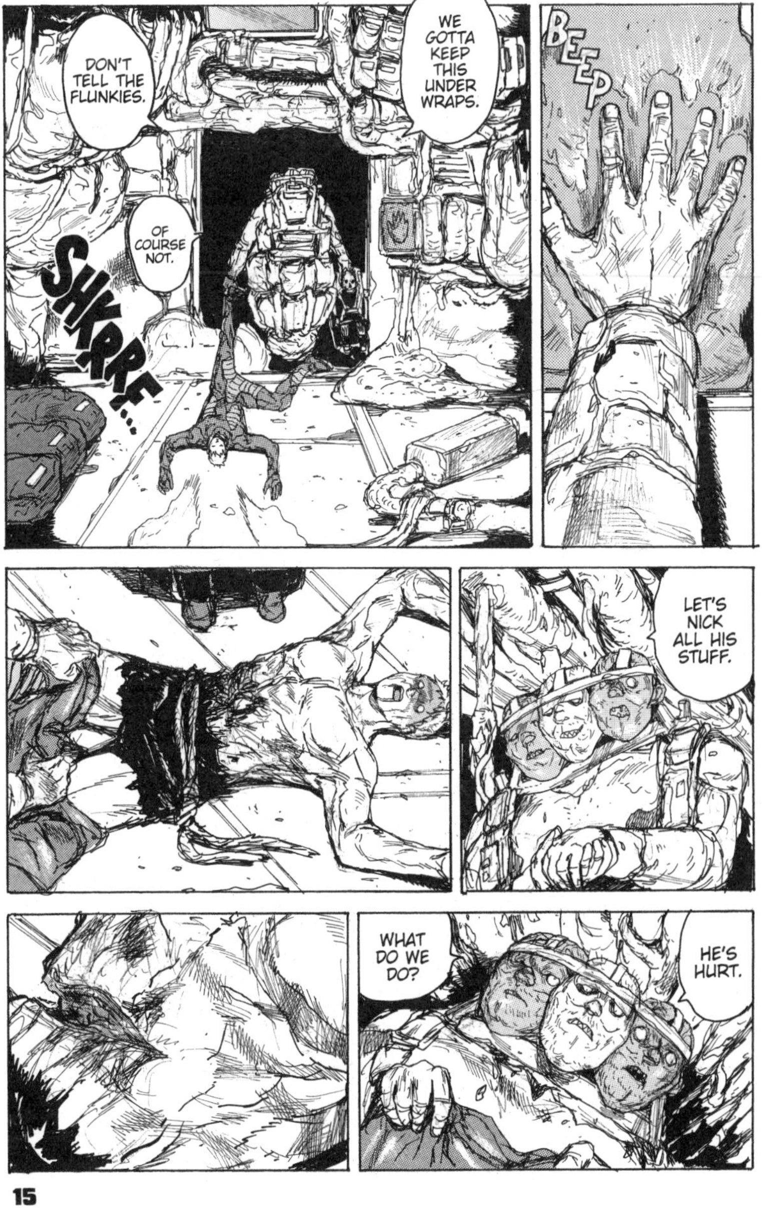
BEEP
WE GOTTA KEEP THIS UNDER WRAPS.
DON'T TELL THE FLUNKIES.
OF COURSE NOT.
SHKRF...
LET'S NICK ALL HIS STUFF.
HE'S HURT.
WHAT DO WE DO?

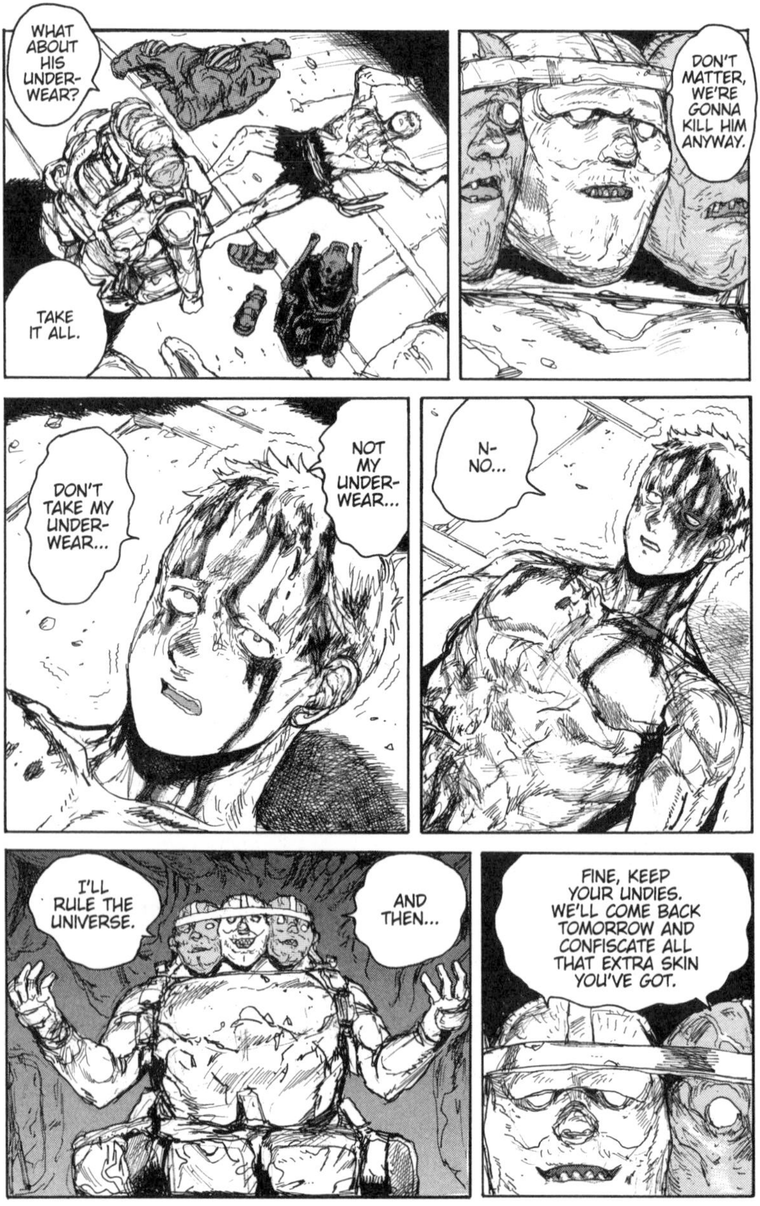
DON'T MATTER, WE'RE GONNA KILL HIM ANYWAY.
WHAT ABOUT HIS UNDER-WEAR?
TAKE IT ALL.
N-NO...
NOT MY UNDER-WEAR...
DON'T TAKE MY UNDER-WEAR...
FINE, KEEP YOUR UNDIES. WE'LL COME BACK TOMORROW AND CONFISCATE ALL THAT EXTRA SKIN YOU'VE GOT.
AND THEN...
I'LL RULE THE UNIVERSE.

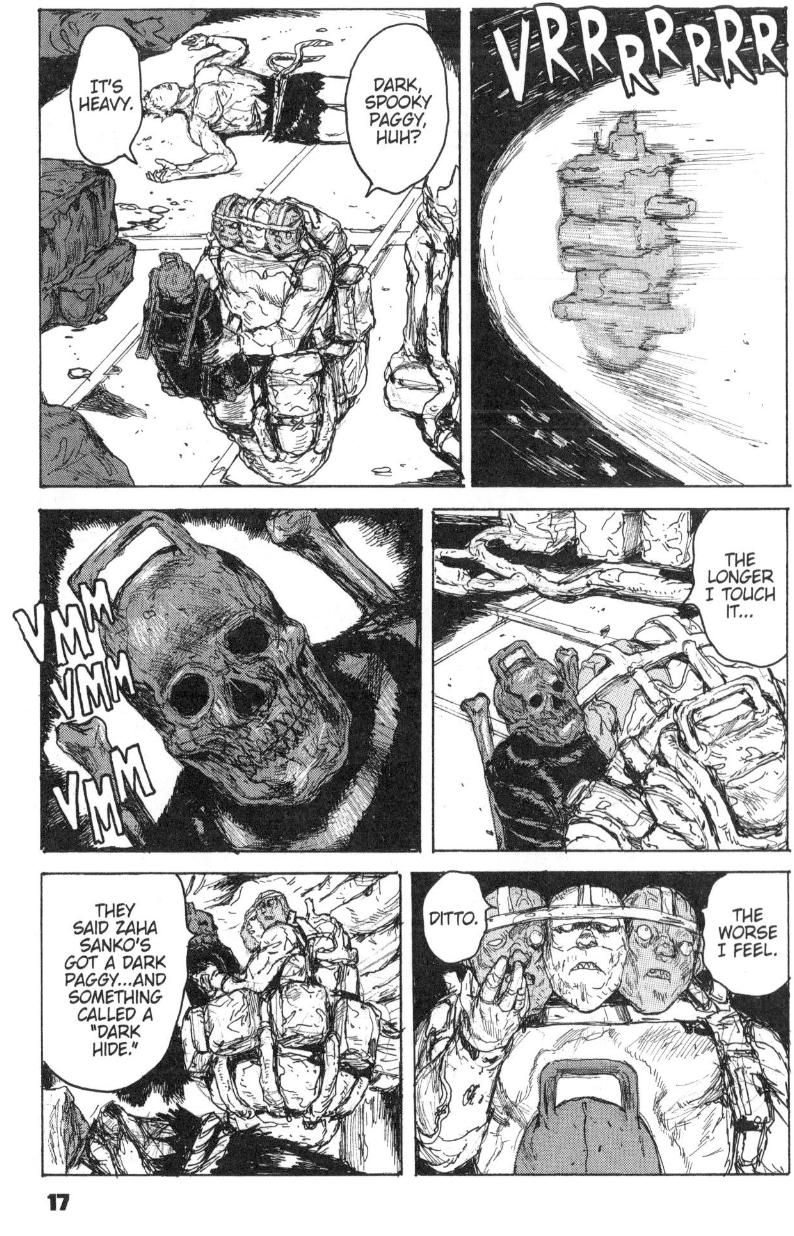
VRRRRRRR
DARK, SPOOKY PAGGY, HUH?
IT'S HEAVY.
THE LONGER I TOUCH IT...
VMM VMM VMM
THE WORSE I FEEL.
DITTO.
THEY SAID ZAHA SANKO'S GOT A DARK PAGGY...AND SOMETHING CALLED A "DARK HIDE."

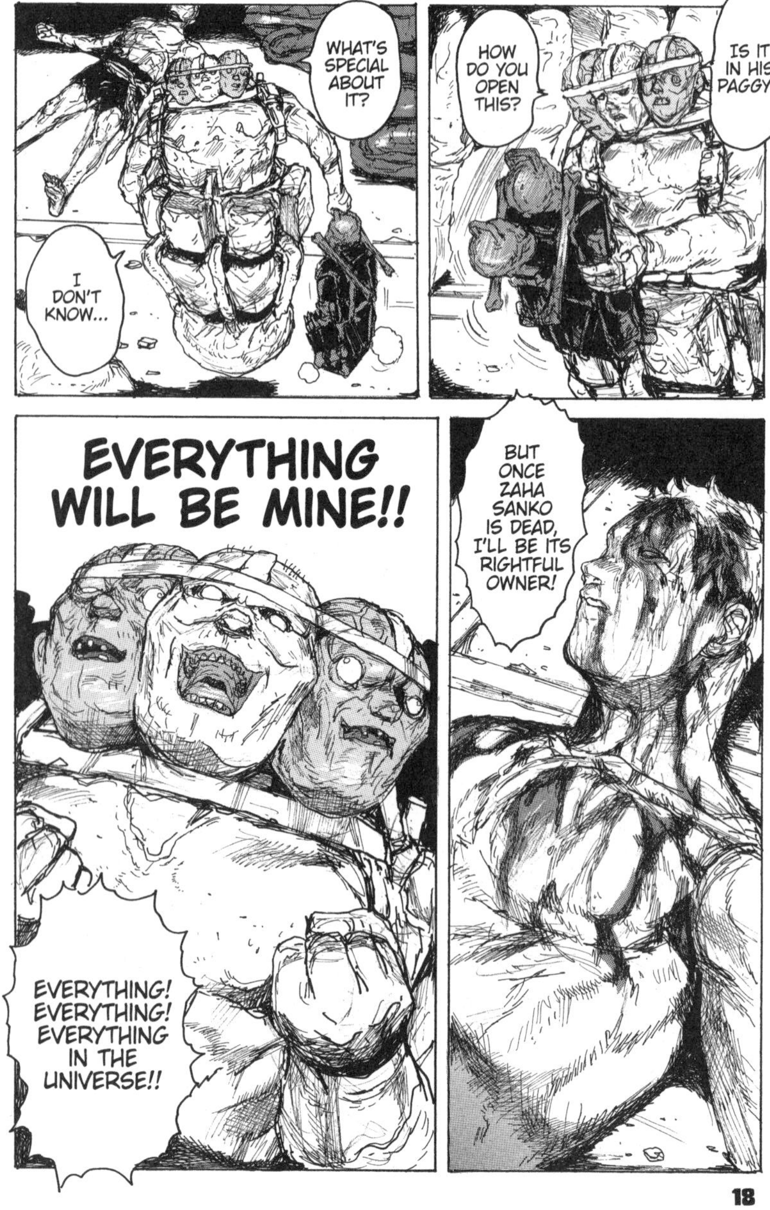
IS IT IN HIS PAGGY?
HOW DO YOU OPEN THIS?
WHAT'S SPECIAL ABOUT IT?
I DON'T KNOW...
BUT ONCE ZAHA SANKO IS DEAD, I'LL BE ITS RIGHTFUL OWNER!
EVERYTHING WILL BE MINE!!
EVERYTHING! EVERYTHING! EVERYTHING IN THE UNIVERSE!!

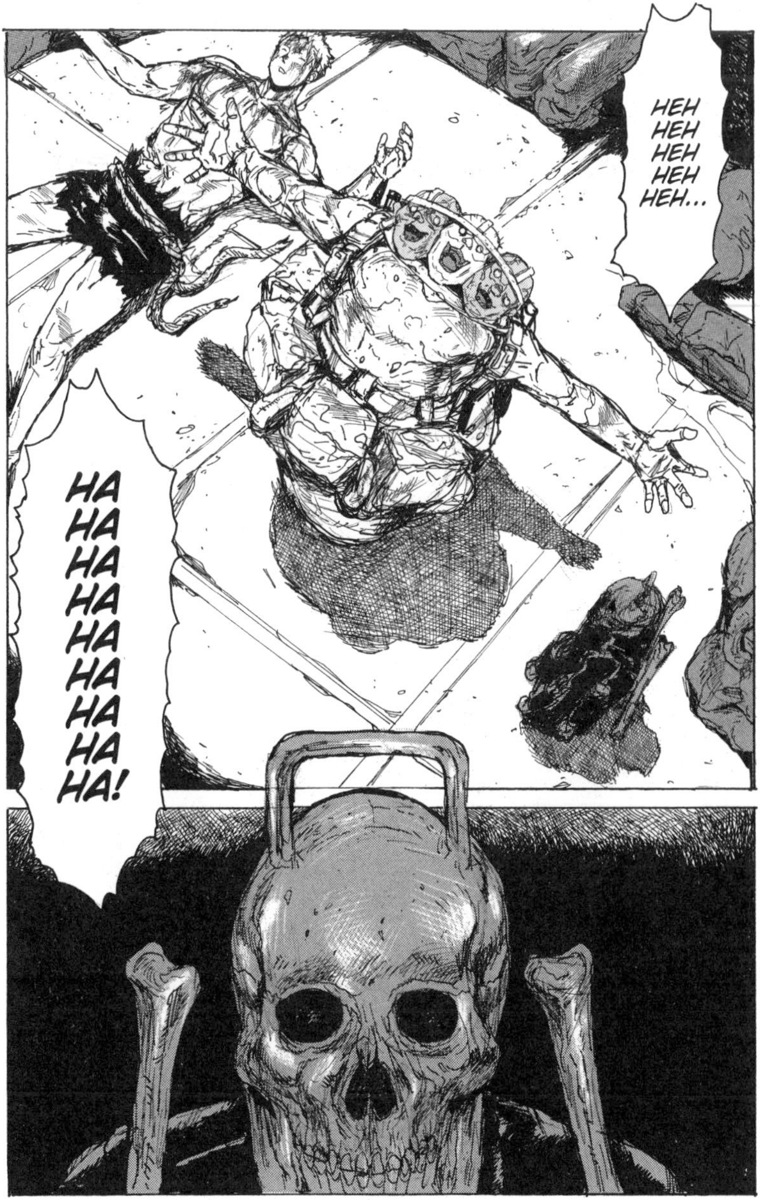
HEH HEH HEH HEH HEH...
HA HA HA HA HA HA HA HA HA HA!

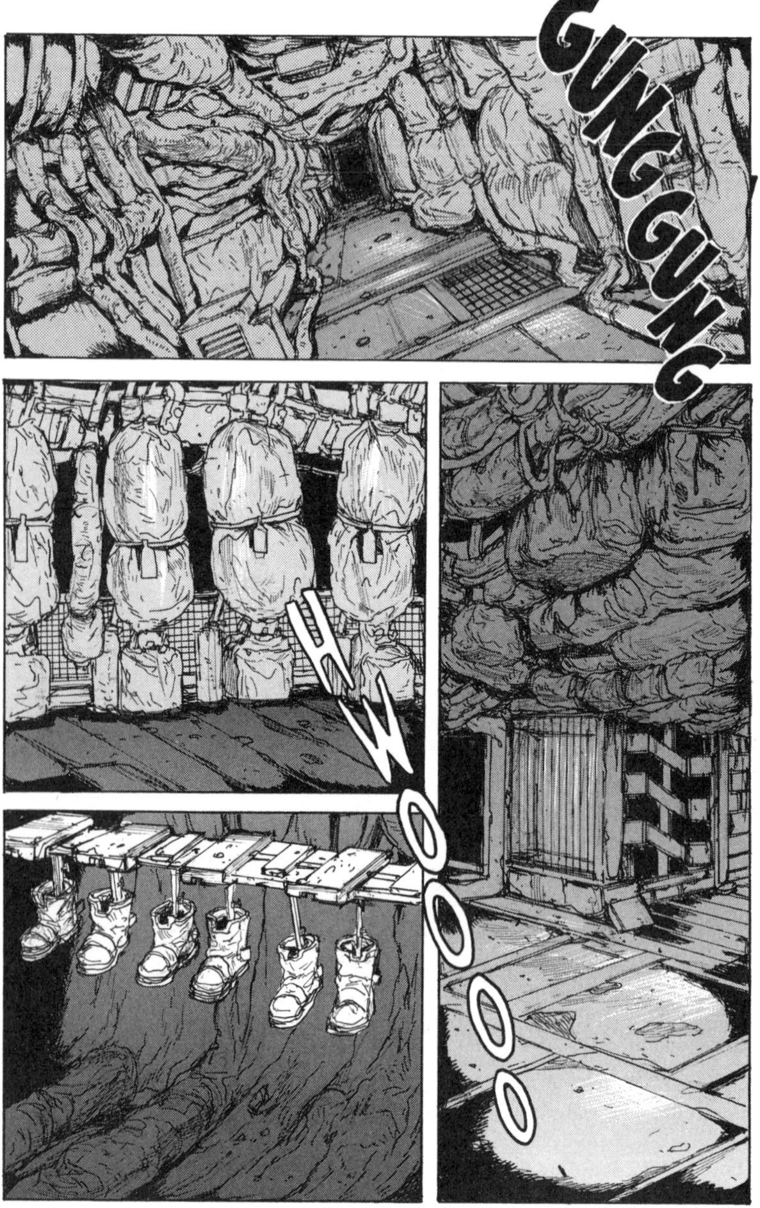
GUNGUNG
HZZOOOOOO

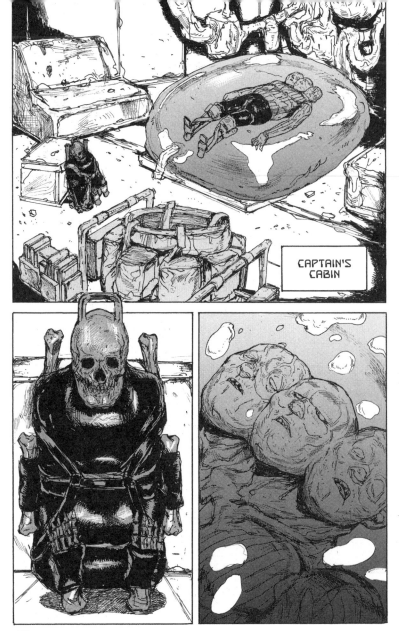

CAPTAIN'S
CABIN

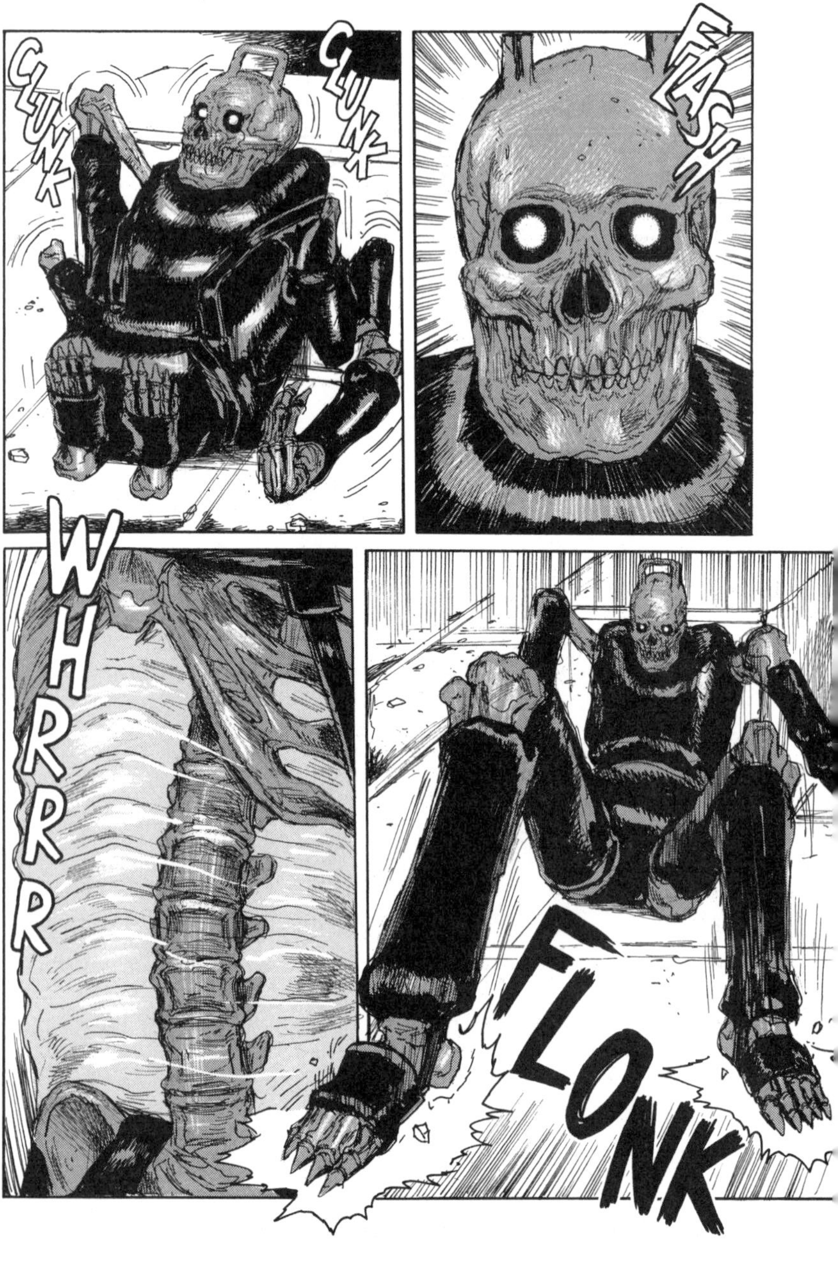
FLASH
CLUNK
CLUNK
FLONK
WHRRRR

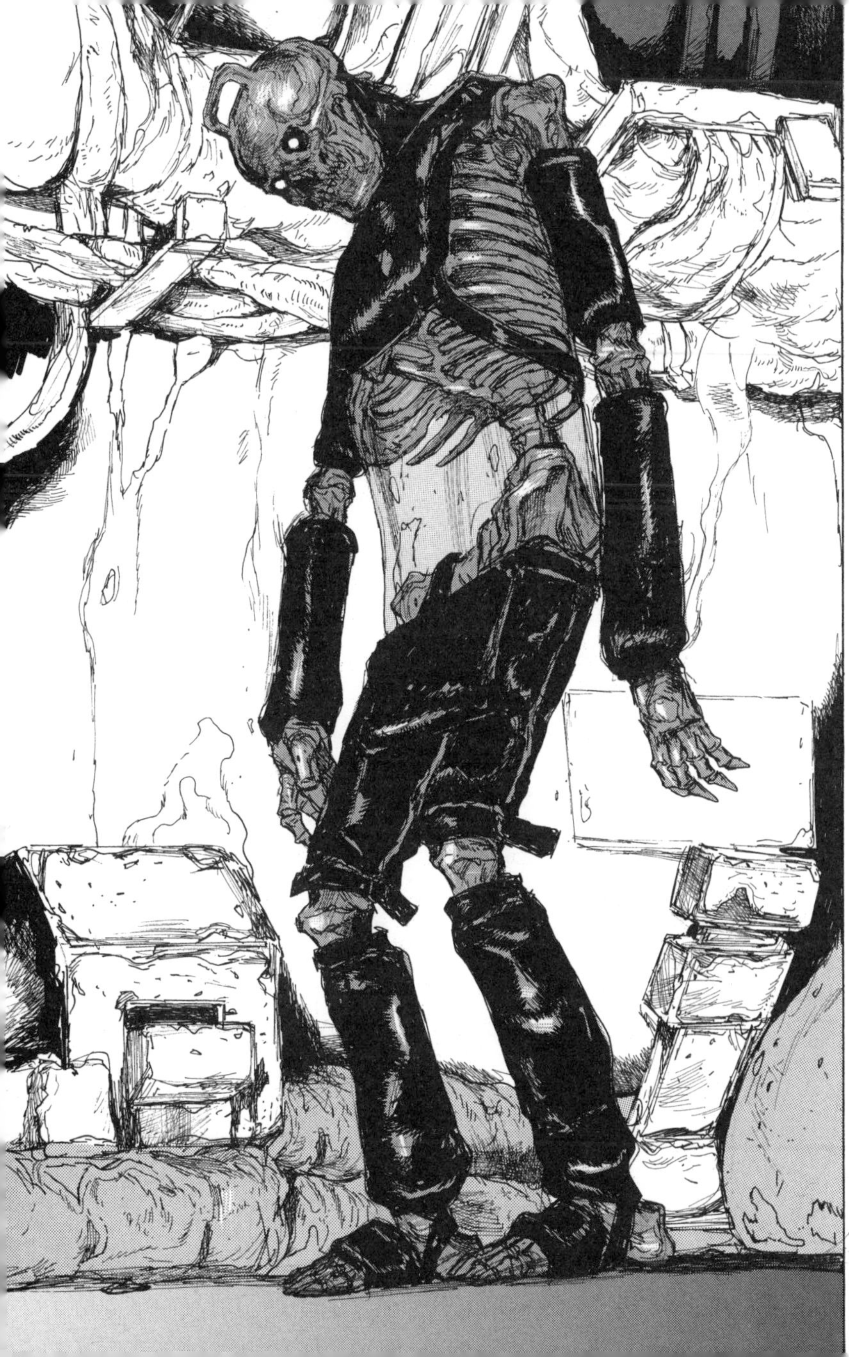

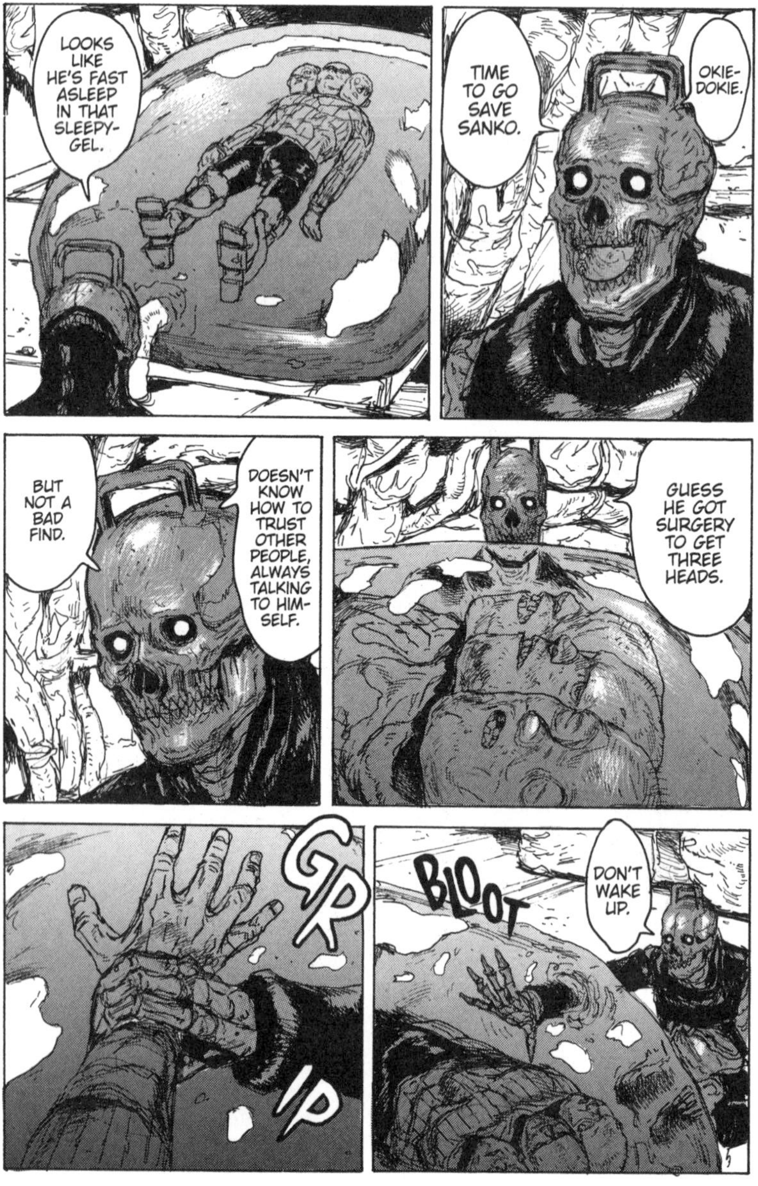
OKIE-DOKIE.
TIME TO GO SAVE SANKO.
LOOKS LIKE HE'S FAST ASLEEP IN THAT SLEEPY-GEL.
GUESS HE GOT SURGERY TO GET THREE HEADS.
DOESN'T KNOW HOW TO TRUST OTHER PEOPLE, ALWAYS TALKING TO HIM-SELF.
BUT NOT A BAD FIND.
DON'T WAKE UP.
BLOOT
GR
IP

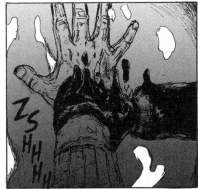

COME, DARK FLESH.

LOOKS LIKE WE'RE IN HYPER-DRIVE...

GUESS THESE GUYS LIVE SCAVENGING JUNK AND RAIDING MERCHANT SHIPS.

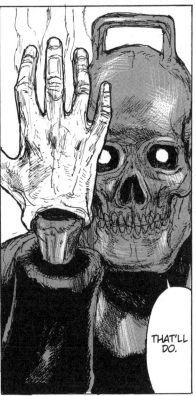

THAT'LL DO.

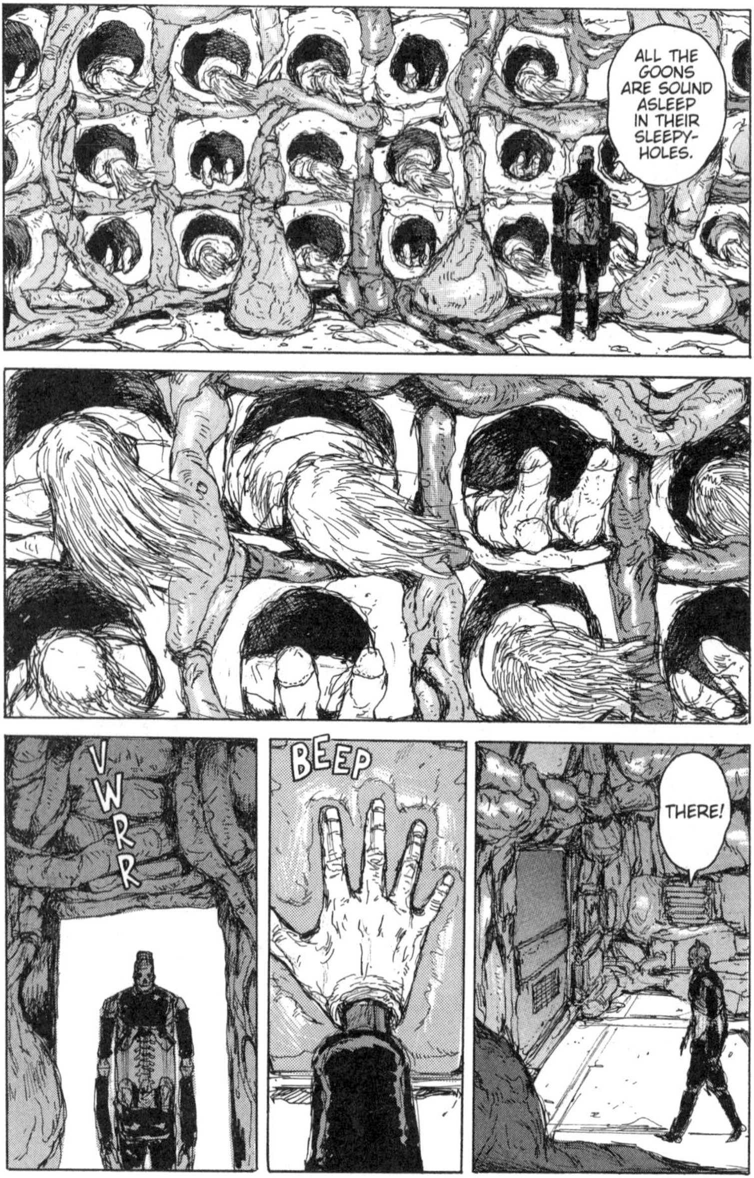
ALL THE GOONS ARE SOUND ASLEEP IN THEIR SLEEPY-HOLES.
THERE!
BEEP
VWRR

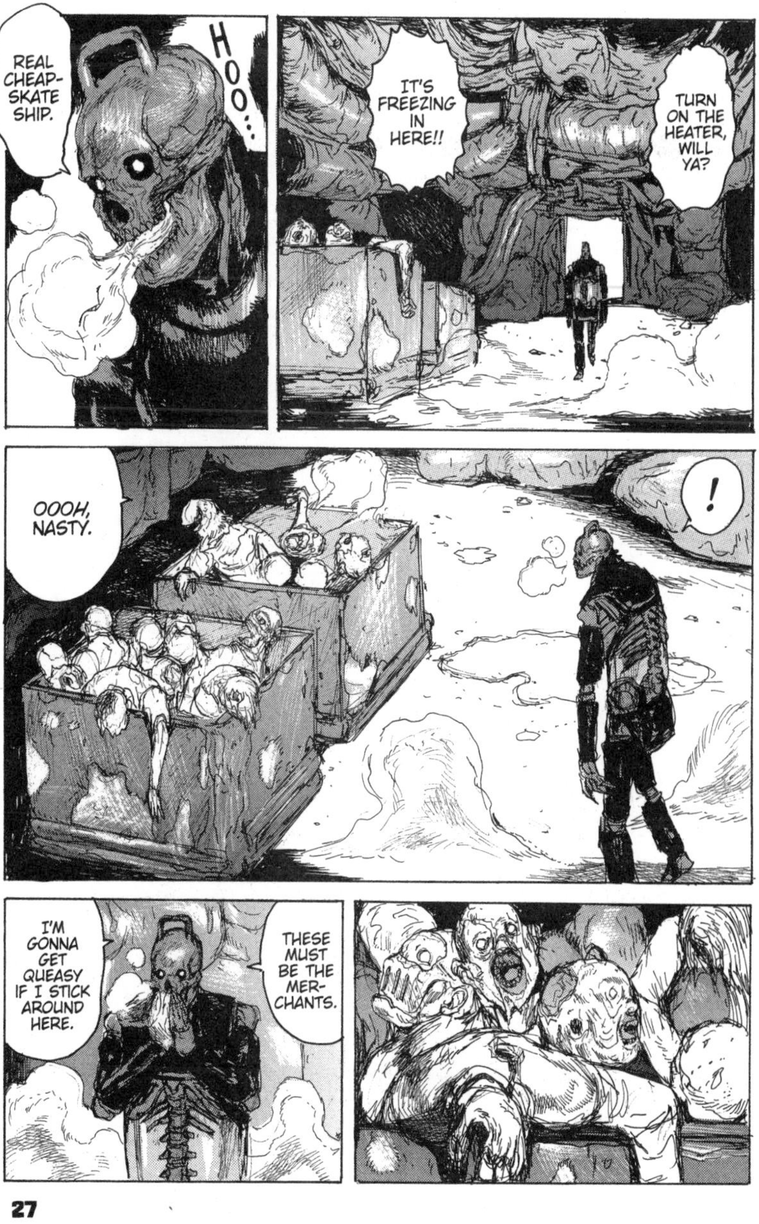
TURN ON THE HEATER, WILL YA?
IT'S FREEZING IN HERE!!
HOO...
REAL CHEAP-SKATE SHIP.
!
OOOH, NASTY.
THESE MUST BE THE MER-CHANTS.
I'M GONNA GET QUEASY IF I STICK AROUND HERE.

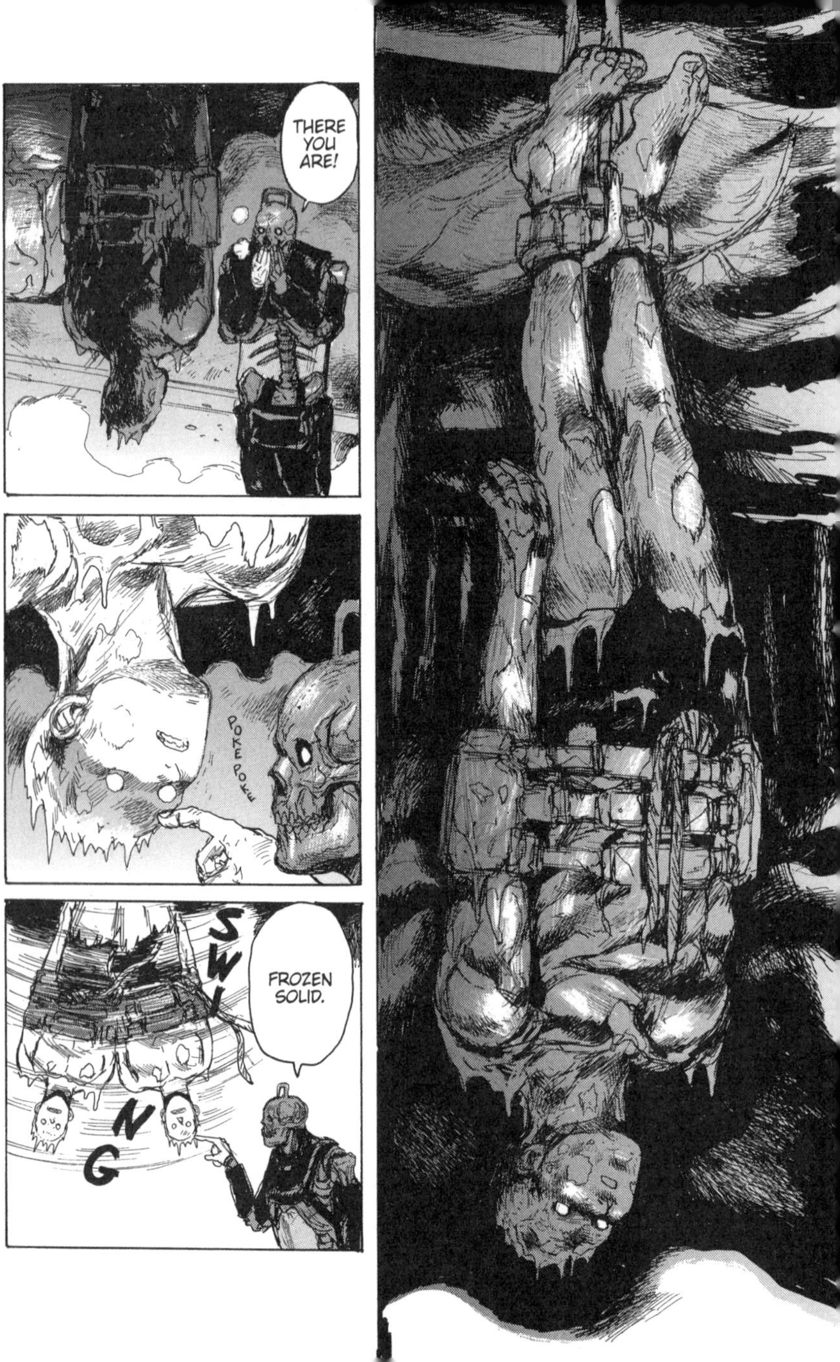
THERE YOU ARE!
POKE POKE
FROZEN SOLID.
SWING

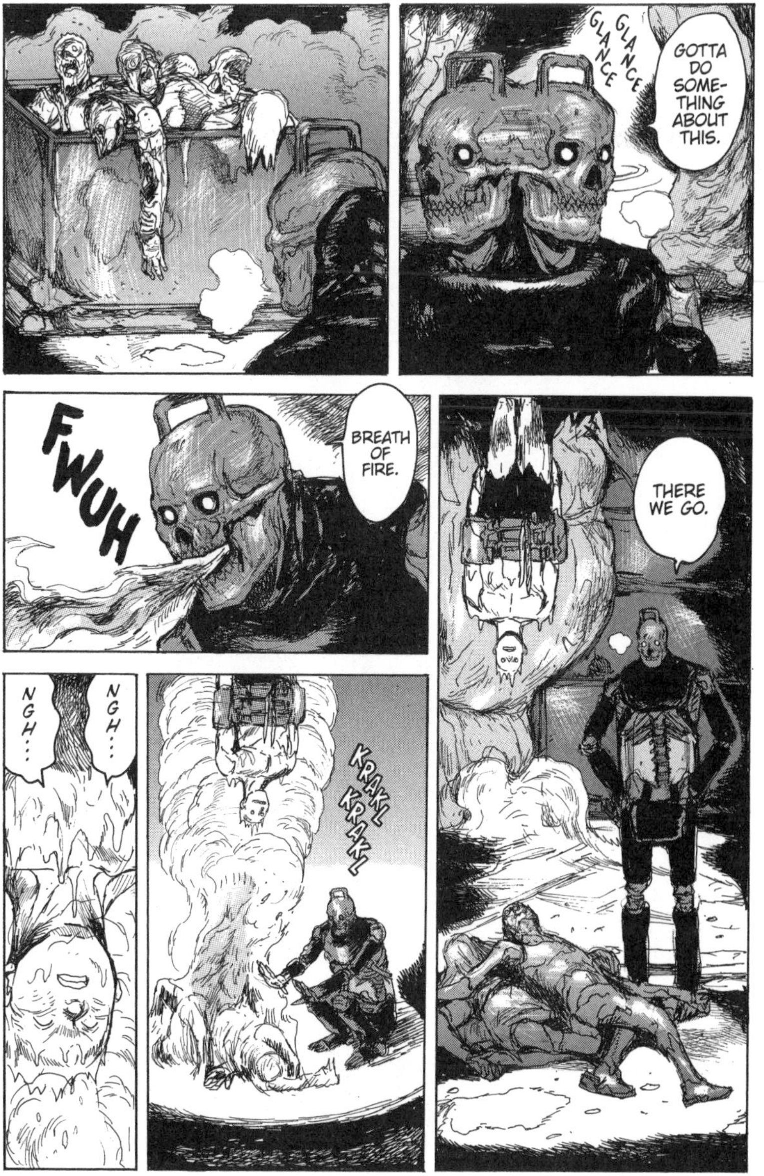

GOTTA DO SOME-THING ABOUT THIS.
GLANCE GLANCE
THERE WE GO.
BREATH OF FIRE.
FWUH
KRAKL KRAKL
NGH...
NGH...

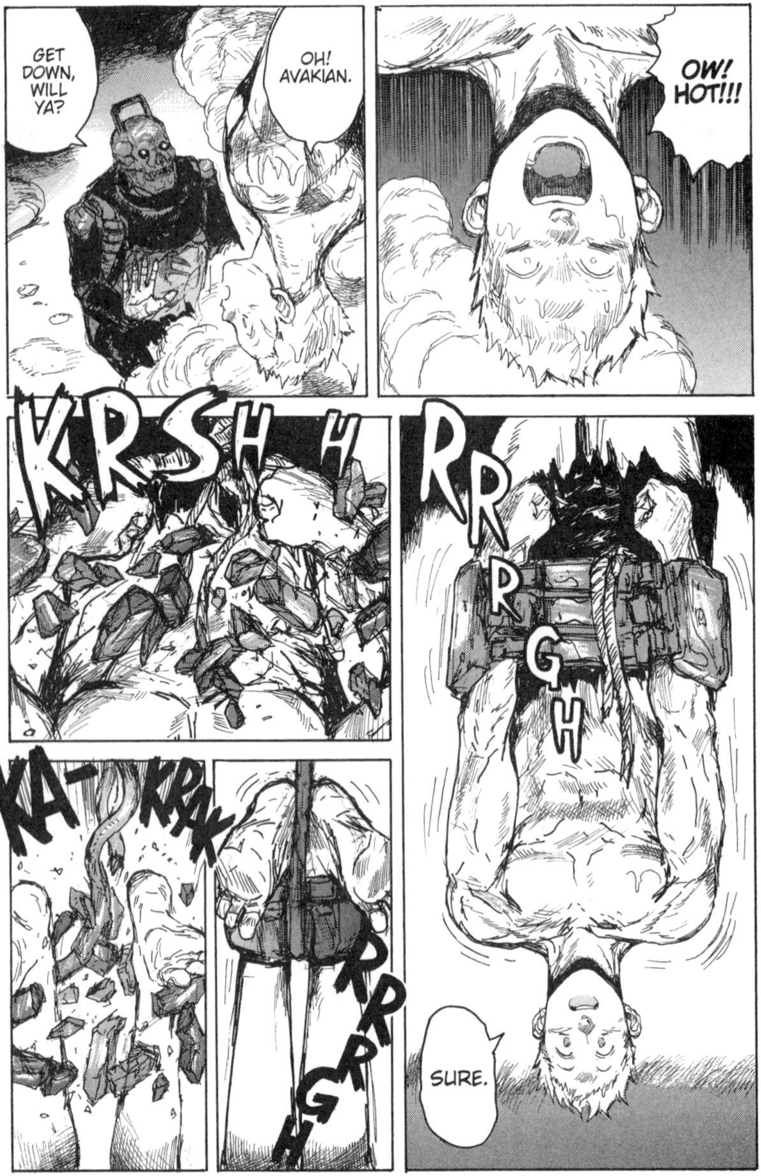
OW! HOT!!!
OH! AVAKIAN.
GET DOWN, WILL YA?
RRRGH
SURE.
KRSHHH
RRRGH
KA-KRAK

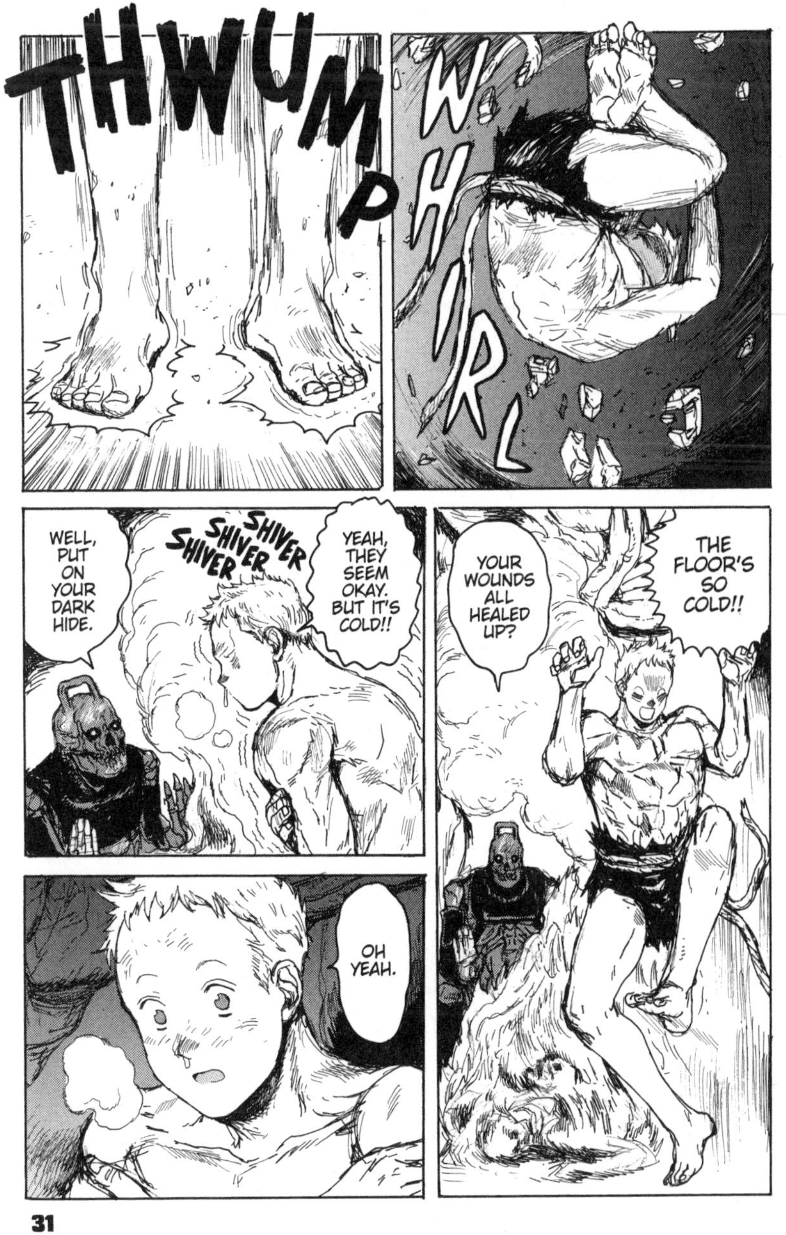
WHIRL
THWUMP
THE FLOOR'S SO COLD!!
YOUR WOUNDS ALL HEALED UP?
YEAH, THEY SEEM OKAY. BUT IT'S COLD!!
SHIVER SHIVER
WELL, PUT ON YOUR DARK HIDE.
OH YEAH.

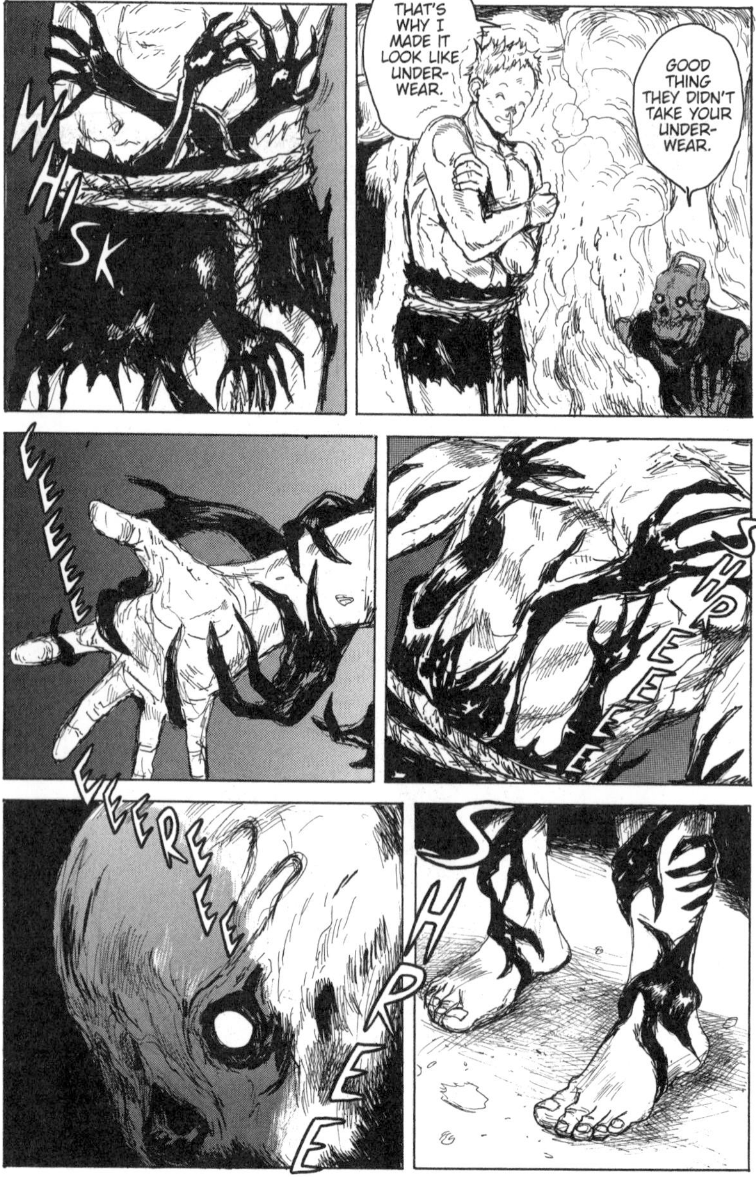
GOOD THING THEY DIDN'T TAKE YOUR UNDER-WEAR.
THAT'S WHY I MADE IT LOOK LIKE UNDER-WEAR.
WHISK
SHREEEEEE
EEEEEE
SHREEE
EEEREEEE

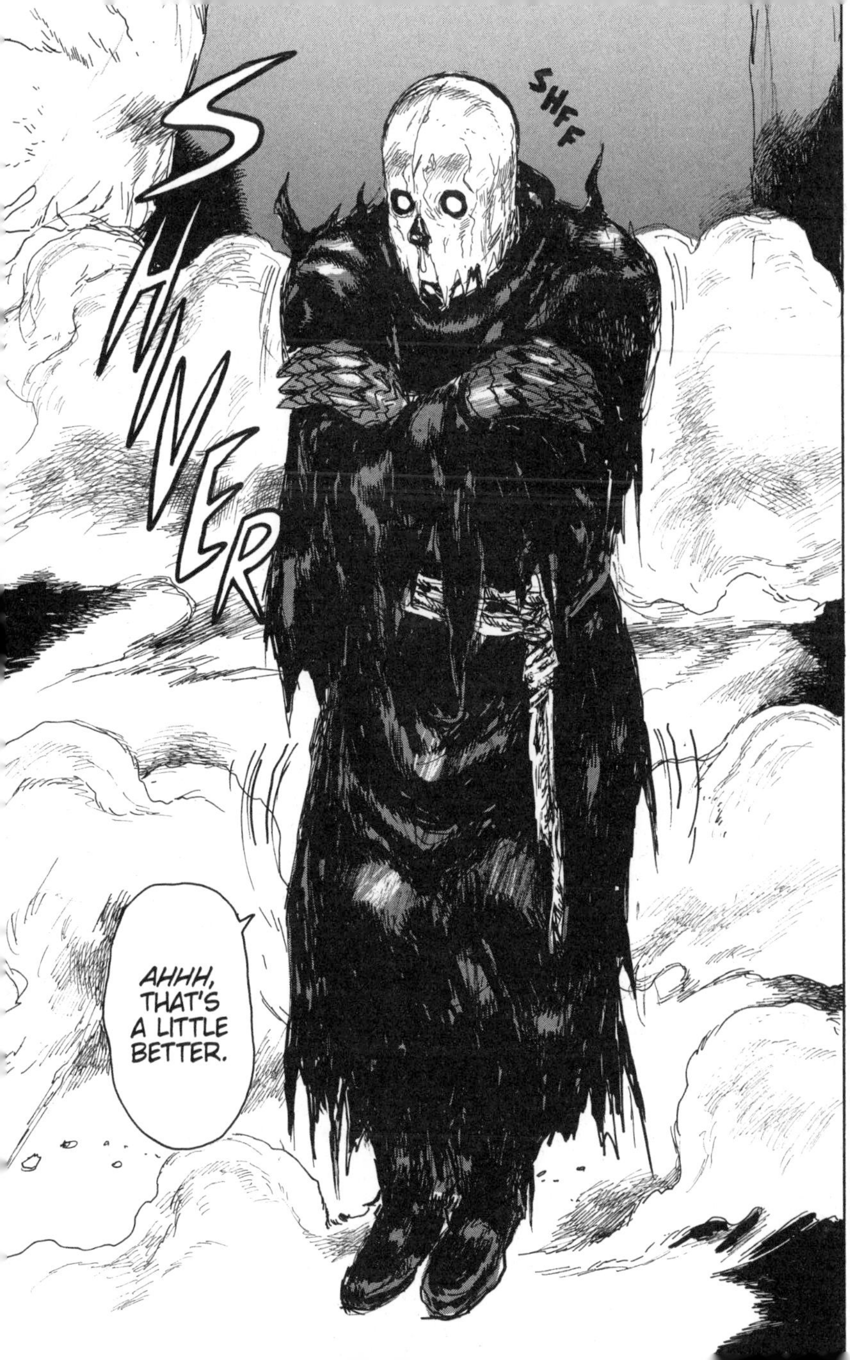
SHFF
SHIVER
AHHH, THAT'S A LITTLE BETTER.

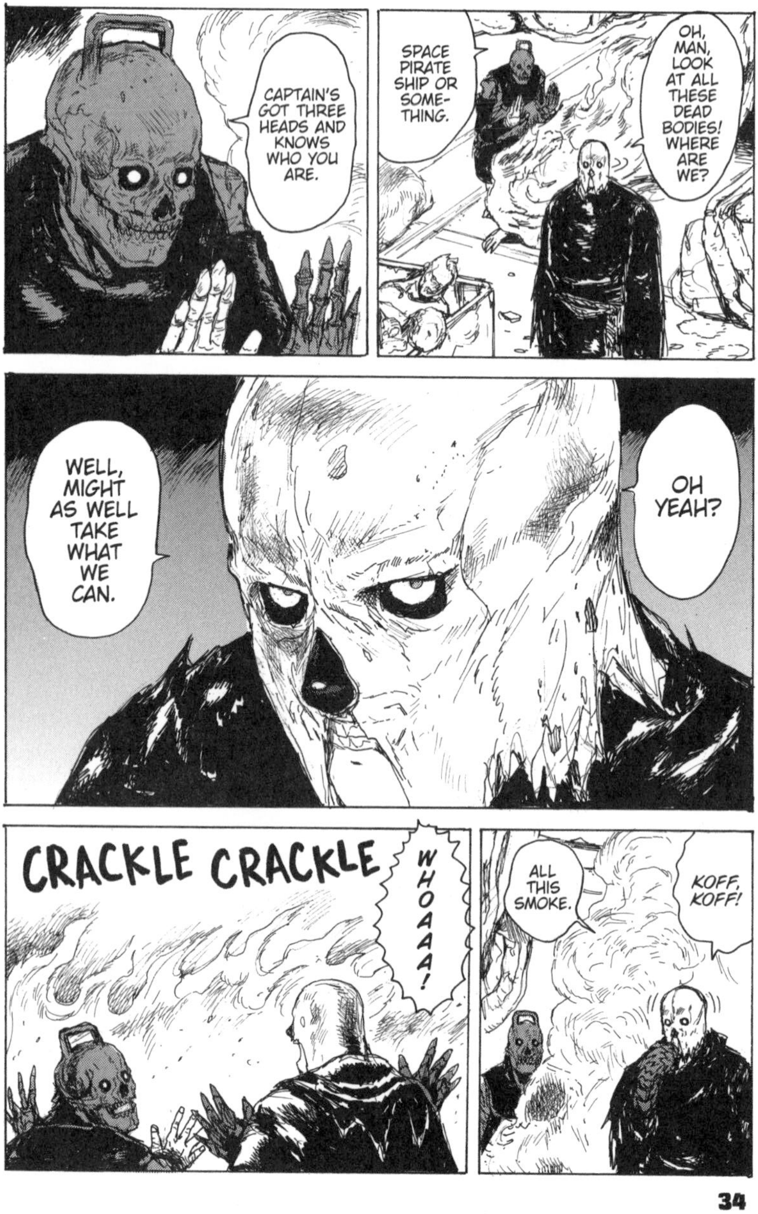
OH, MAN, LOOK AT ALL THESE DEAD BODIES! WHERE ARE WE?
SPACE PIRATE SHIP OR SOME-THING.
CAPTAIN'S GOT THREE HEADS AND KNOWS WHO YOU ARE.
OH YEAH?
WELL, MIGHT AS WELL TAKE WHAT WE CAN.
KOFF, KOFF!
ALL THIS SMOKE.
WHOAAAA!
CRACKLE CRACKLE

★ Design of the undersuit (of darkness)

UNDERSUIT
(OF DARKNESS)

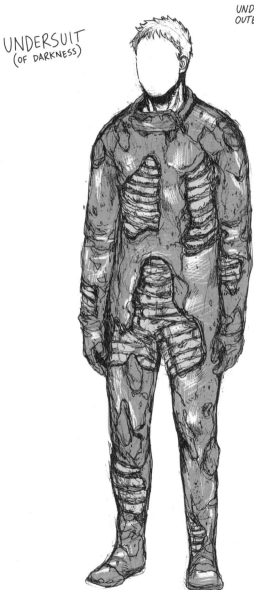

UNDER THE
OUTERWEAR

OUTERWEAR:

PAGGY
(OF DARKNESS)

DARK HIDE

BOOTS

PAGGY FEATURES

○ HELMET
○ PROPULSION
○ COMMUNICATION
○ ILLUMINATION
○ POWERED BY DARKNES
○ RESPIRATION

★ Design of Avakian (1)

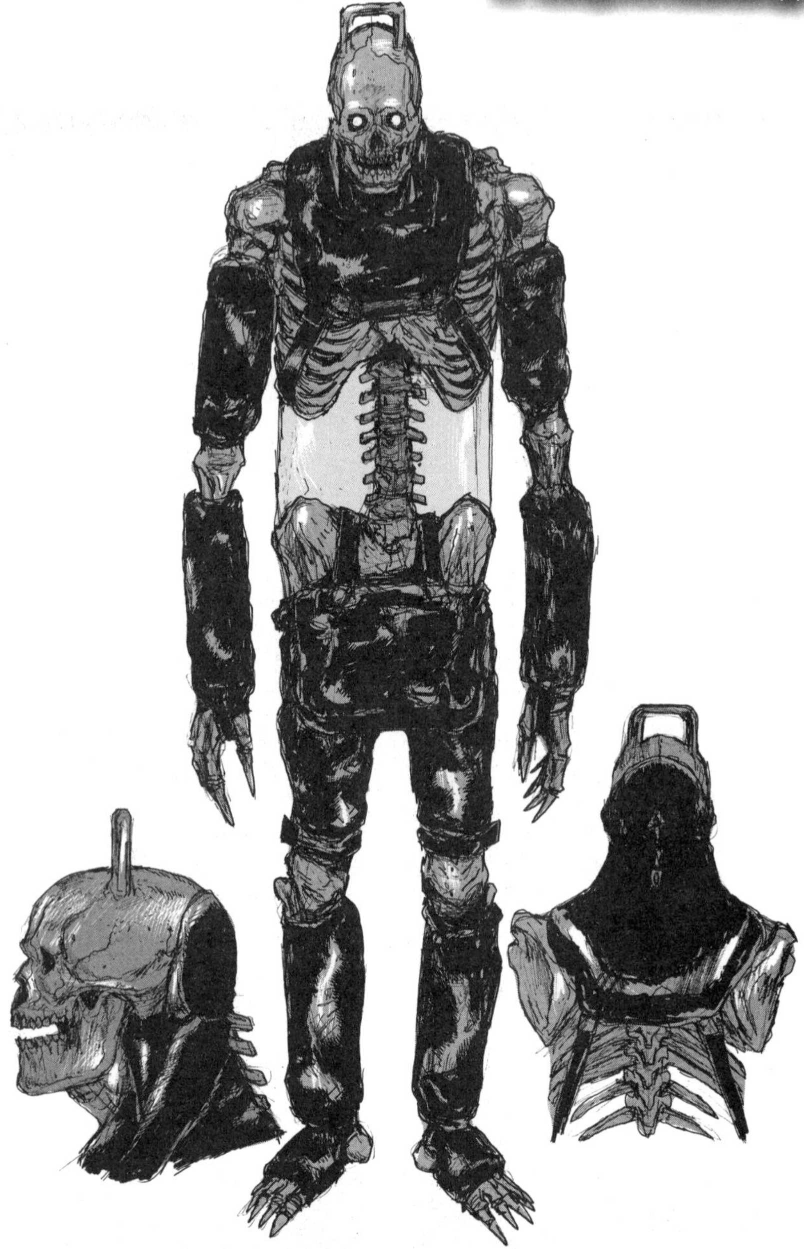

DAI DARK

DAI DARK

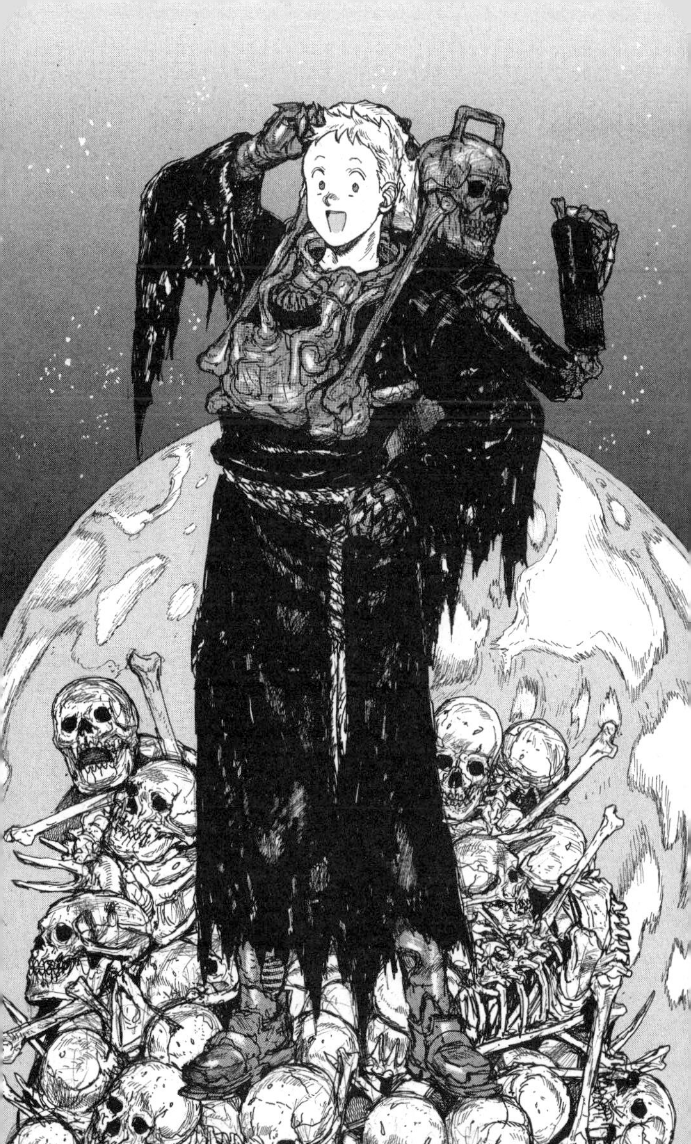

Bone 2: Fireball Mad Ax

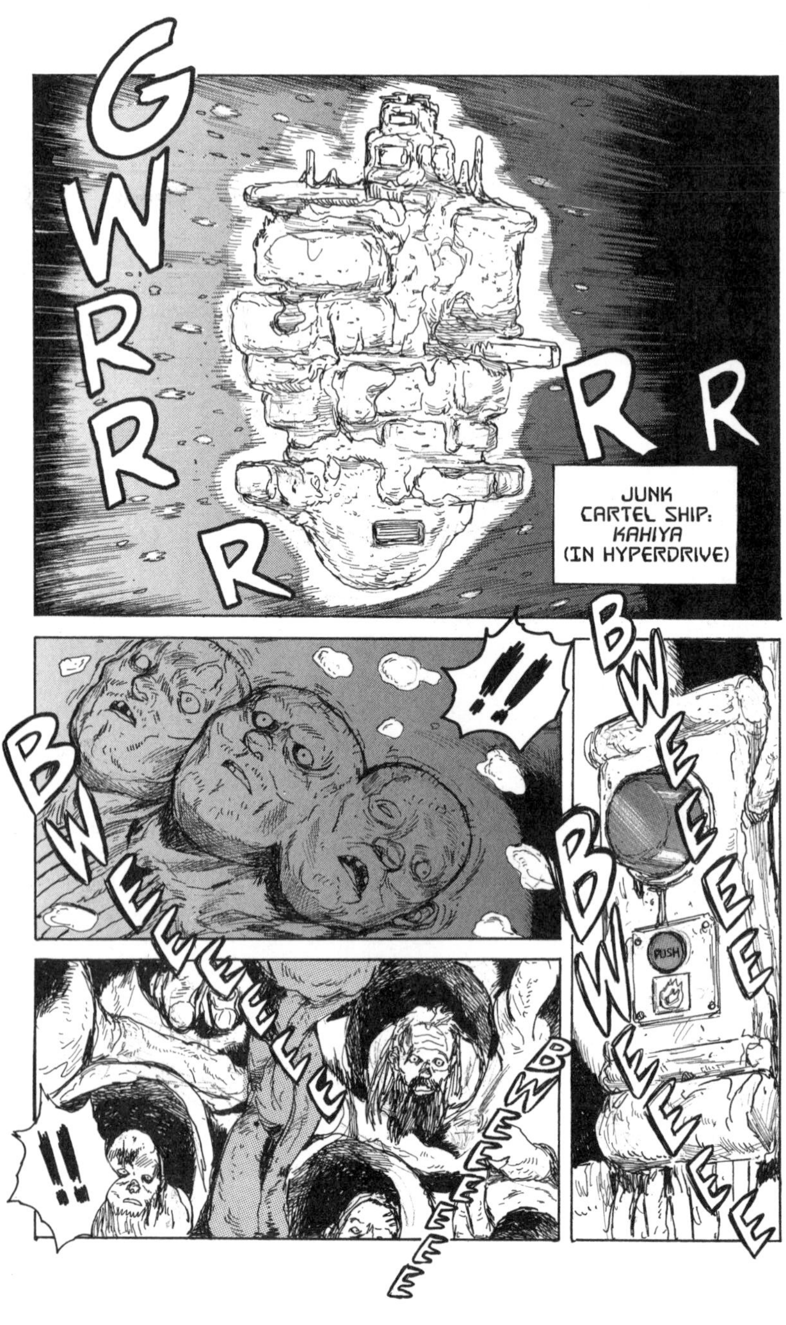
GWRRRRR
JUNK CARTEL SHIP: KAHIYA (IN HYPERDRIVE)
BWEEEEE
BWEEEEEE
!!
BWEEEEEEE
!!
BWEEEEEEE

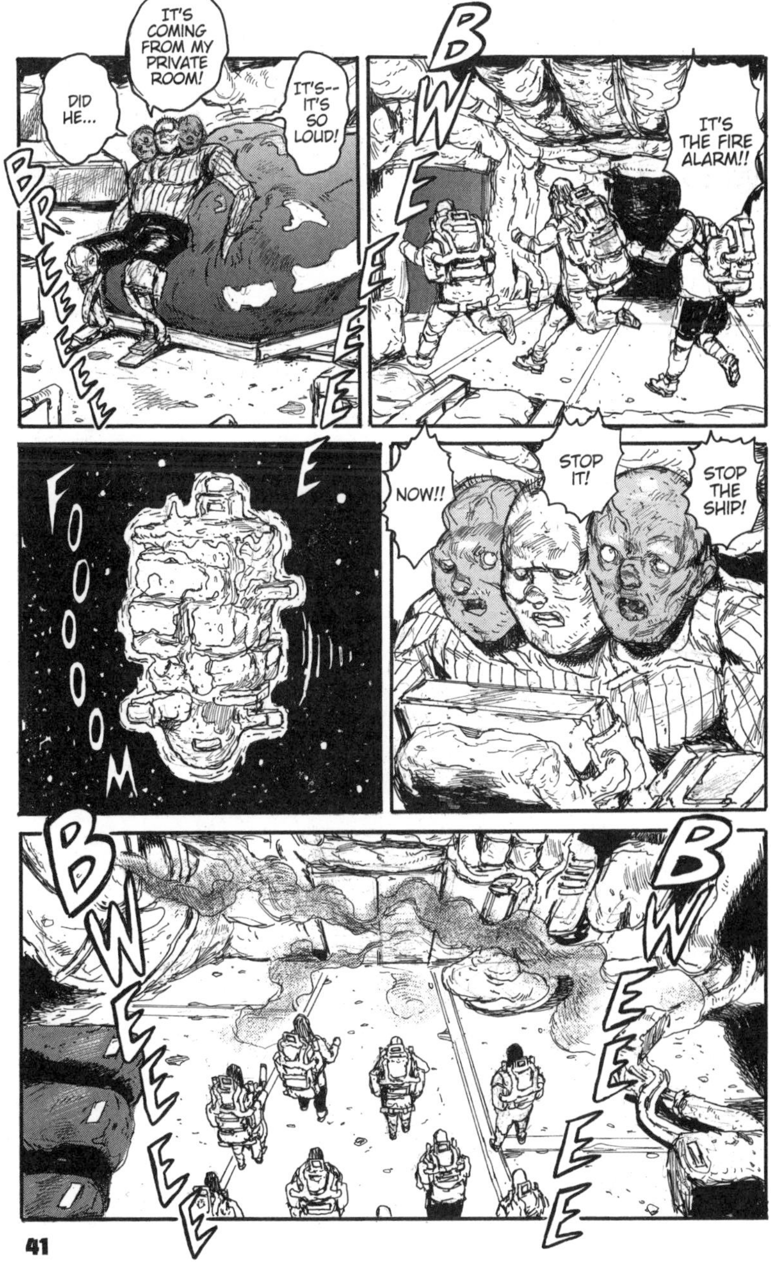
BWEEEEEE
IT'S THE FIRE ALARM!!
IT'S COMING FROM MY PRIVATE ROOM!
IT'S-- IT'S SO LOUD!
DID HE...
BREEEEEEE
STOP THE SHIP!
STOP IT!
NOW!!
FOOOOOOM
BWEEEEEE
BWEEEEEE

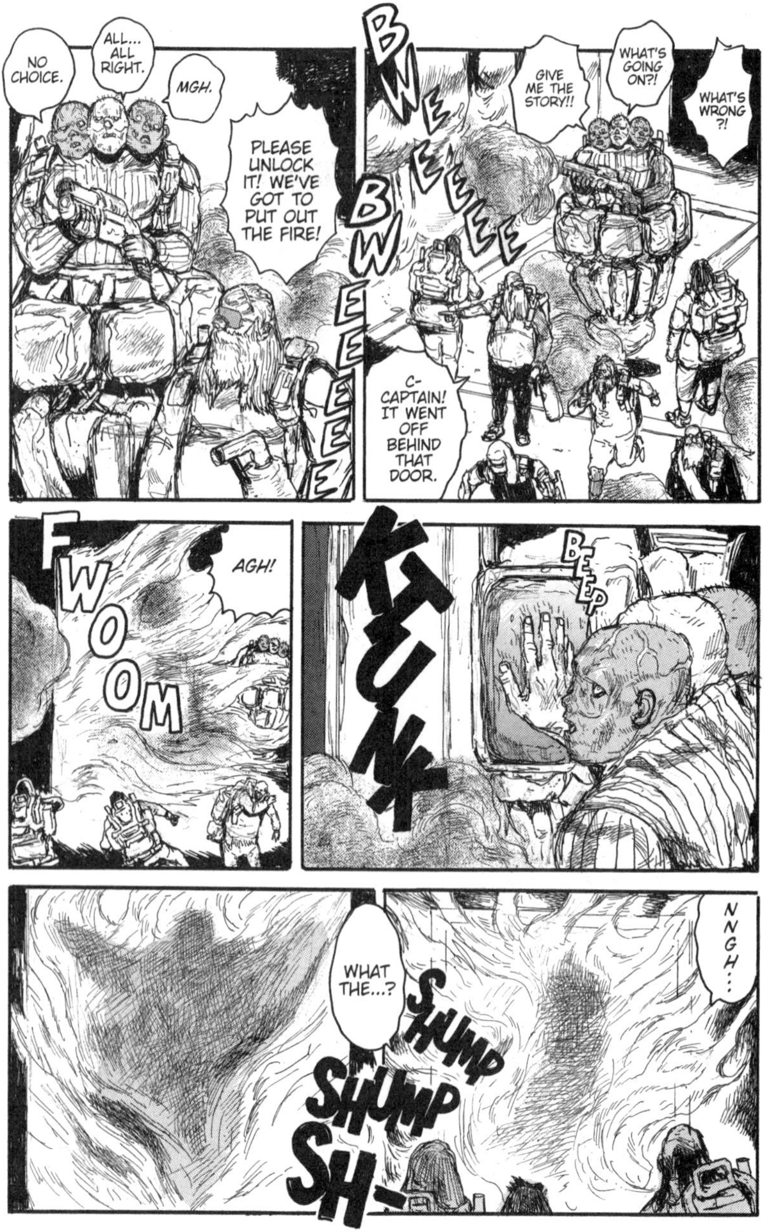
BWEEEEE
WHAT'S GOING ON?!
WHAT'S WRONG?!
GIVE ME THE STORY!!
BWEEEEEE
C-CAPTAIN! IT WENT OFF BEHIND THAT DOOR.
PLEASE UNLOCK IT! WE'VE GOT TO PUT OUT THE FIRE!
MGH.
ALL... ALL RIGHT.
NO CHOICE.
BEEP
KTUNK
AGH!
FWOOM
NNGH...
WHAT THE...?
SHUMP
SHUMP
SH-

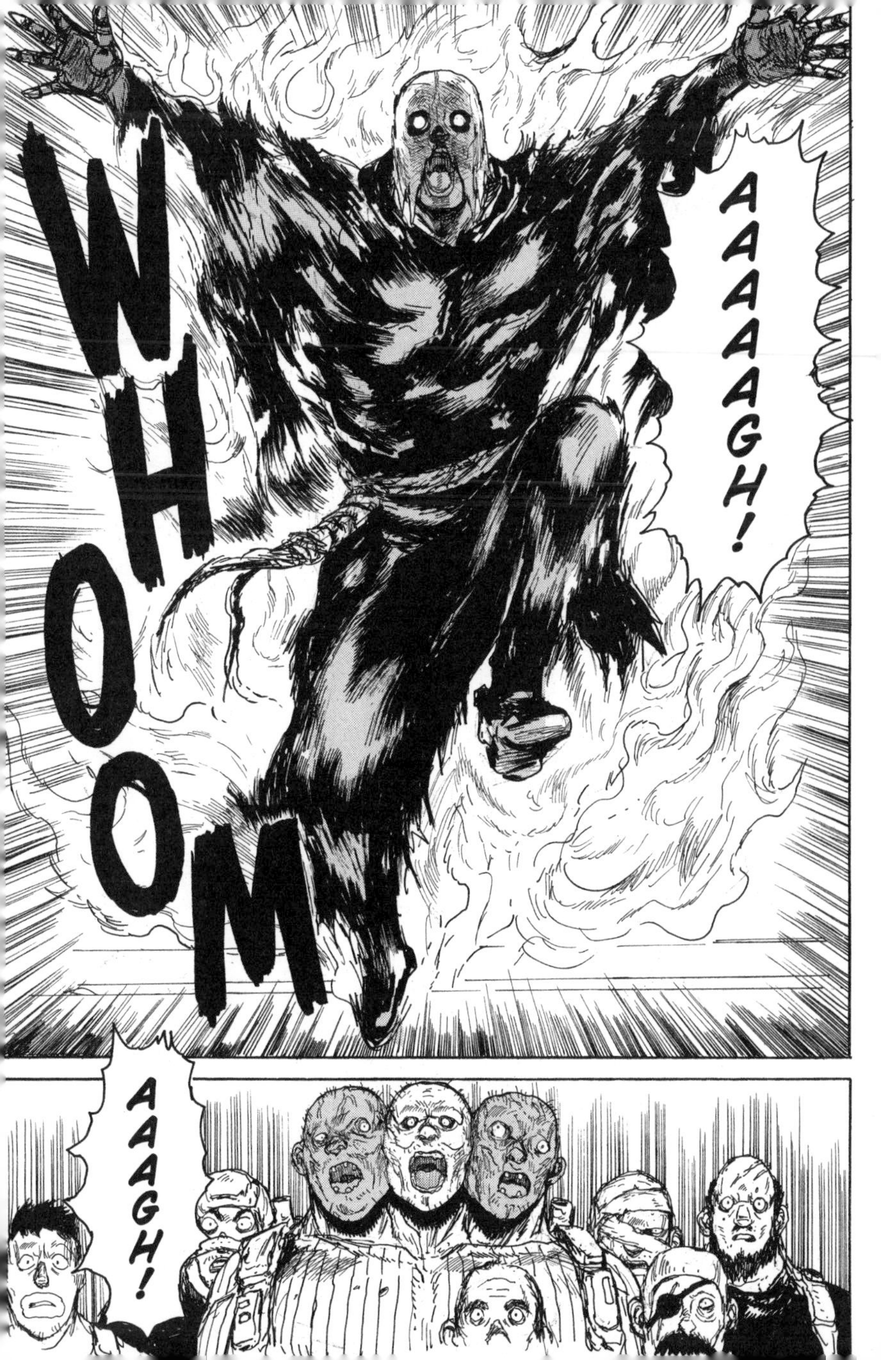
AAAAAAAGH!
WHOOOM!
AAAAGH!

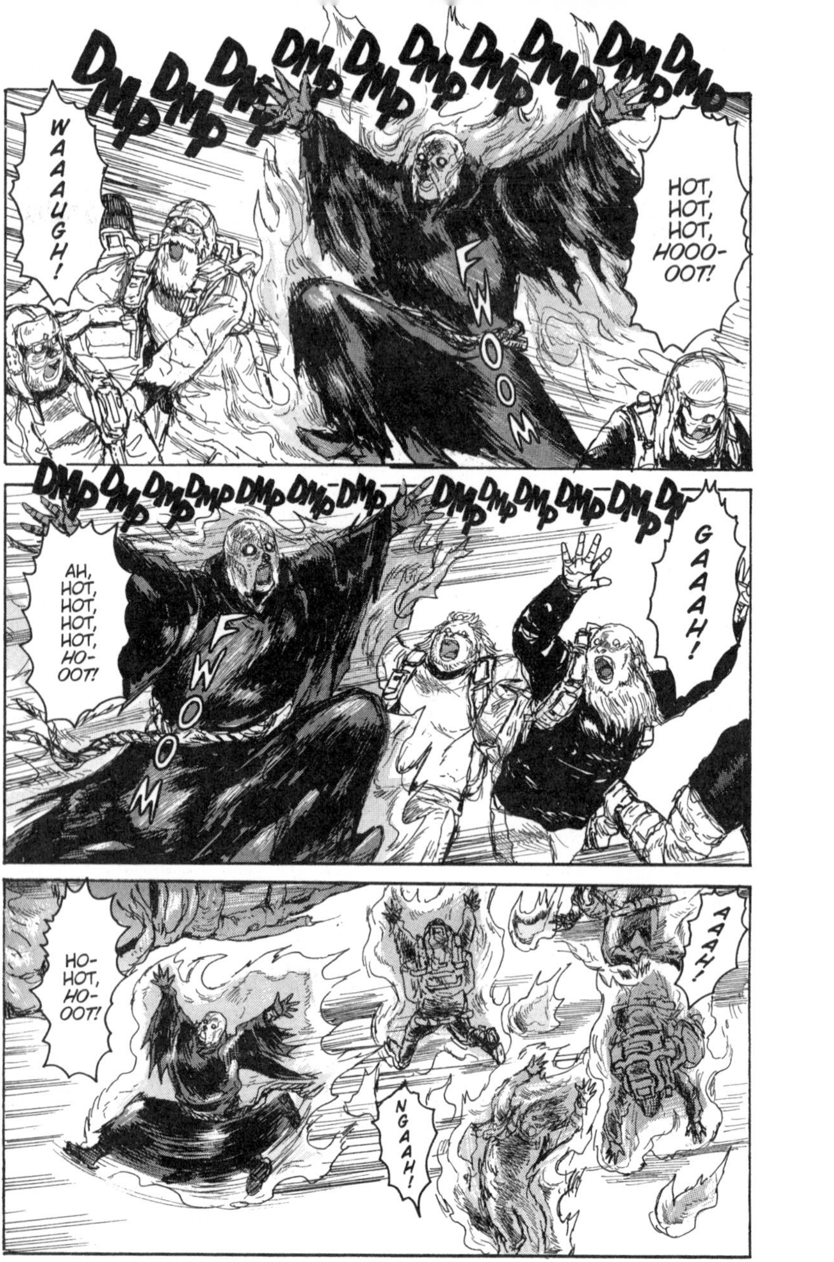
DMP DMP DMP DMP DMP DMP DMP DMP DMP DMP DMP
HOT, HOT, HOT, HOOOO-OOT!
FWOOM
WAAAAUGH!
DMP DMP DMP DMP DMP DMP DMP DMP DMP DMP DMP DMP DMP
GAAAAH!
FWOOM
AH, HOT, HOT, HOT, HOT, HO-OOT!
AAAAH!
NGAAAH!
HO-HOT, HO-OOT!

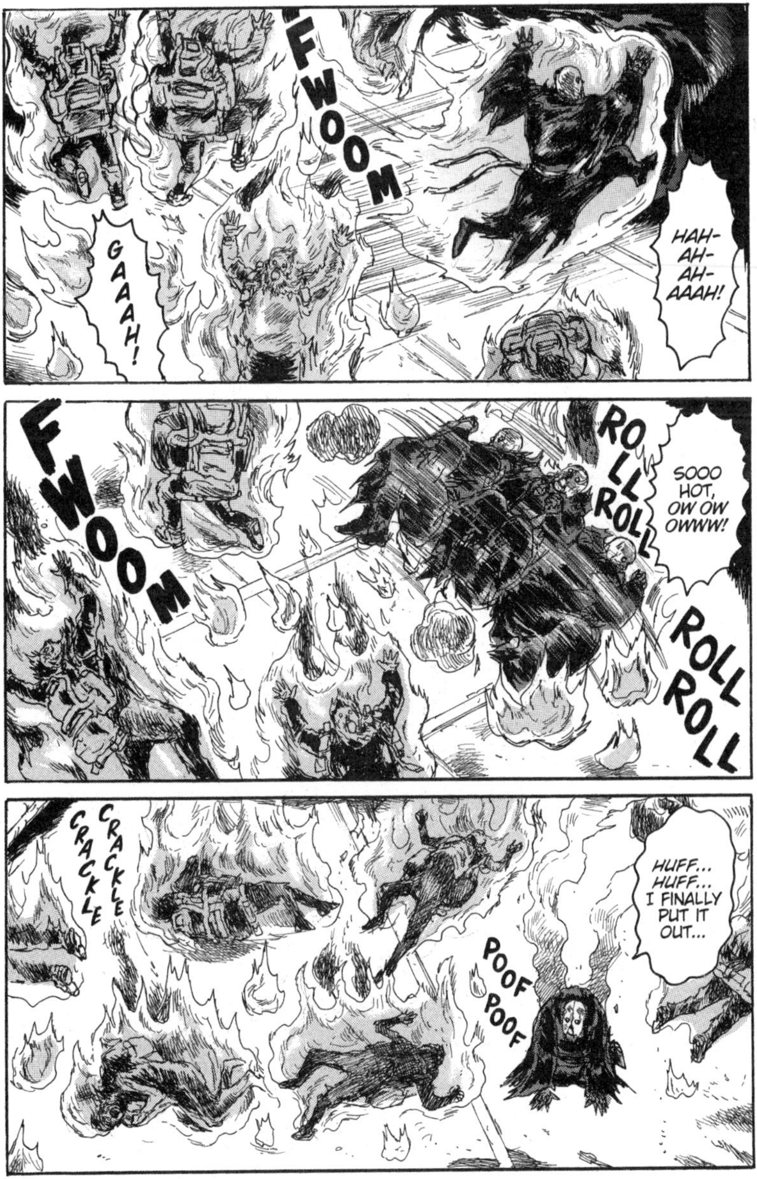
HAH-AH-AH-AAAH!
FWOOM
GAAAAH!
SOOO HOT, OW OW OWWW!
ROLL ROLL
ROLL ROLL ROLL
FWOOM
HUFF... HUFF... I FINALLY PUT IT OUT...
POOF POOF
CRACKLE CRACKLE

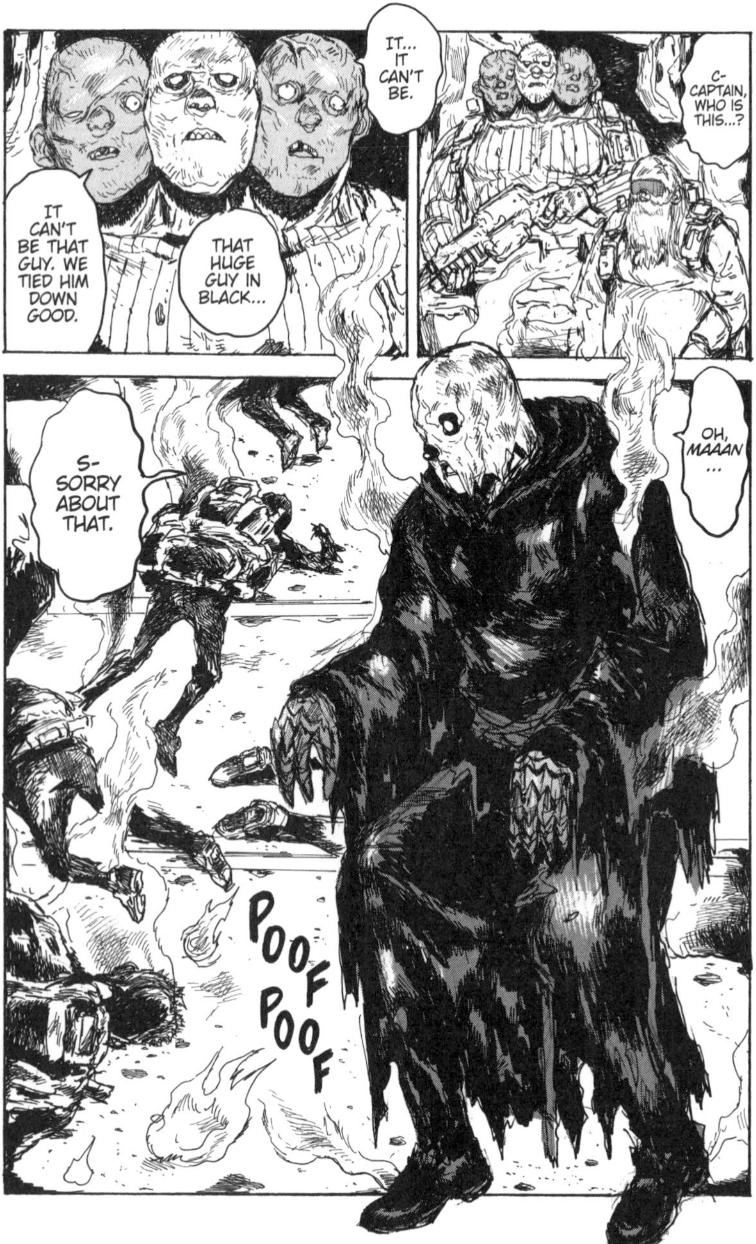
C-CAPTAIN, WHO IS THIS...?
IT... IT CAN'T BE.
THAT HUGE GUY IN BLACK...
IT CAN'T BE THAT GUY. WE TIED HIM DOWN GOOD.
OH, MAAAN ...
S-SORRY ABOUT THAT.
POOF POOF

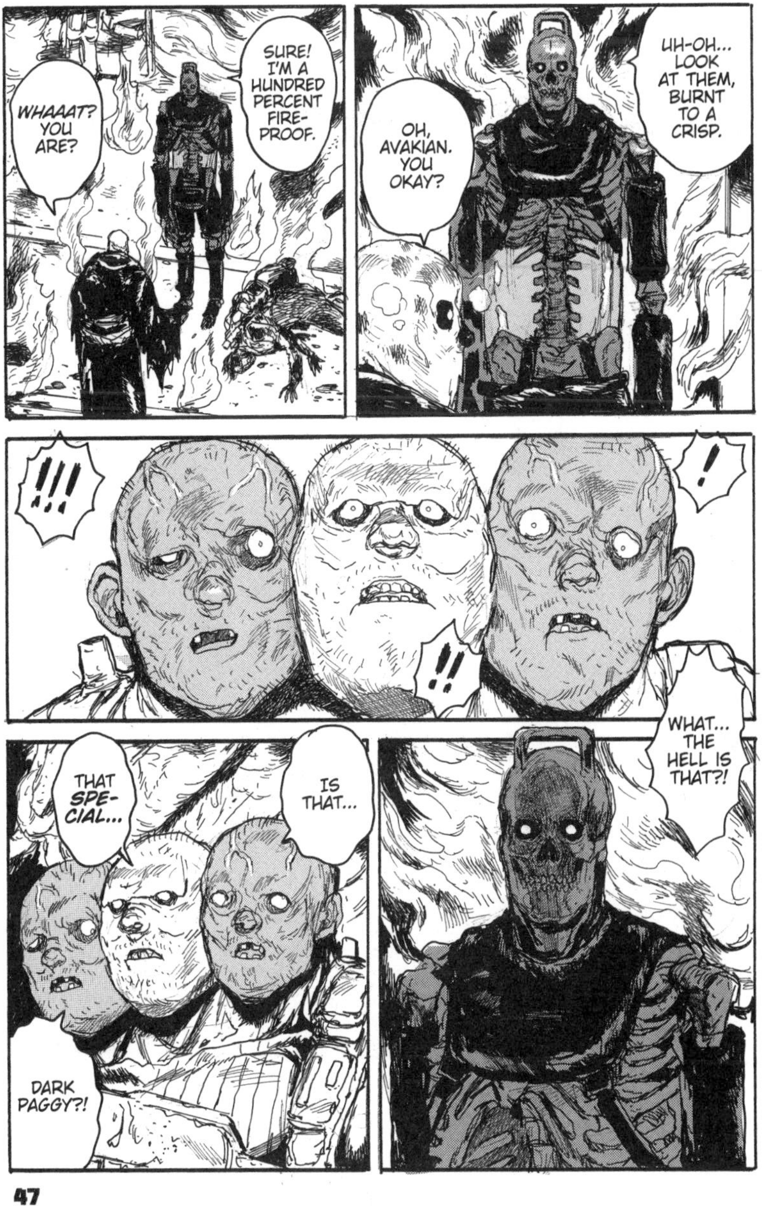
UH-OH... LOOK AT THEM, BURNT TO A CRISP.
OH, AVAKIAN. YOU OKAY?
SURE! I'M A HUNDRED PERCENT FIRE-PROOF.
WHAAAT? YOU ARE?
!
!!!
!!
WHAT... THE HELL IS THAT?!
IS THAT...
THAT *SPE-CIAL...*
DARK PAGGY?!

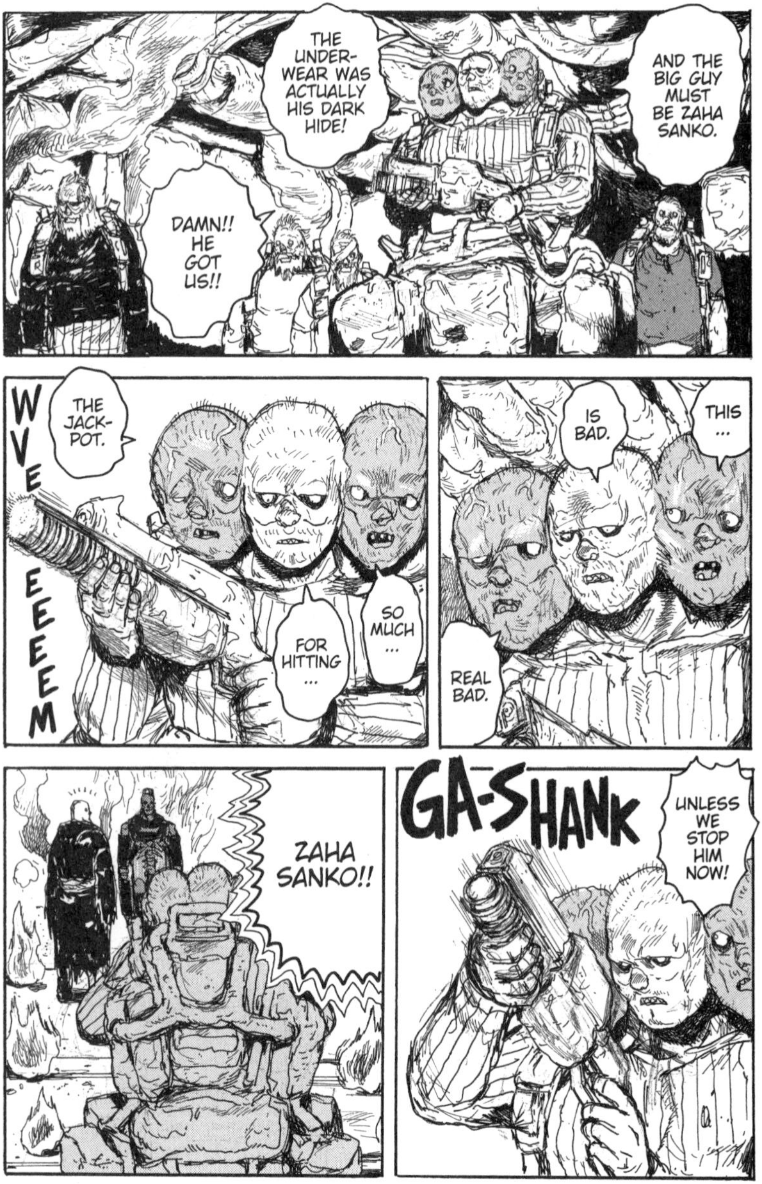
AND THE BIG GUY MUST BE ZAHA SANKO.
THE UNDER-WEAR WAS ACTUALLY HIS DARK HIDE!
DAMN!! HE GOT US!!
THIS ...
IS BAD.
REAL BAD.
THE JACK-POT.
SO MUCH ...
FOR HITTING ...
WVEEEEEM
UNLESS WE STOP HIM NOW!
GA-SHANK
ZAHA SANKO!!

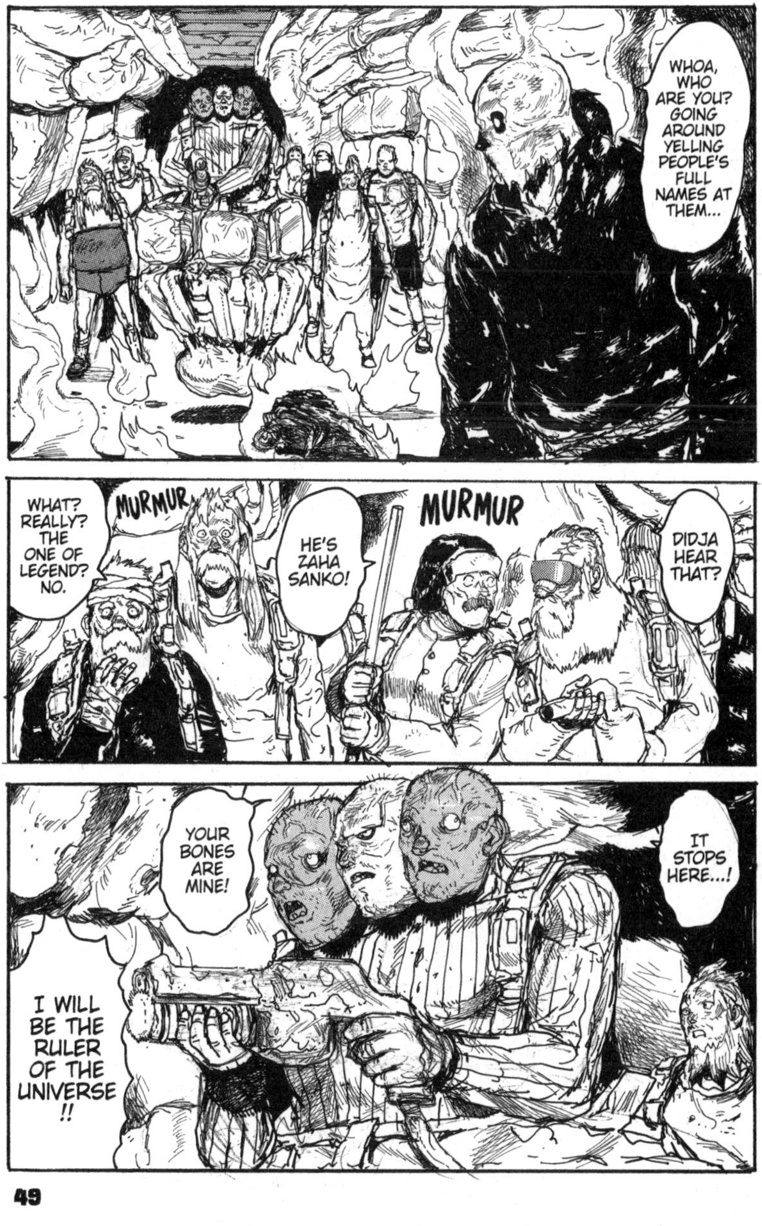
WHOA, WHO ARE YOU? GOING AROUND YELLING PEOPLE'S FULL NAMES AT THEM...
DIDJA HEAR THAT?
MURMUR
HE'S ZAHA SANKO!
MURMUR
WHAT? REALLY? THE ONE OF LEGEND? NO.
IT STOPS HERE...!
YOUR BONES ARE MINE!
I WILL BE THE RULER OF THE UNIVERSE!!

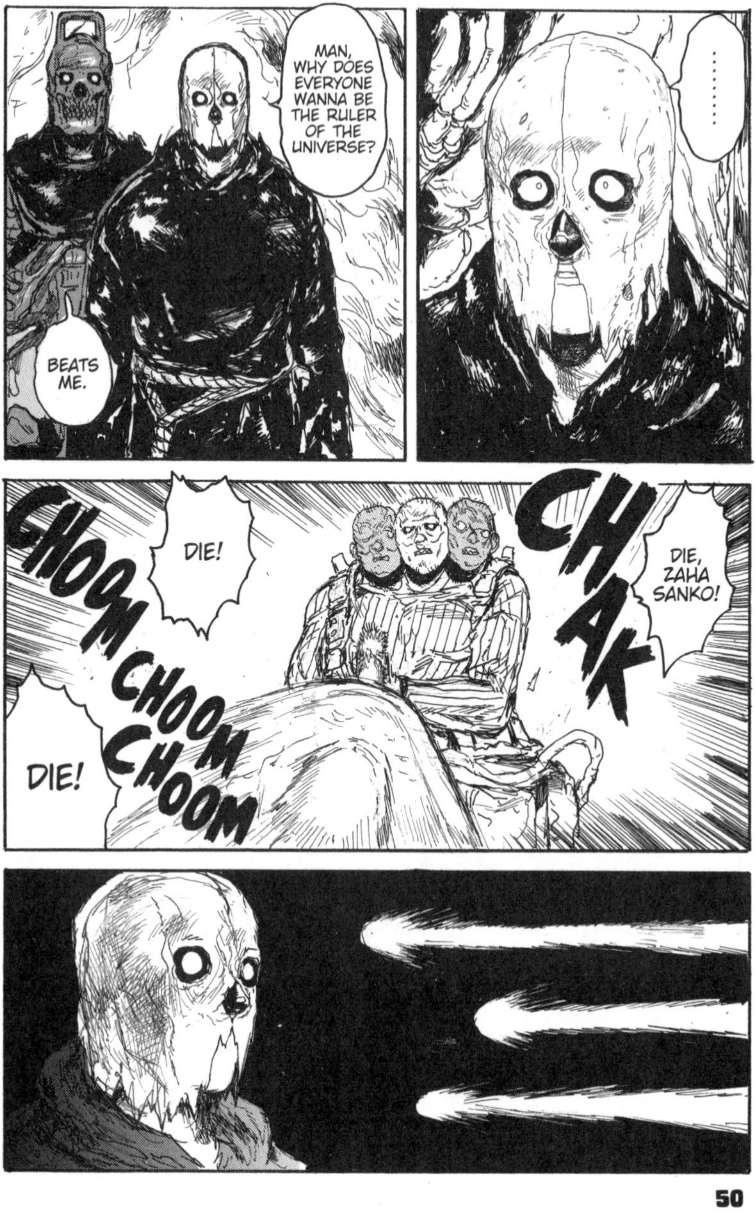
......
MAN, WHY DOES EVERYONE WANNA BE THE RULER OF THE UNIVERSE?
BEATS ME.
CHAK
DIE, ZAHA SANKO!
DIE!
CHOOM CHOOM CHOOM CHOOM
DIE!

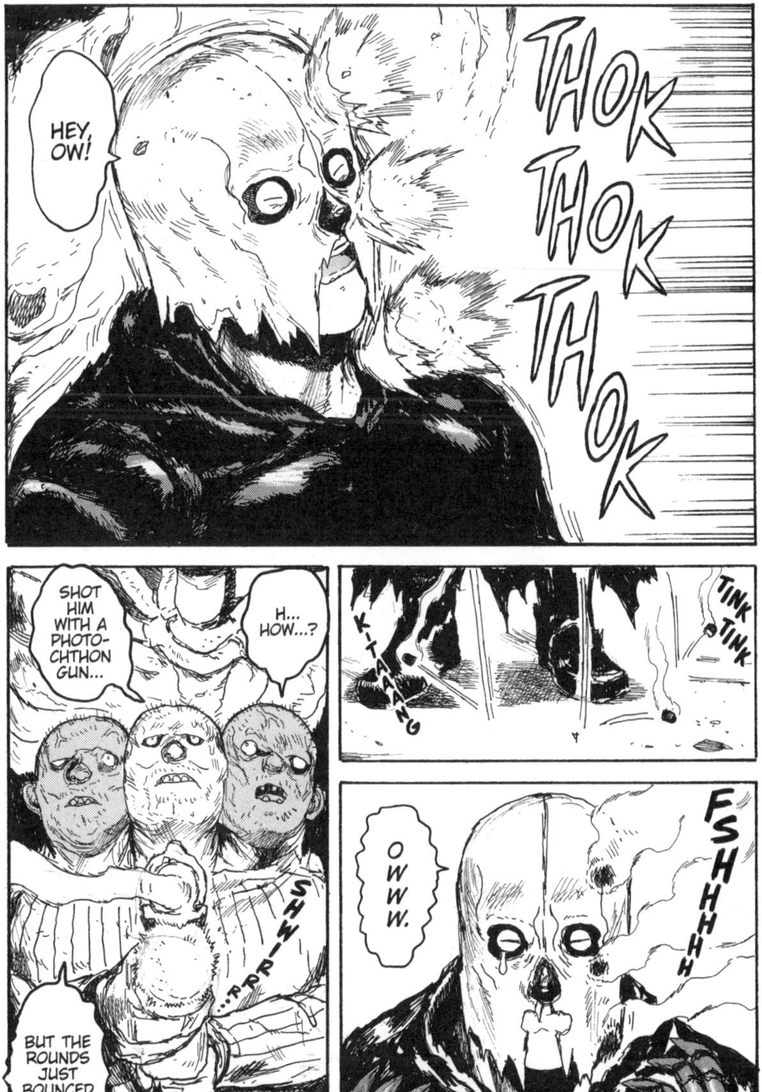
THOK THOK THOK
HEY, OW!
TINK TINK
KITAAANG
FSHHHHH
OWWW.
H... HOW...?
SHOT HIM WITH A PHOTO-CHTHON GUN...
SHWIRRR...
BUT THE ROUNDS JUST BOUNCED OFF.

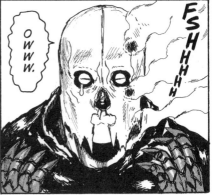

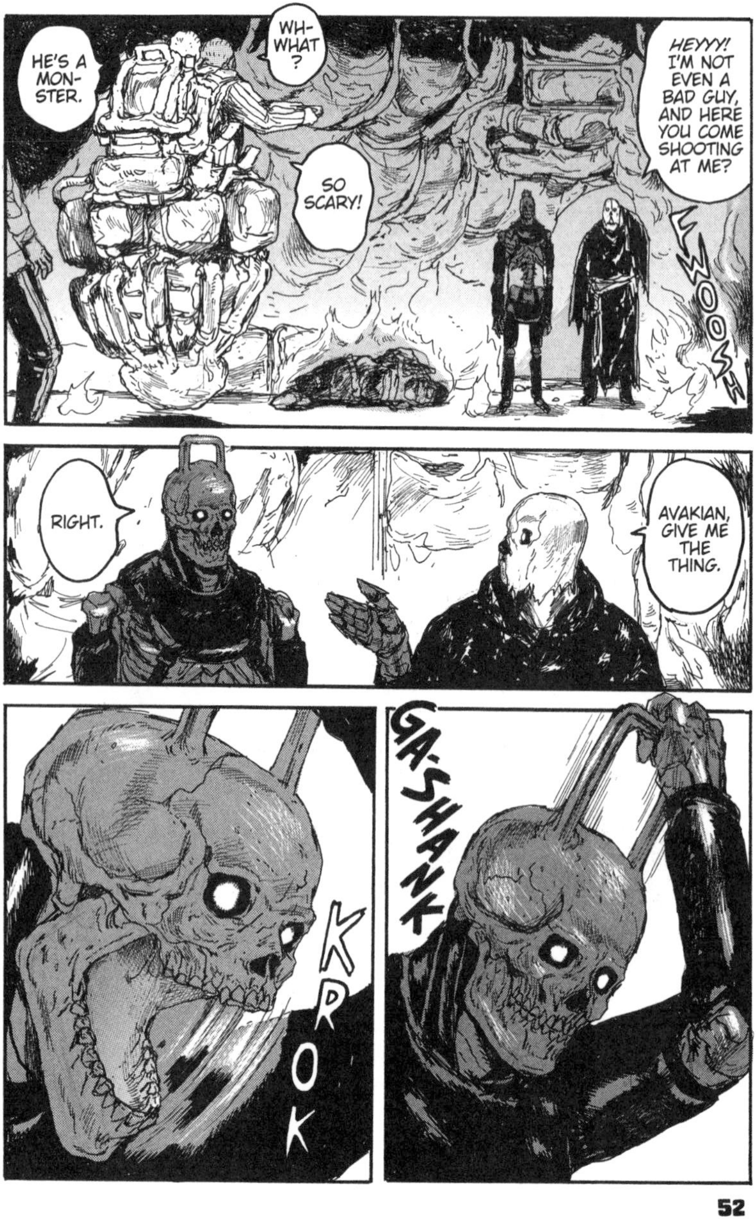
HEYYY! I'M NOT EVEN A BAD GUY, AND HERE YOU COME SHOOTING AT ME?
FWOOSH
SO SCARY!
WH-WHAT?
HE'S A MON-STER.
AVAKIAN, GIVE ME THE THING.
RIGHT.
GA'SHANK
KROK

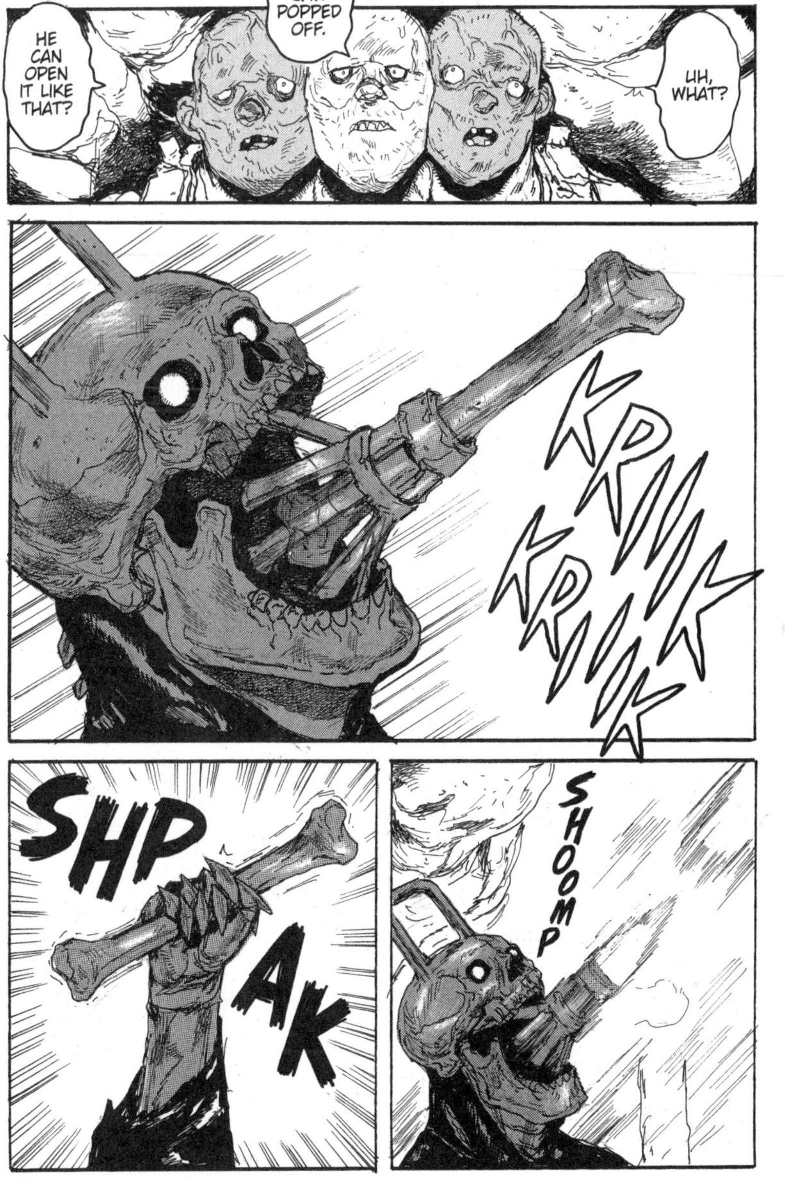
UH, WHAT?
HIS JAW POPPED OFF.
HE CAN OPEN IT LIKE THAT?
KRIIK KRIIK
SHOOMP
SHP AK

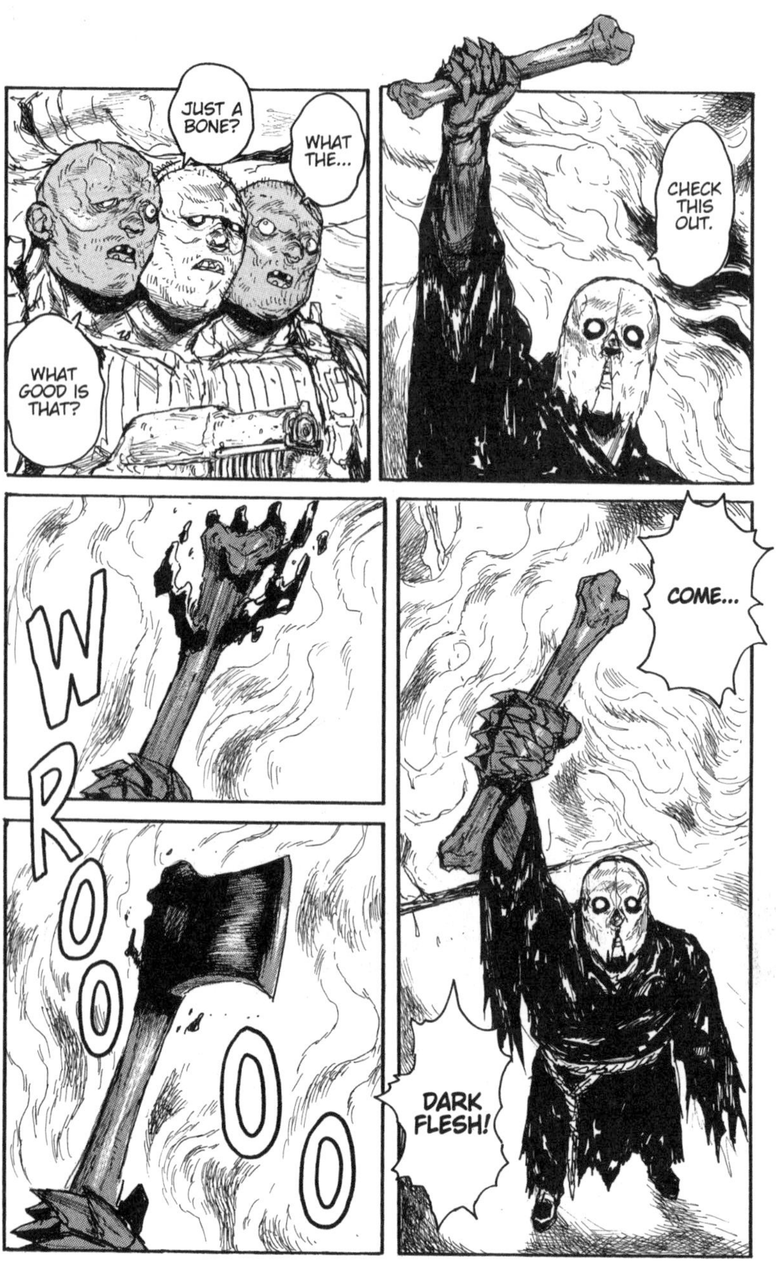
CHECK THIS OUT.
WHAT THE...
JUST A BONE?
WHAT GOOD IS THAT?
COME...
DARK FLESH!
WROOOO

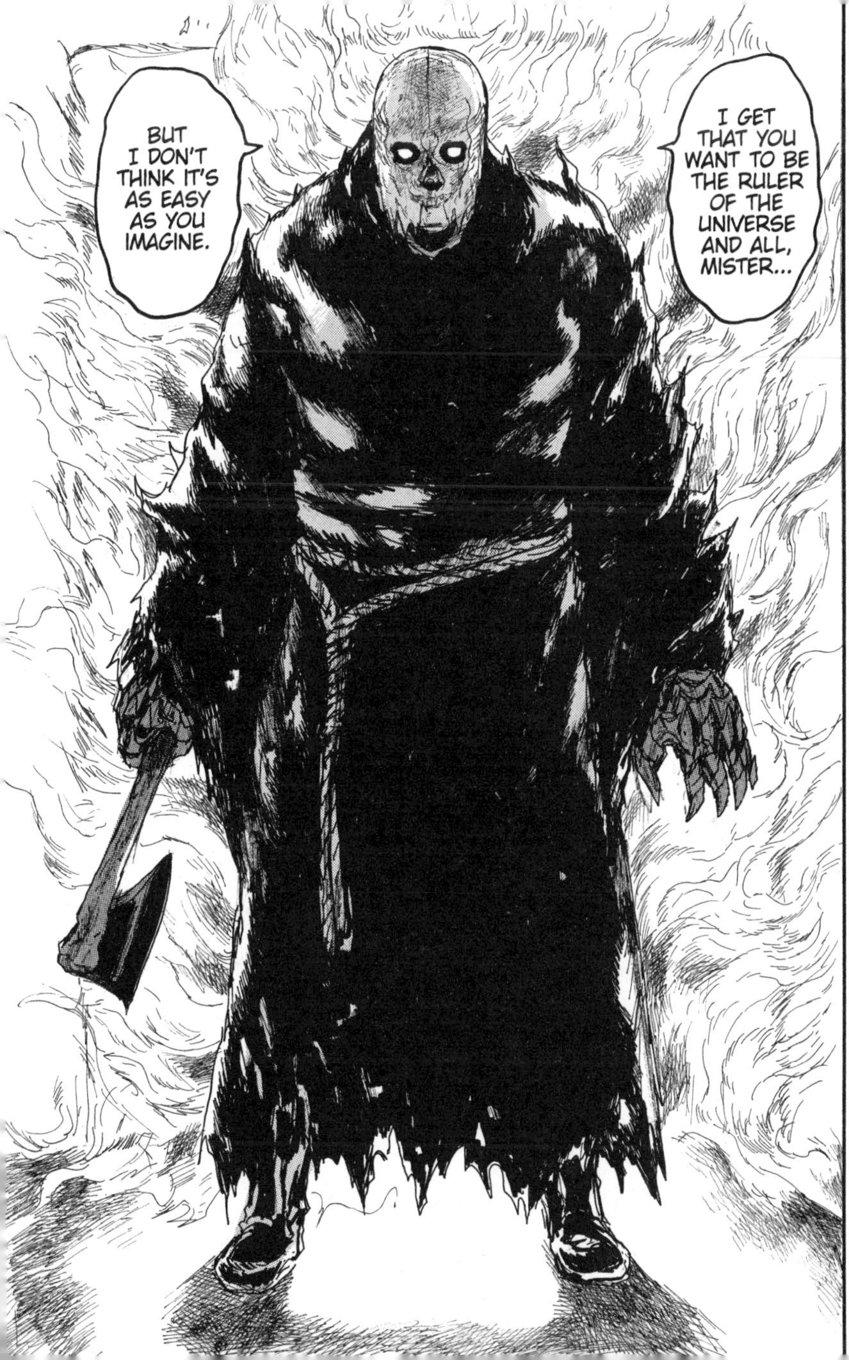
I GET THAT YOU WANT TO BE THE RULER OF THE UNIVERSE AND ALL, MISTER...
BUT I DON'T THINK IT'S AS EASY AS YOU IMAGINE.

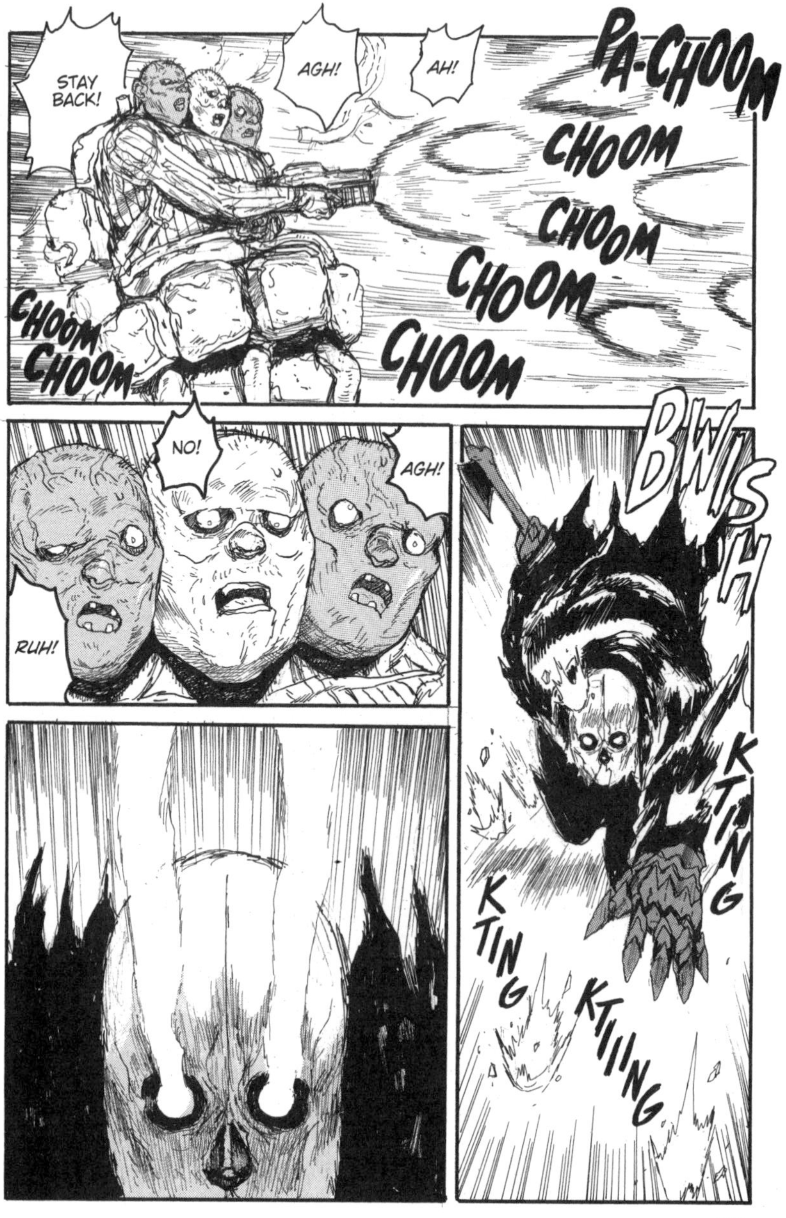
PA-CHOOM
AH!
AGH!
STAY BACK!
CHOOM
CHOOM
CHOOM
CHOOM
CHOOM CHOOM
BWISH
KTING
KTING
KTIIING
AGH!
NO!
RUH!

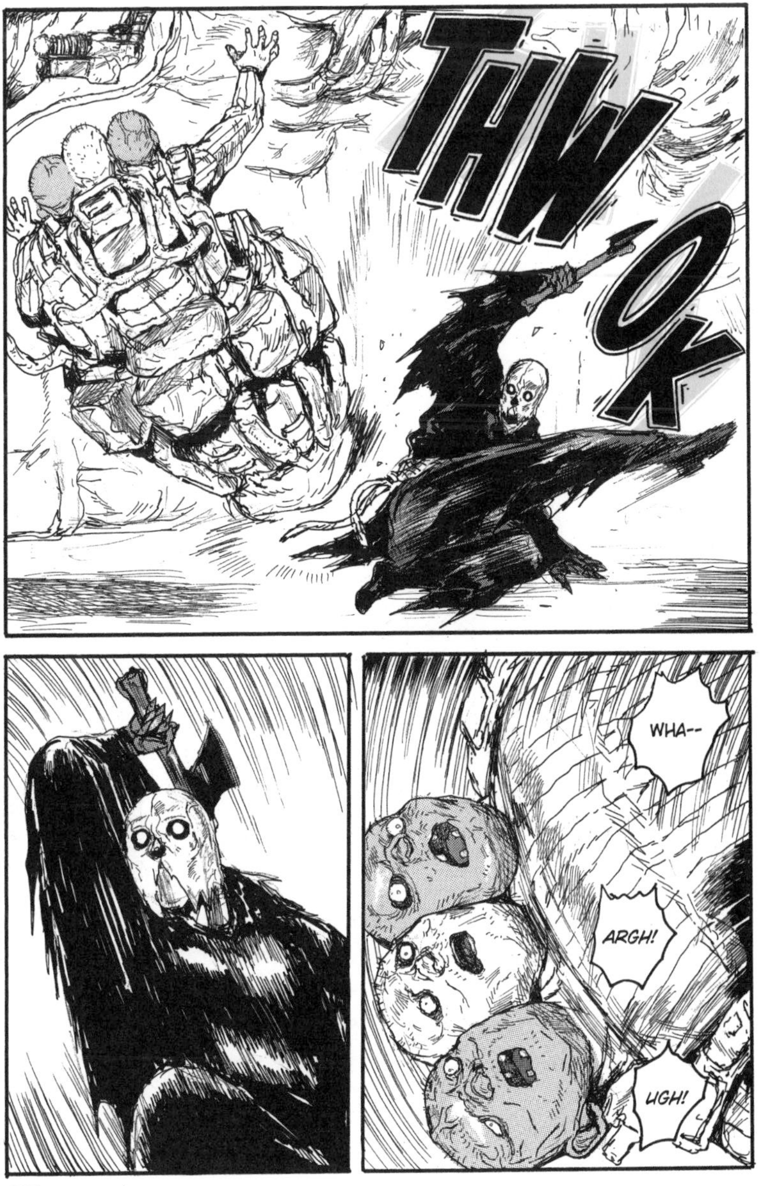
THWOK
WHA--
ARGH!
UGH!

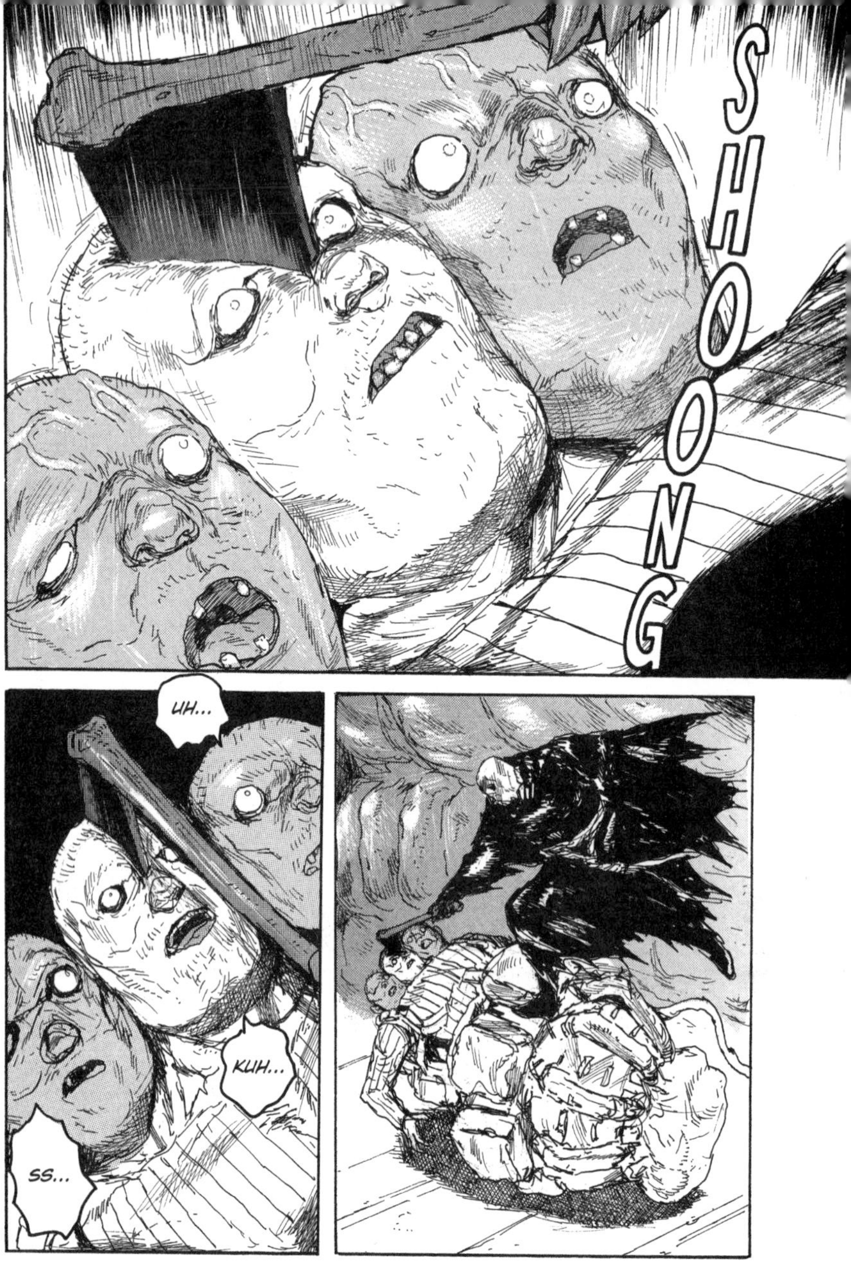
SHOOONG
UH...
KUH...
SS...

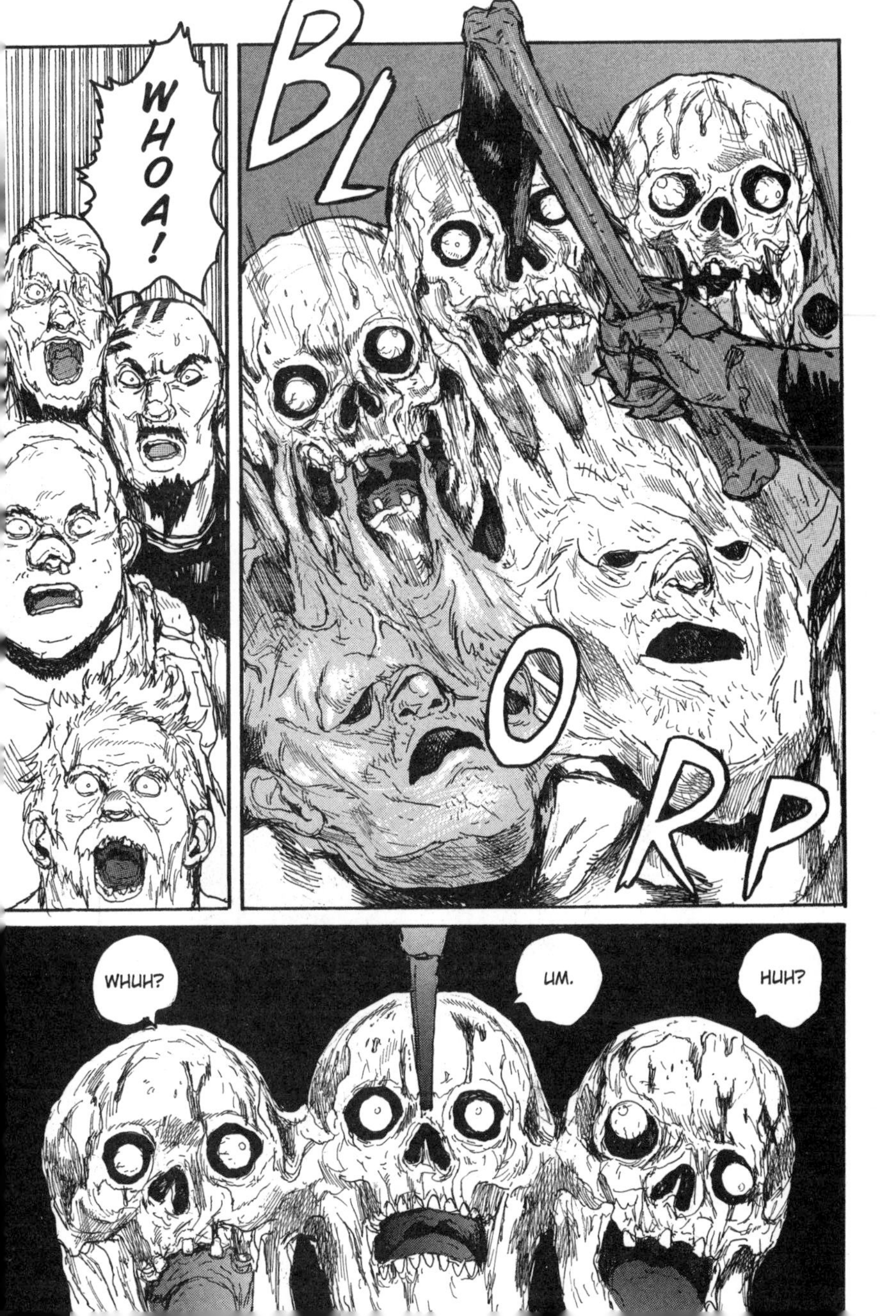
BLORP
WHOA!
HUH?
UM.
WHUH?

SPOOSH
BLURP
THUNK
FLUMP
BLOOSH

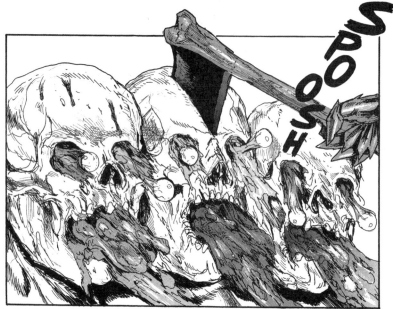

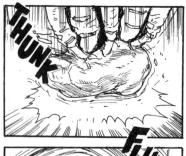

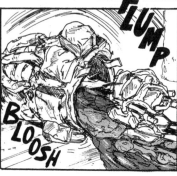

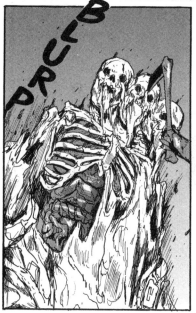

AAAH!

C-CAPTAIN!

BUT...

HE'S ZAHA SANKO...

ANY WISH YOU DESIRE, RIGHT?

THAT'S WHAT THEY SAY.

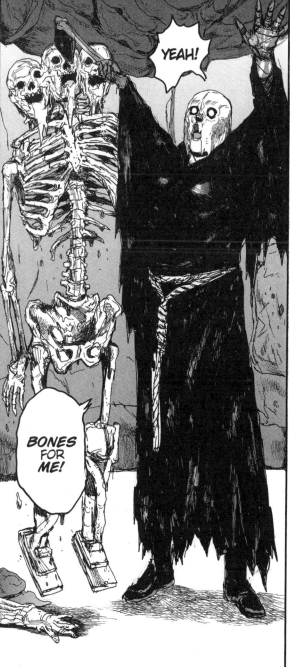

YEAH!

BONES FOR ME!

61

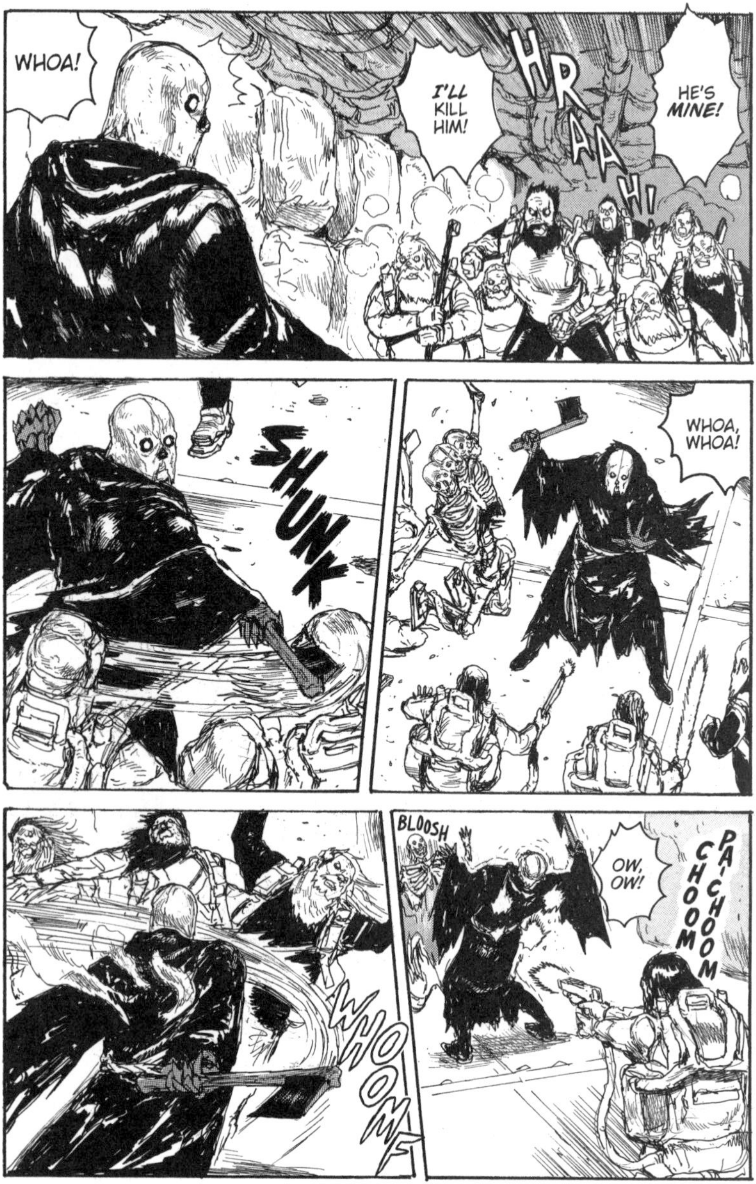
HE'S MINE!
HRAAAH!
I'LL KILL HIM!
WHOA!
WHOA, WHOA!
SHUNK
PAICHOOM
CHOOM
OW, OW!
BLOOSH
WHOOMF

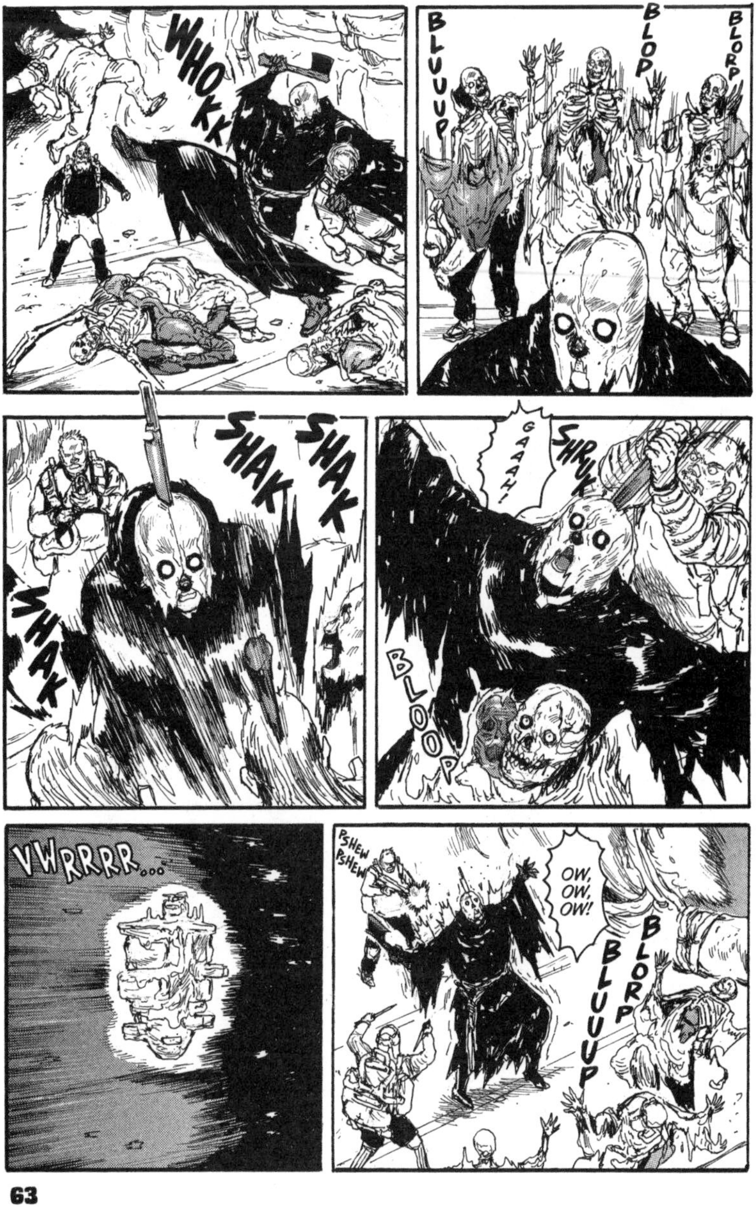

BLORP
BLOP
BLUUUP
WHOKKK
GAAAH!
SHRUK
BLOOOP
SHAK
SHAK
SHAK
OW, OW, OW!
BLORP
BLUUUP
PSHEW PSHEW
VWRRRR...

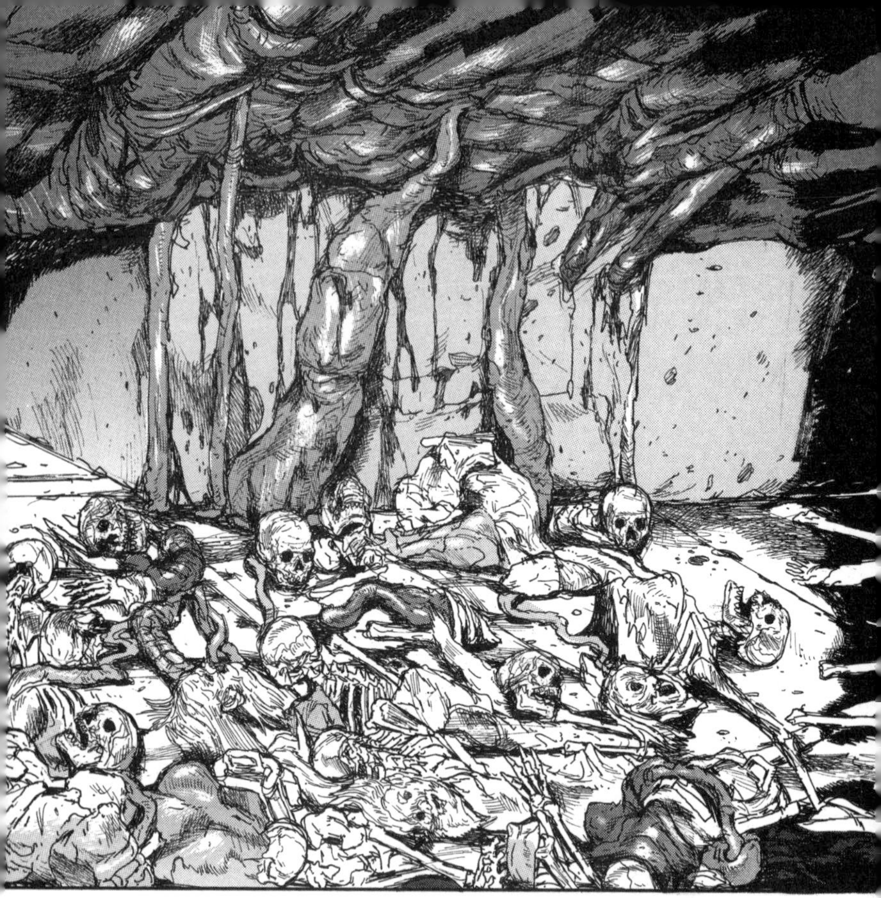

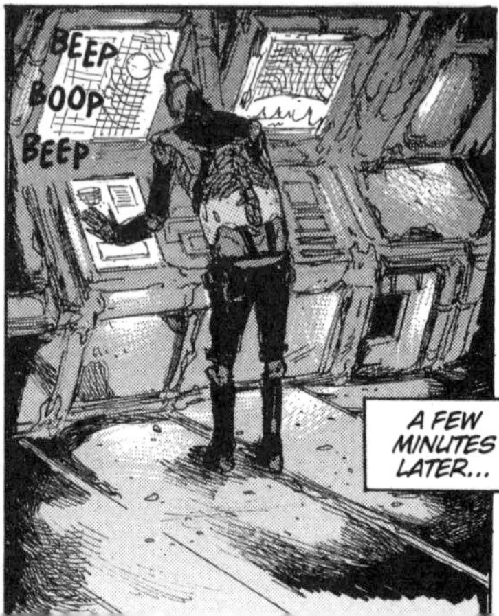
BEEP
BOOP
BEEP
A FEW MINUTES LATER...

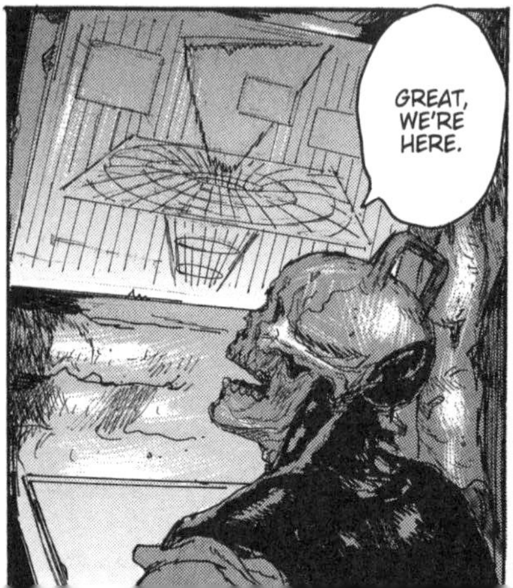
GREAT, WE'RE HERE.

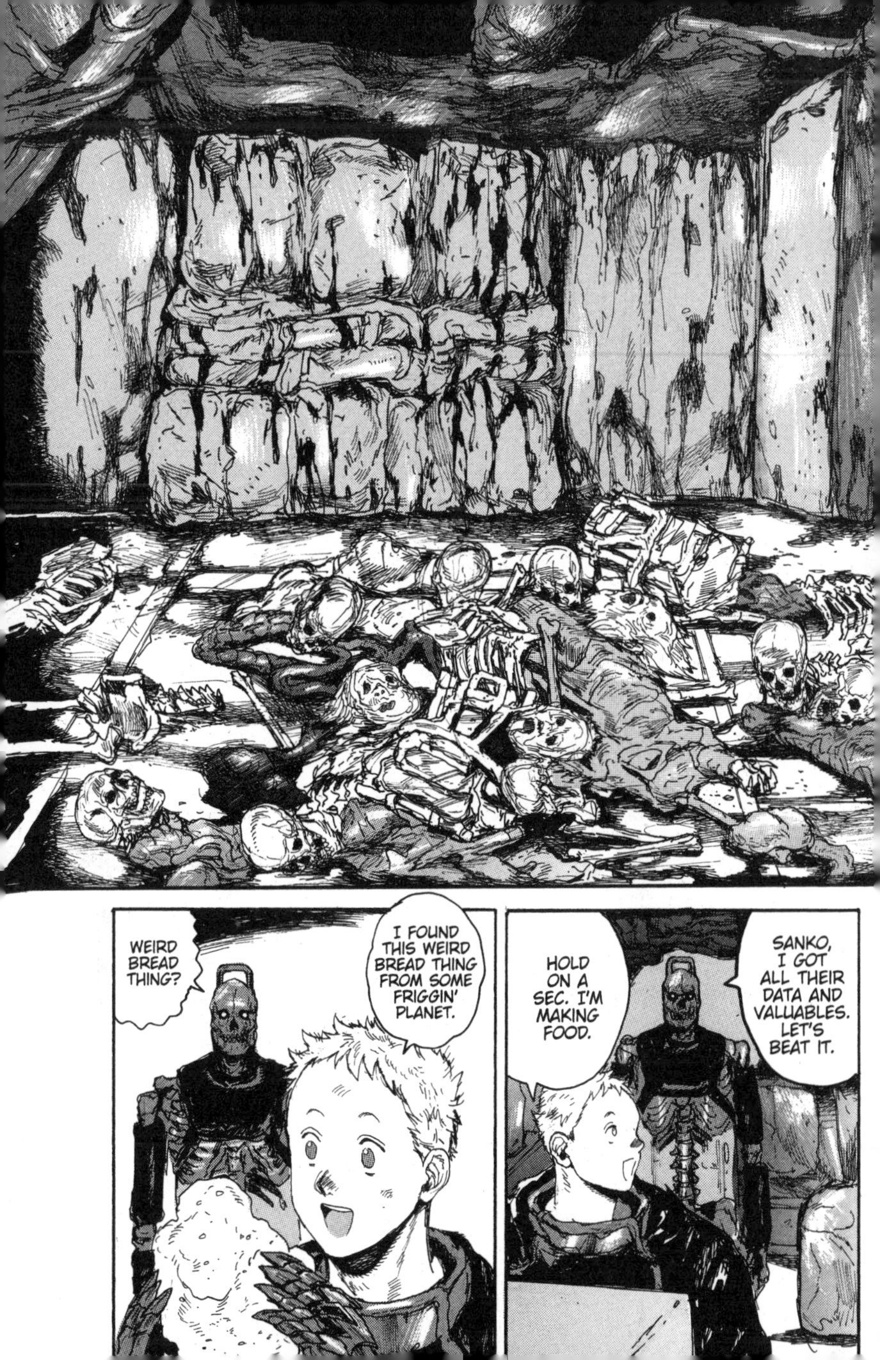
SANKO, I GOT ALL THEIR DATA AND VALUABLES. LET'S BEAT IT.
HOLD ON A SEC. I'M MAKING FOOD.
I FOUND THIS WEIRD BREAD THING FROM SOME FRIGGIN' PLANET.
WEIRD BREAD THING?

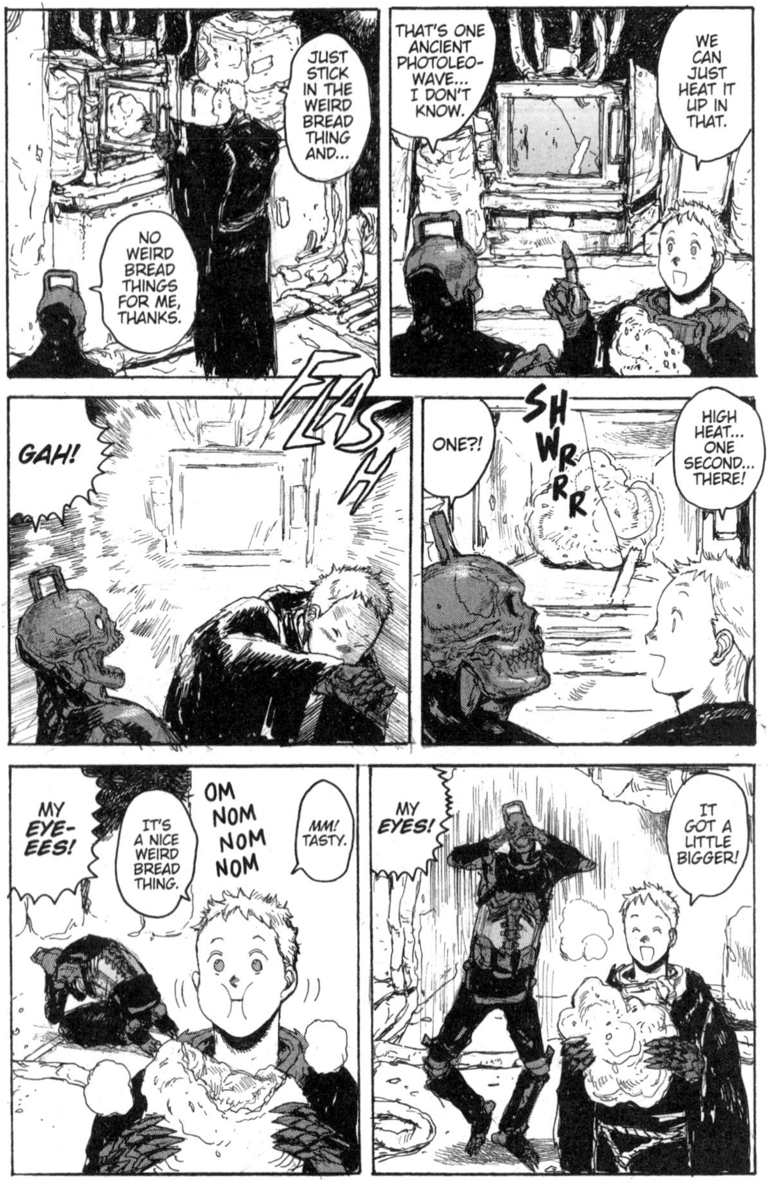
WE CAN JUST HEAT IT UP IN THAT.
THAT'S ONE ANCIENT PHOTOLEO-WAVE... I DON'T KNOW.
JUST STICK IN THE WEIRD BREAD THING AND...
NO WEIRD BREAD THINGS FOR ME, THANKS.
HIGH HEAT... ONE SECOND... THERE!
SHWRRR
ONE?!
FLASH
GAH!
IT GOT A LITTLE BIGGER!
MY EYES!
MM! TASTY.
OM NOM NOM NOM
IT'S A NICE WEIRD BREAD THING.
MY EYE-EES!

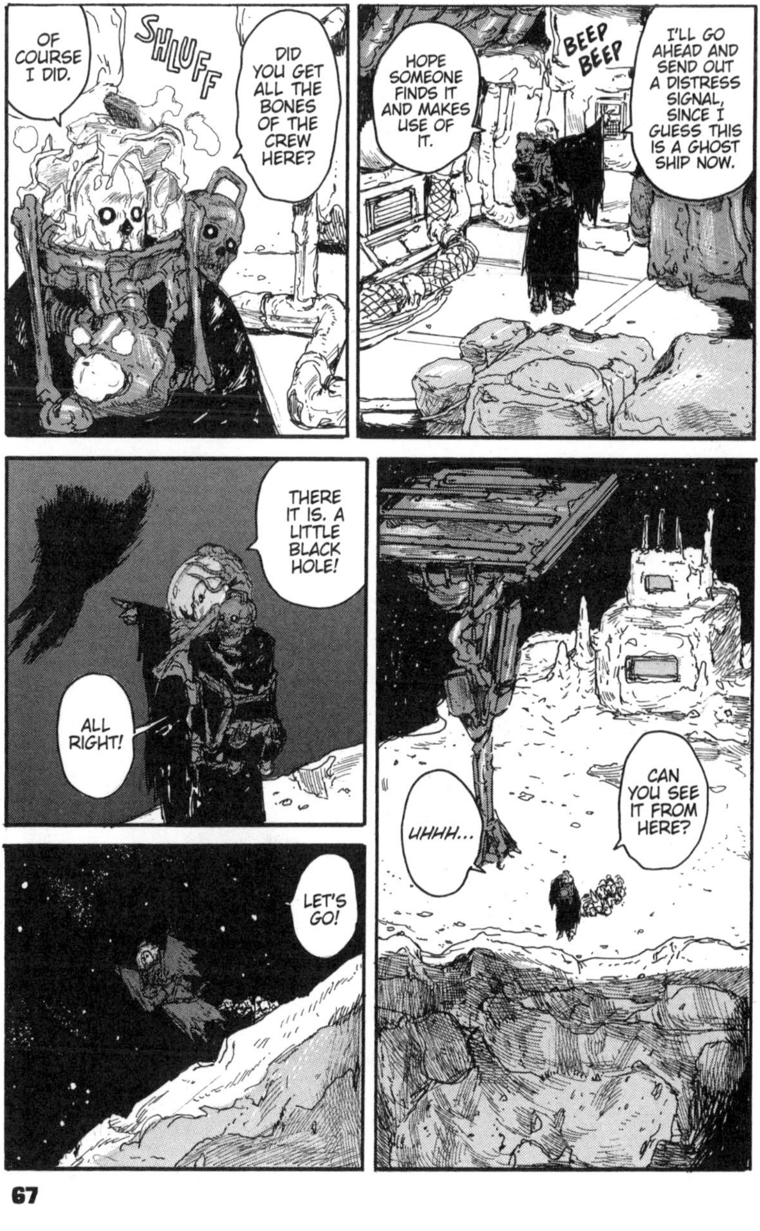
I'LL GO AHEAD AND SEND OUT A DISTRESS SIGNAL, SINCE I GUESS THIS IS A GHOST SHIP NOW.
BEEP BEEP
HOPE SOMEONE FINDS IT AND MAKES USE OF IT.
DID YOU GET ALL THE BONES OF THE CREW HERE?
SHLUFF
OF COURSE I DID.
CAN YOU SEE IT FROM HERE?
UHHH...
THERE IT IS. A LITTLE BLACK HOLE!
ALL RIGHT!
LET'S GO!

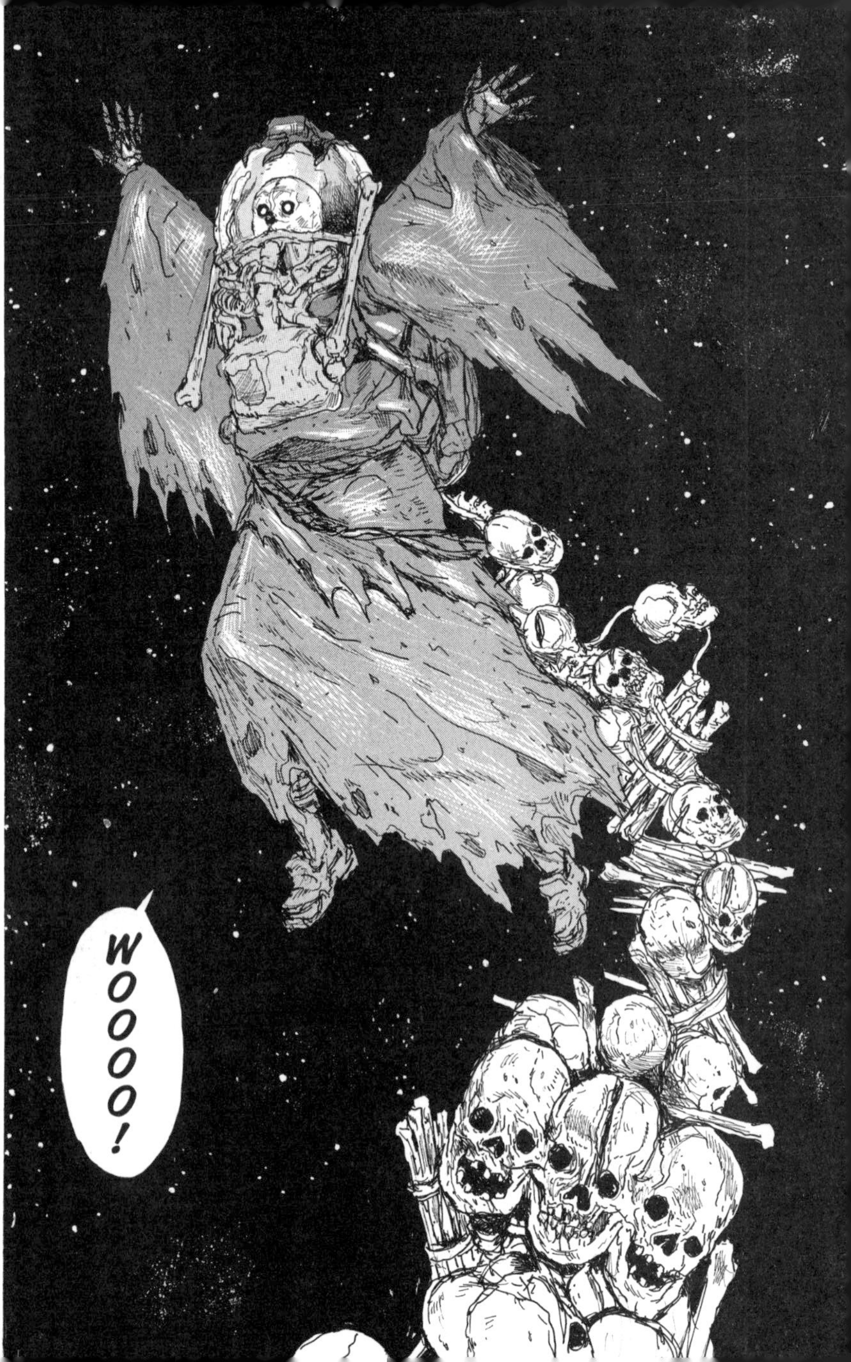
WOOOO!

★ Design of Zaha Sanko

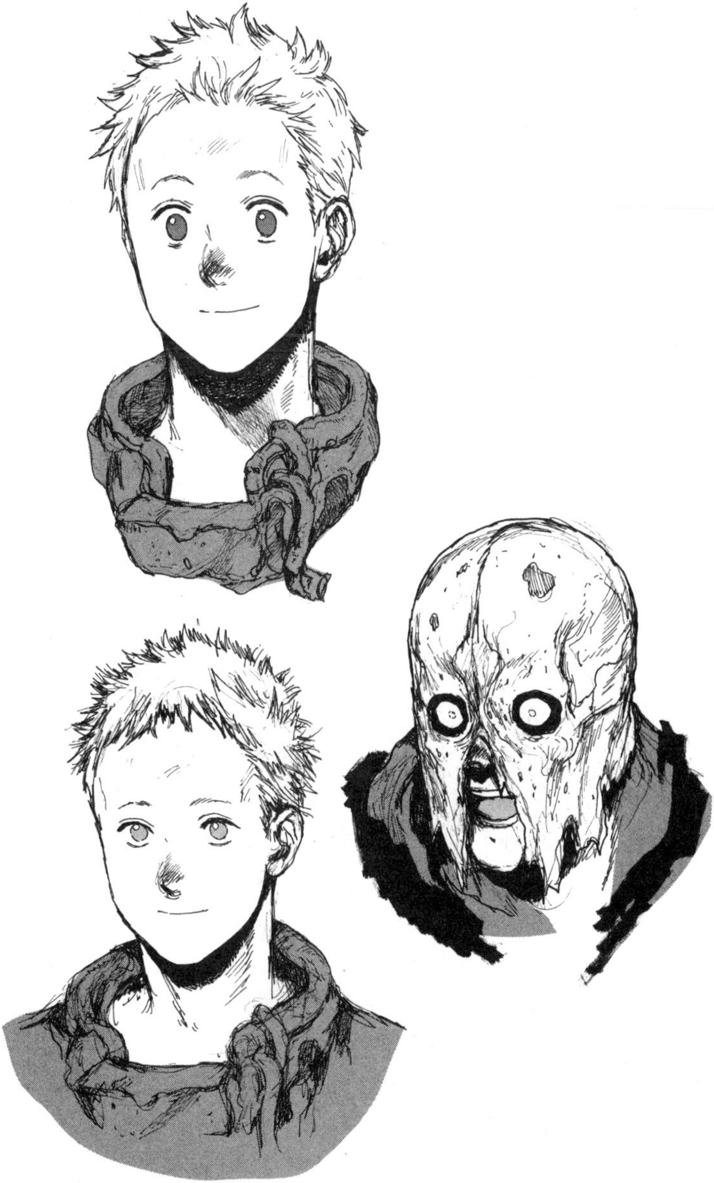

★ Design of Avakian (2)

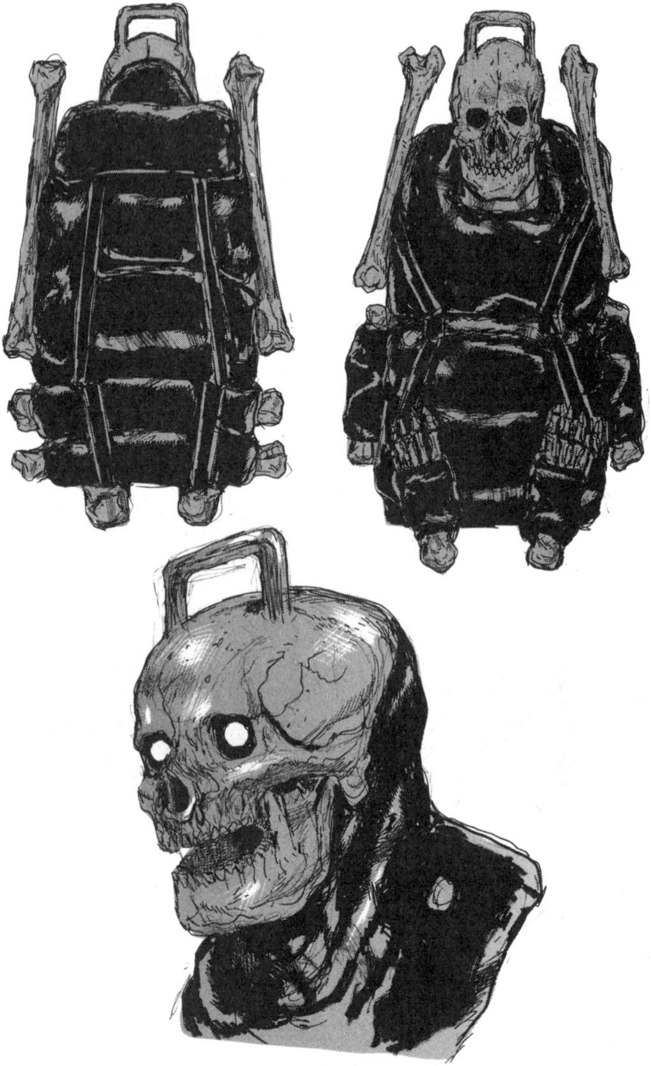

DAI DARK

DAI DARK

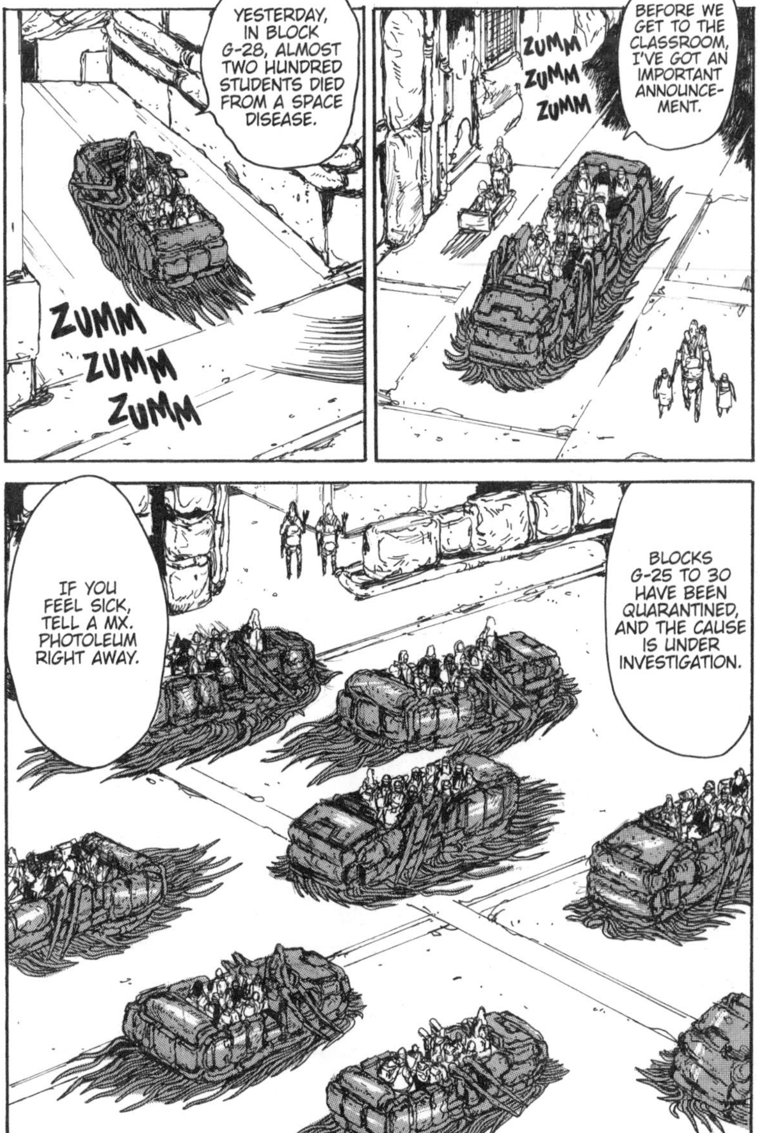
BEFORE WE GET TO THE CLASSROOM, I'VE GOT AN IMPORTANT ANNOUNCE-MENT.
ZUMM ZUMM ZUMM
YESTERDAY, IN BLOCK G-28, ALMOST TWO HUNDRED STUDENTS DIED FROM A SPACE DISEASE.
ZUMM ZUMM ZUMM
BLOCKS G-25 TO 30 HAVE BEEN QUARANTINED, AND THE CAUSE IS UNDER INVESTIGATION.
IF YOU FEEL SICK, TELL A MX. PHOTOLEUM RIGHT AWAY.

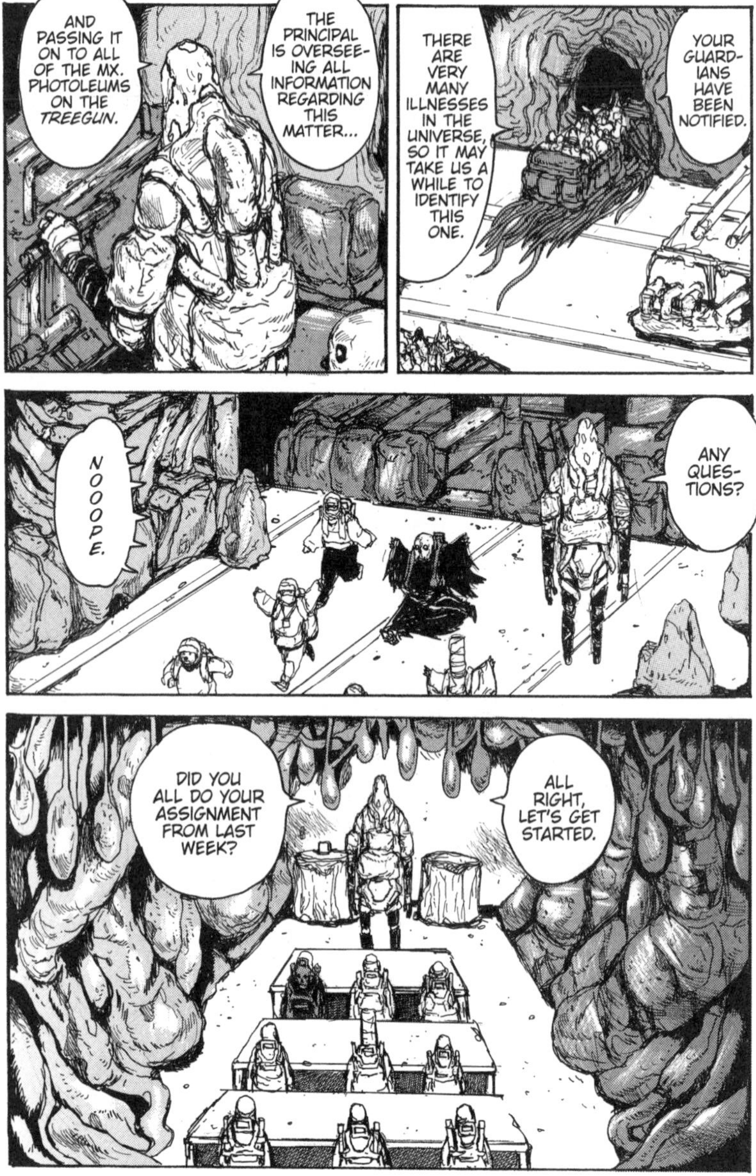
YOUR GUARDIANS HAVE BEEN NOTIFIED.
THERE ARE VERY MANY ILLNESSES IN THE UNIVERSE, SO IT MAY TAKE US A WHILE TO IDENTIFY THIS ONE.
THE PRINCIPAL IS OVERSEEING ALL INFORMATION REGARDING THIS MATTER...
AND PASSING IT ON TO ALL OF THE MX. PHOTOLEUMS ON THE *TREEGUN*.
ANY QUESTIONS?
NOOOOPE.
ALL RIGHT, LET'S GET STARTED.
DID YOU ALL DO YOUR ASSIGNMENT FROM LAST WEEK?

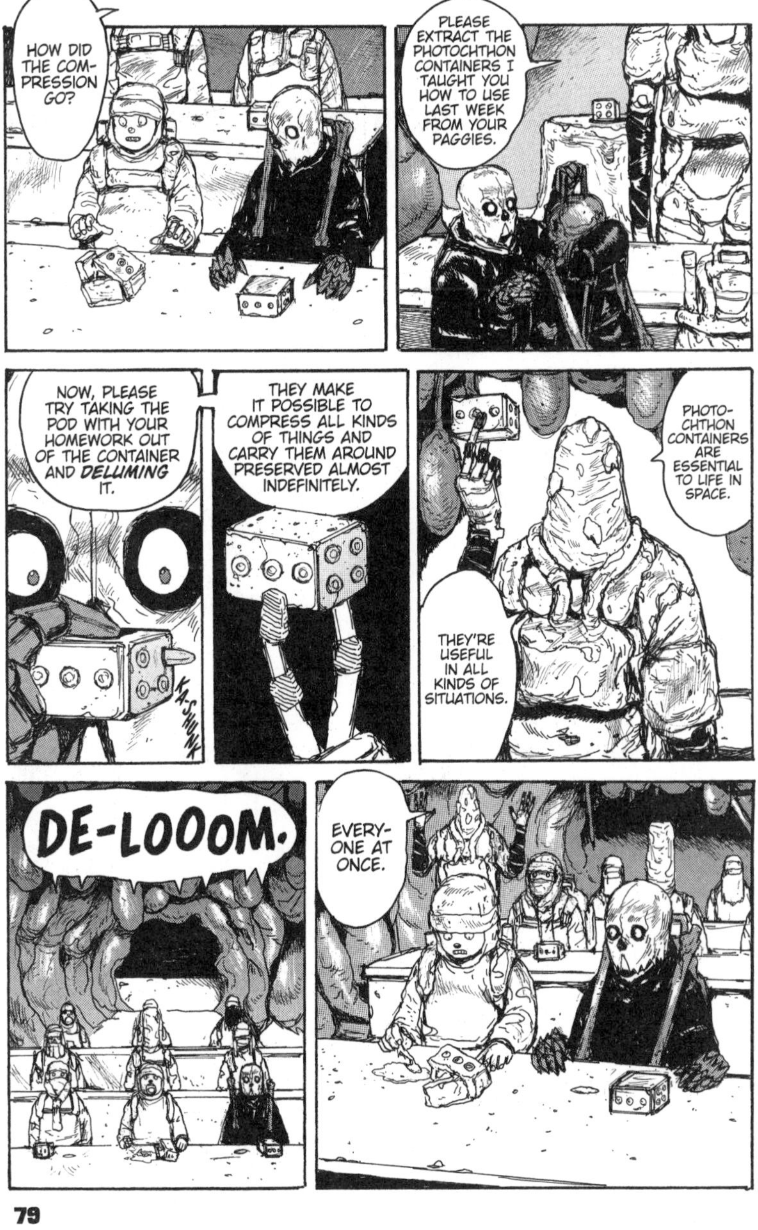

PLEASE EXTRACT THE PHOTOCHTHON CONTAINERS I TAUGHT YOU HOW TO USE LAST WEEK FROM YOUR PAGGIES.
HOW DID THE COM-PRESSION GO?
PHOTO-CHTHON CONTAINERS ARE ESSENTIAL TO LIFE IN SPACE.
THEY'RE USEFUL IN ALL KINDS OF SITUATIONS.
THEY MAKE IT POSSIBLE TO COMPRESS ALL KINDS OF THINGS AND CARRY THEM AROUND PRESERVED ALMOST INDEFINITELY.
NOW, PLEASE TRY TAKING THE POD WITH YOUR HOMEWORK OUT OF THE CONTAINER AND ***DELUMING*** IT.
KA-SHUNK
EVERY-ONE AT ONCE.
DE-LOOOM.

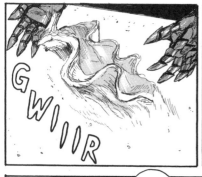

BURB BURB BURB
GWIIIR
BOOM
NGH!
UGH!
YAY!
I ASKED YOU TO MAKE YOUR FAVORITE FOOD.
DOES IT STILL LOOK THE WAY IT DID WHEN YOU COOKED IT?
WHAT'S THAT YOU MADE?
A MEAP-SWICH.
BEEEE?
WHAT IS A MEAP-SWICH?

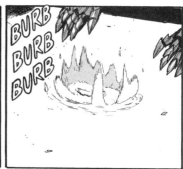

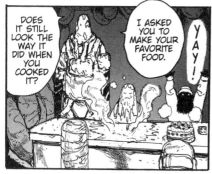

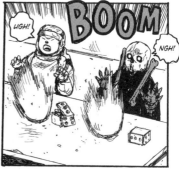

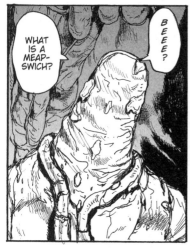

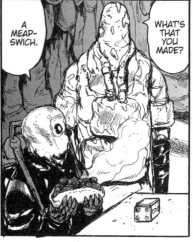

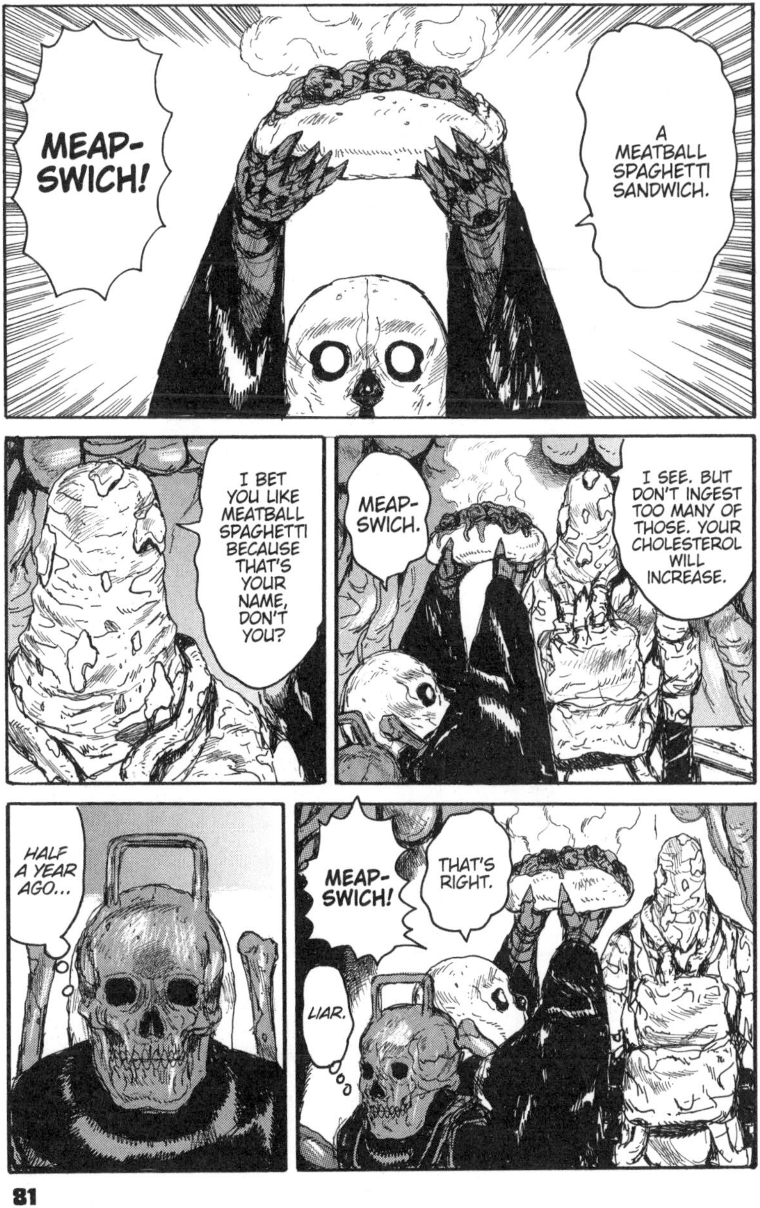
A MEATBALL SPAGHETTI SANDWICH.
MEAP-SWICH!
I SEE. BUT DON'T INGEST TOO MANY OF THOSE. YOUR CHOLESTEROL WILL INCREASE.
MEAP-SWICH.
I BET YOU LIKE MEATBALL SPAGHETTI BECAUSE THAT'S YOUR NAME, DON'T YOU?
THAT'S RIGHT.
MEAP-SWICH!
LIAR.
HALF A YEAR AGO...

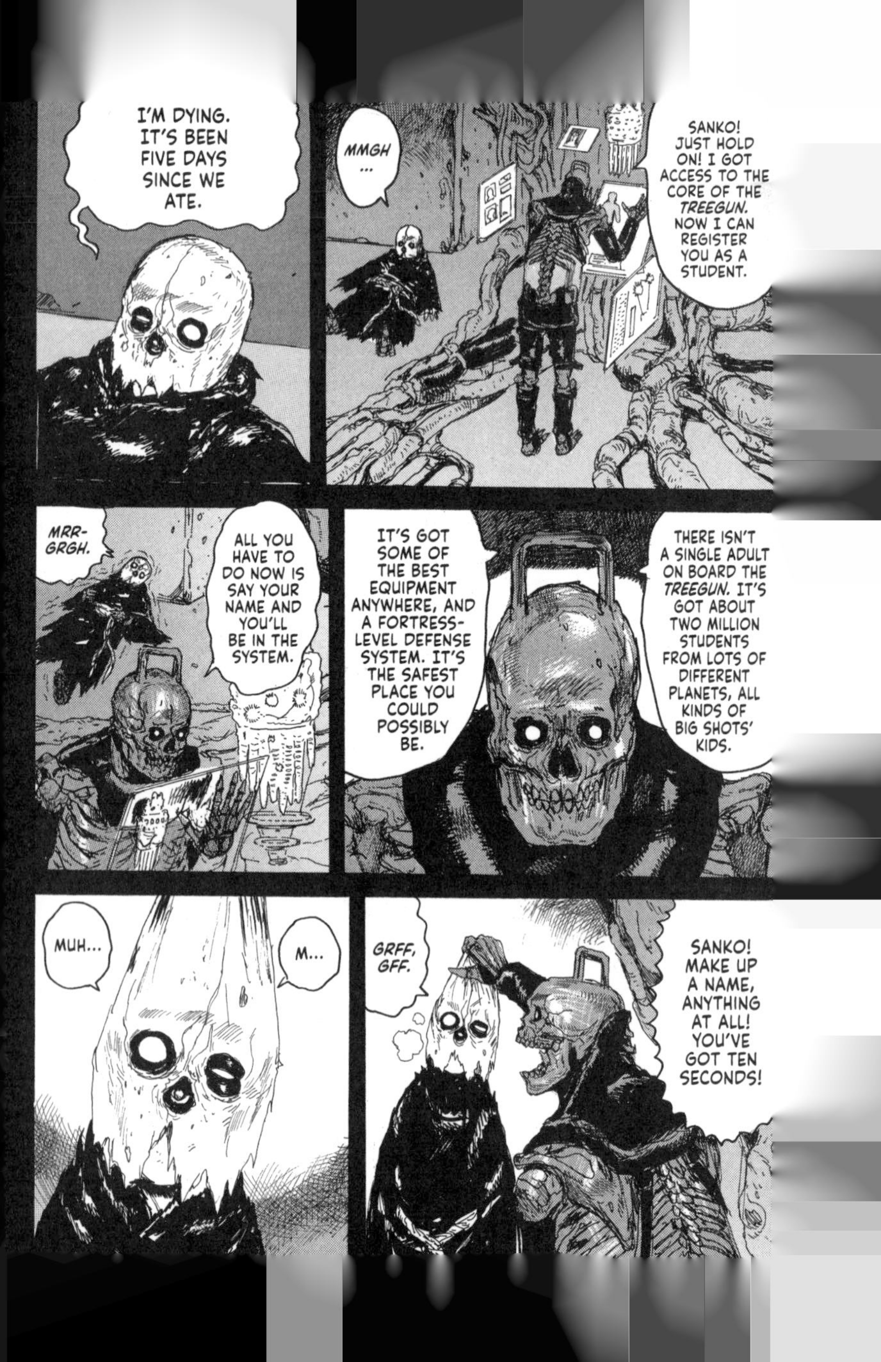
SANKO! JUST HOLD ON! I GOT ACCESS TO THE CORE OF THE *TREEGUN.* NOW I CAN REGISTER YOU AS A STUDENT.
MMGH ...
I'M DYING. IT'S BEEN FIVE DAYS SINCE WE ATE.
THERE ISN'T A SINGLE ADULT ON BOARD THE *TREEGUN.* IT'S GOT ABOUT TWO MILLION STUDENTS FROM LOTS OF DIFFERENT PLANETS, ALL KINDS OF BIG SHOTS' KIDS.
IT'S GOT SOME OF THE BEST EQUIPMENT ANYWHERE, AND A FORTRESS-LEVEL DEFENSE SYSTEM. IT'S THE SAFEST PLACE YOU COULD POSSIBLY BE.
ALL YOU HAVE TO DO NOW IS SAY YOUR NAME AND YOU'LL BE IN THE SYSTEM.
MRR-GRGH.
SANKO! MAKE UP A NAME, ANYTHING AT ALL! YOU'VE GOT TEN SECONDS!
GRFF, GFF.
M...
MUH...

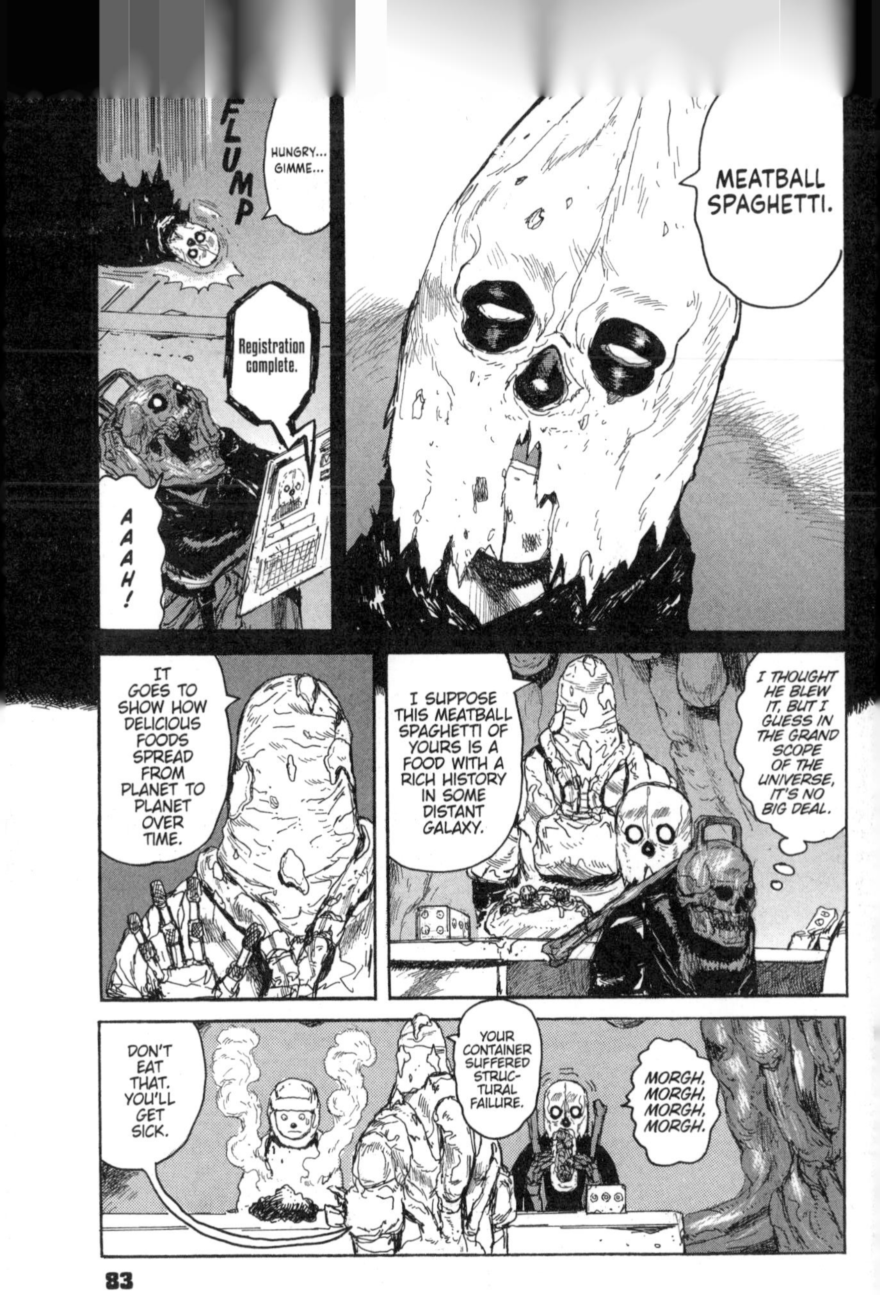

MEATBALL SPAGHETTI.
HUNGRY... GIMME...
FLUMP
Registration complete.
AAAAH!
I THOUGHT HE BLEW IT, BUT I GUESS IN THE GRAND SCOPE OF THE UNIVERSE, IT'S NO BIG DEAL.
I SUPPOSE THIS MEATBALL SPAGHETTI OF YOURS IS A FOOD WITH A RICH HISTORY IN SOME DISTANT GALAXY.
IT GOES TO SHOW HOW DELICIOUS FOODS SPREAD FROM PLANET TO PLANET OVER TIME.
MORGH, MORGH, MORGH, MORGH.
YOUR CONTAINER SUFFERED STRUCTURAL FAILURE.
DON'T EAT THAT. YOU'LL GET SICK.

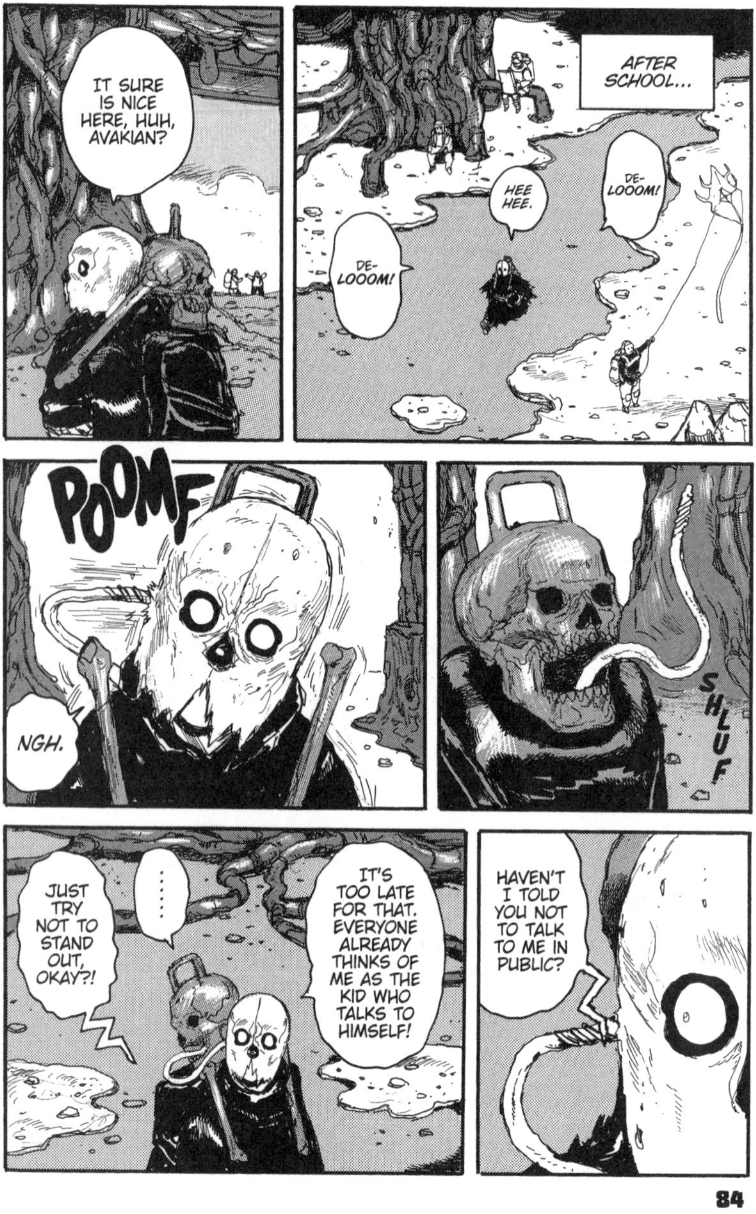
AFTER SCHOOL...
DE-LOOOM!
HEE HEE.
DE-LOOOM!
IT SURE IS NICE HERE, HUH, AVAKIAN?
SHLUF
POOMF
NGH.
HAVEN'T I TOLD YOU NOT TO TALK TO ME IN PUBLIC?
IT'S TOO LATE FOR THAT. EVERYONE ALREADY THINKS OF ME AS THE KID WHO TALKS TO HIMSELF!
......
JUST TRY NOT TO STAND OUT, OKAY?!

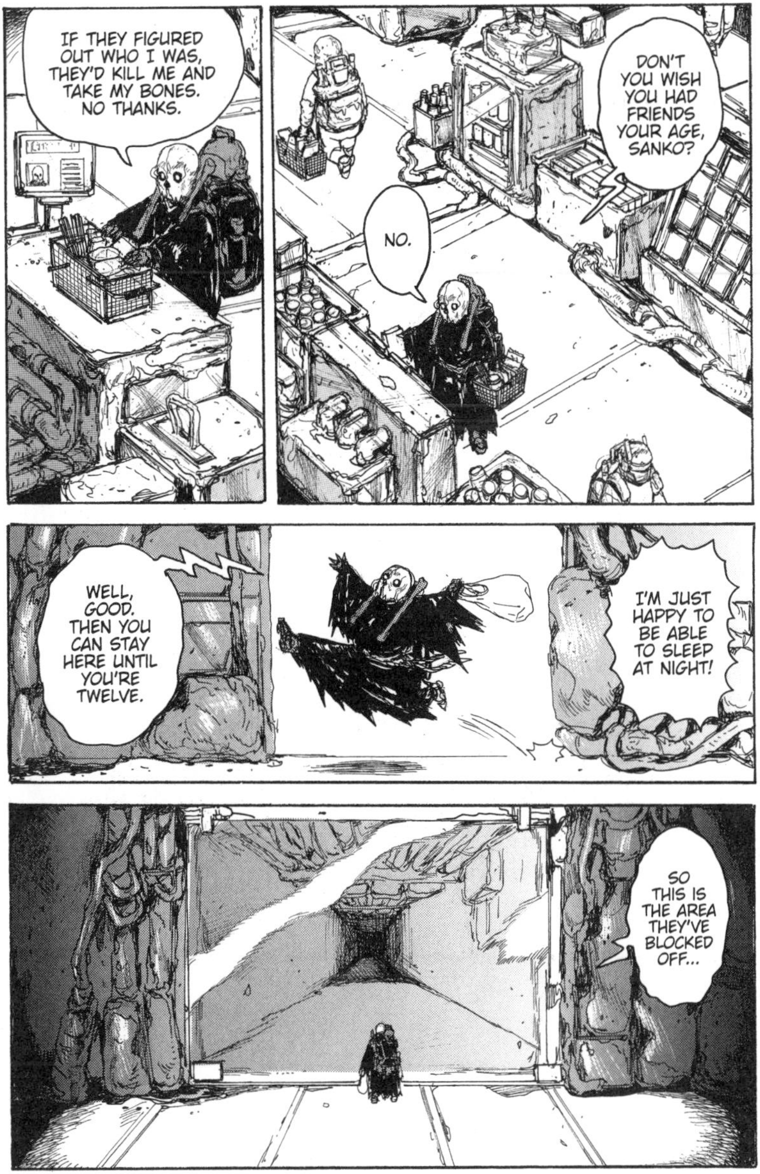
DON'T YOU WISH YOU HAD FRIENDS YOUR AGE, SANKO?
NO.
IF THEY FIGURED OUT WHO I WAS, THEY'D KILL ME AND TAKE MY BONES. NO THANKS.
I'M JUST HAPPY TO BE ABLE TO SLEEP AT NIGHT!
WELL, GOOD. THEN YOU CAN STAY HERE UNTIL YOU'RE TWELVE.
SO THIS IS THE AREA THEY'VE BLOCKED OFF...

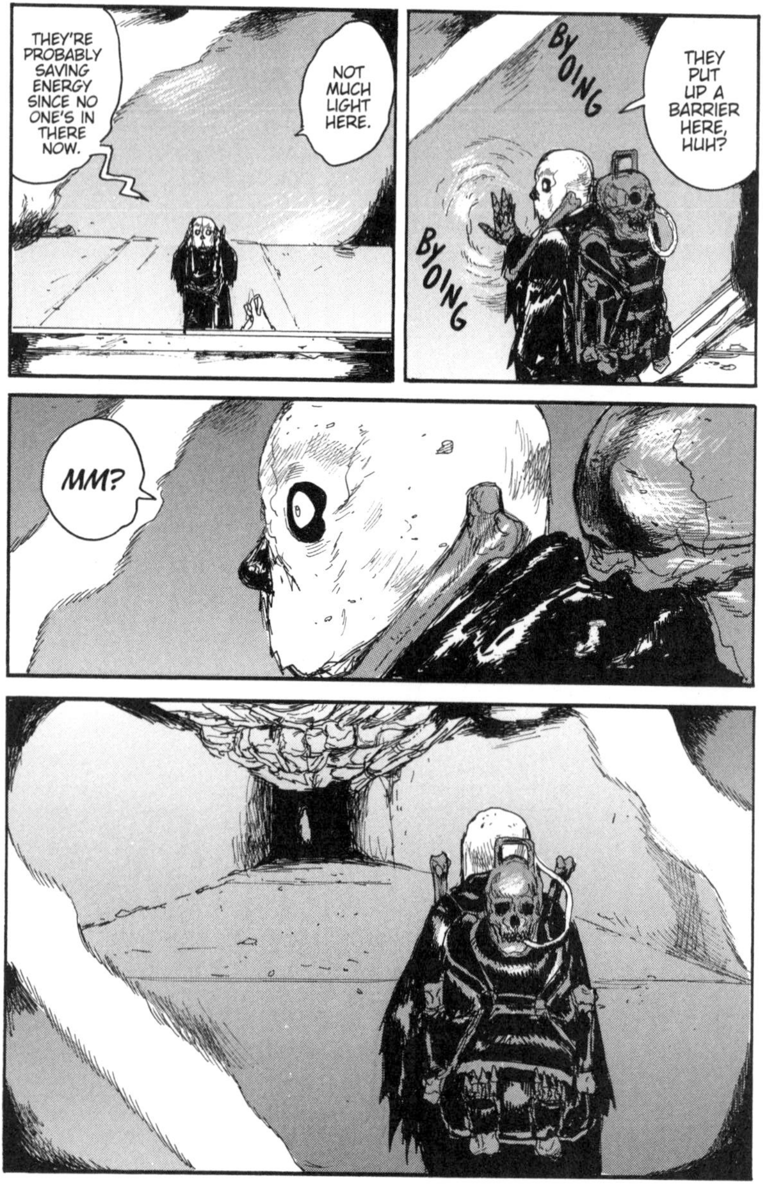
THEY PUT UP A BARRIER HERE, HUH?
BYOING
BYOING
NOT MUCH LIGHT HERE.
THEY'RE PROBABLY SAVING ENERGY SINCE NO ONE'S IN THERE NOW.
MM?

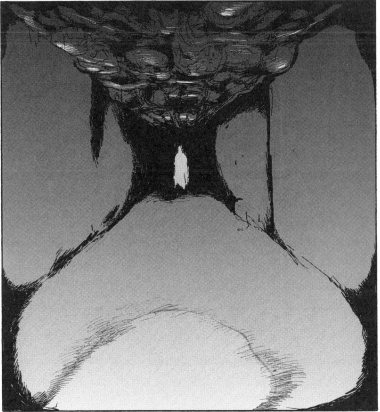

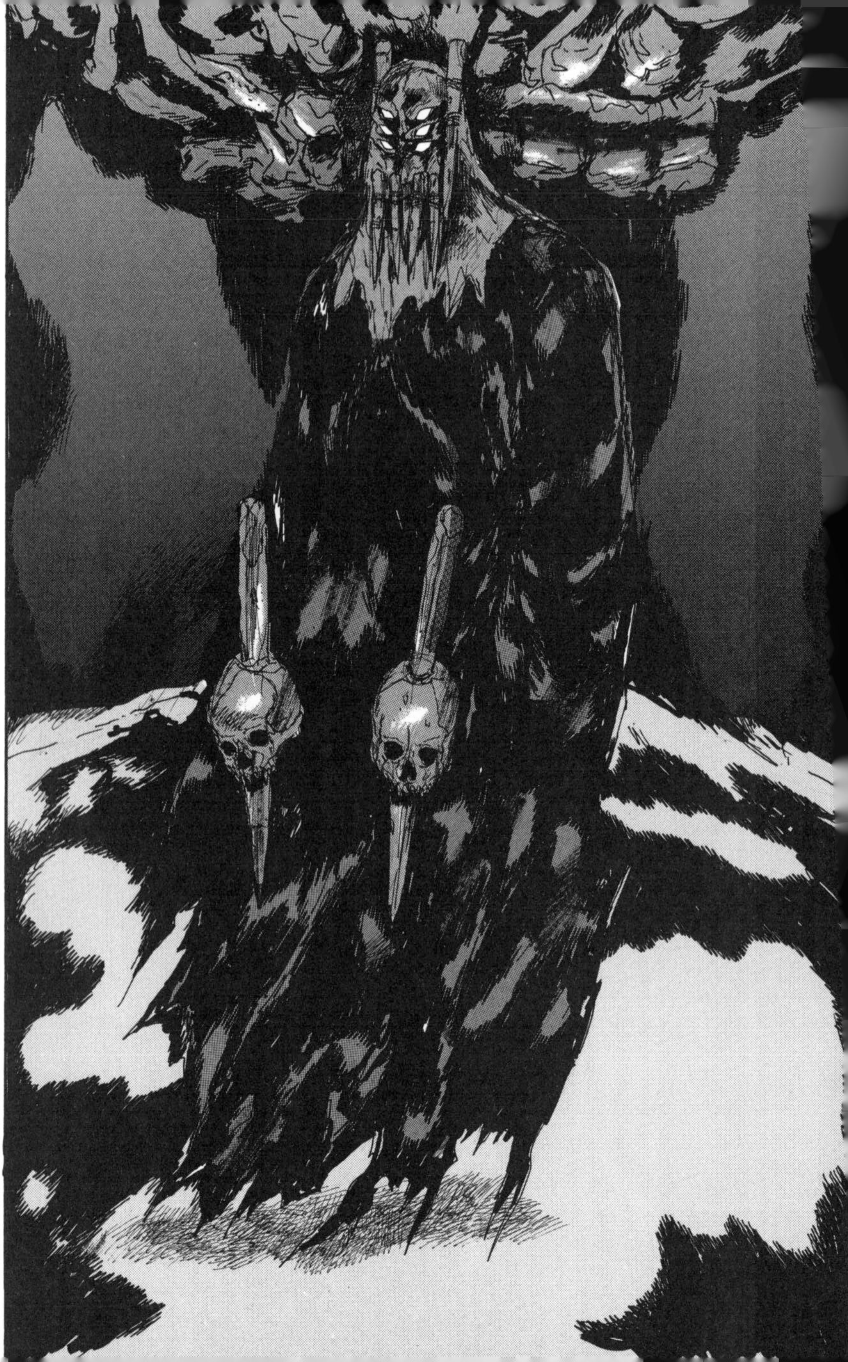

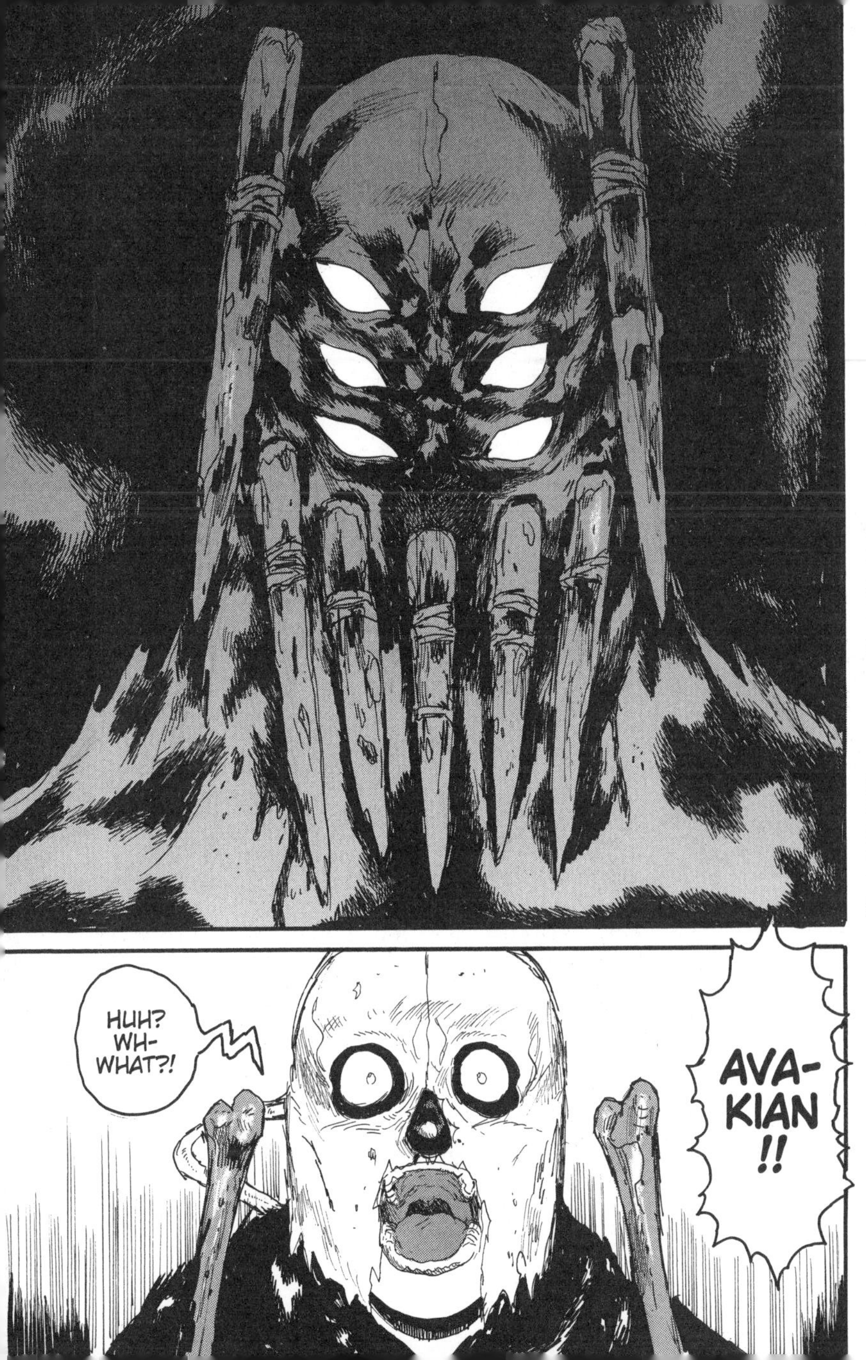
AVA-KIAN!!
HUH? WH-WHAT?!

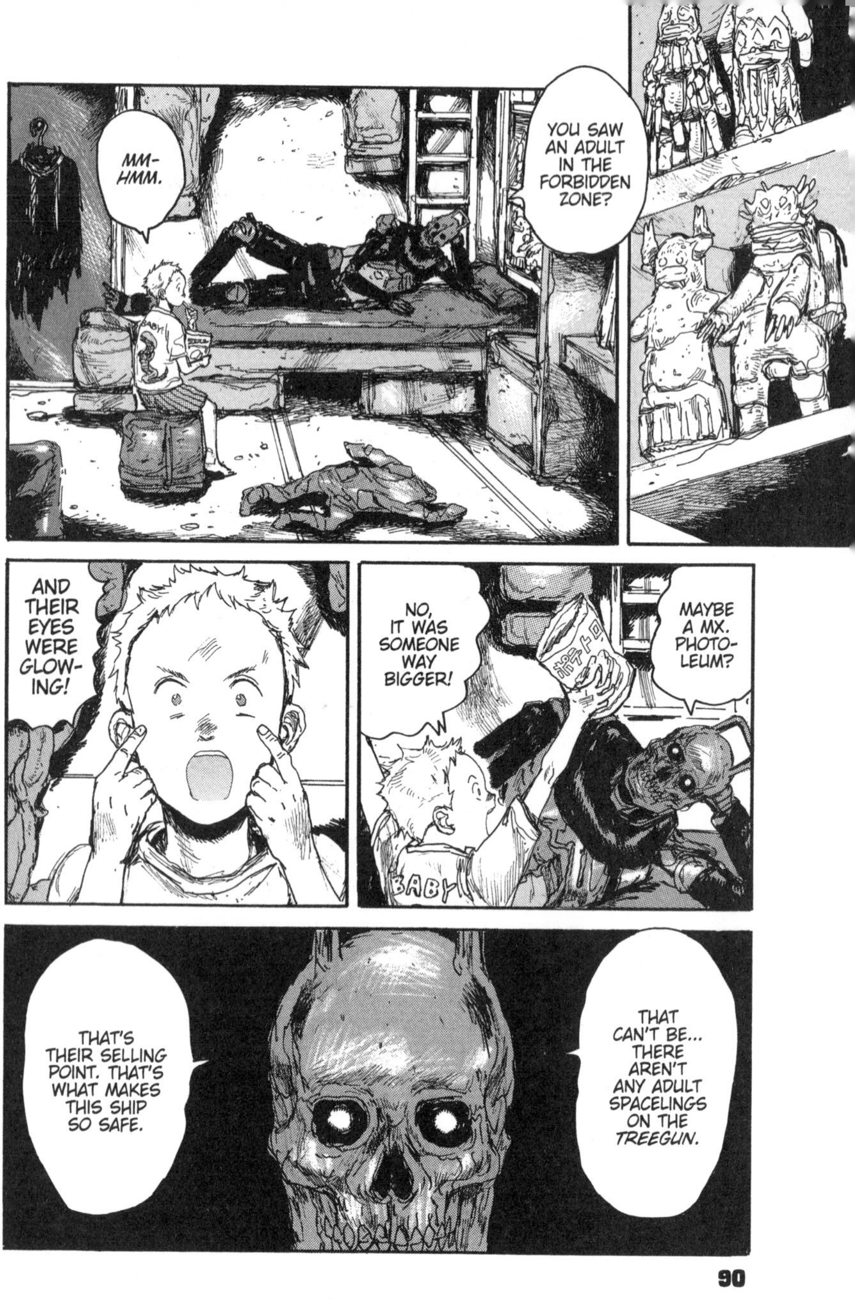
YOU SAW AN ADULT IN THE FORBIDDEN ZONE?
MM-HMM.
MAYBE A MX. PHOTOLEUM?
NO, IT WAS SOMEONE WAY BIGGER!
AND THEIR EYES WERE GLOWING!
THAT CAN'T BE... THERE AREN'T ANY ADULT SPACELINGS ON THE *TREEGUN*.
THAT'S THEIR SELLING POINT. THAT'S WHAT MAKES THIS SHIP SO SAFE.

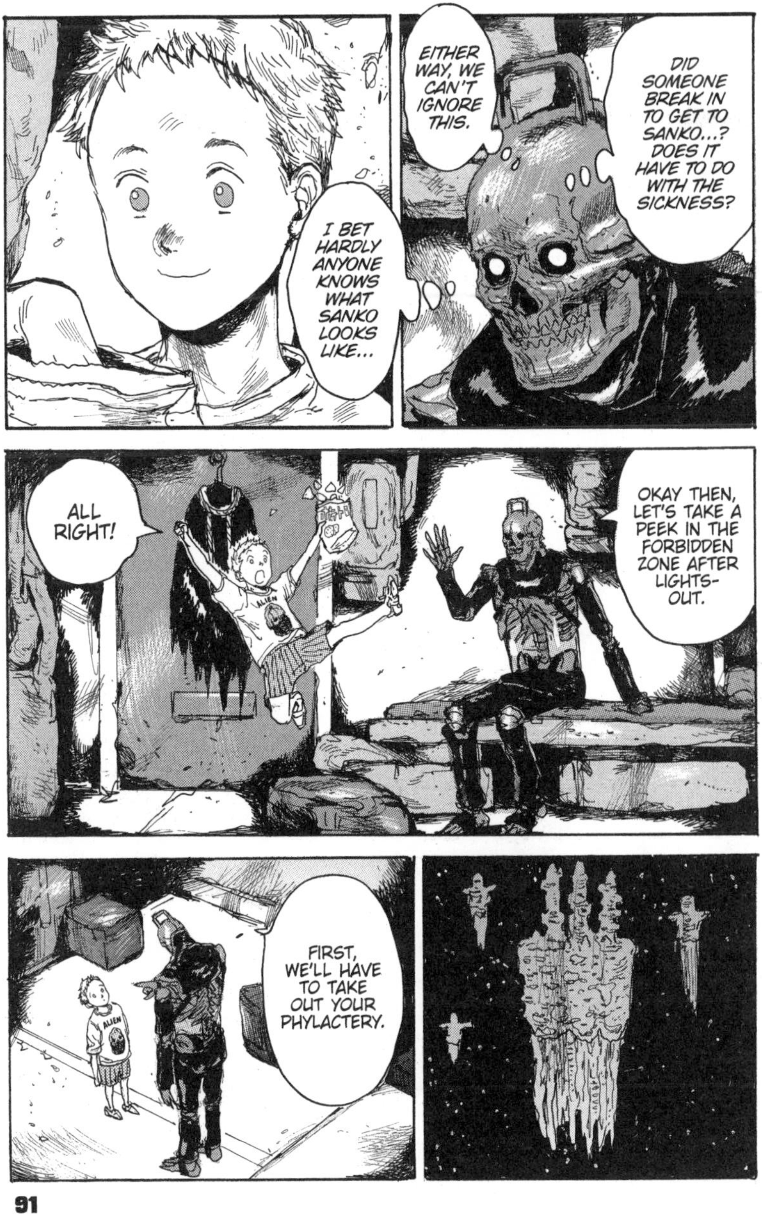
DID SOMEONE BREAK IN TO GET TO SANKO...? DOES IT HAVE TO DO WITH THE SICKNESS?
EITHER WAY, WE CAN'T IGNORE THIS.
I BET HARDLY ANYONE KNOWS WHAT SANKO LOOKS LIKE...
OKAY THEN, LET'S TAKE A PEEK IN THE FORBIDDEN ZONE AFTER LIGHTS-OUT.
ALL RIGHT!
ALIEN
FIRST, WE'LL HAVE TO TAKE OUT YOUR PHYLACTERY.

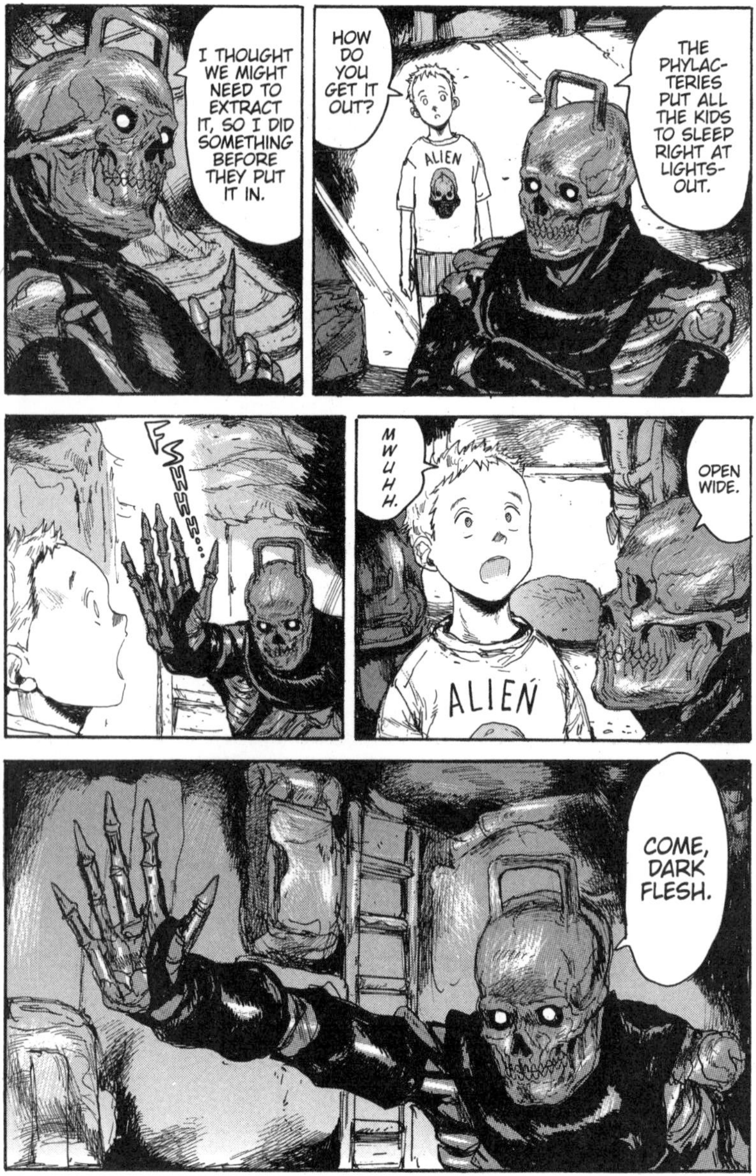
THE PHYLACTERIES PUT ALL THE KIDS TO SLEEP RIGHT AT LIGHTS-OUT.
HOW DO YOU GET IT OUT?
ALIEN
I THOUGHT WE MIGHT NEED TO EXTRACT IT, SO I DID SOMETHING BEFORE THEY PUT IT IN.
OPEN WIDE.
MWUHH.
ALIEN
FSHHHH...
COME, DARK FLESH.

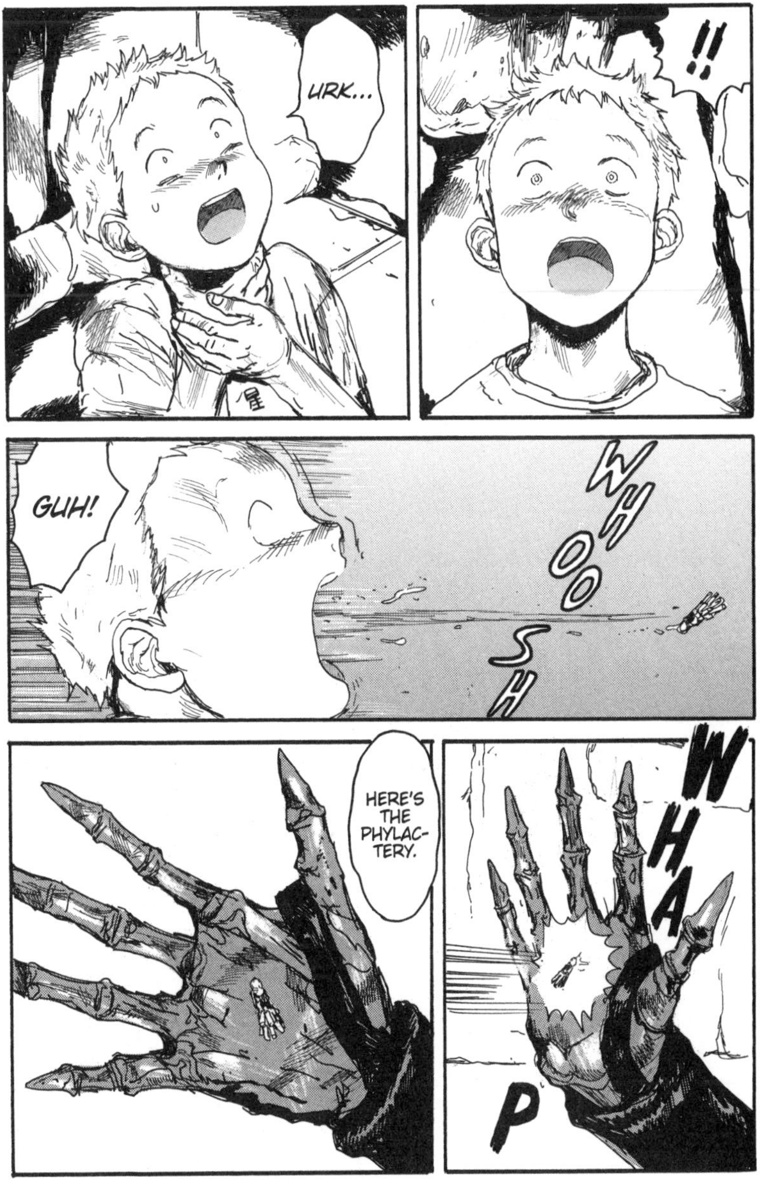
!!
URK...
屋
WHOOSH
GUH!
WHAP
HERE'S THE PHYLACTERY.

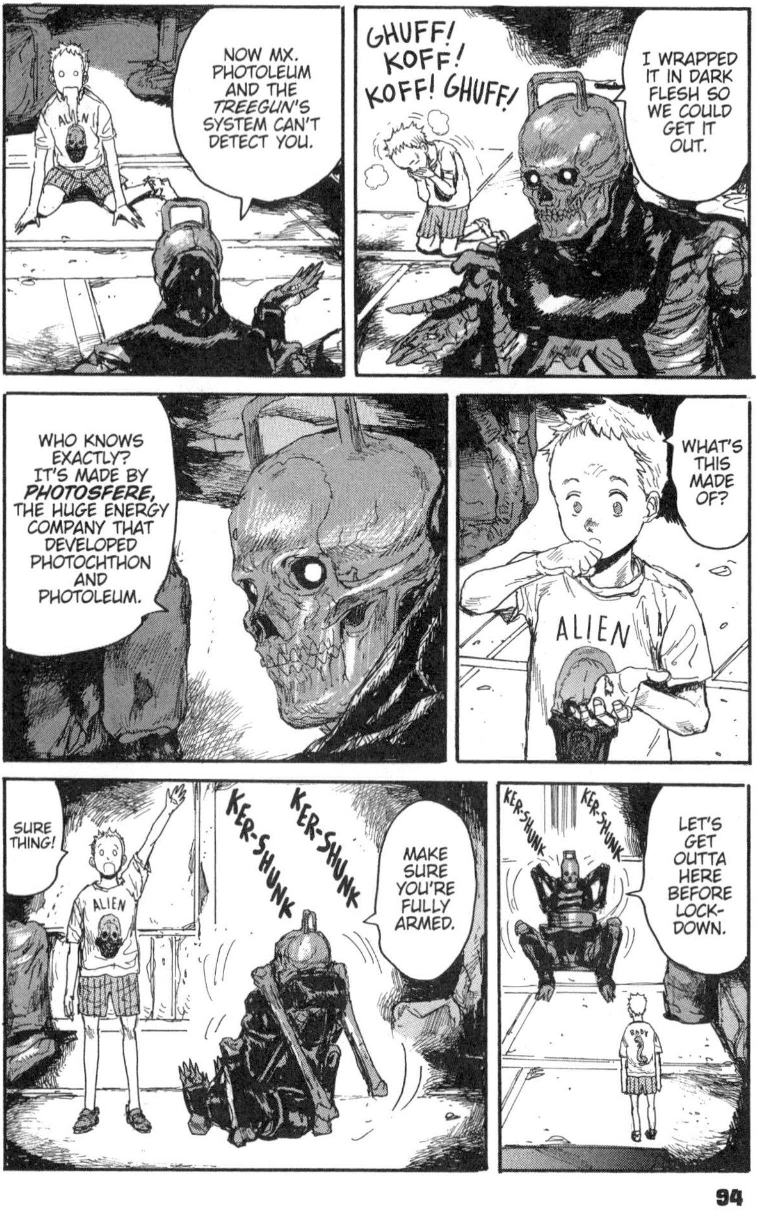

GHUFF! KOFF! KOFF! GHUFF!
I WRAPPED IT IN DARK FLESH SO WE COULD GET IT OUT.
NOW MX. PHOTOLEUM AND THE *TREEGUN*'S SYSTEM CAN'T DETECT YOU.
WHAT'S THIS MADE OF?
ALIEN
WHO KNOWS EXACTLY? IT'S MADE BY ***PHOTOSFERE,*** THE HUGE ENERGY COMPANY THAT DEVELOPED PHOTOCHTHON AND PHOTOLEUM.
KER-SHUNK
KER-SHUNK
LET'S GET OUTTA HERE BEFORE LOCK-DOWN.
KER-SHUNK
KER-SHUNK
MAKE SURE YOU'RE FULLY ARMED.
SURE THING!
ALIEN

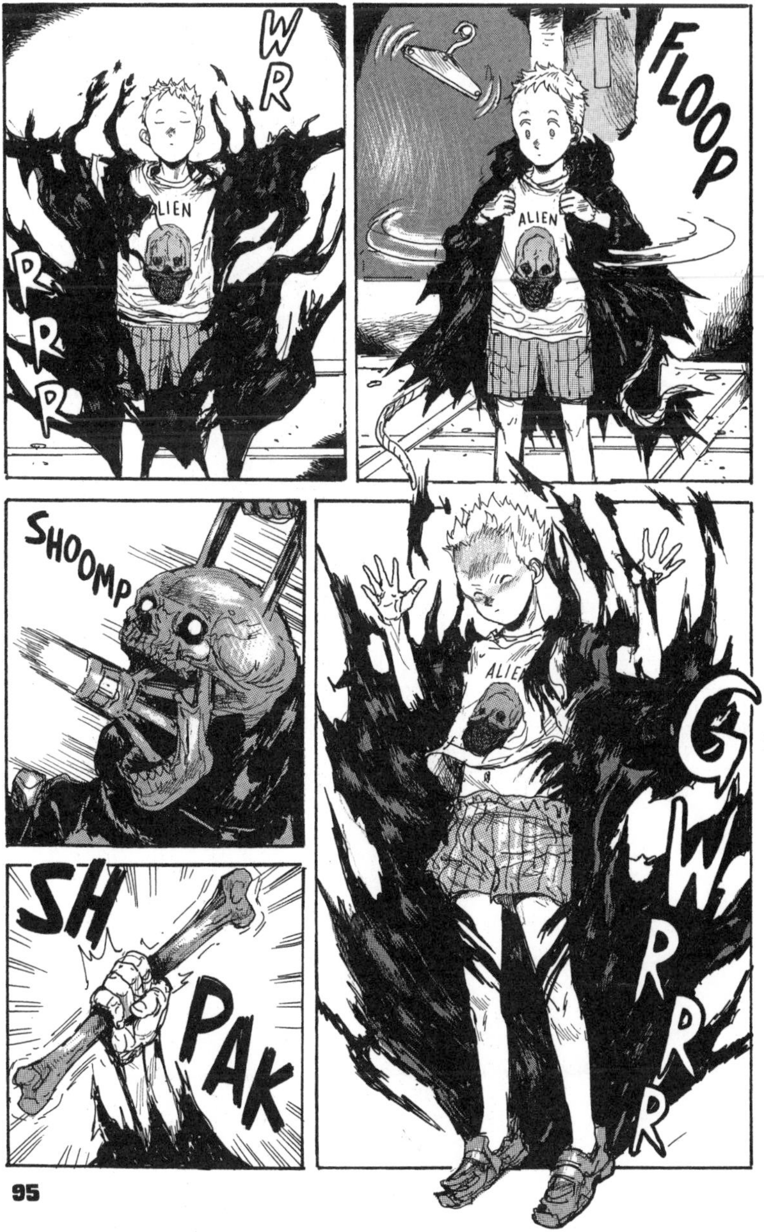
FLOOP
ALIEN
WR
RRR
ALIEN
ALIEN
GWRRRR
SHOOMP
SH
PAK

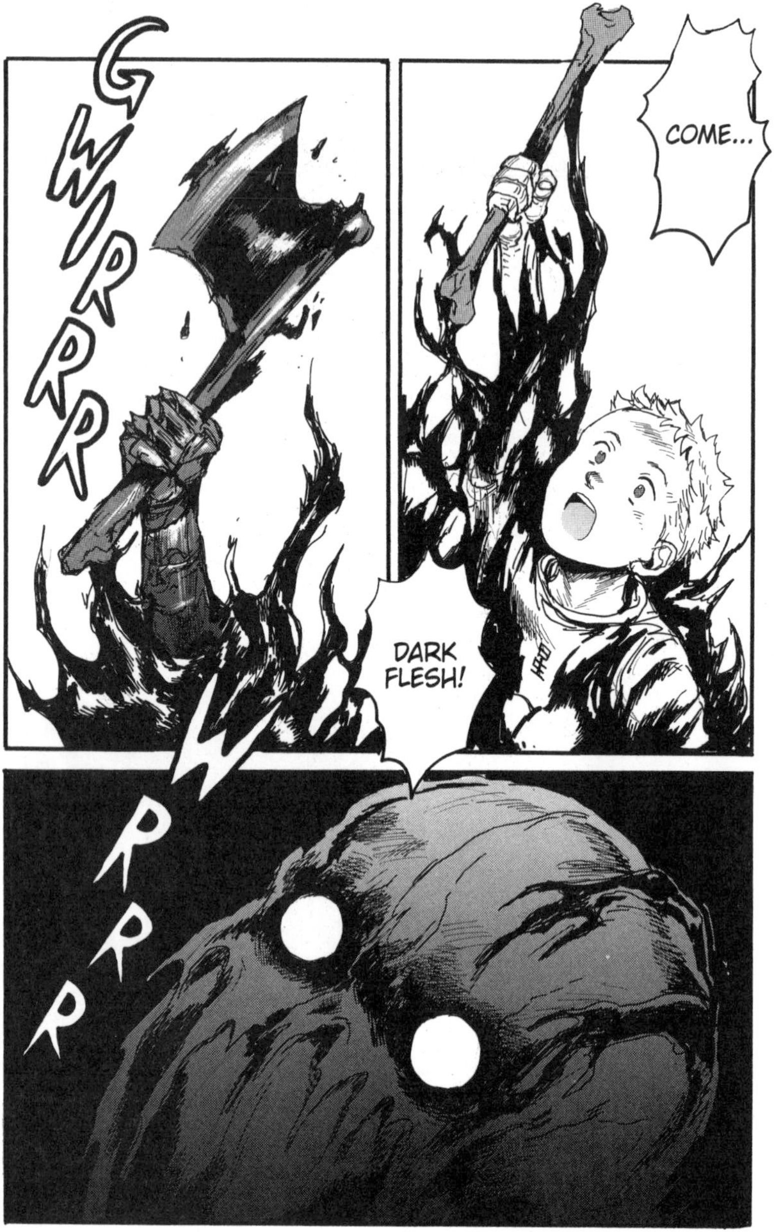
COME...
GWRRR
DARK FLESH!
WRRR

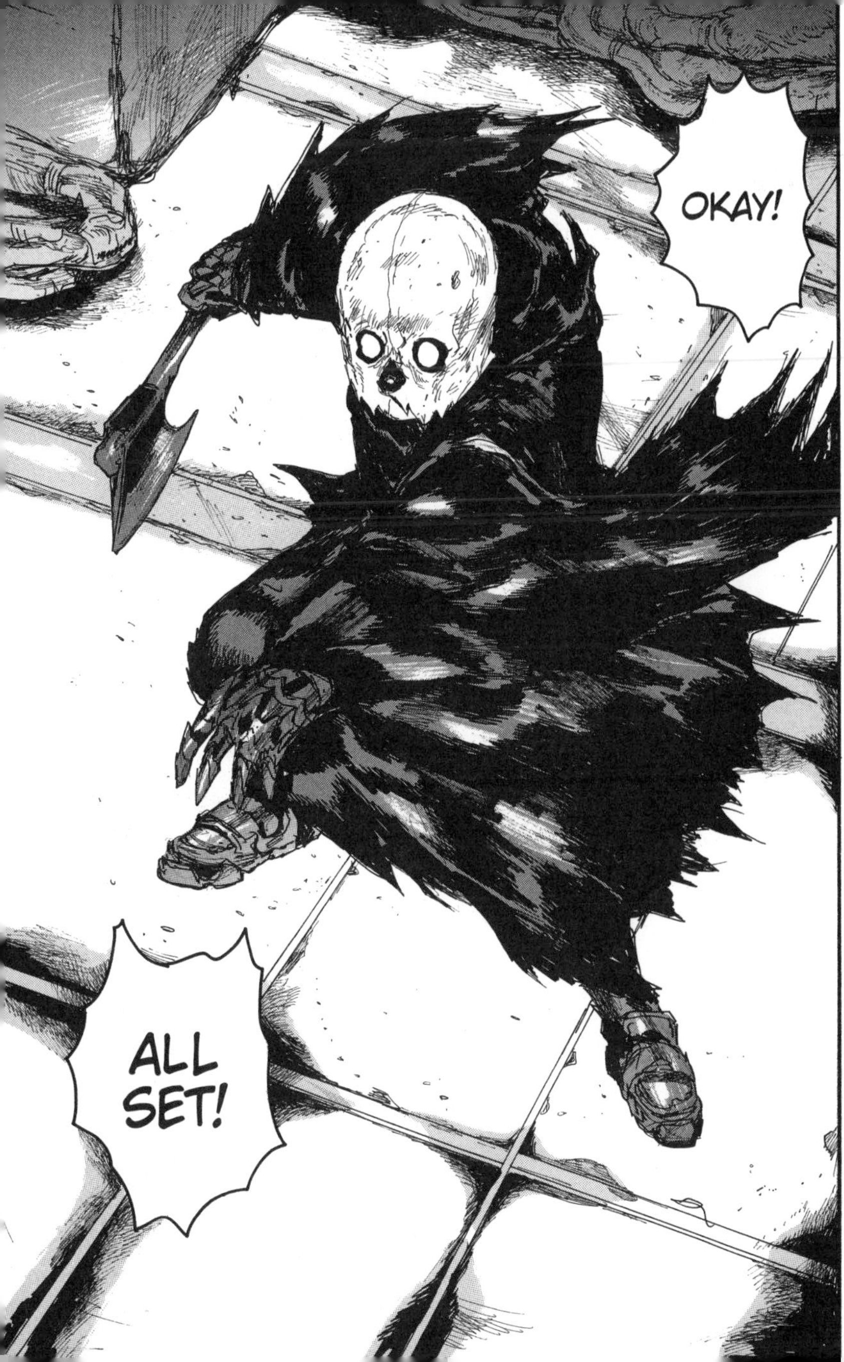
OKAY!
ALL SET!

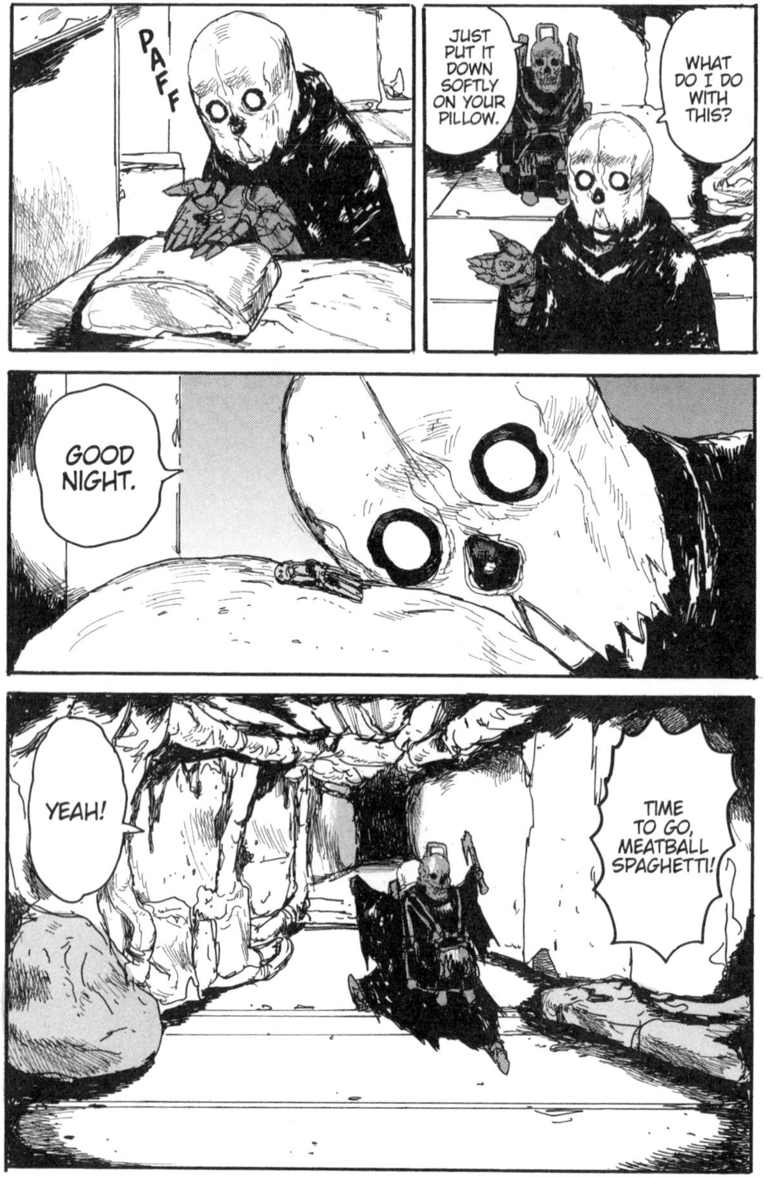
WHAT DO I DO WITH THIS?
JUST PUT IT DOWN SOFTLY ON YOUR PILLOW.
PAFF
GOOD NIGHT.
TIME TO GO, MEATBALL SPAGHETTI!
YEAH!

★ Cover art for the *Monthly Shonen Sunday* 10th anniversary issue.

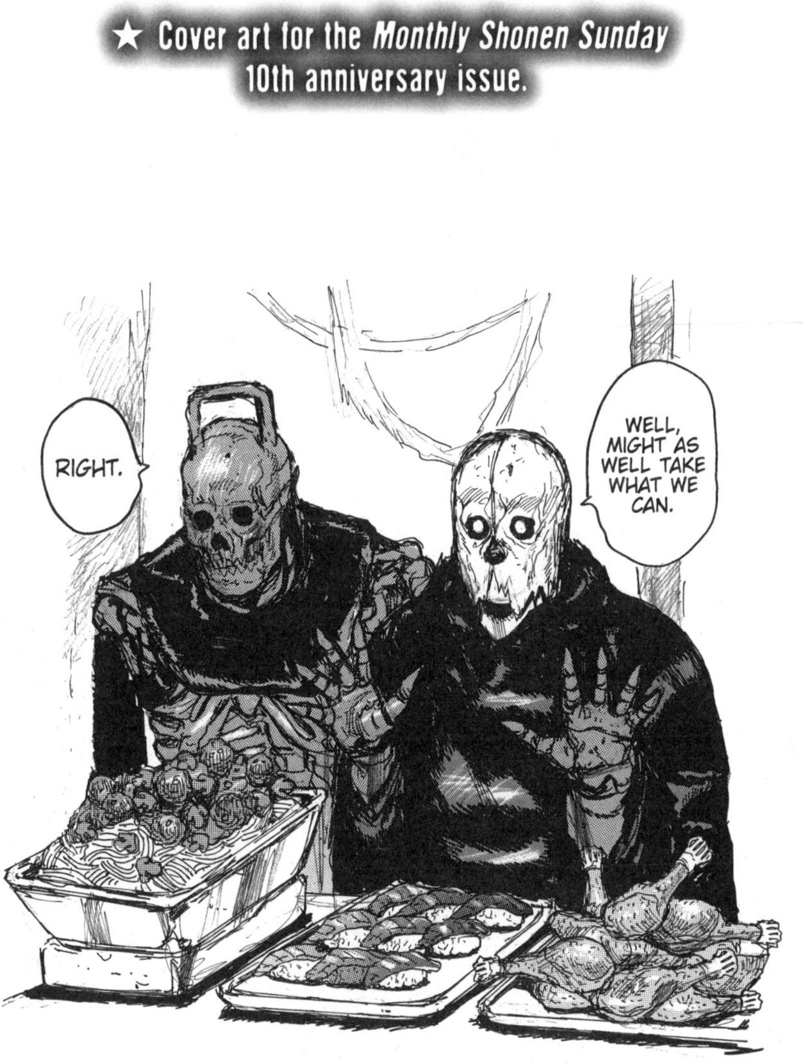
WELL, MIGHT AS WELL TAKE WHAT WE CAN.
RIGHT.

★ Art for the *Monthly Shonen Sunday* 10th anniversary issue.

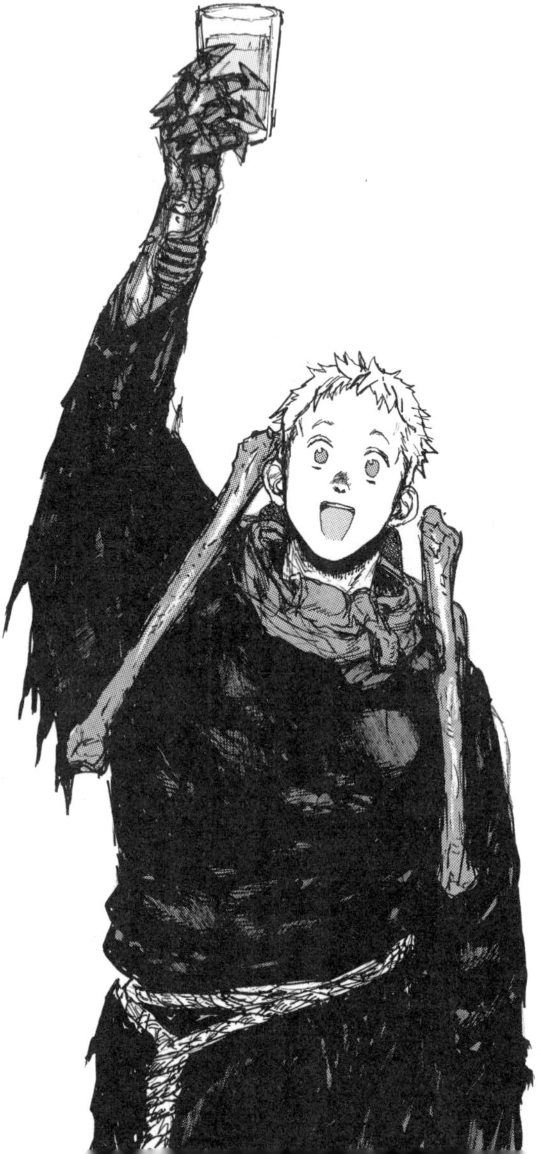

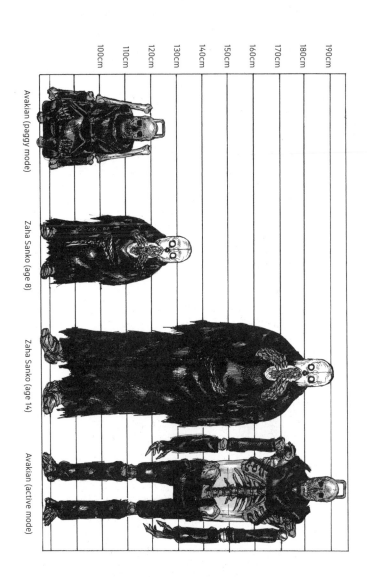

190cm
180cm
170cm
160cm
150cm
140cm
130cm
120cm
110cm
100cm

Avakian (paggy mode)

Zaha Sanko (age 8)

Zaha Sanko (age 14)

Avakian (active mode)

Bone 4: Allow Me to Kill You

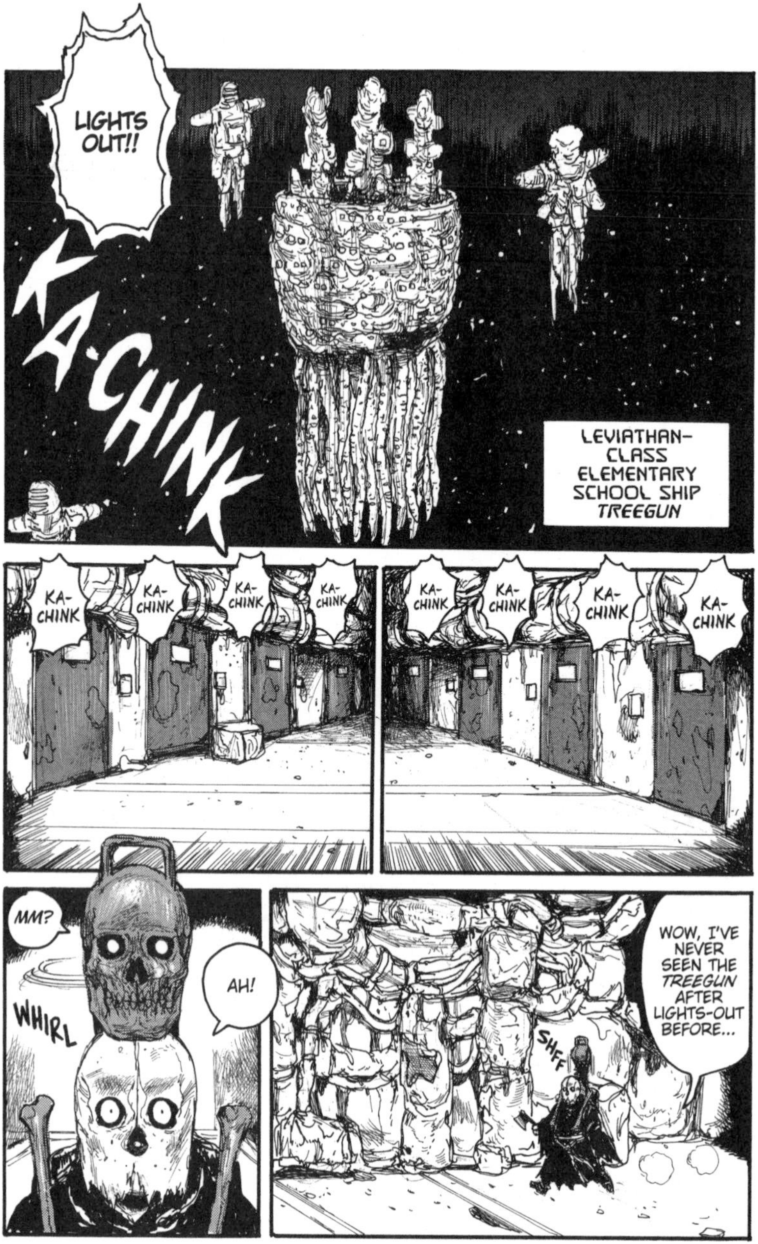
LIGHTS OUT!!
LEVIATHAN-CLASS ELEMENTARY SCHOOL SHIP *TREEGUN*
KA-CHINK
KA-CHINK
KA-CHINK
KA-CHINK
KA-CHINK
KA-CHINK
KA-CHINK
KA-CHINK
KA-CHINK
WOW, I'VE NEVER SEEN THE *TREEGUN* AFTER LIGHTS-OUT BEFORE...
SHFF
MM?
AH!
WHIRL

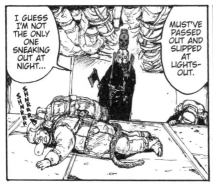

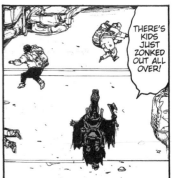

THERE'S KIDS JUST ZONKED OUT ALL OVER!
MUST'VE PASSED OUT AND SLIPPED AT LIGHTS-OUT.
I GUESS I'M NOT THE ONLY ONE SNEAKING OUT AT NIGHT...
SHNRRR
SHNRRR
!
KER-SHUNK
WHOA!
ZHUP

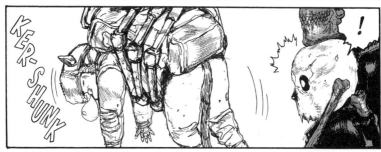

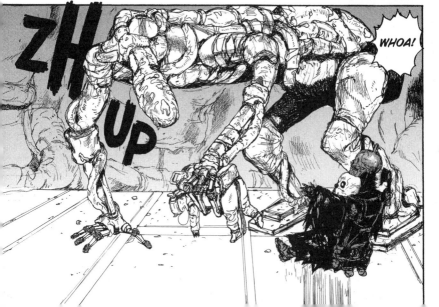

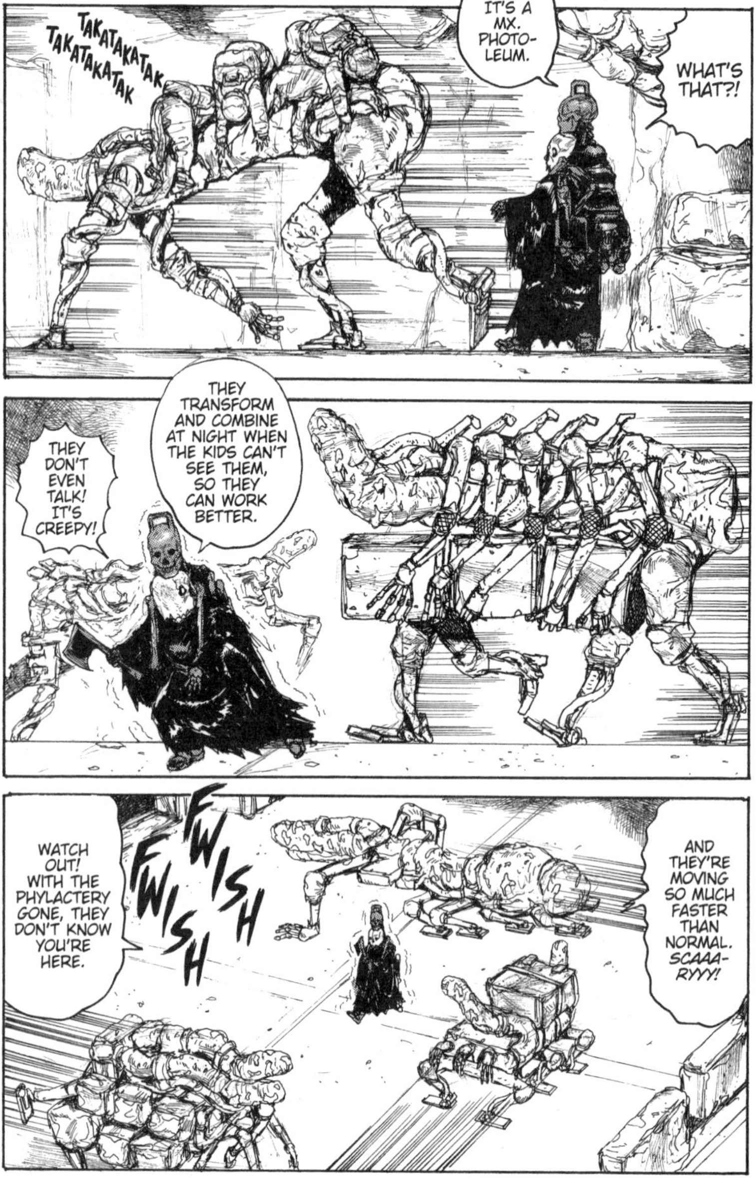
WHAT'S THAT?!
WHAT? IT'S A MX. PHOTO-LEUM.
TAKATAKATAK TAKATAKATAK
THEY TRANSFORM AND COMBINE AT NIGHT WHEN THE KIDS CAN'T SEE THEM, SO THEY CAN WORK BETTER.
THEY DON'T EVEN TALK! IT'S CREEPY!
AND THEY'RE MOVING SO MUCH FASTER THAN NORMAL. *SCAAA-RYYY!*
FWISH FWISH
WATCH OUT! WITH THE PHYLACTERY GONE, THEY DON'T KNOW YOU'RE HERE.

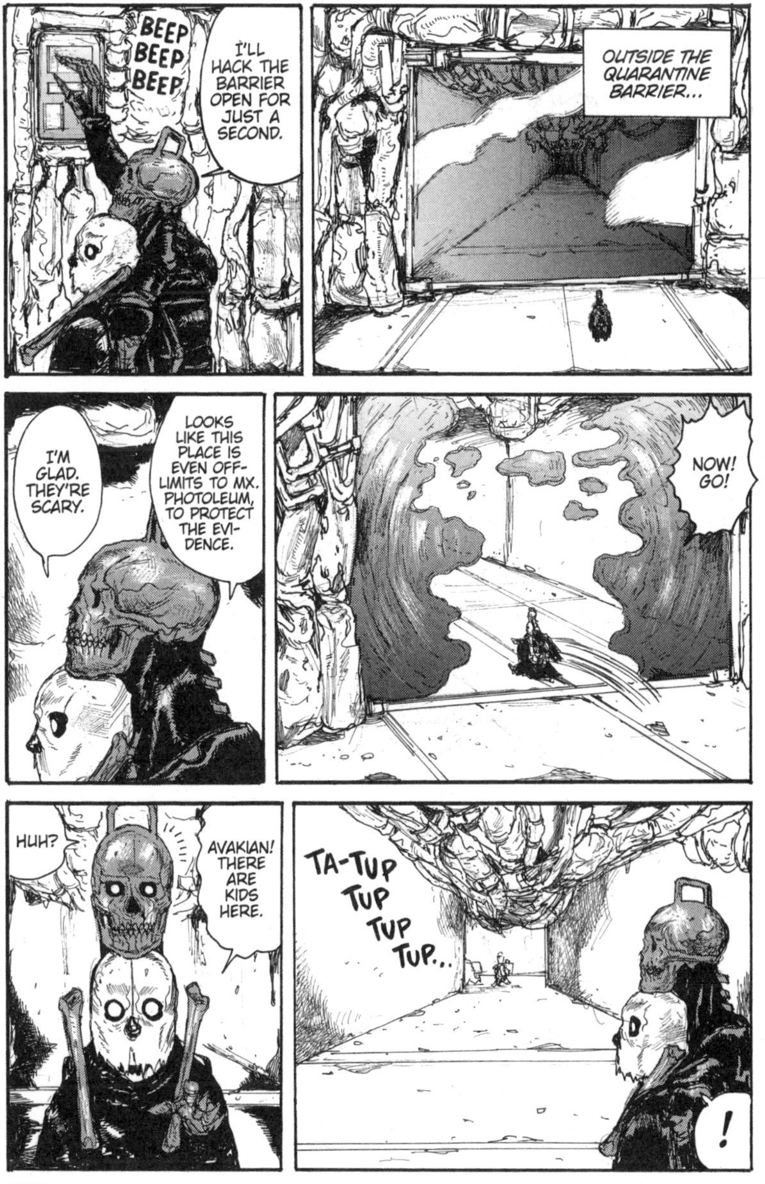
OUTSIDE THE QUARANTINE BARRIER...
I'LL HACK THE BARRIER OPEN FOR JUST A SECOND.
BEEP BEEP BEEP
NOW! GO!
LOOKS LIKE THIS PLACE IS EVEN OFF-LIMITS TO MX. PHOTOLEUM, TO PROTECT THE EVI-DENCE.
I'M GLAD. THEY'RE SCARY.
TA-TUP TUP TUP TUP...
!
AVAKIAN! THERE ARE KIDS HERE.
HUH?

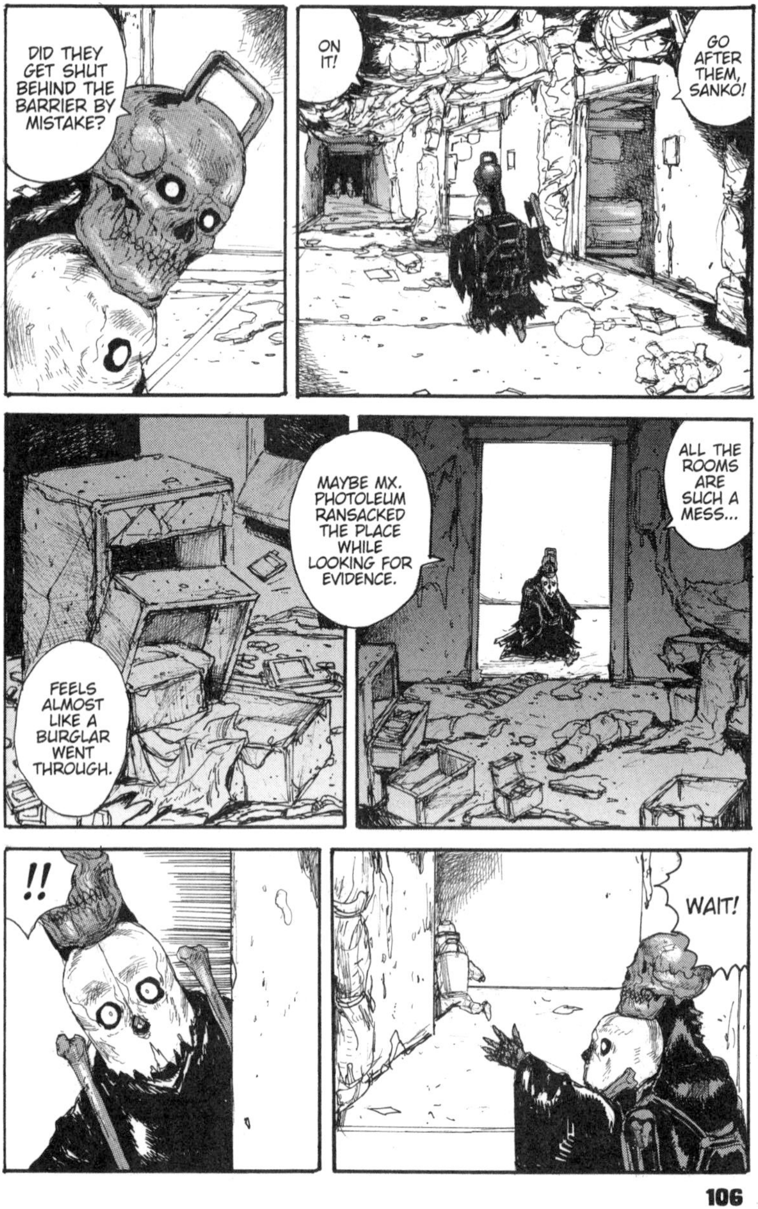
GO AFTER THEM, SANKO!
ON IT!
DID THEY GET SHUT BEHIND THE BARRIER BY MISTAKE?
ALL THE ROOMS ARE SUCH A MESS...
MAYBE MX. PHOTOLEUM RANSACKED THE PLACE WHILE LOOKING FOR EVIDENCE.
FEELS ALMOST LIKE A BURGLAR WENT THROUGH.
WAIT!
!!

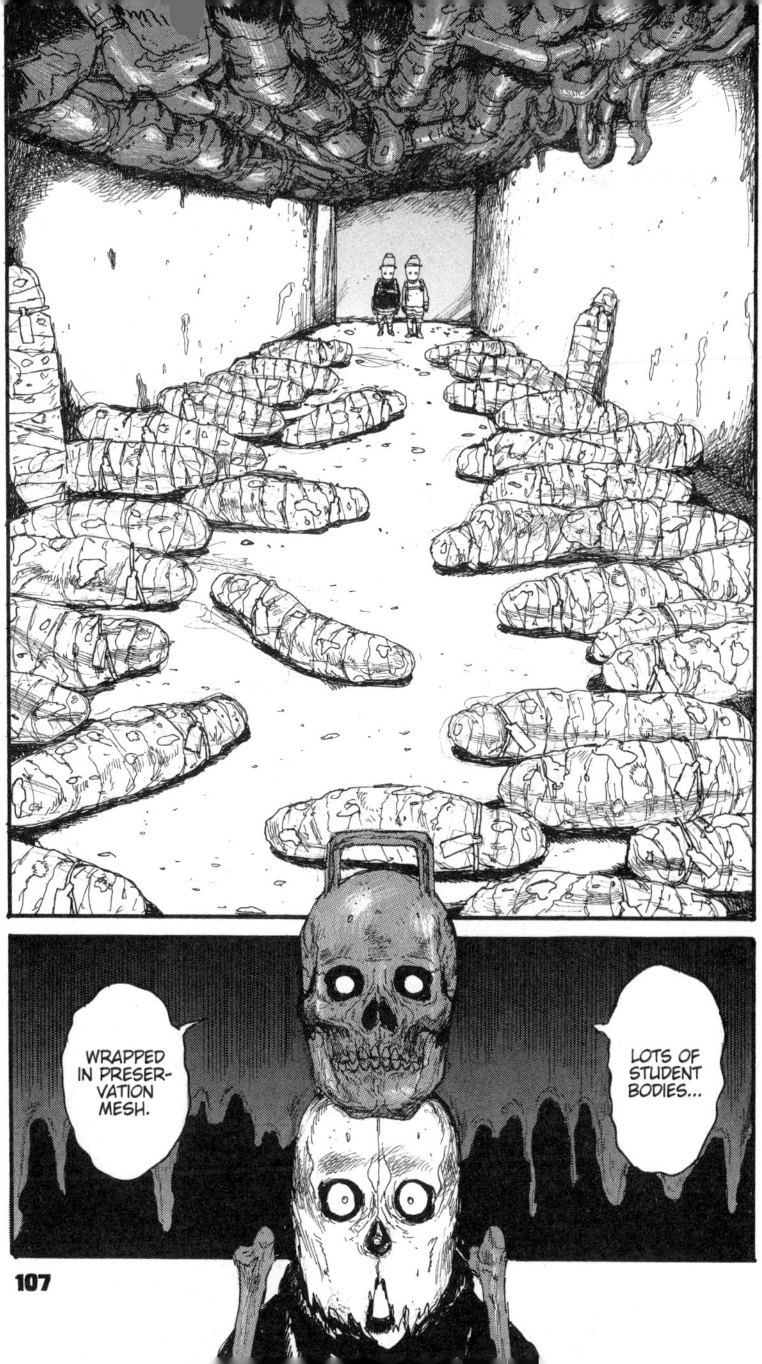
LOTS OF STUDENT BODIES...
WRAPPED IN PRESER-VATION MESH.

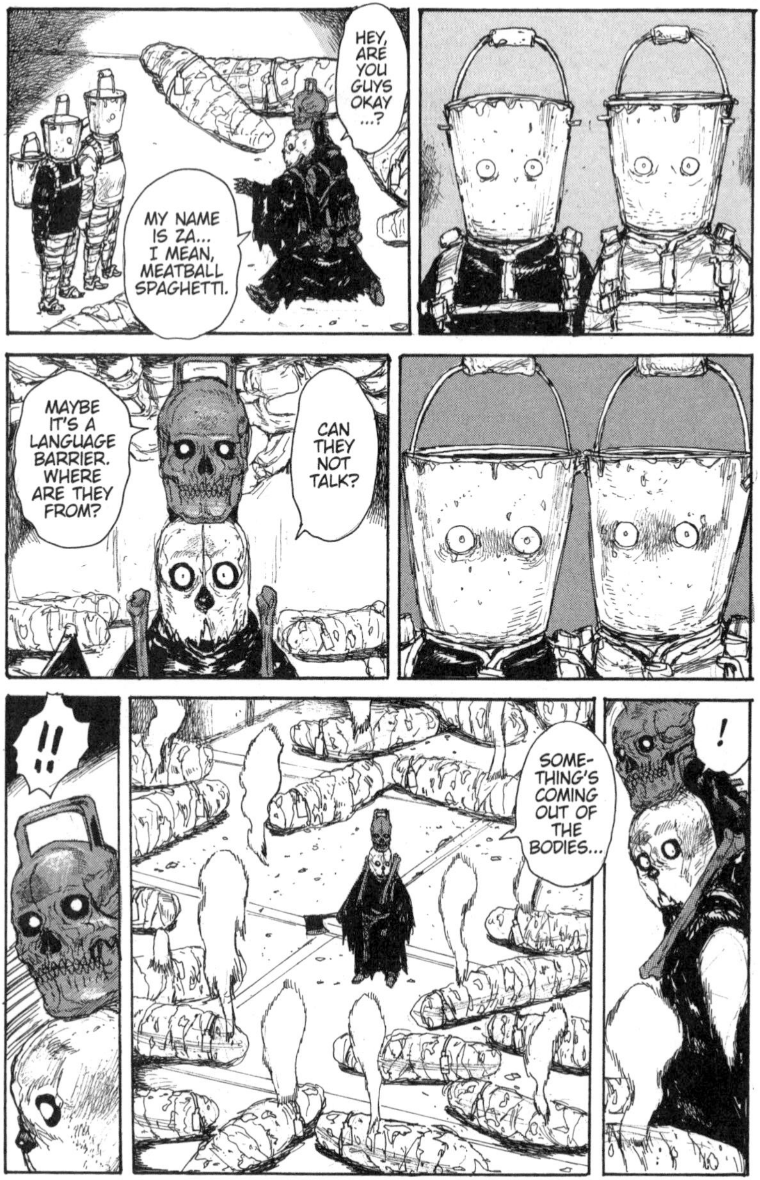
HEY, ARE YOU GUYS OKAY ...?
MY NAME IS ZA... I MEAN, MEATBALL SPAGHETTI.
CAN THEY NOT TALK?
MAYBE IT'S A LANGUAGE BARRIER. WHERE ARE THEY FROM?
!
SOME-THING'S COMING OUT OF THE BODIES...
!!

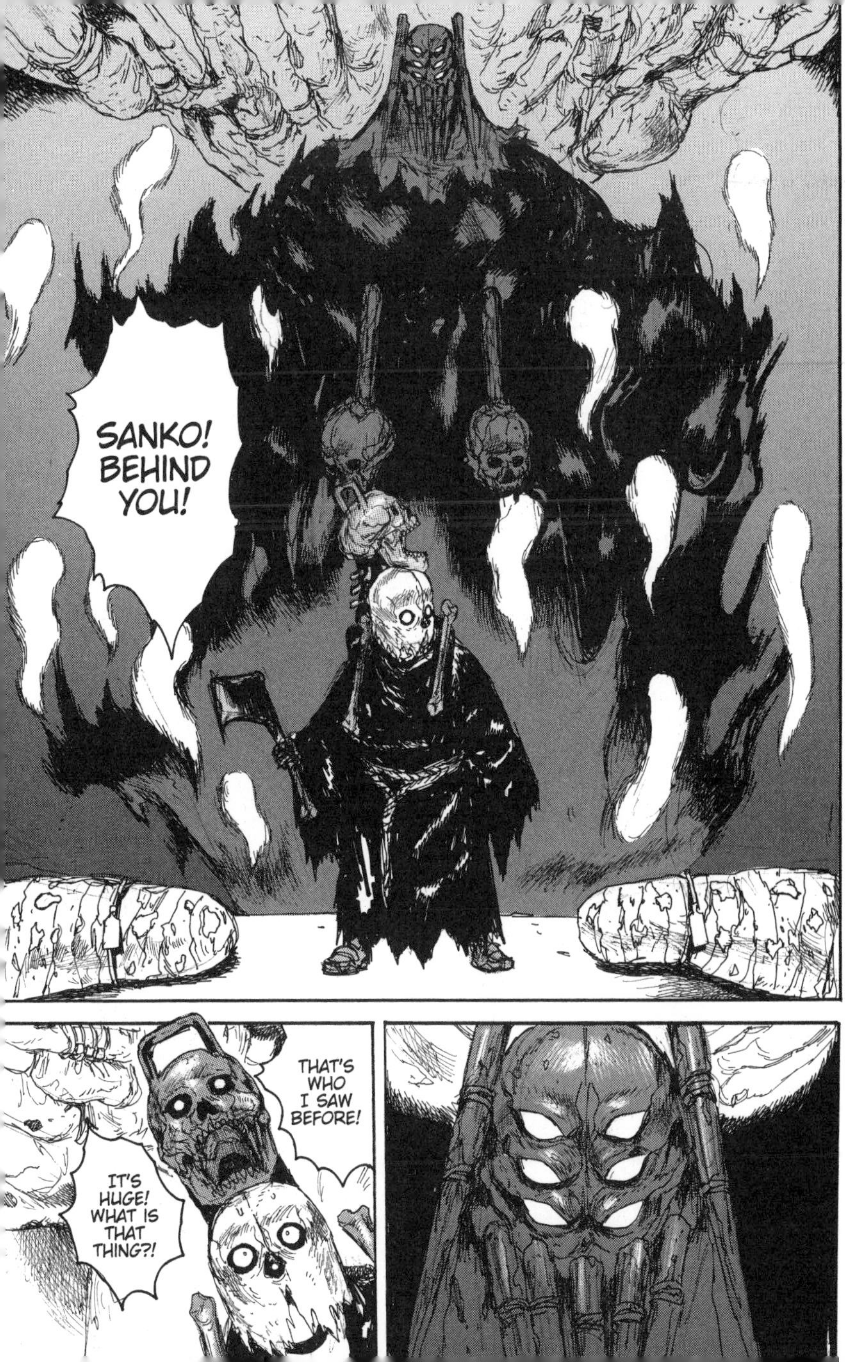
SANKO! BEHIND YOU!
THAT'S WHO I SAW BEFORE!
IT'S HUGE! WHAT IS THAT THING?!

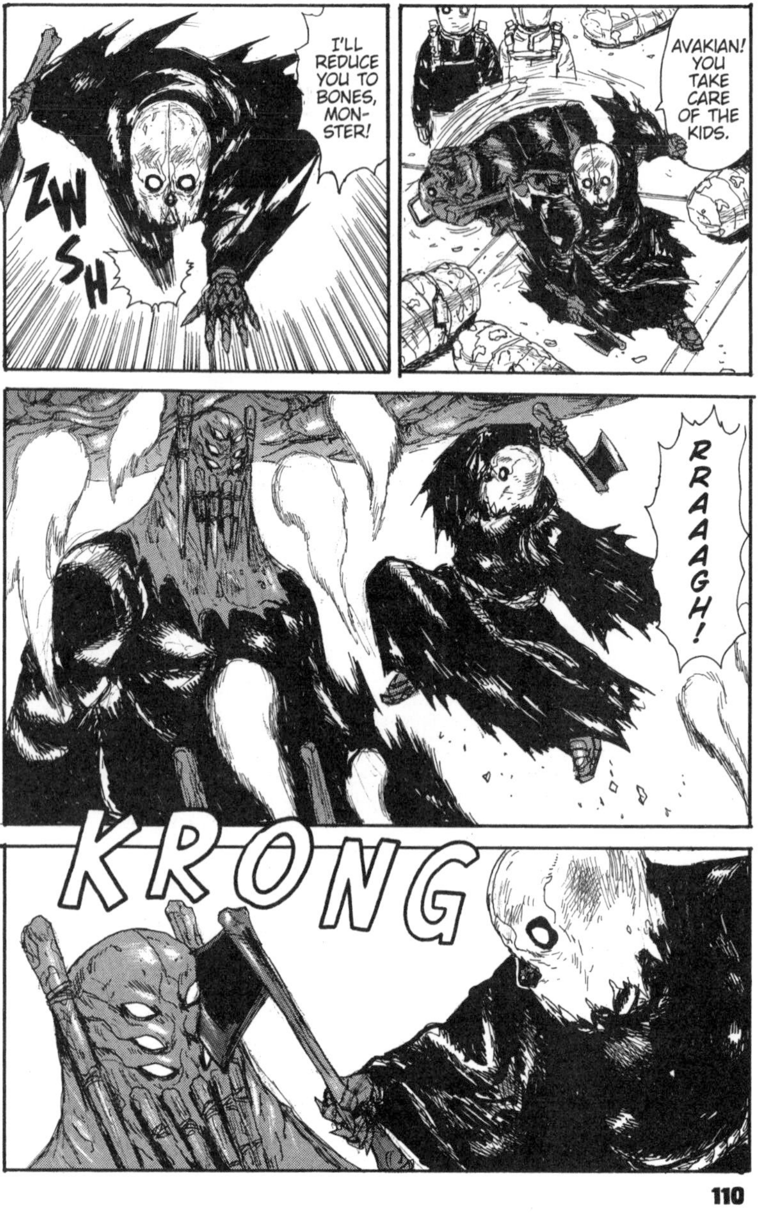
AVAKIAN! YOU TAKE CARE OF THE KIDS.
I'LL REDUCE YOU TO BONES, MON-STER!
ZWSH
RRAAAAGH!
KRONG

THWAP

YOU'RE IN MY WAY.

GAH!

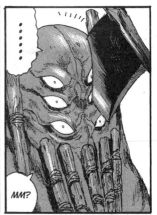

· · · ·

MM?

WHAT WAS THAT? MY AX OF DARK FLESH DIDN'T WORK...

CRUMBLE

SAN-KO!!

KRUNK

THWUNK

QUIT IT.

YAAAGH!

BUT I'LL TRY AGAIN!!

WHO THE HELL ARE YOU?
YOU GOT BEEF WITH ME?
AREN'T YOU HERE TO KILL ME?
WHO DO YOU THINK YOU ARE? AS IF I CARE ABOUT SOME BRAT.
HE DOESN'T KNOW WHO I AM.
KER-SHUNK
......
WHO ARE YOU?
WHAT ARE YOU DOING ON THE *TREE-GUN*?
HEH HEH HEH. AH, YOU WANT TO KNOW, DO YOU?
VERY WELL. I SHALL TELL YOU.

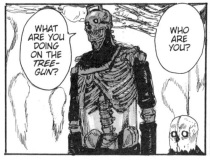

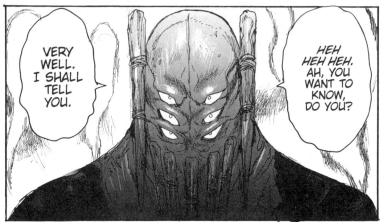

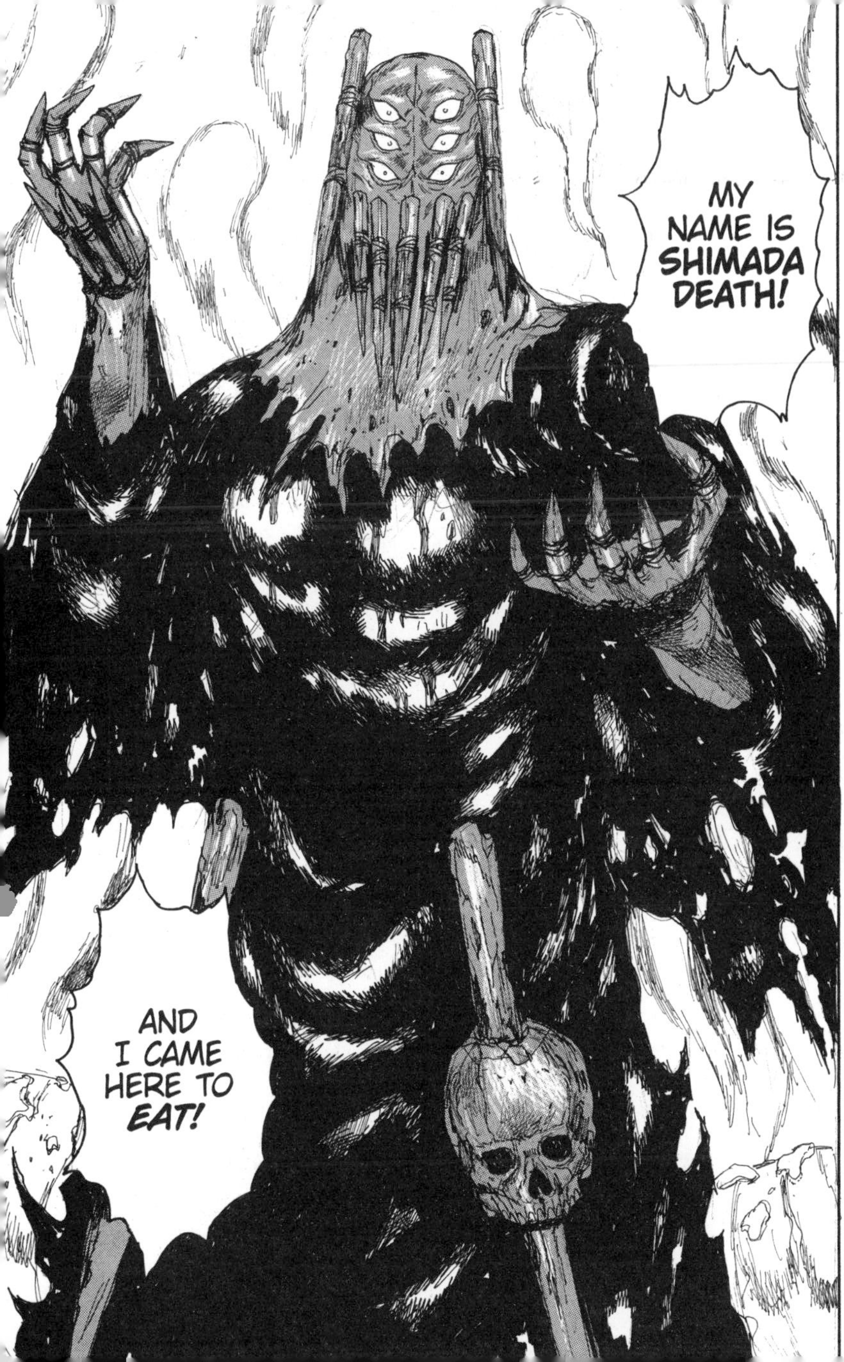
MY NAME IS SHIMADA DEATH!
AND I CAME HERE TO EAT!

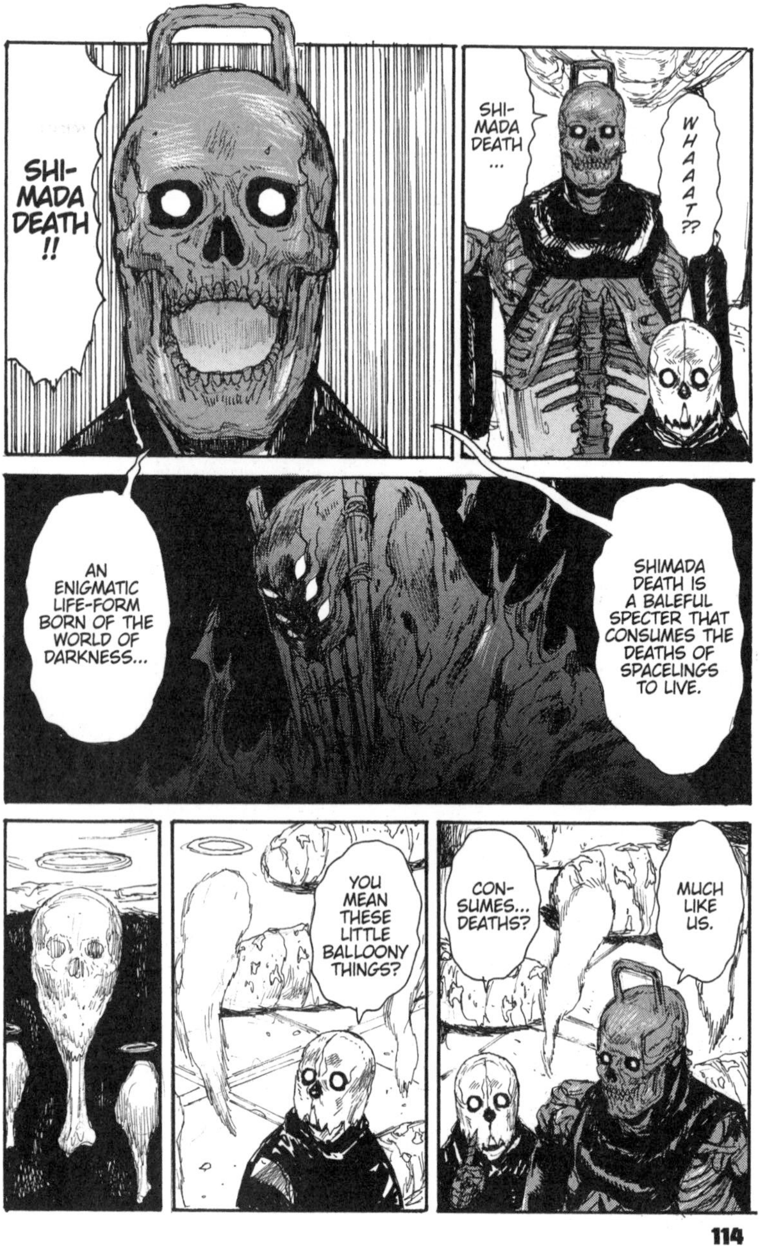
WHAAAT??
SHI-MADA DEATH...
SHI-MADA DEATH!!
SHIMADA DEATH IS A BALEFUL SPECTER THAT CONSUMES THE DEATHS OF SPACELINGS TO LIVE.
AN ENIGMATIC LIFE-FORM BORN OF THE WORLD OF DARKNESS...
MUCH LIKE US.
CON-SUMES... DEATHS?
YOU MEAN THESE LITTLE BALLOONY THINGS?

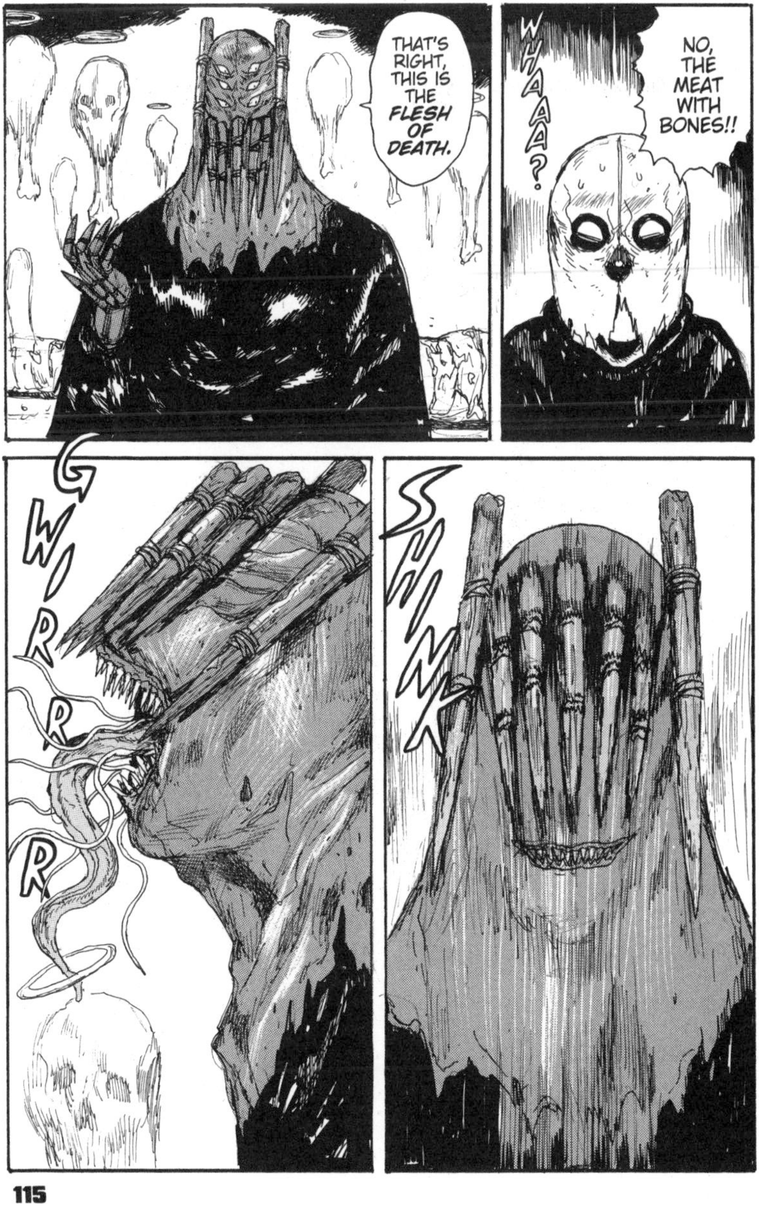
WHAAAA?
NO, THE MEAT WITH BONES!!
THAT'S RIGHT, THIS IS THE *FLESH OF DEATH.*
SHINK
GWIRRR

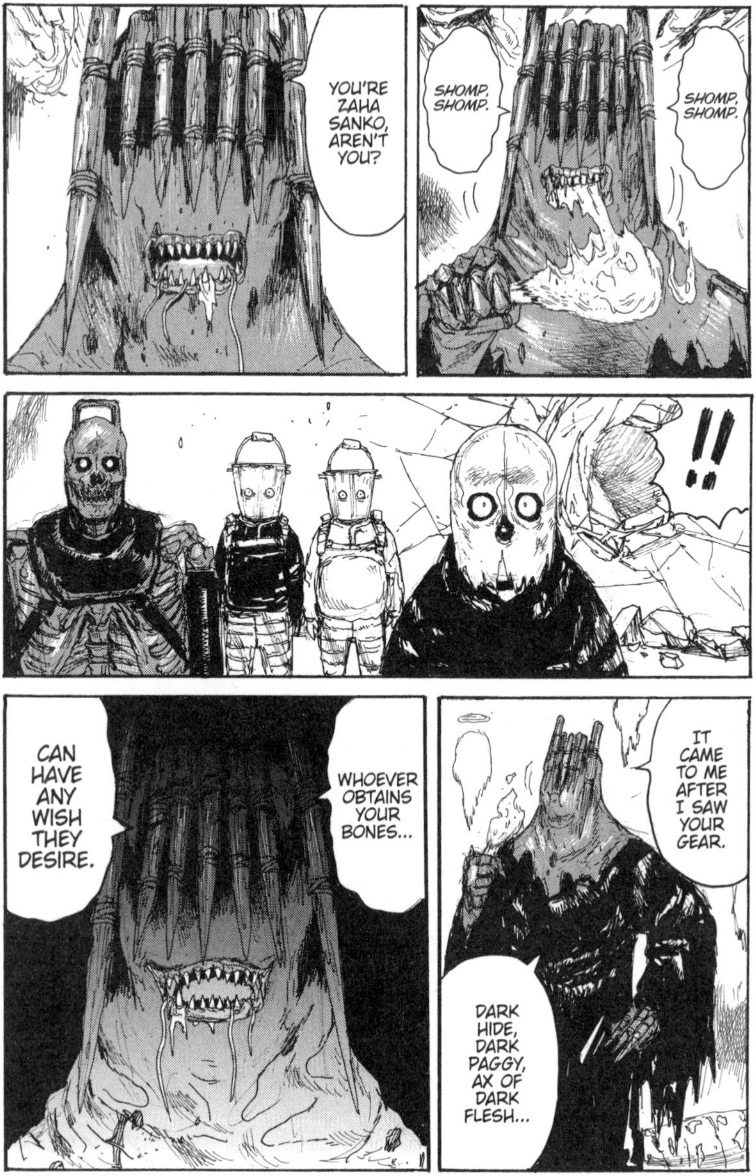
SHOMP, SHOMP.
SHOMP, SHOMP.
YOU'RE ZAHA SANKO, AREN'T YOU?
!!
IT CAME TO ME AFTER I SAW YOUR GEAR.
DARK HIDE, DARK PAGGY, AX OF DARK FLESH...
WHOEVER OBTAINS YOUR BONES...
CAN HAVE ANY WISH THEY DESIRE.

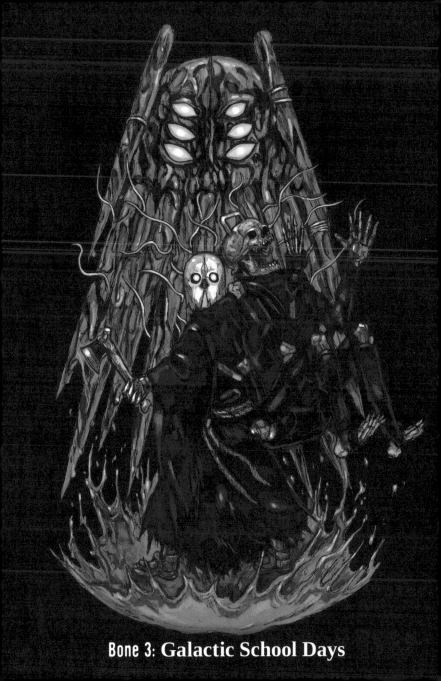

Bone 3: Galactic School Days

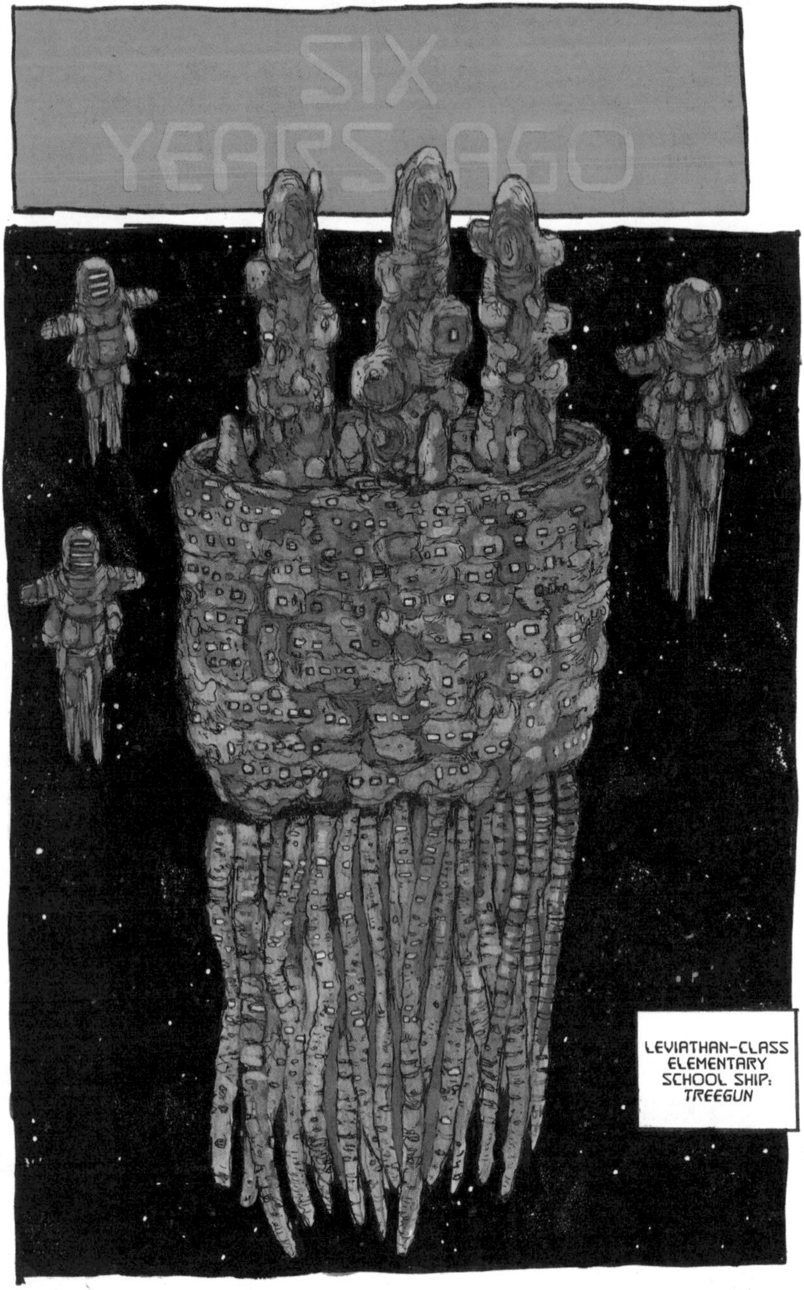
SIX YEARS AGO
LEVIATHAN-CLASS ELEMENTARY SCHOOL SHIP: *TREEGUN*

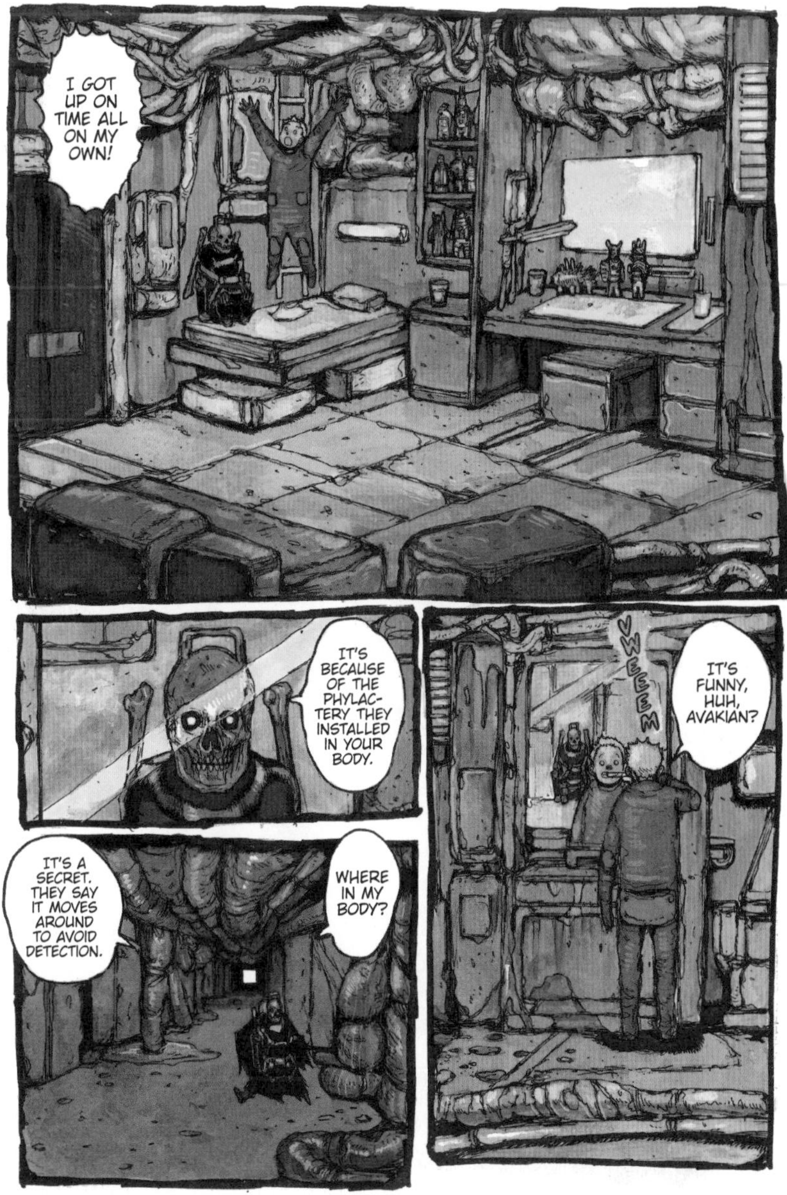
I GOT UP ON TIME ALL ON MY OWN!
VWEEEM
IT'S FUNNY, HUH, AVAKIAN?
IT'S BECAUSE OF THE PHYLAC-TERY THEY INSTALLED IN YOUR BODY.
WHERE IN MY BODY?
IT'S A SECRET. THEY SAY IT MOVES AROUND TO AVOID DETECTION.

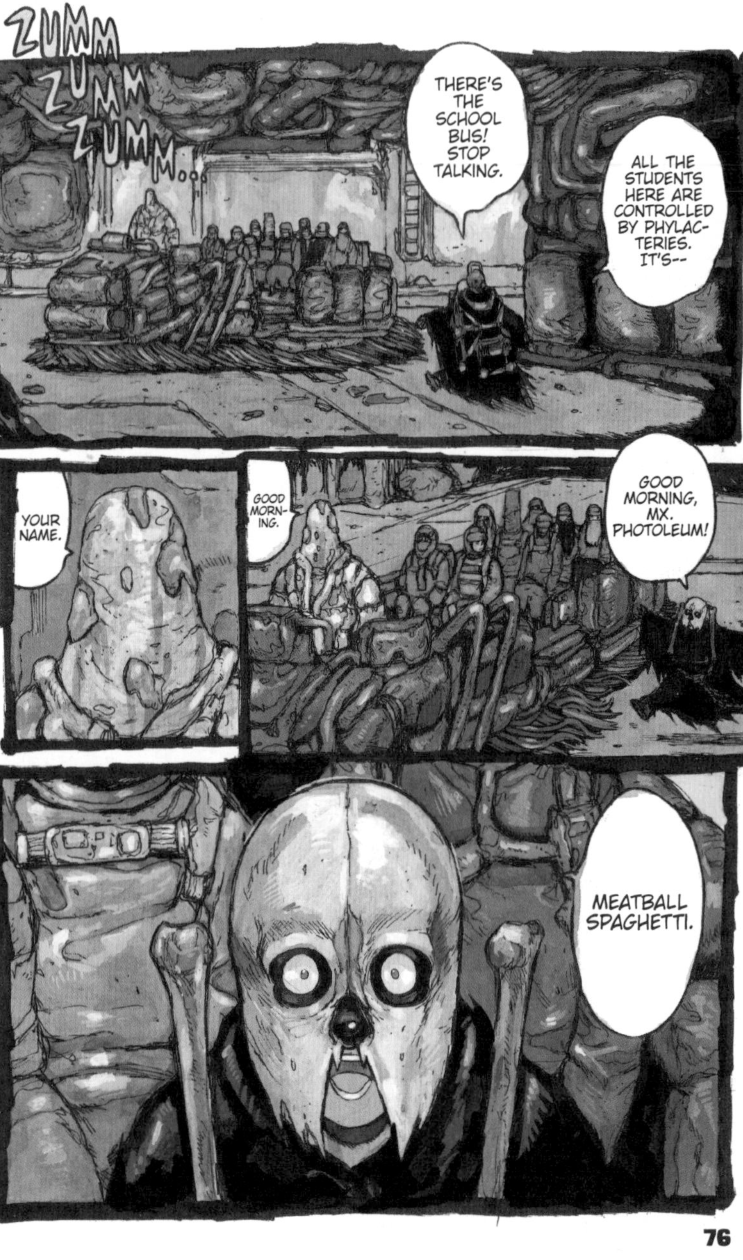
ALL THE STUDENTS HERE ARE CONTROLLED BY PHYLACTERIES. IT'S--
THERE'S THE SCHOOL BUS! STOP TALKING.
ZUMM ZUMM ZUMM...
GOOD MORNING, MX. PHOTOLEUM!
GOOD MORNING.
YOUR NAME.
MEATBALL SPAGHETTI.

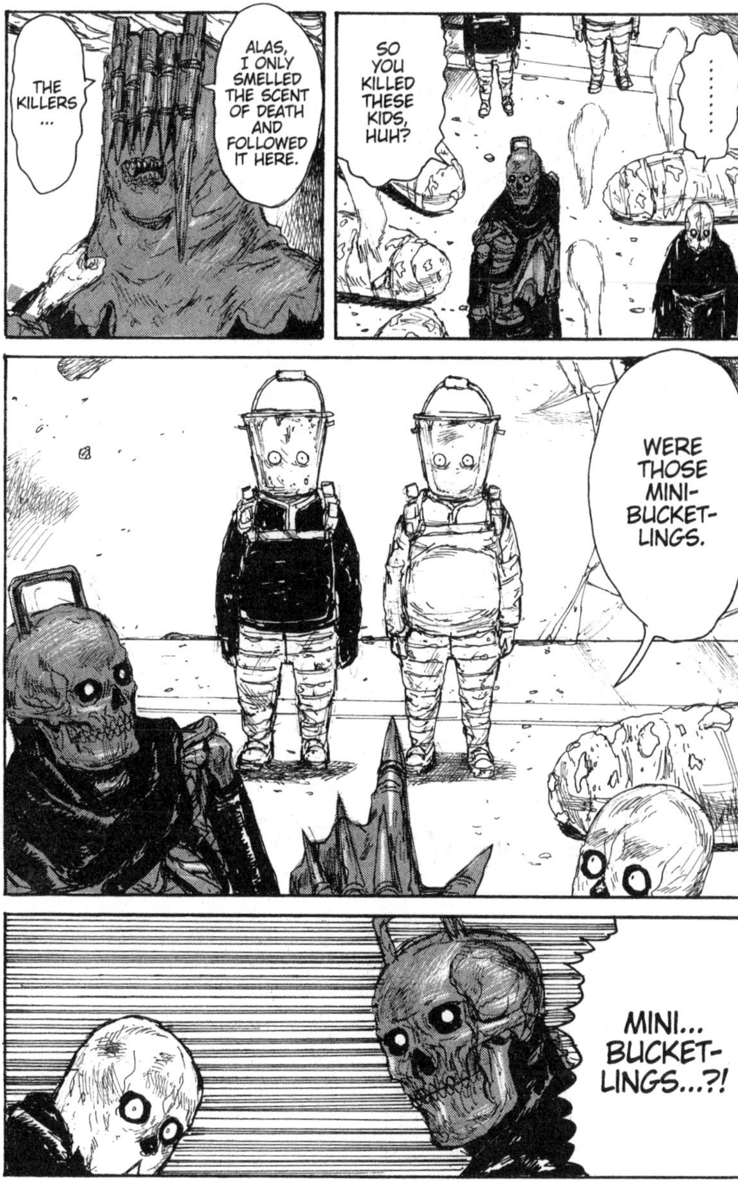
......
SO YOU KILLED THESE KIDS, HUH?
ALAS, I ONLY SMELLED THE SCENT OF DEATH AND FOLLOWED IT HERE.
THE KILLERS ...
WERE THOSE MINI-BUCKET-LINGS.
MINI... BUCKET-LINGS...?!

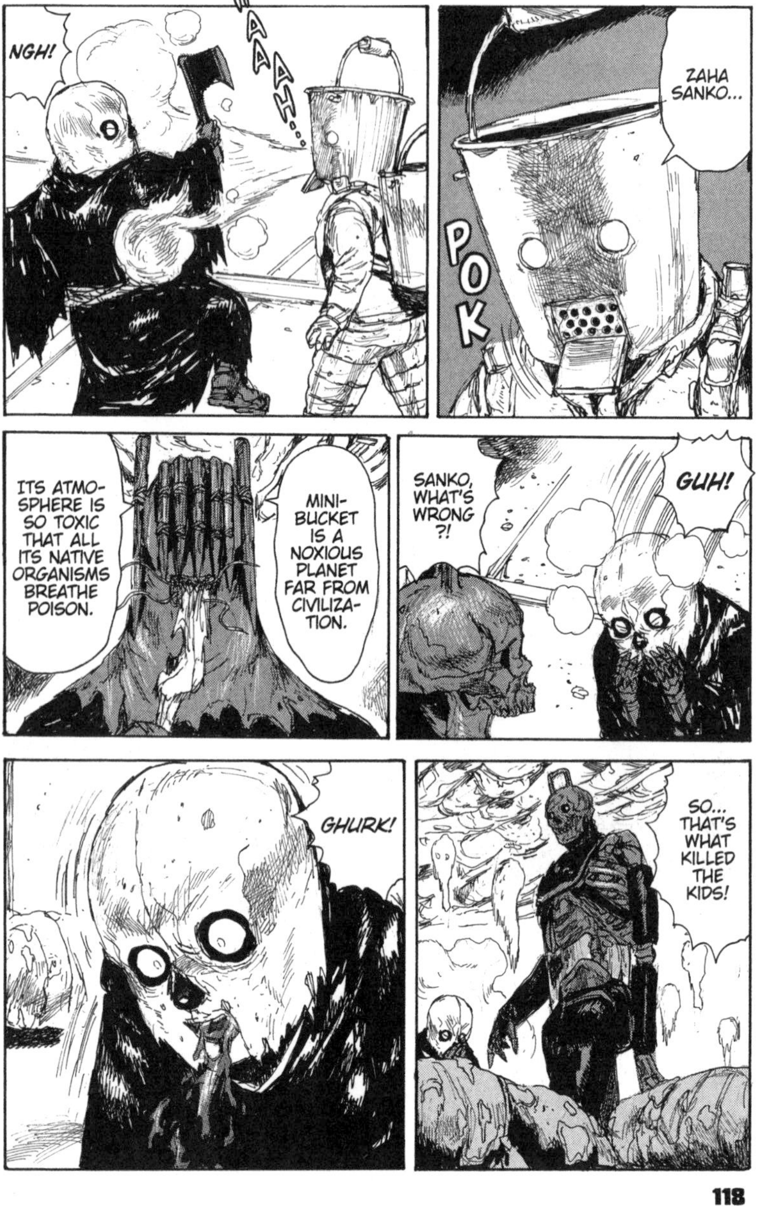
ZAHA SANKO...
POK
HAAAAH...
NGH!
GUH!
SANKO, WHAT'S WRONG ?!
MINI-BUCKET IS A NOXIOUS PLANET FAR FROM CIVILIZATION.
ITS ATMOSPHERE IS SO TOXIC THAT ALL ITS NATIVE ORGANISMS BREATHE POISON.
SO... THAT'S WHAT KILLED THE KIDS!
GHURK!

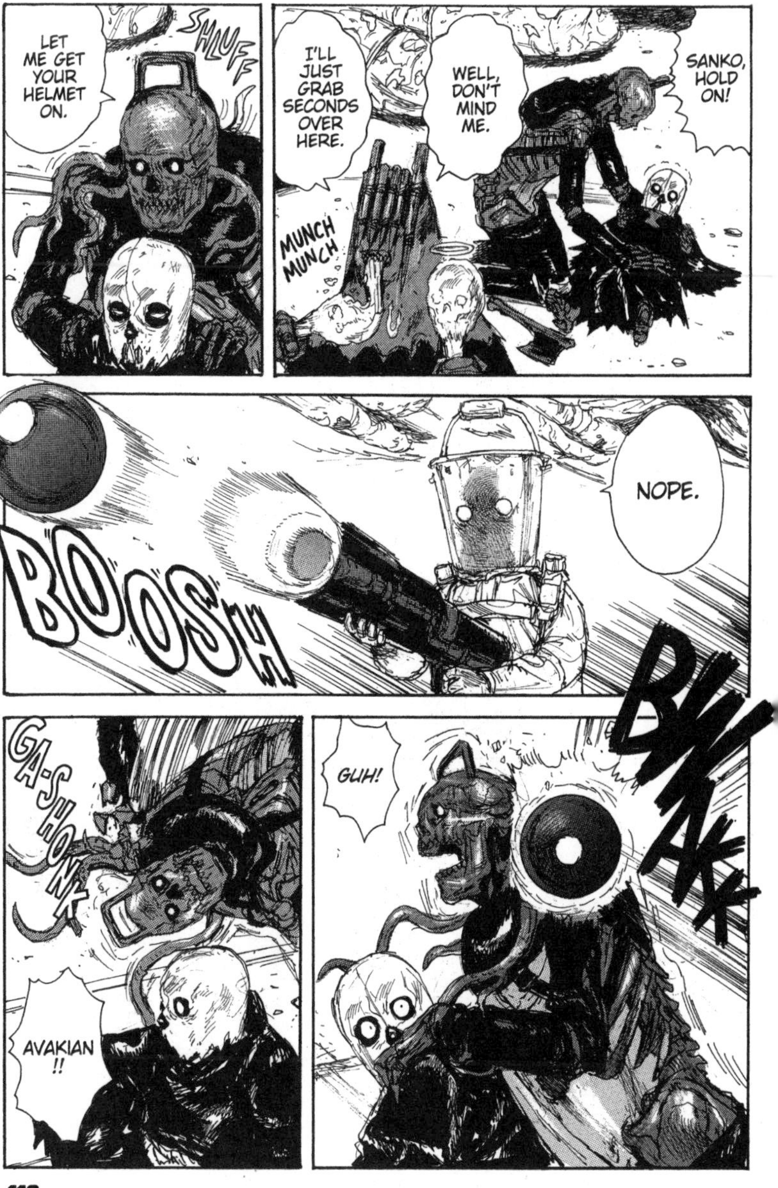
SANKO, HOLD ON!
WELL, DON'T MIND ME.
I'LL JUST GRAB SECONDS OVER HERE.
MUNCH MUNCH
SHLUFF
LET ME GET YOUR HELMET ON.
NOPE.
BOOSHH
BWAKK
GUH!
GA-SHONK
AVAKIAN !!

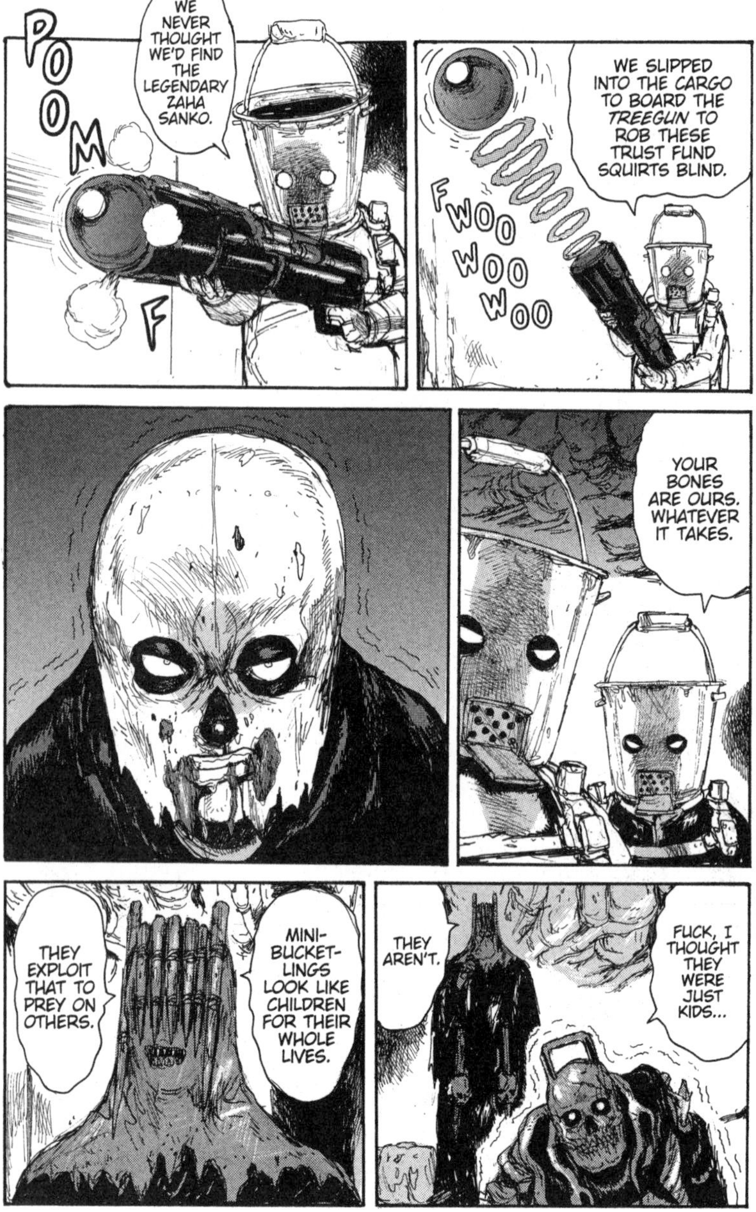
WE SLIPPED INTO THE CARGO TO BOARD THE *TREEGUN* TO ROB THESE TRUST FUND SQUIRTS BLIND.
FWOO WOO WOO WOO
WE NEVER THOUGHT WE'D FIND THE LEGENDARY ZAHA SANKO.
POOMF
YOUR BONES ARE OURS. WHATEVER IT TAKES.
FUCK, I THOUGHT THEY WERE JUST KIDS...
THEY AREN'T.
MINI-BUCKET-LINGS LOOK LIKE CHILDREN FOR THEIR WHOLE LIVES.
THEY EXPLOIT THAT TO PREY ON OTHERS.

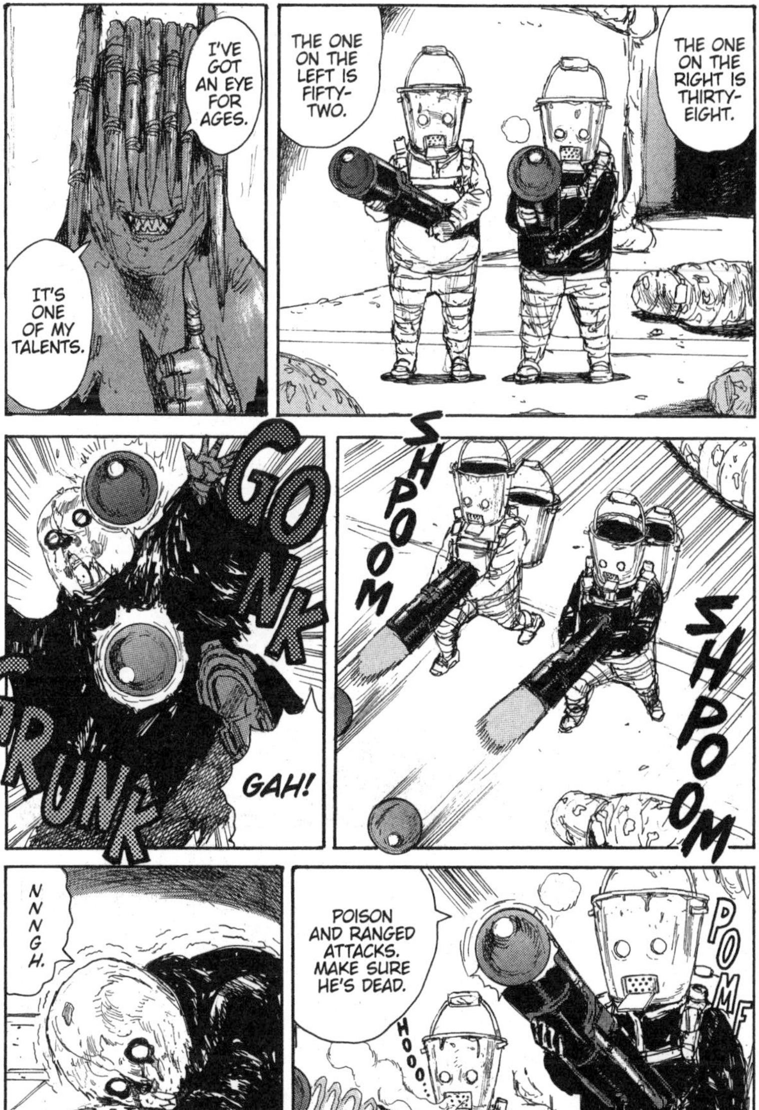
THE ONE ON THE RIGHT IS THIRTY-EIGHT.
THE ONE ON THE LEFT IS FIFTY-TWO.
I'VE GOT AN EYE FOR AGES.
IT'S ONE OF MY TALENTS.
SHPOOOM
SHPOOOM
GONK
GRUNK
GAH!
POMF
POISON AND RANGED ATTACKS. MAKE SURE HE'S DEAD.
HOOOO...
NNNGH.

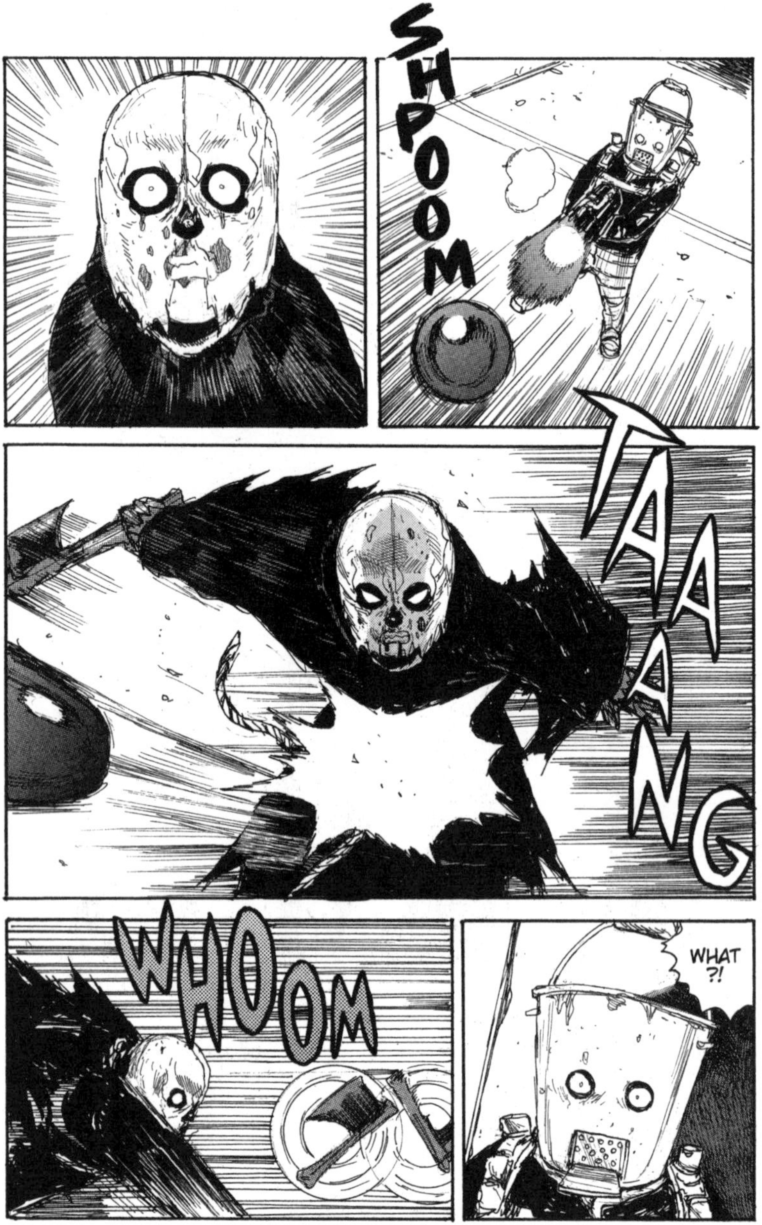
SHPOOM
TAAAANG
WHAT ?!
WHOOM

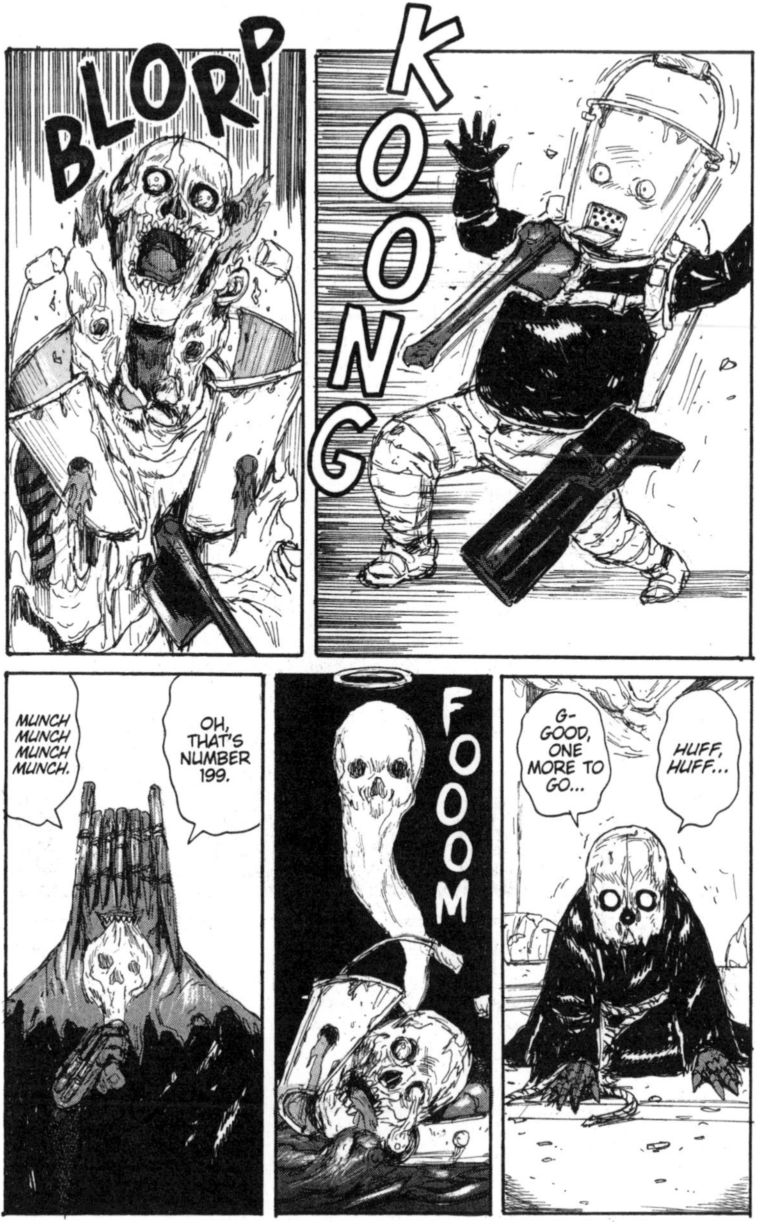
KOONG
BLORP
HUFF, HUFF...
G-GOOD, ONE MORE TO GO...
FOOOM
OH, THAT'S NUMBER 199.
MUNCH MUNCH MUNCH MUNCH.

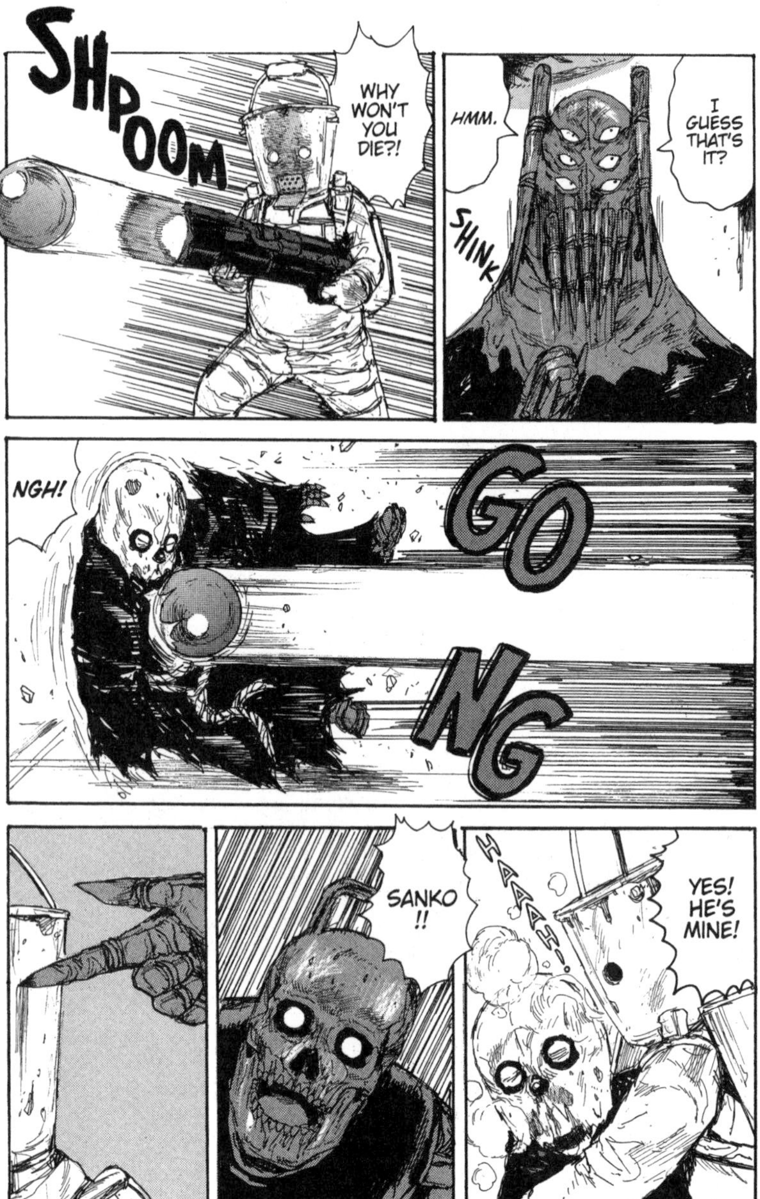
I GUESS THAT'S IT?
HMM.
SHINK
WHY WON'T YOU DIE?!
SHPOOM
NGH!
GONG
YES! HE'S MINE!
HAAAH!
SANKO!!

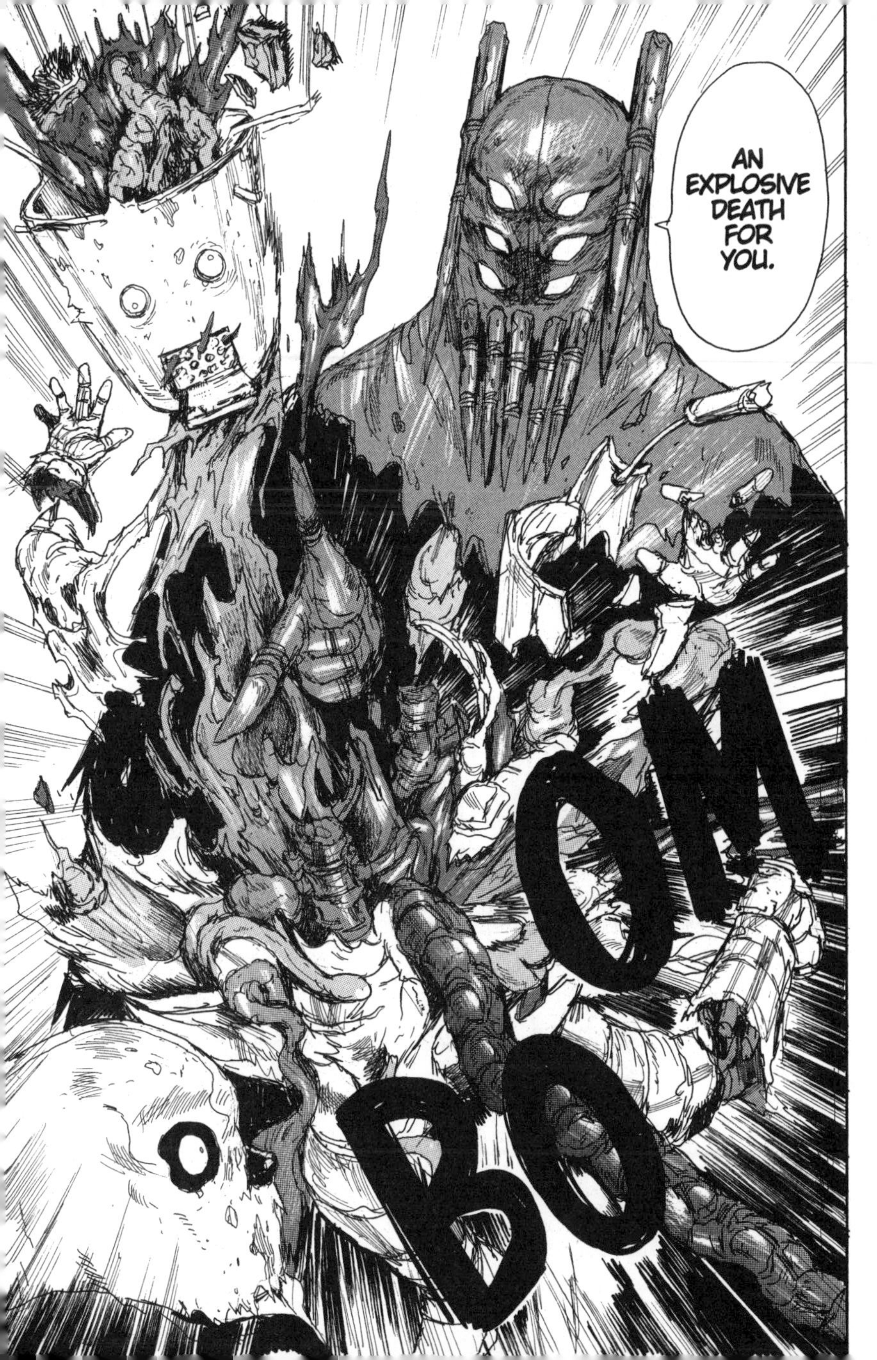
AN EXPLOSIVE DEATH FOR YOU.
BOOM

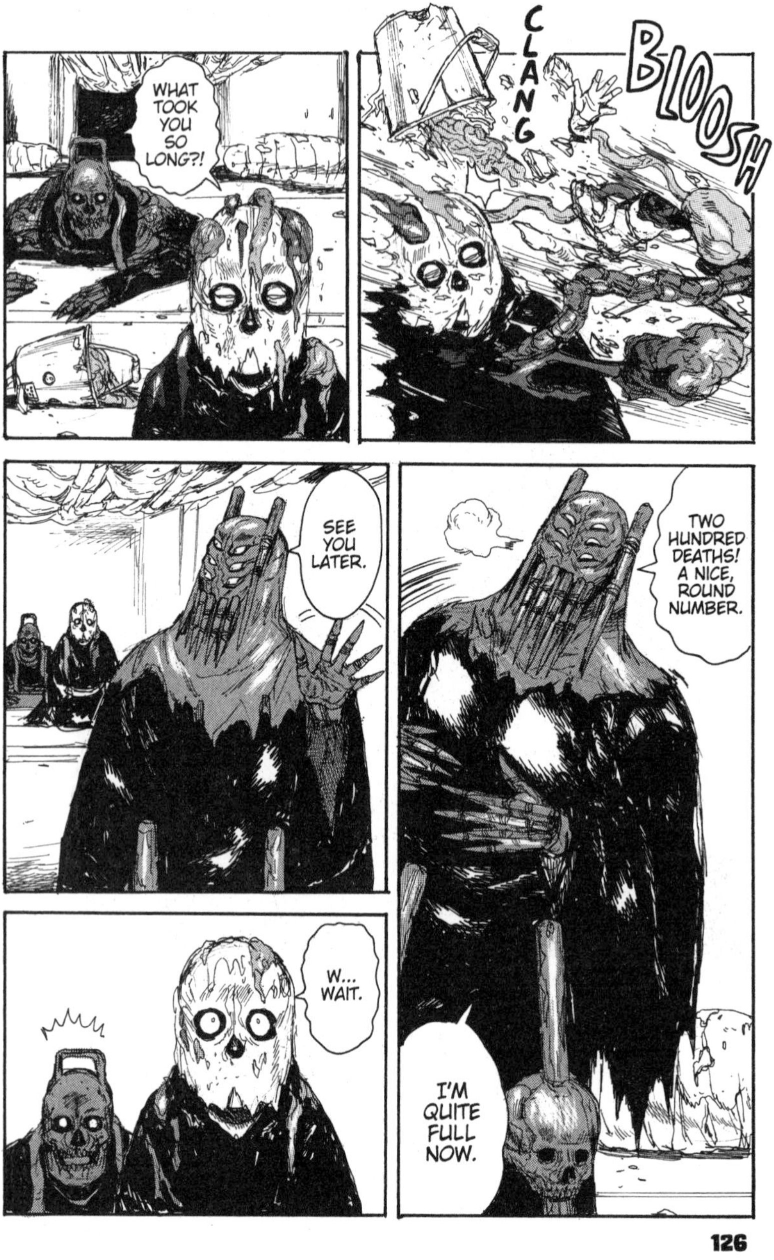
CLANG
BLOOSH
WHAT TOOK YOU SO LONG?!
TWO HUNDRED DEATHS! A NICE, ROUND NUMBER.
I'M QUITE FULL NOW.
SEE YOU LATER.
W... WAIT.

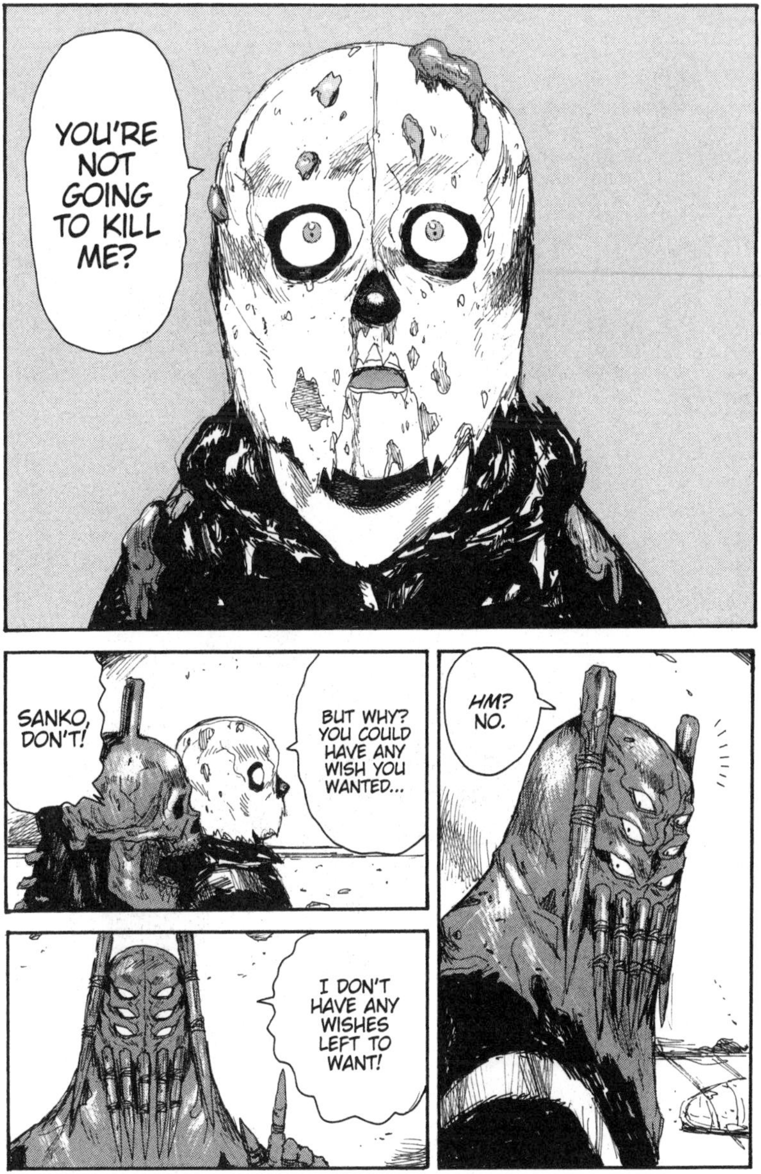
YOU'RE NOT GOING TO KILL ME?
HM? NO.
BUT WHY? YOU COULD HAVE ANY WISH YOU WANTED...
SANKO, DON'T!
I DON'T HAVE ANY WISHES LEFT TO WANT!

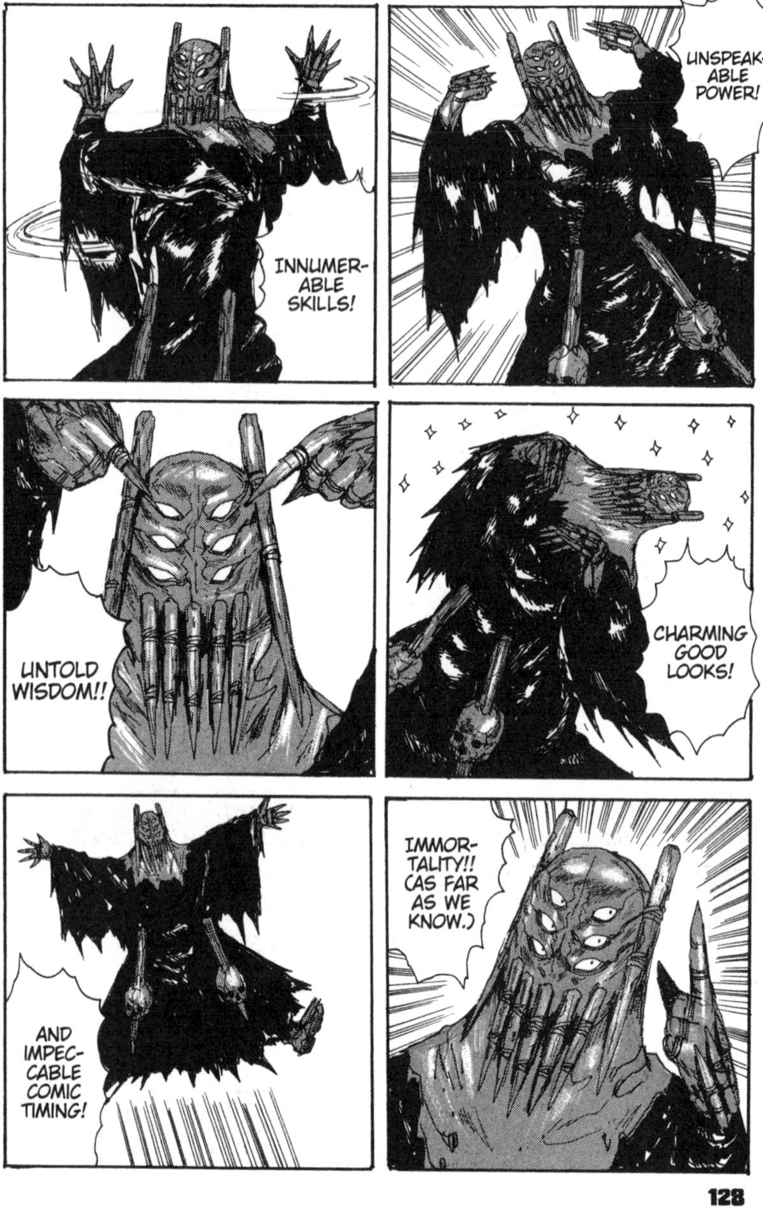
UNSPEAK-
ABLE
POWER!
INNUMER-
ABLE
SKILLS!
CHARMING
GOOD
LOOKS!
UNTOLD
WISDOM!!
IMMOR-
TALITY!!
(AS FAR
AS WE
KNOW.)
AND
IMPEC-
CABLE
COMIC
TIMING!

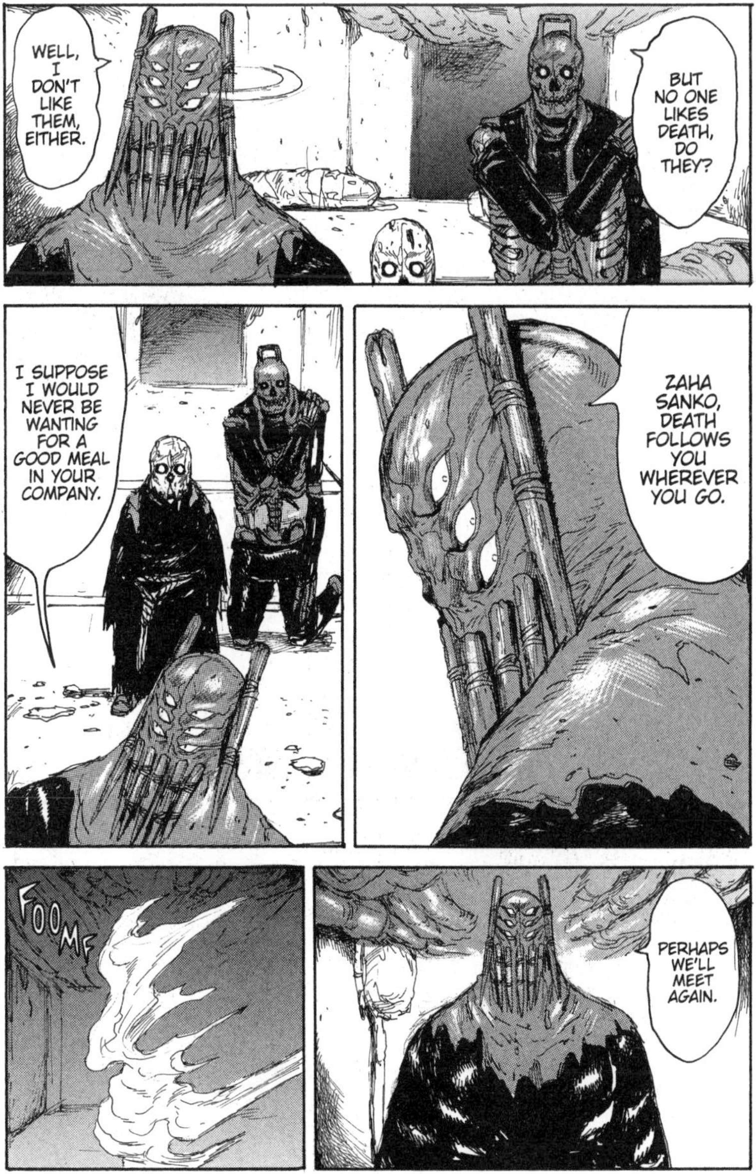
BUT NO ONE LIKES DEATH, DO THEY?
WELL, I DON'T LIKE THEM, EITHER.
ZAHA SANKO, DEATH FOLLOWS YOU WHEREVER YOU GO.
I SUPPOSE I WOULD NEVER BE WANTING FOR A GOOD MEAL IN YOUR COMPANY.
PERHAPS WE'LL MEET AGAIN.
FOOMF

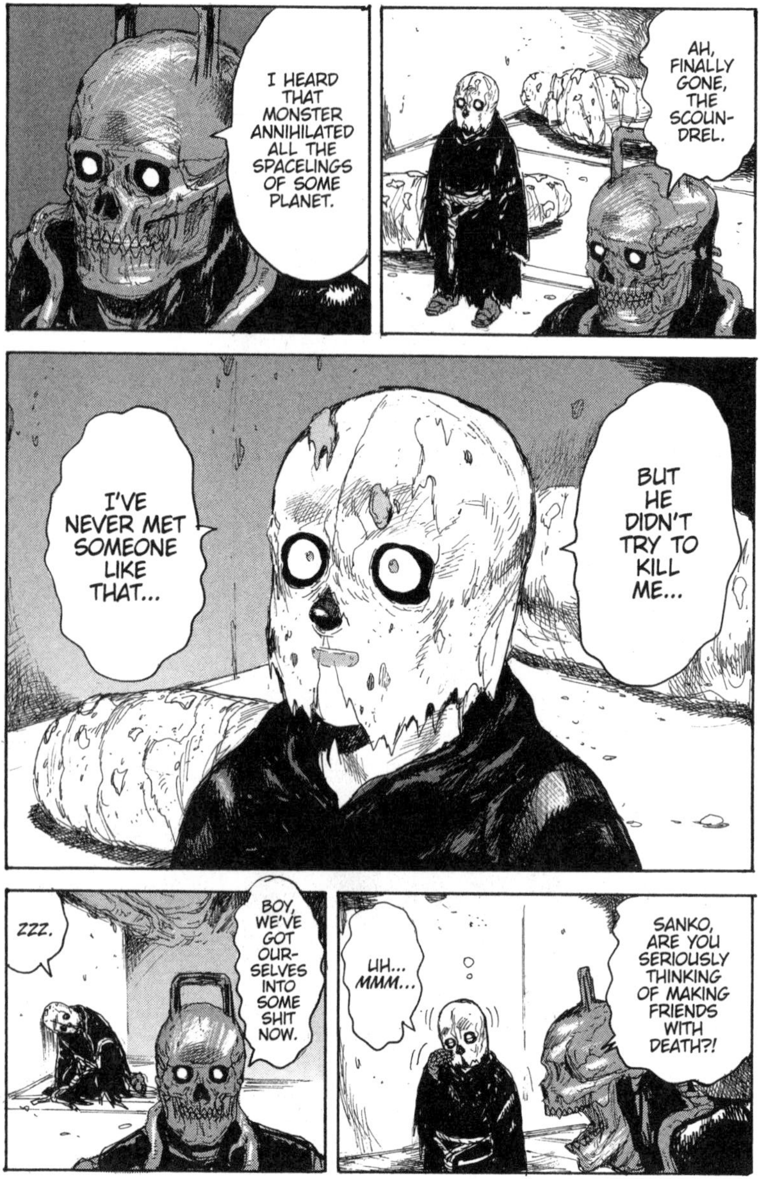
AH, FINALLY GONE, THE SCOUN-DREL.
I HEARD THAT MONSTER ANNIHILATED ALL THE SPACELINGS OF SOME PLANET.
BUT HE DIDN'T TRY TO KILL ME...
I'VE NEVER MET SOMEONE LIKE THAT...
SANKO, ARE YOU SERIOUSLY THINKING OF MAKING FRIENDS WITH DEATH?!
UH... MMM...
BOY, WE'VE GOT OUR-SELVES INTO SOME SHIT NOW.
ZZZ.

★ Design of Shimada Death (1)

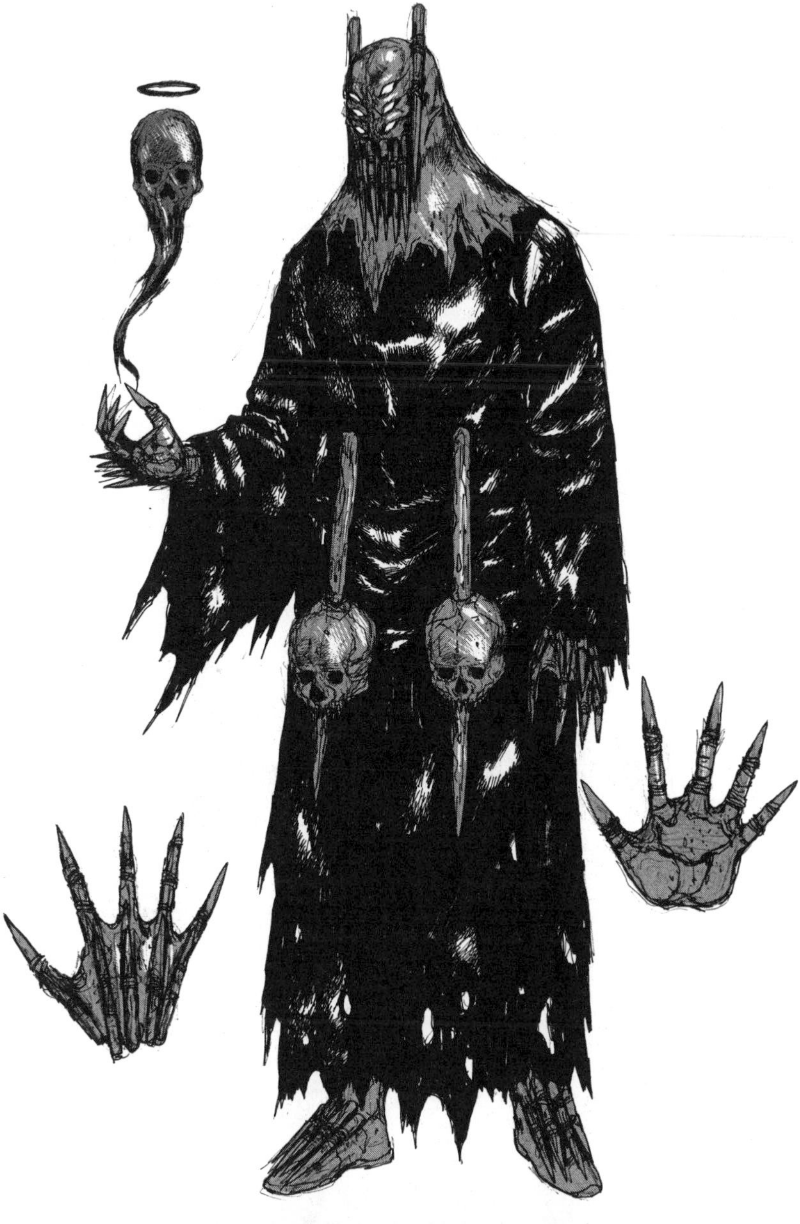

★ *Dai Dark* preview art

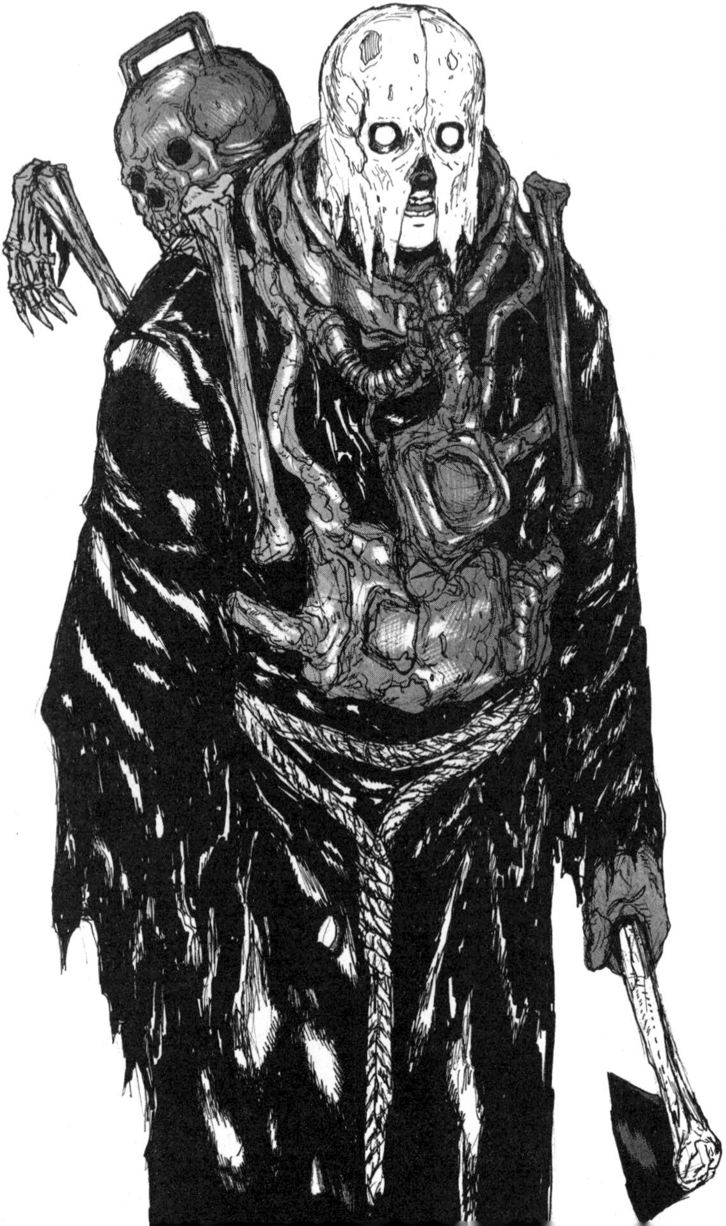

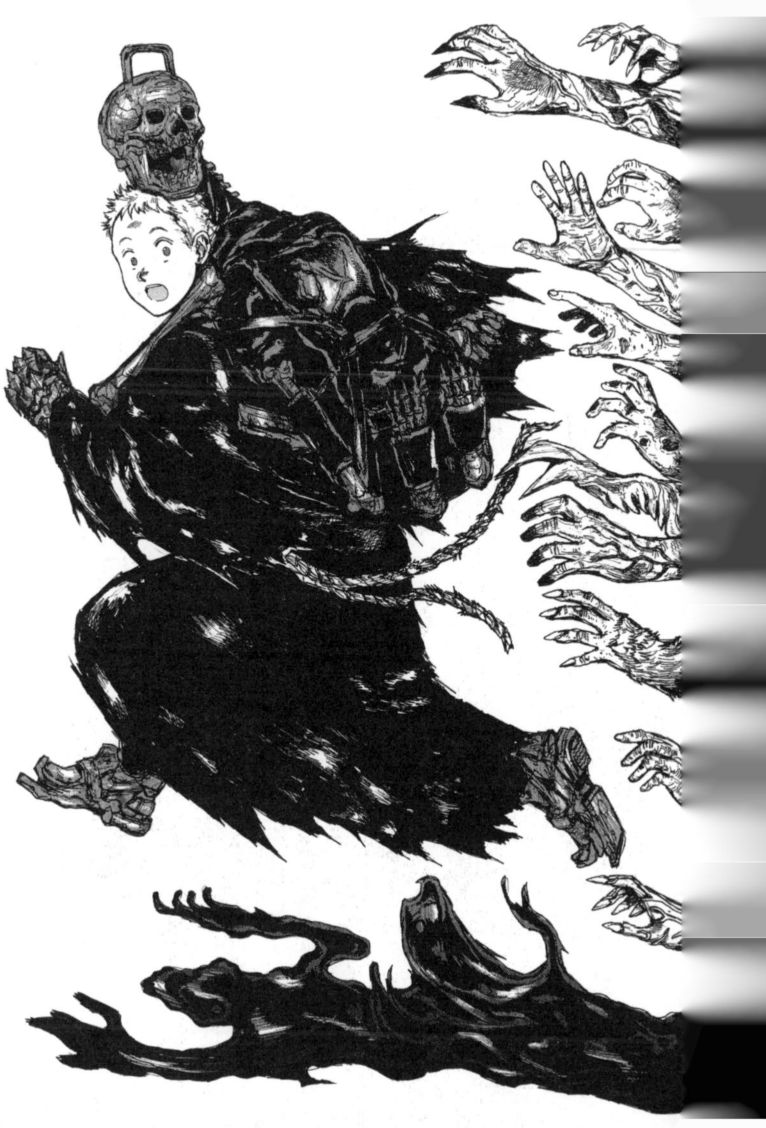

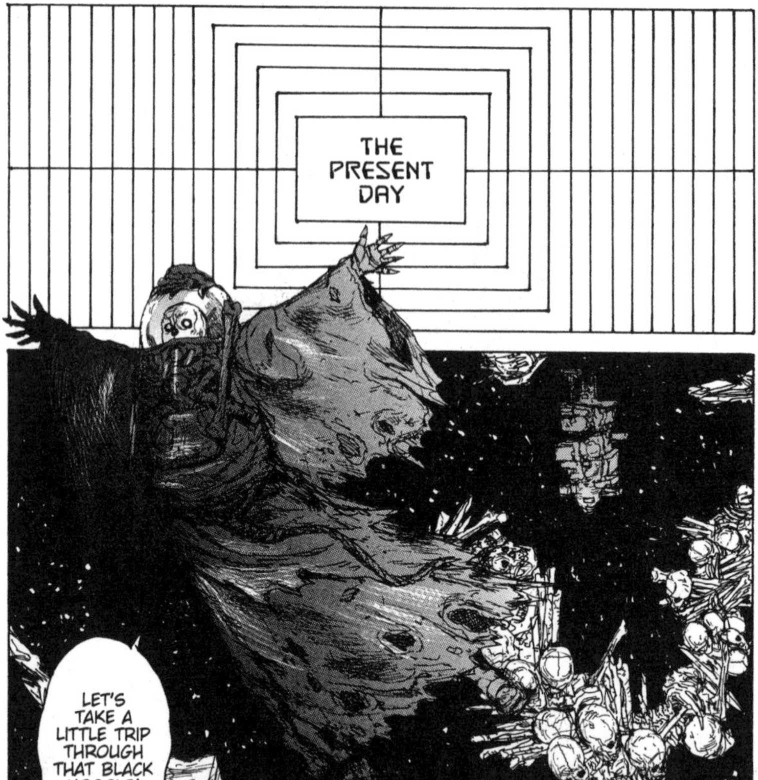
THE PRESENT DAY
LET'S TAKE A LITTLE TRIP THROUGH THAT BLACK HOOOLE!

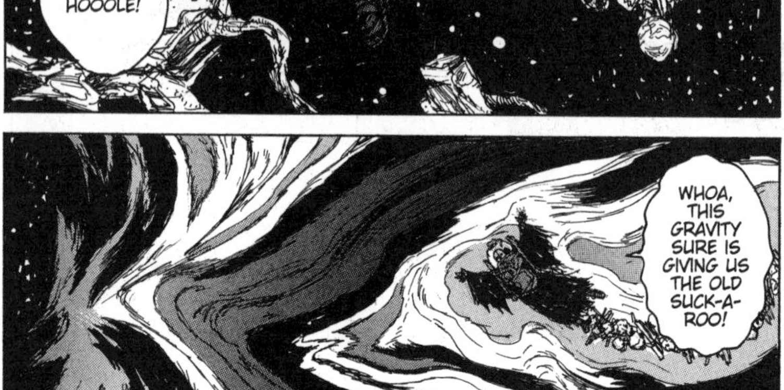
WHOA, THIS GRAVITY SURE IS GIVING US THE OLD SUCK-A-ROO!

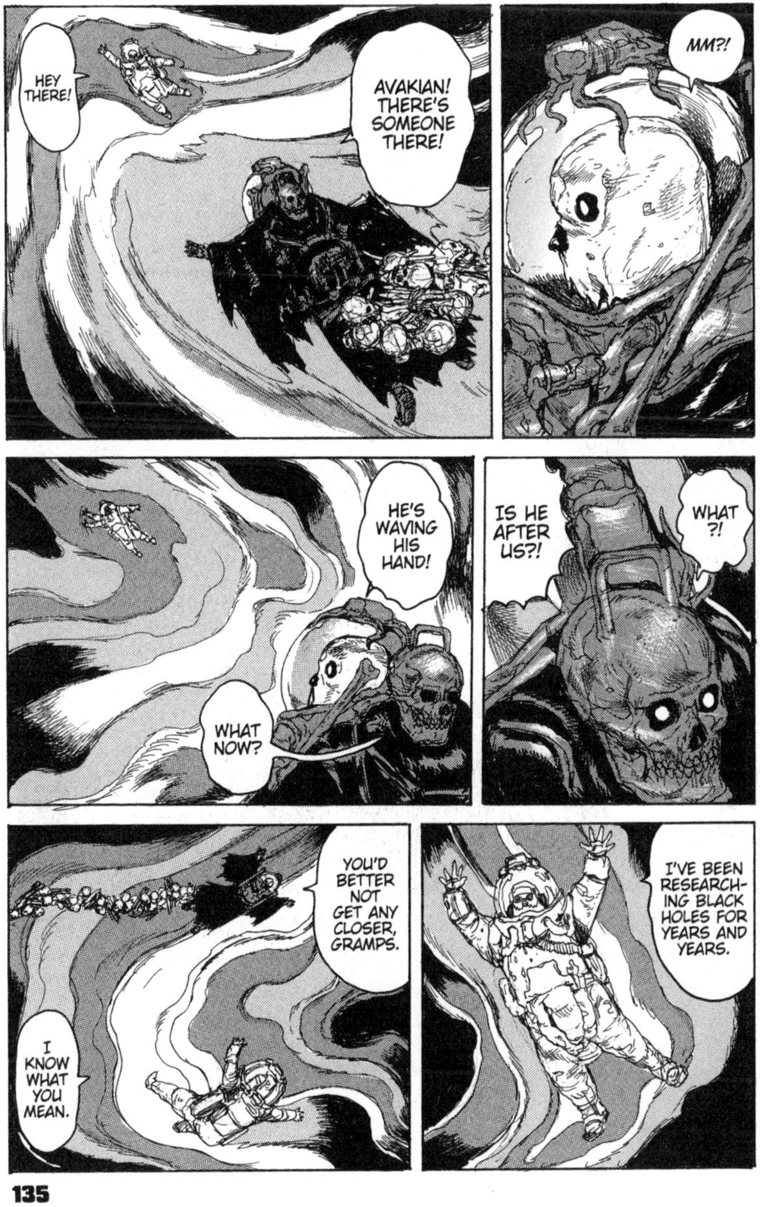
MM?!
AVAKIAN! THERE'S SOMEONE THERE!
HEY THERE!
WHAT ?!
IS HE AFTER US?!
HE'S WAVING HIS HAND!
WHAT NOW?
I'VE BEEN RESEARCH-ING BLACK HOLES FOR YEARS AND YEARS.
YOU'D BETTER NOT GET ANY CLOSER, GRAMPS.
I KNOW WHAT YOU MEAN.

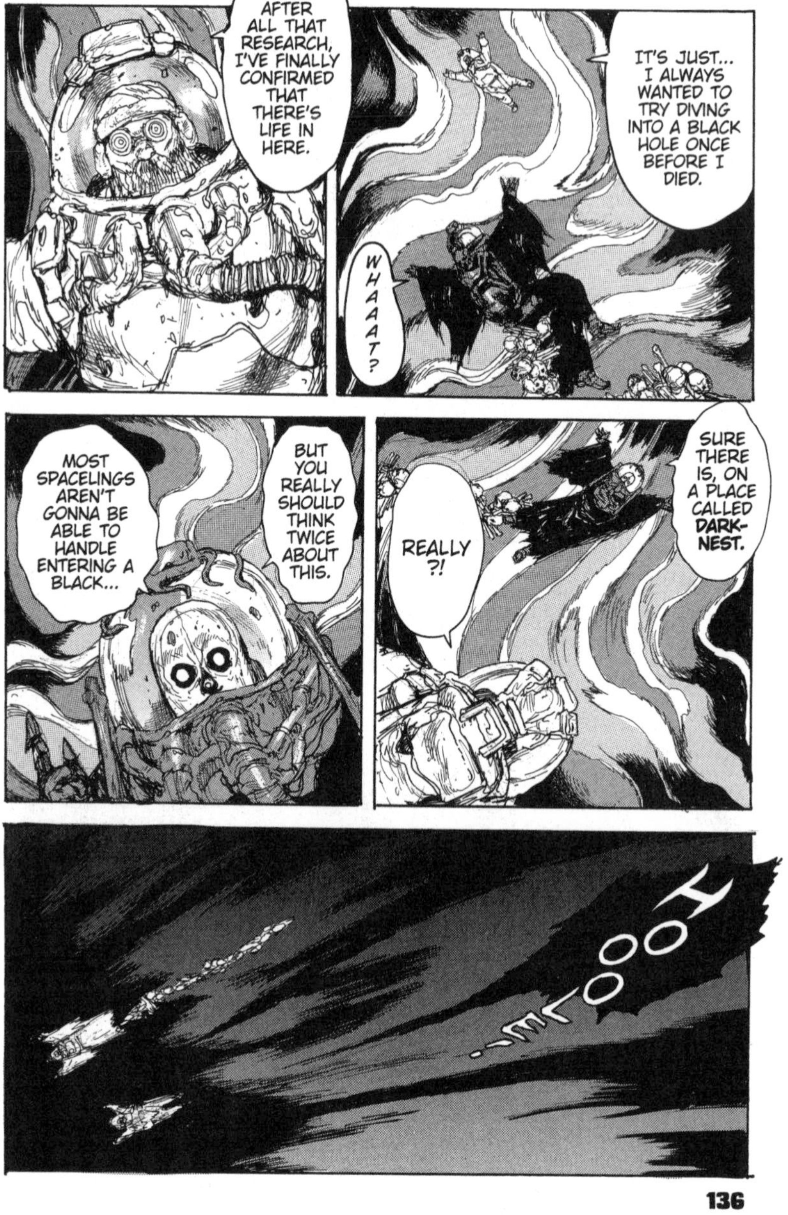
IT'S JUST... I ALWAYS WANTED TO TRY DIVING INTO A BLACK HOLE ONCE BEFORE I DIED.
WHAAAAT?
AFTER ALL THAT RESEARCH, I'VE FINALLY CONFIRMED THAT THERE'S LIFE IN HERE.
SURE THERE IS, ON A PLACE CALLED **DARK-NEST.**
REALLY?!
BUT YOU REALLY SHOULD THINK TWICE ABOUT THIS.
MOST SPACELINGS AREN'T GONNA BE ABLE TO HANDLE ENTERING A BLACK...
HOOOOM!-

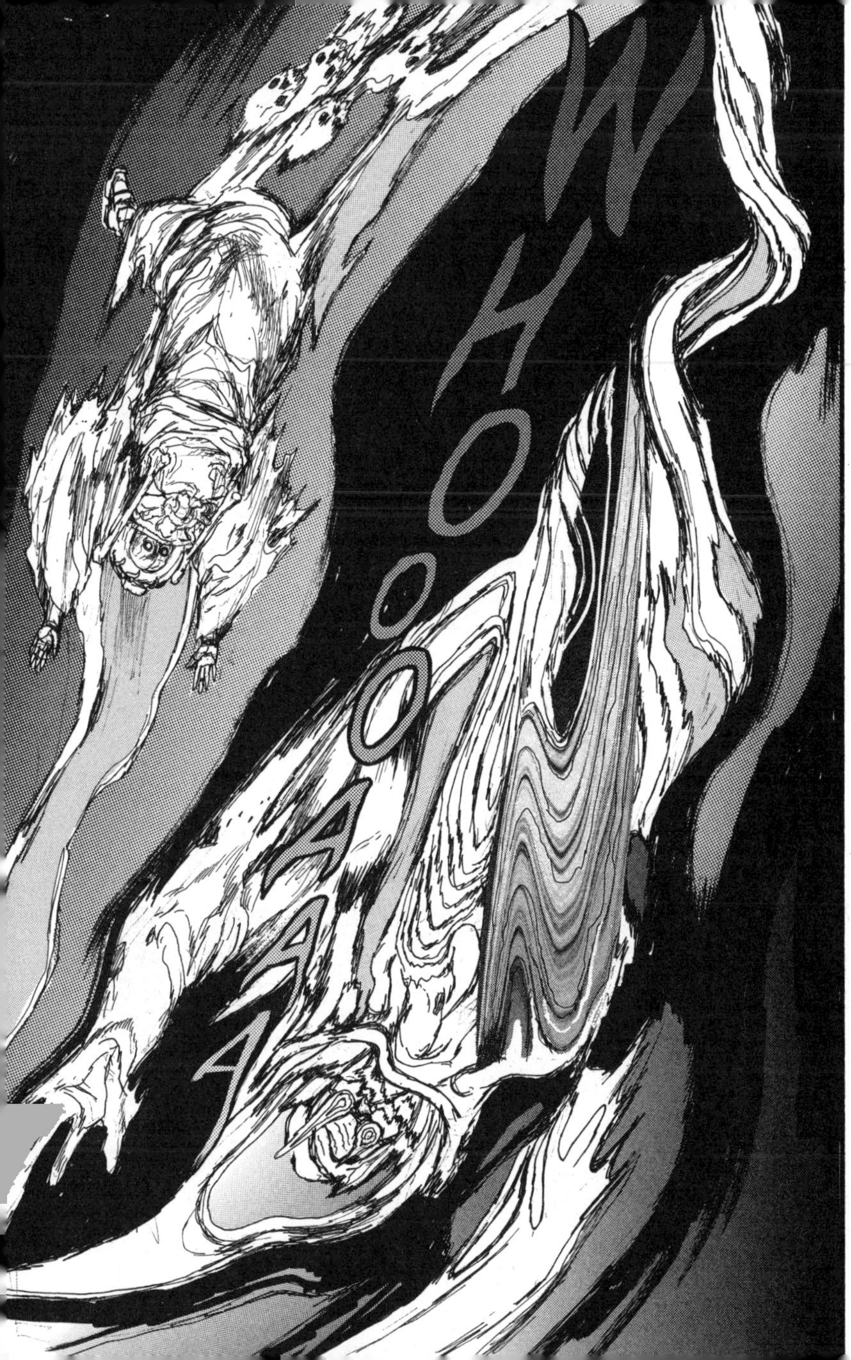
WHOOOAAA

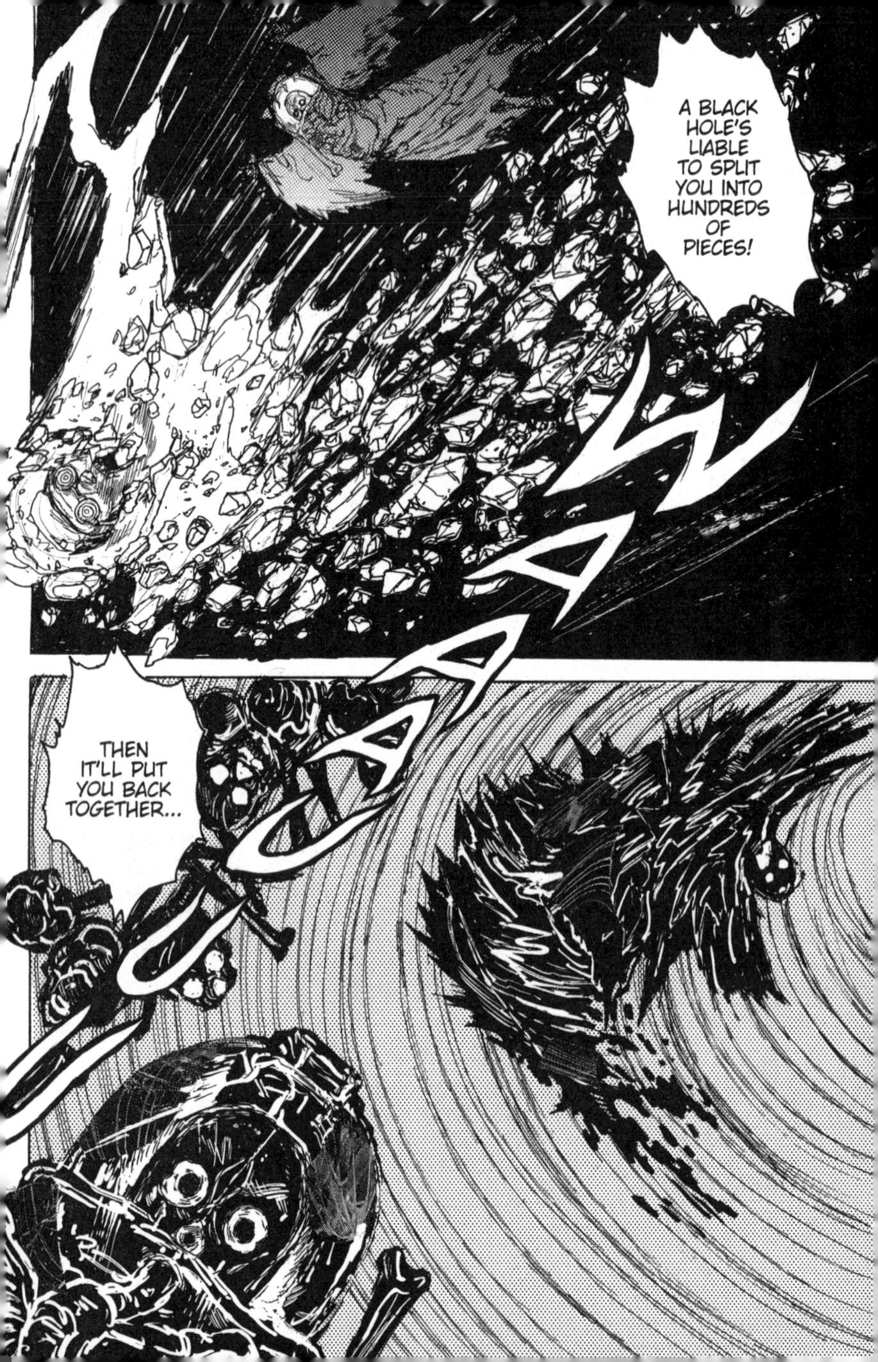
A BLACK HOLE'S LIABLE TO SPLIT YOU INTO HUNDREDS OF PIECES!
THEN IT'LL PUT YOU BACK TOGETHER...

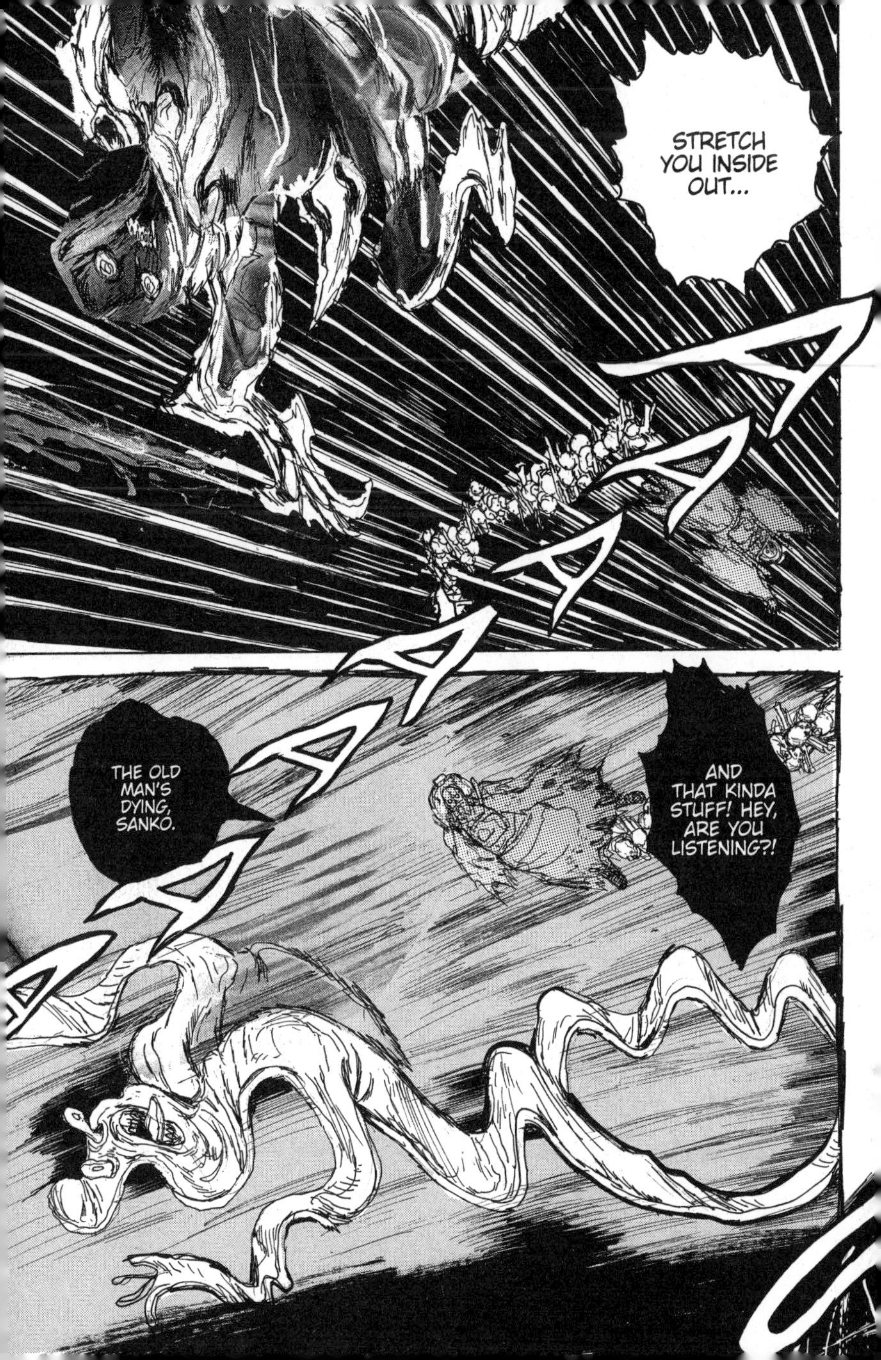
STRETCH YOU INSIDE OUT...
AAAAAAAA
AND THAT KINDA STUFF! HEY, ARE YOU LISTENING?!
THE OLD MAN'S DYING, SANKO.

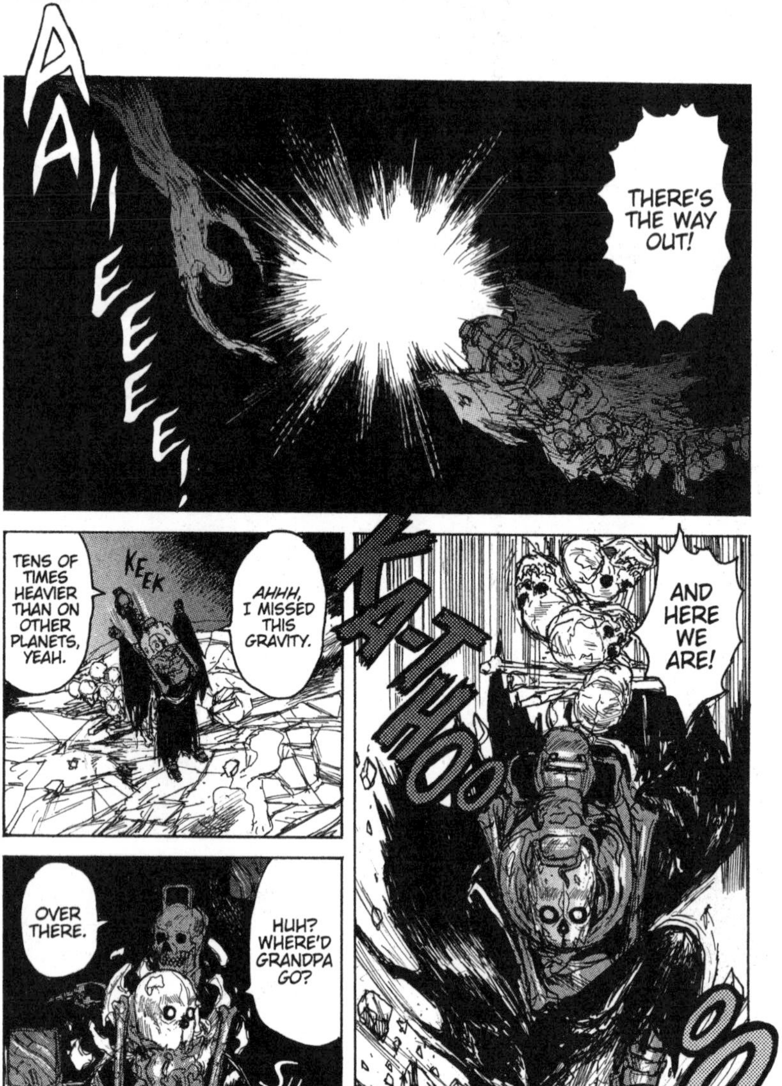
THERE'S THE WAY OUT!
AAIIEEEE!
AND HERE WE ARE!
KA-THOOOOOOOM
AHHH, I MISSED THIS GRAVITY.
TENS OF TIMES HEAVIER THAN ON OTHER PLANETS, YEAH.
KEEK
HUH? WHERE'D GRANDPA GO?
OVER THERE.
SHLUF

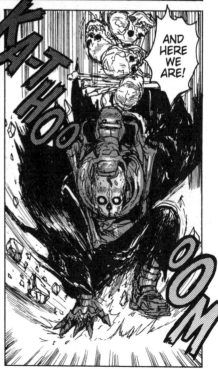

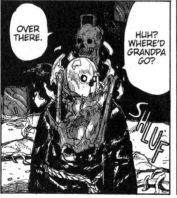

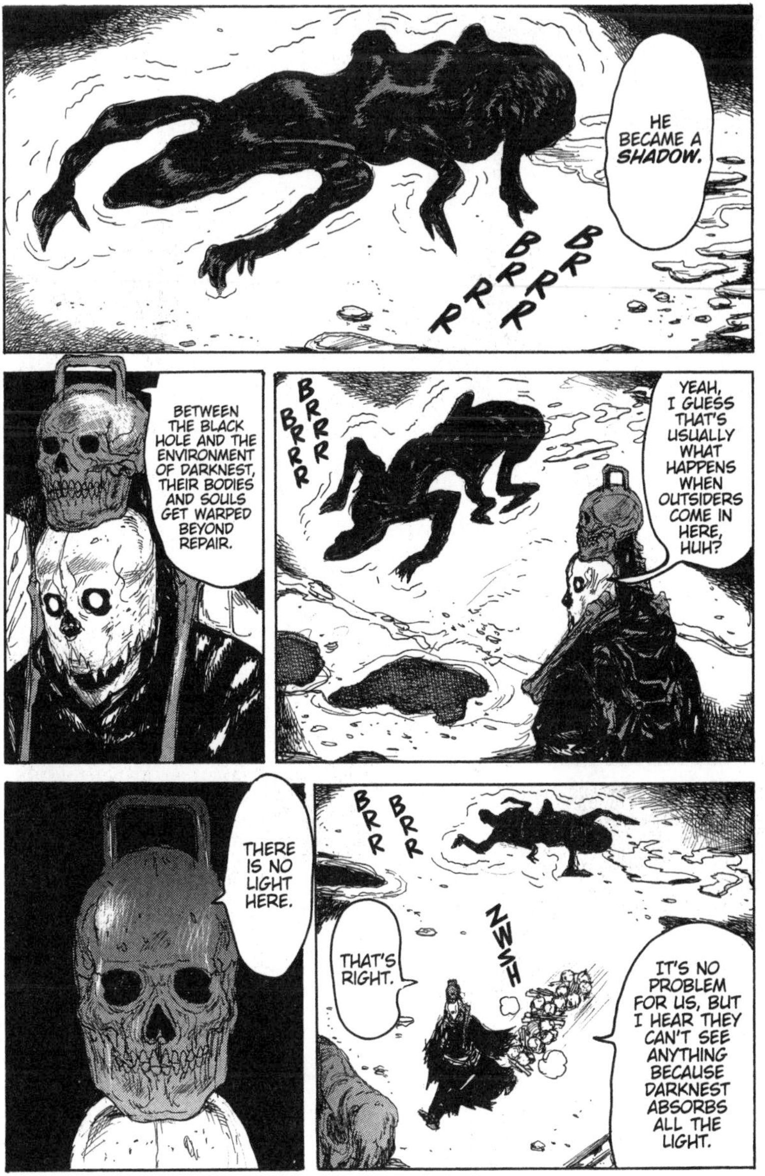
HE BECAME A SHADOW.
BRRRR
BRRRR
YEAH, I GUESS THAT'S USUALLY WHAT HAPPENS WHEN OUTSIDERS COME IN HERE, HUH?
BRRR
BRRR
BETWEEN THE BLACK HOLE AND THE ENVIRONMENT OF DARKNEST, THEIR BODIES AND SOULS GET WARPED BEYOND REPAIR.
BRR
BRR
ZWSH
IT'S NO PROBLEM FOR US, BUT I HEAR THEY CAN'T SEE ANYTHING BECAUSE DARKNEST ABSORBS ALL THE LIGHT.
THAT'S RIGHT.
THERE IS NO LIGHT HERE.

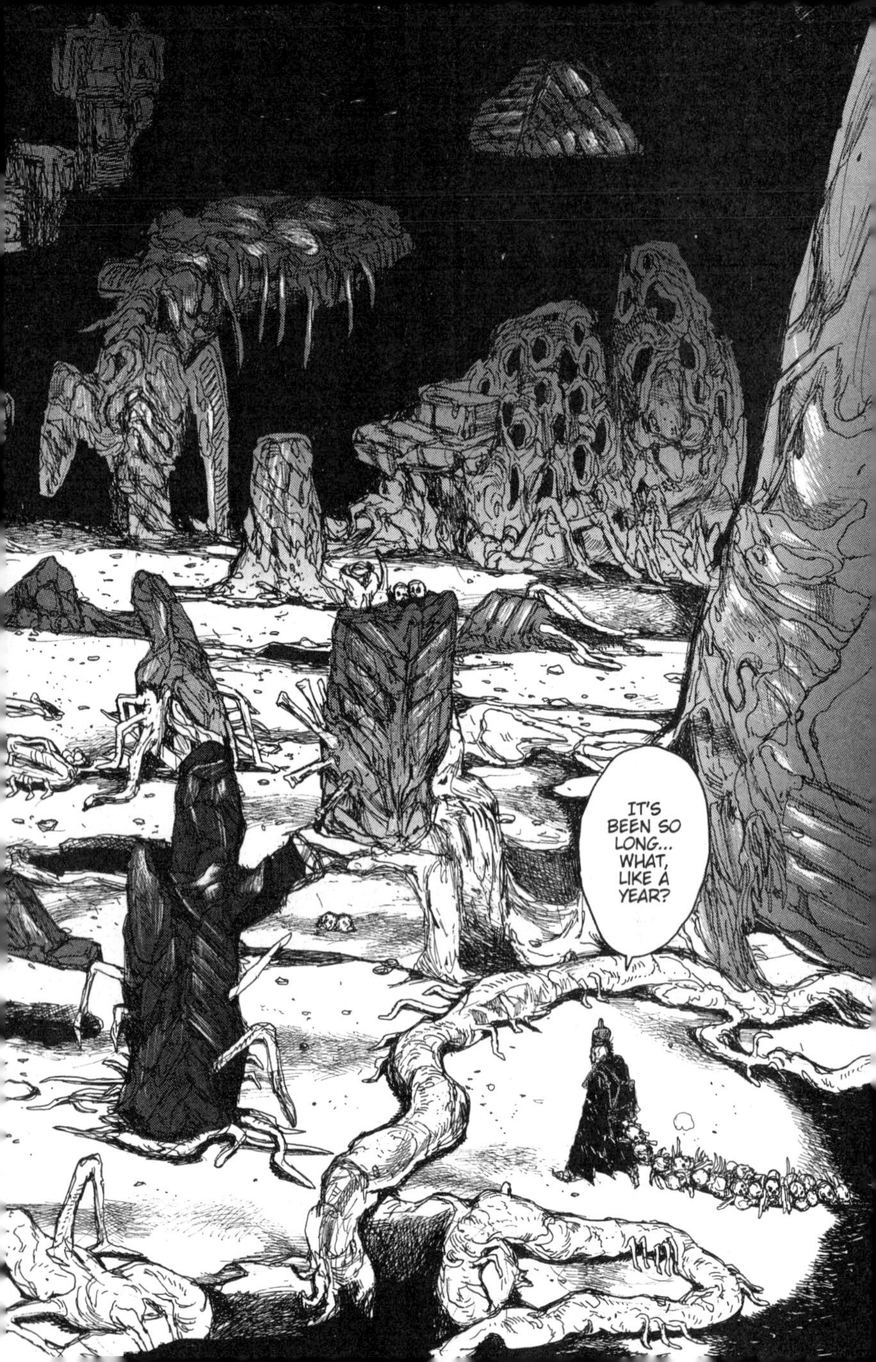
IT'S BEEN SO LONG... WHAT, LIKE A YEAR?

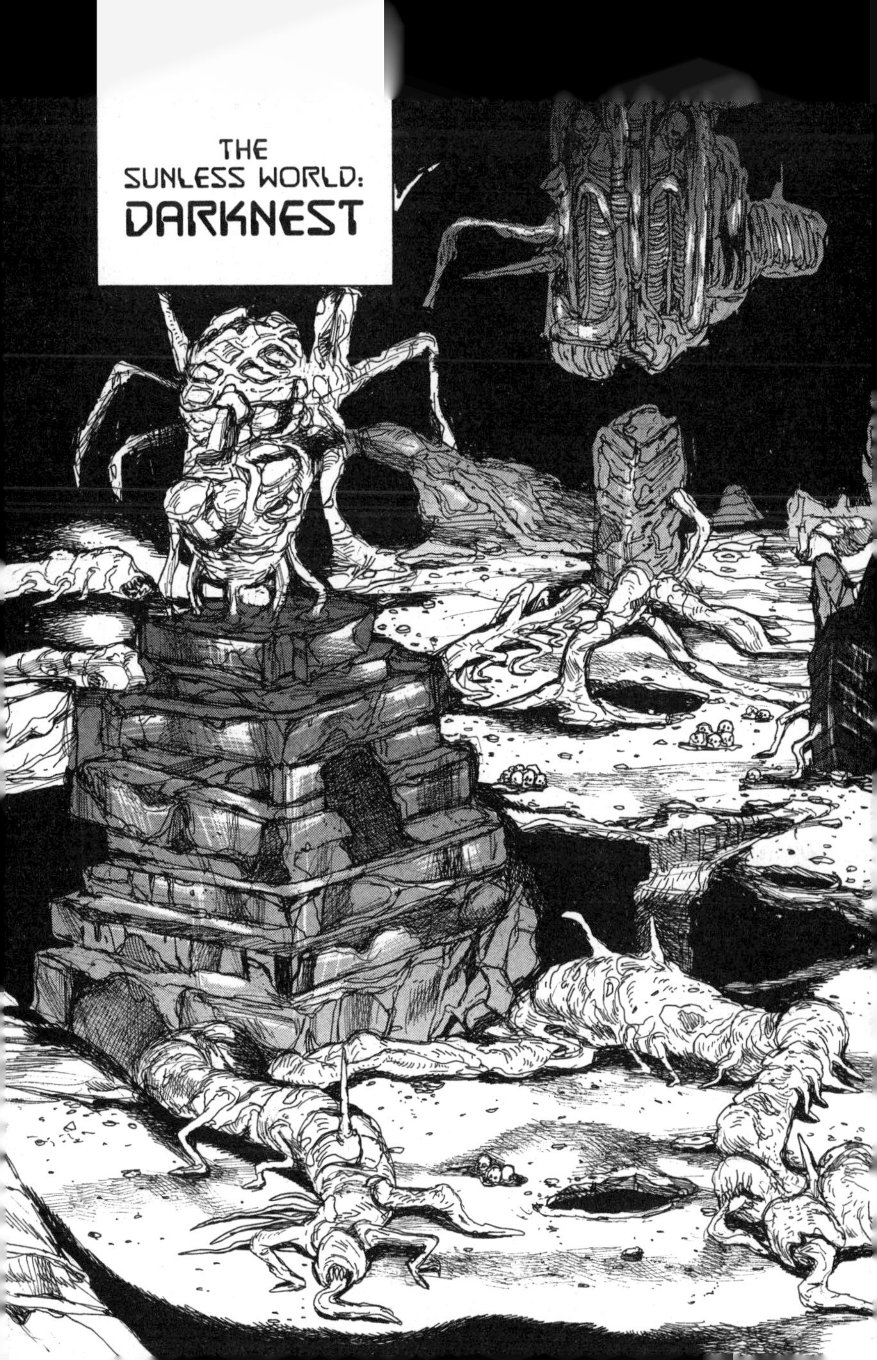
THE
SUNLESS WORLD:
DARKNEST

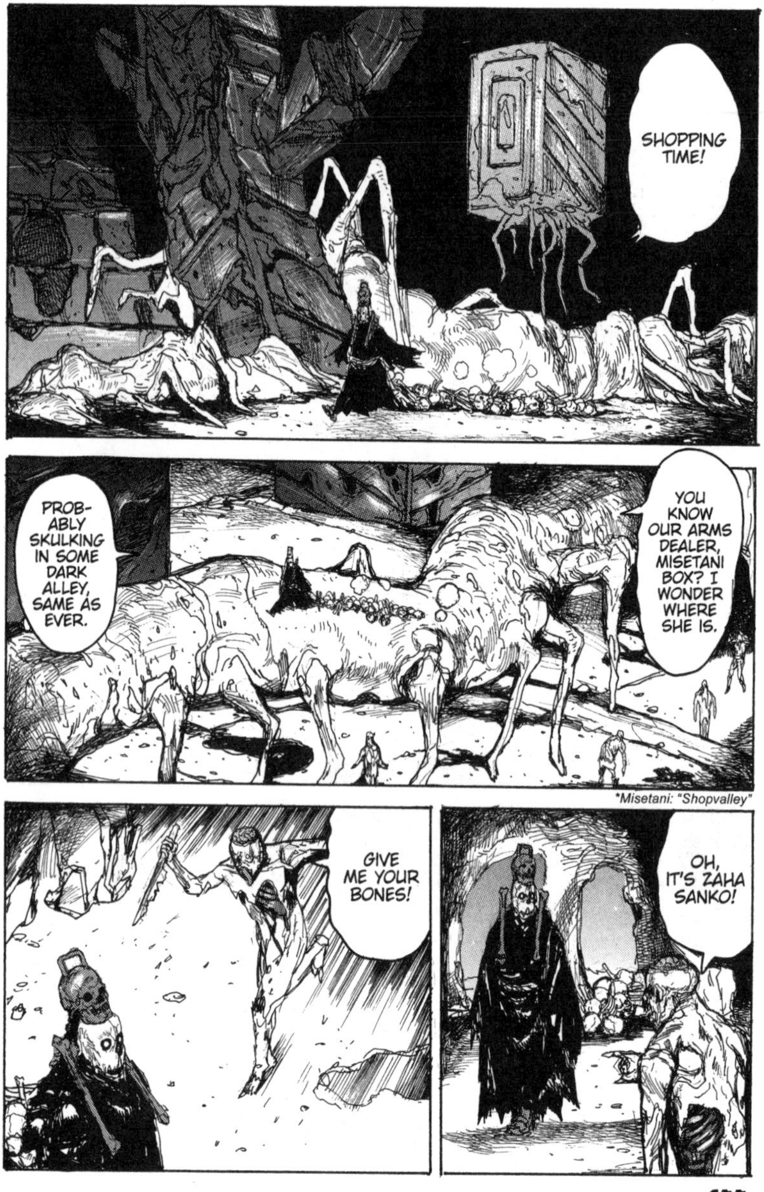
SHOPPING TIME!
YOU KNOW OUR ARMS DEALER, MISETANI BOX? I WONDER WHERE SHE IS.
PROB-ABLY SKULKING IN SOME DARK ALLEY, SAME AS EVER.
*Misetani: "Shopvalley"
OH, IT'S ZAHA SANKO!
GIVE ME YOUR BONES!

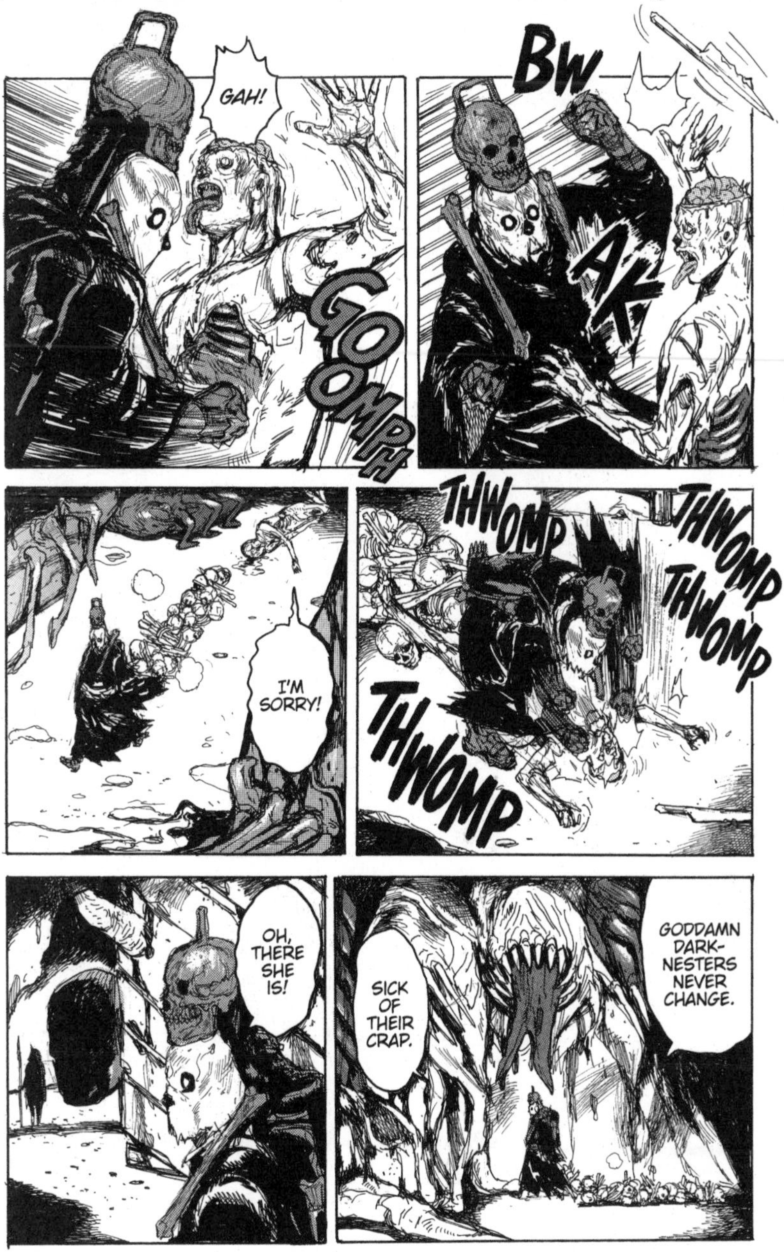
BW
AK
GAH!
GOOMPH
THWOMP
THWOMP
THWOMP
THWOMP
I'M SORRY!
GODDAMN DARK-NESTERS NEVER CHANGE.
SICK OF THEIR CRAP.
OH, THERE SHE IS!

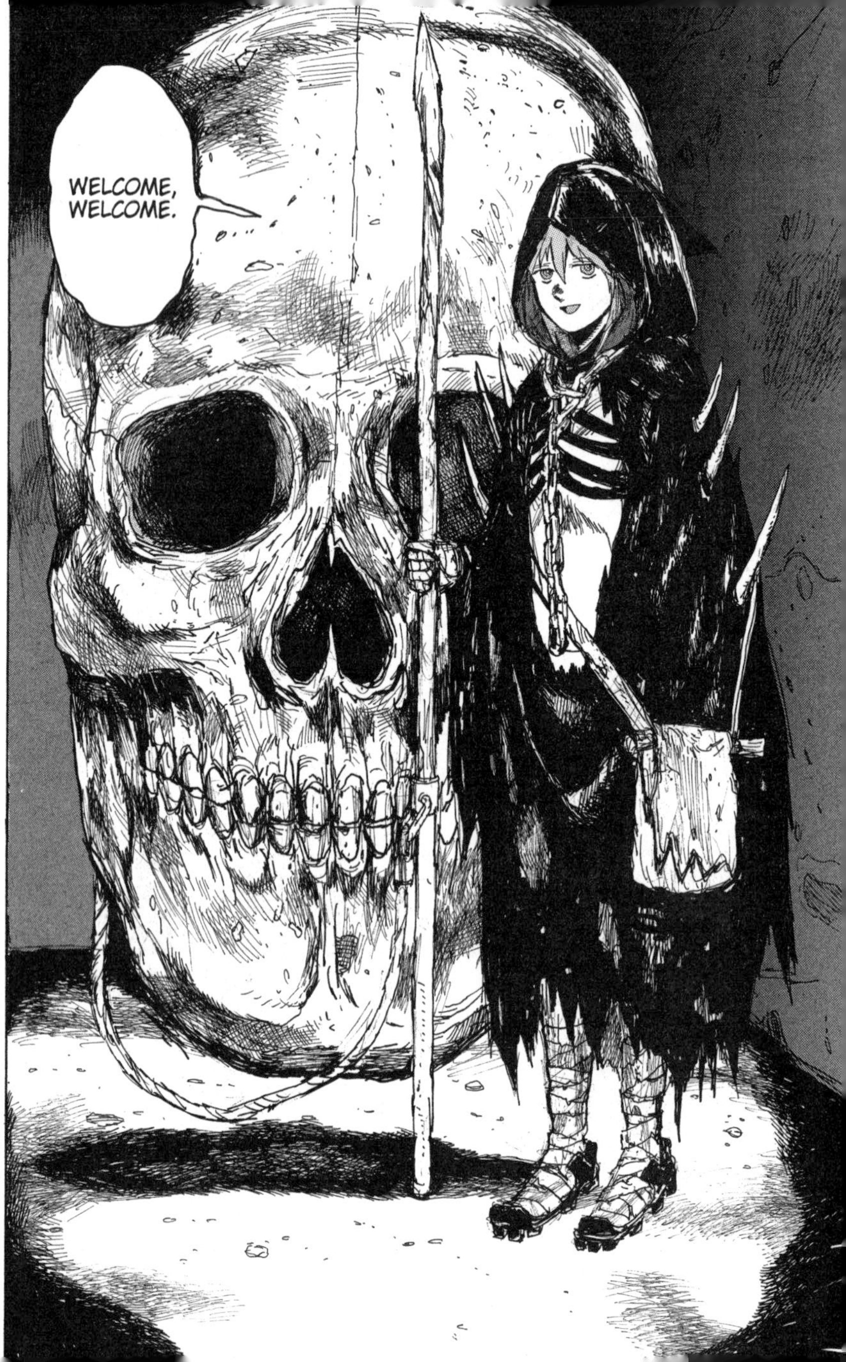
WELCOME, WELCOME.

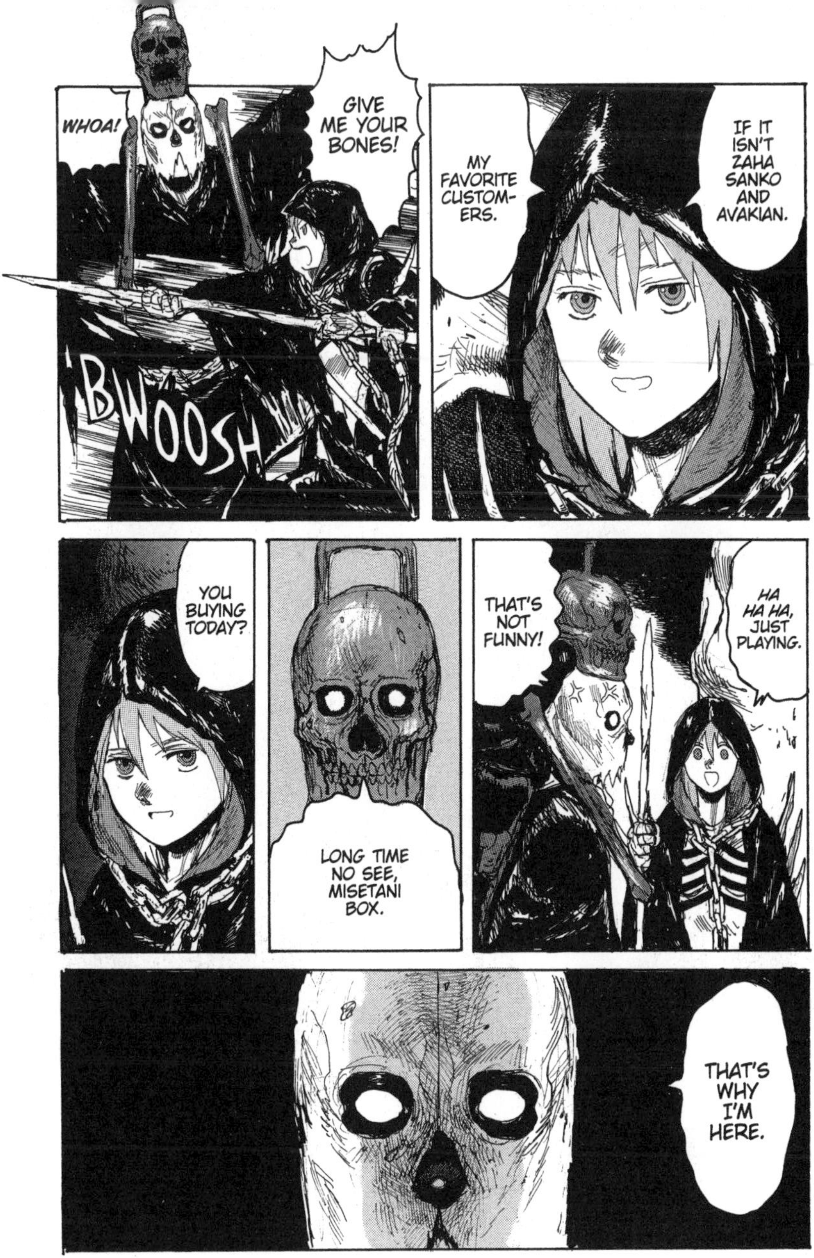
IF IT ISN'T ZAHA SANKO AND AVAKIAN.
MY FAVORITE CUSTOMERS.
GIVE ME YOUR BONES!
WHOA!
BWOOSH
HA HA HA, JUST PLAYING.
THAT'S NOT FUNNY!
LONG TIME NO SEE, MISETANI BOX.
YOU BUYING TODAY?
THAT'S WHY I'M HERE.

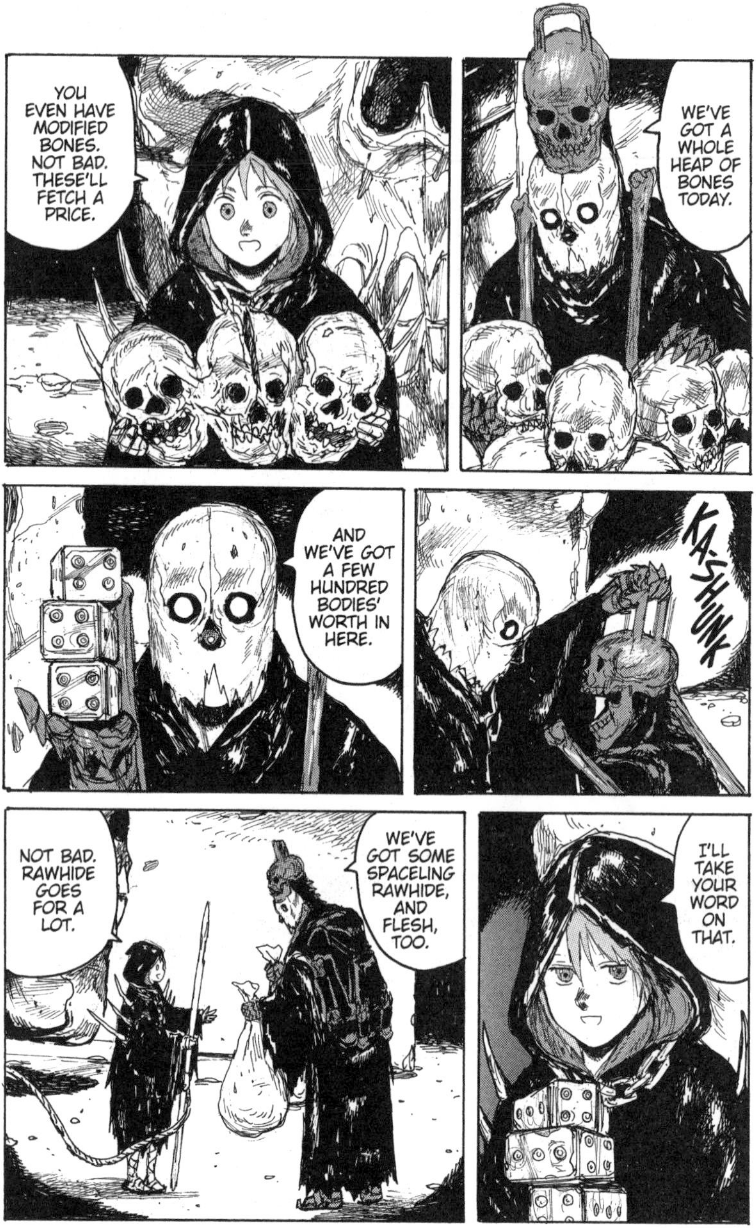
WE'VE GOT A WHOLE HEAP OF BONES TODAY.
YOU EVEN HAVE MODIFIED BONES. NOT BAD. THESE'LL FETCH A PRICE.
KA-SHUNK
AND WE'VE GOT A FEW HUNDRED BODIES' WORTH IN HERE.
I'LL TAKE YOUR WORD ON THAT.
WE'VE GOT SOME SPACELING RAWHIDE, AND FLESH, TOO.
NOT BAD. RAWHIDE GOES FOR A LOT.

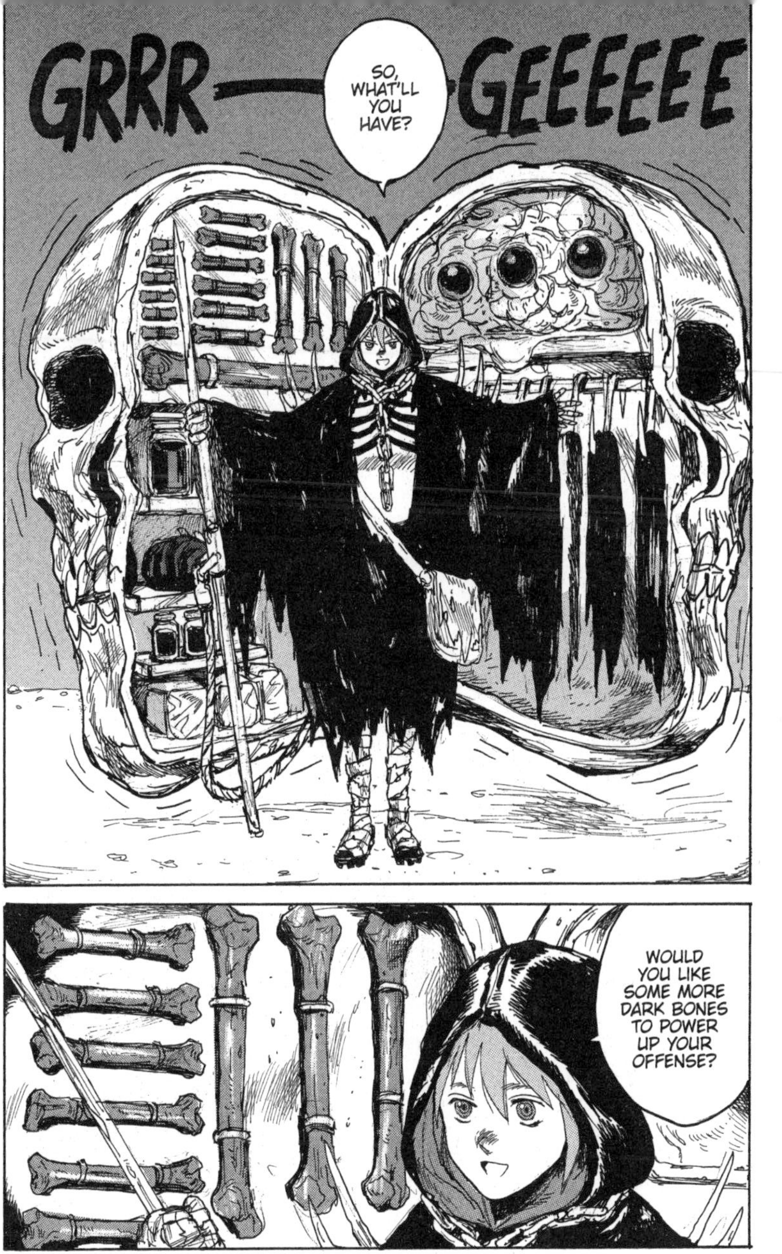
SO, WHAT'LL YOU HAVE?
GRRR—GEEEEEE
WOULD YOU LIKE SOME MORE DARK BONES TO POWER UP YOUR OFFENSE?

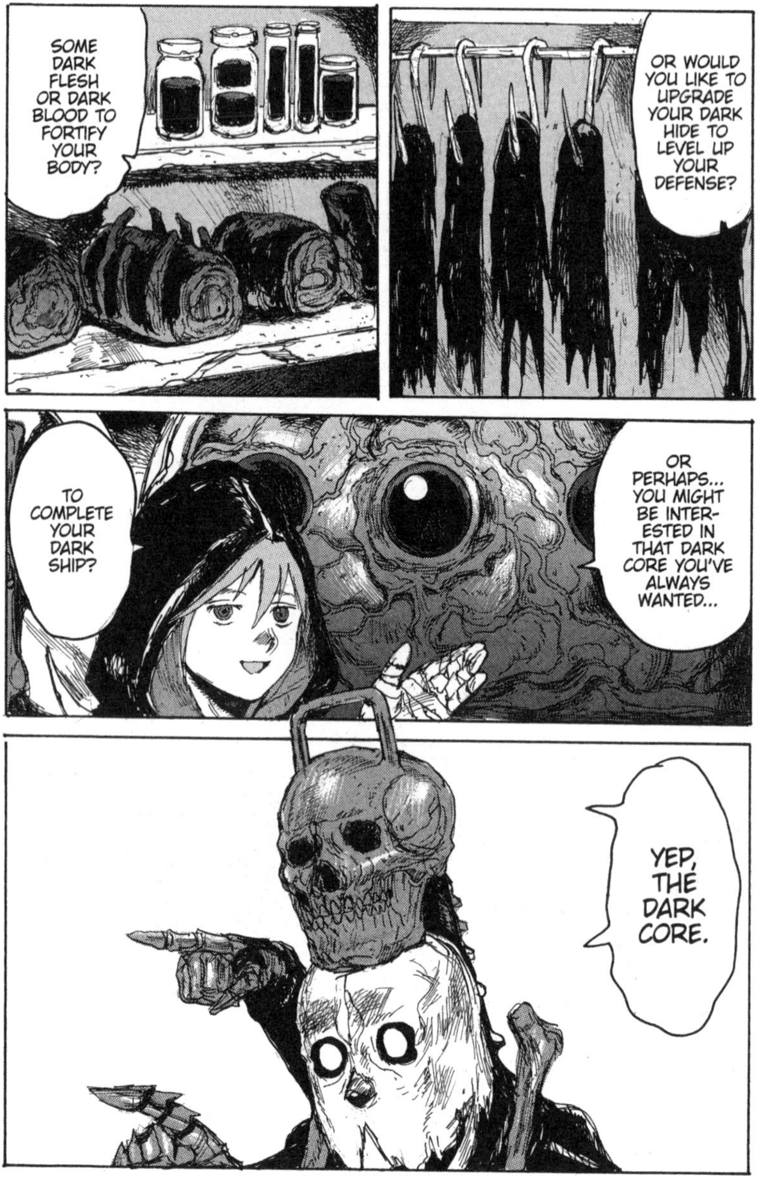
OR WOULD YOU LIKE TO UPGRADE YOUR DARK HIDE TO LEVEL UP YOUR DEFENSE?
SOME DARK FLESH OR DARK BLOOD TO FORTIFY YOUR BODY?
OR PERHAPS... YOU MIGHT BE INTER-ESTED IN THAT DARK CORE YOU'VE ALWAYS WANTED...
TO COMPLETE YOUR DARK SHIP?
YEP, THE DARK CORE.

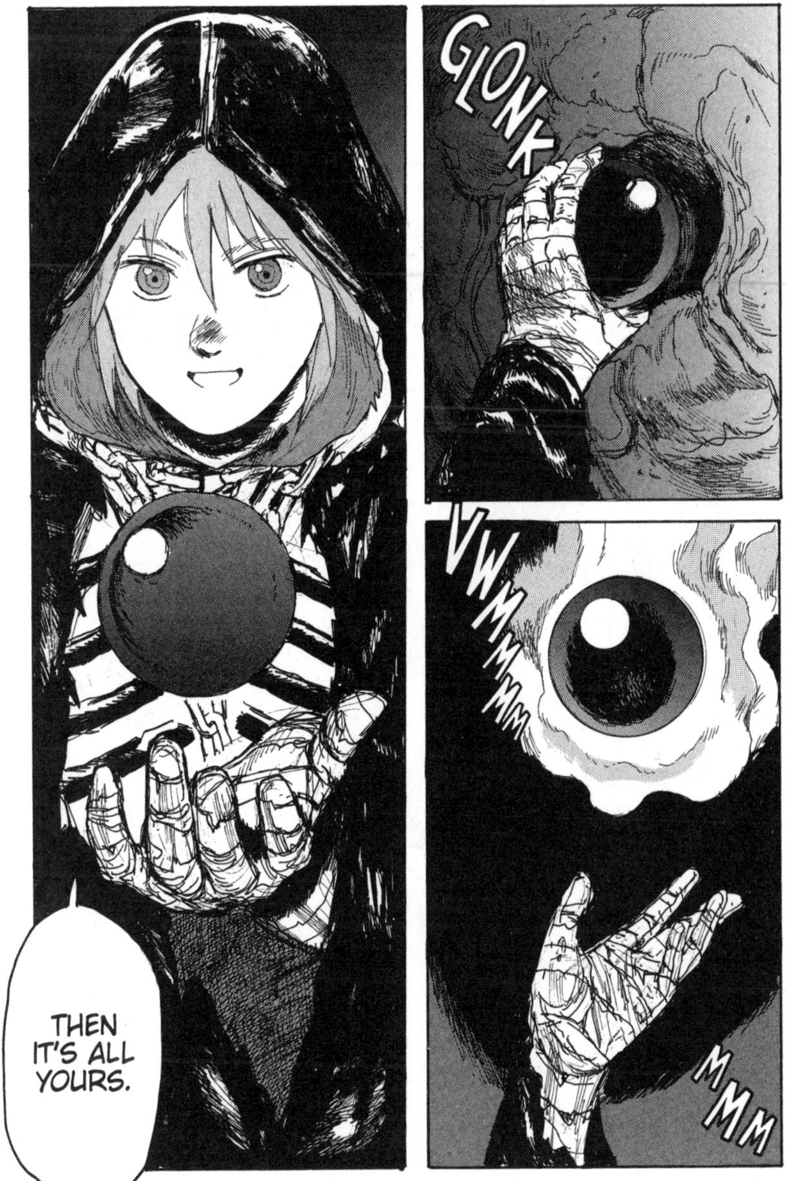
GLONK
VWMMMM
MMM
THEN IT'S ALL YOURS.

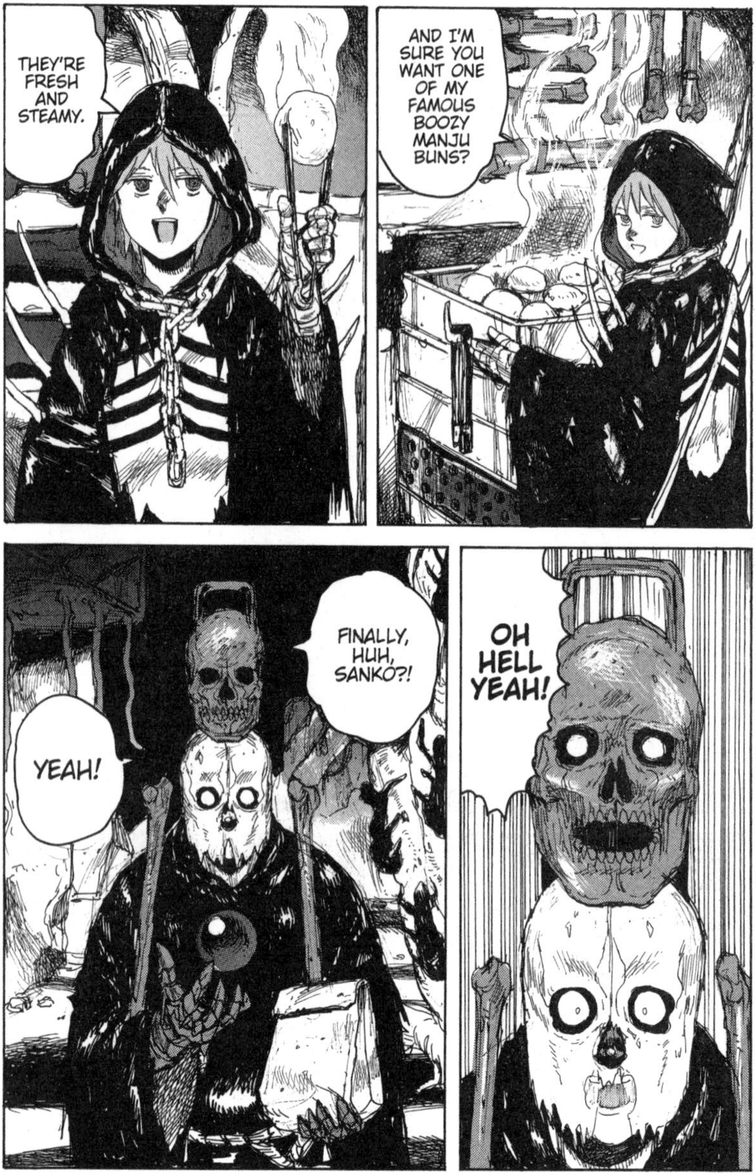
AND I'M SURE YOU WANT ONE OF MY FAMOUS BOOZY MANJU BUNS?
THEY'RE FRESH AND STEAMY.
OH HELL YEAH!
FINALLY, HUH, SANKO?!
YEAH!

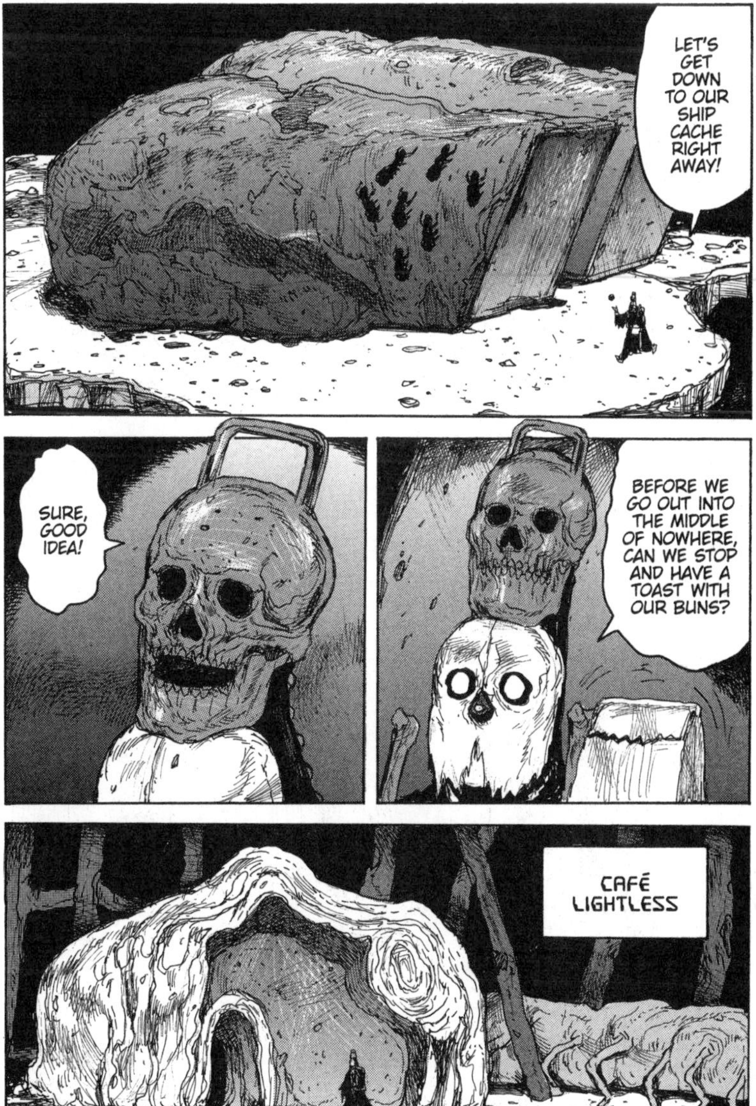
LET'S GET DOWN TO OUR SHIP CACHE RIGHT AWAY!
BEFORE WE GO OUT INTO THE MIDDLE OF NOWHERE, CAN WE STOP AND HAVE A TOAST WITH OUR BUNS?
SURE, GOOD IDEA!
CAFÉ LIGHTLESS

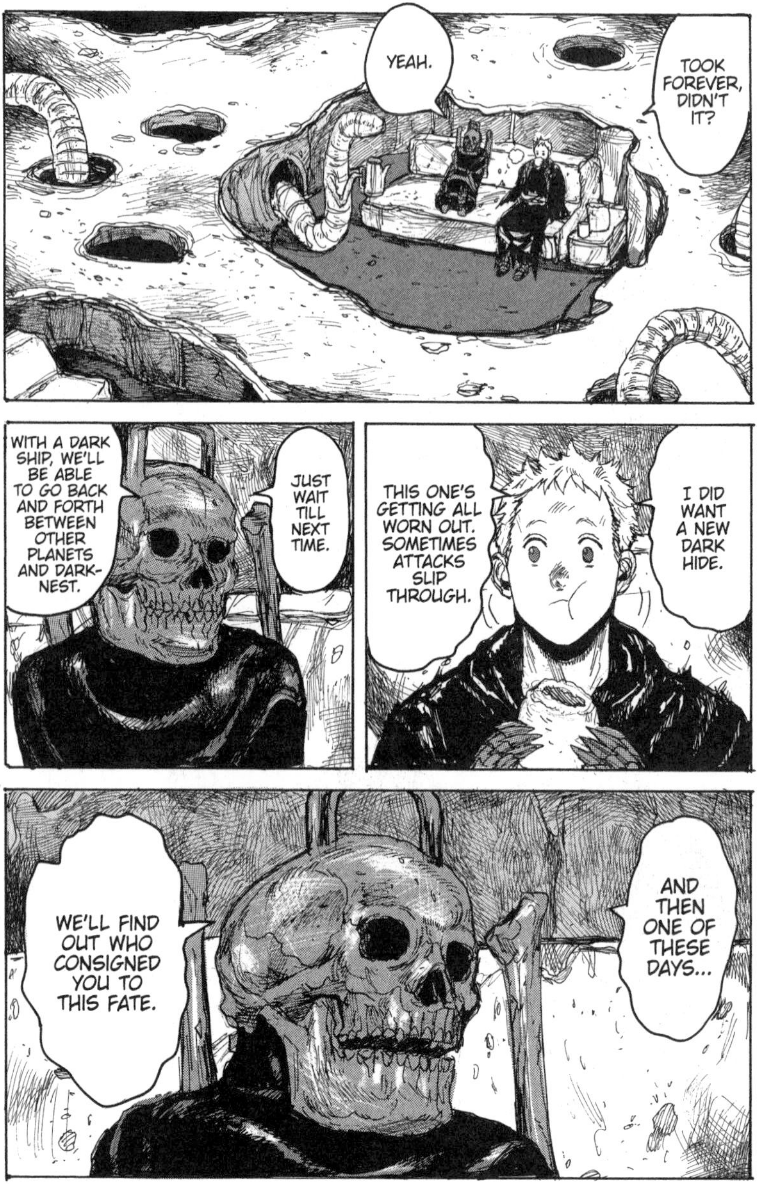
TOOK FOREVER, DIDN'T IT?
YEAH.
I DID WANT A NEW DARK HIDE.
THIS ONE'S GETTING ALL WORN OUT. SOMETIMES ATTACKS SLIP THROUGH.
JUST WAIT TILL NEXT TIME.
WITH A DARK SHIP, WE'LL BE ABLE TO GO BACK AND FORTH BETWEEN OTHER PLANETS AND DARK-NEST.
AND THEN ONE OF THESE DAYS...
WE'LL FIND OUT WHO CONSIGNED YOU TO THIS FATE.

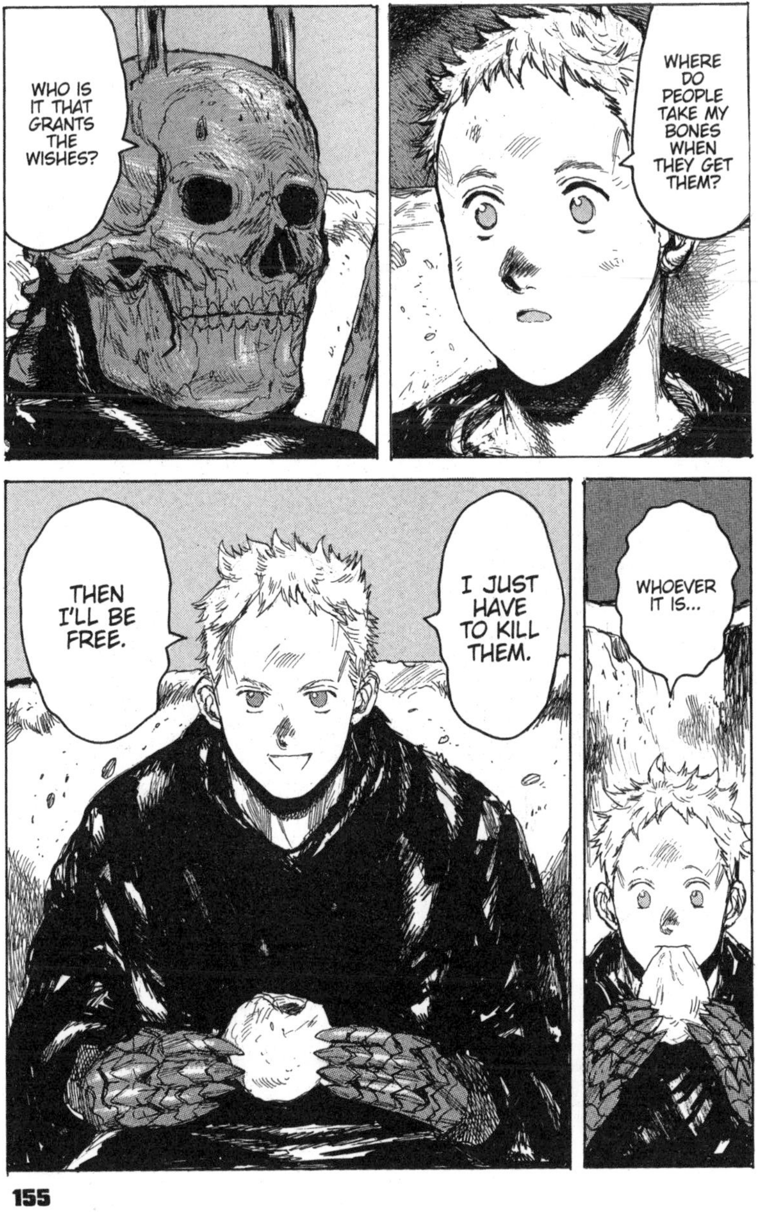
WHERE DO PEOPLE TAKE MY BONES WHEN THEY GET THEM?
WHO IS IT THAT GRANTS THE WISHES?
WHOEVER IT IS...
I JUST HAVE TO KILL THEM.
THEN I'LL BE FREE.

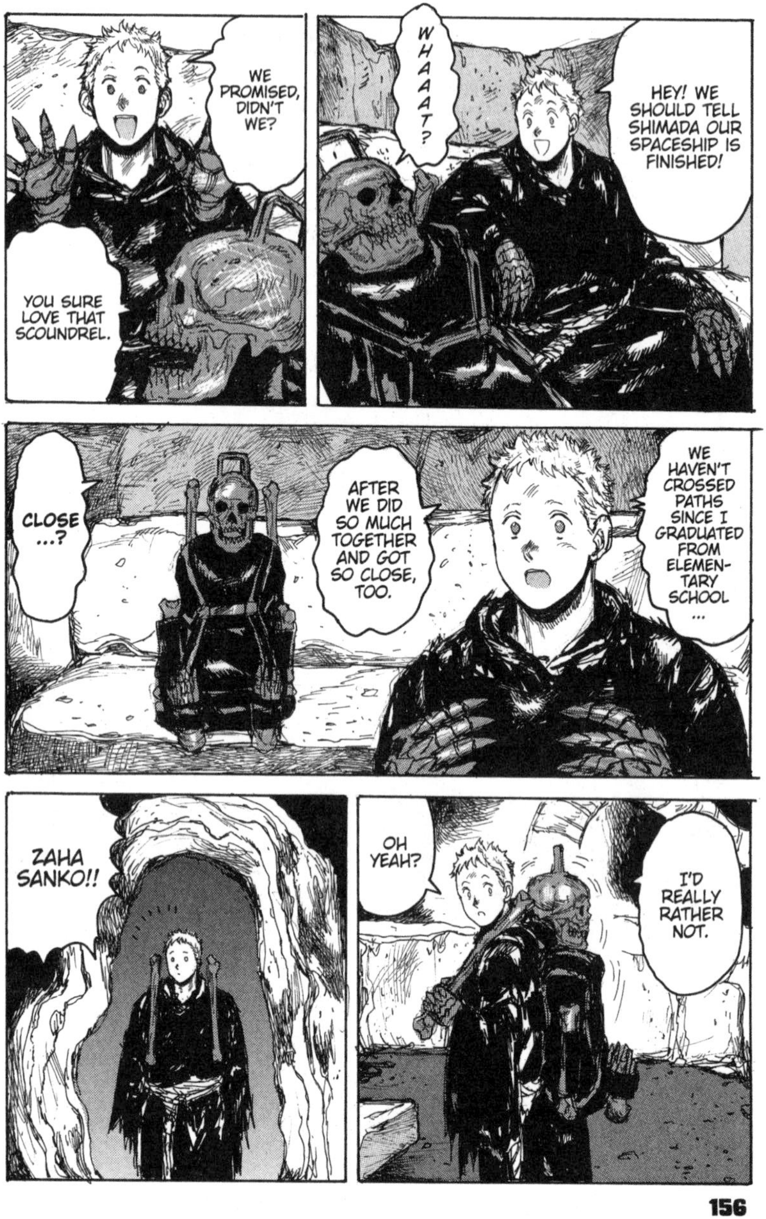
HEY! WE SHOULD TELL SHIMADA OUR SPACESHIP IS FINISHED!
WHAAAT?
WE PROMISED, DIDN'T WE?
YOU SURE LOVE THAT SCOUNDREL.
WE HAVEN'T CROSSED PATHS SINCE I GRADUATED FROM ELEMENTARY SCHOOL ...
AFTER WE DID SO MUCH TOGETHER AND GOT SO CLOSE, TOO.
CLOSE ...?
I'D REALLY RATHER NOT.
OH YEAH?
ZAHA SANKO!!

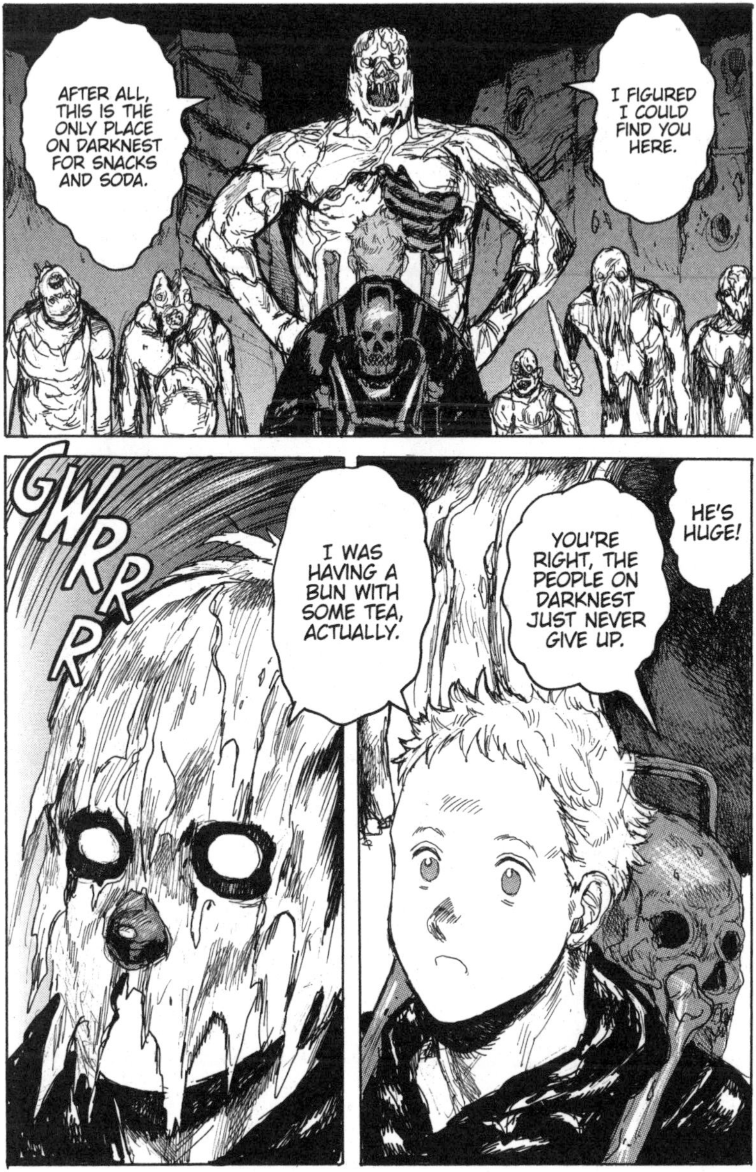
I FIGURED I COULD FIND YOU HERE.
AFTER ALL, THIS IS THE ONLY PLACE ON DARKNEST FOR SNACKS AND SODA.
HE'S HUGE!
YOU'RE RIGHT, THE PEOPLE ON DARKNEST JUST NEVER GIVE UP.
I WAS HAVING A BUN WITH SOME TEA, ACTUALLY.
GWRRRR

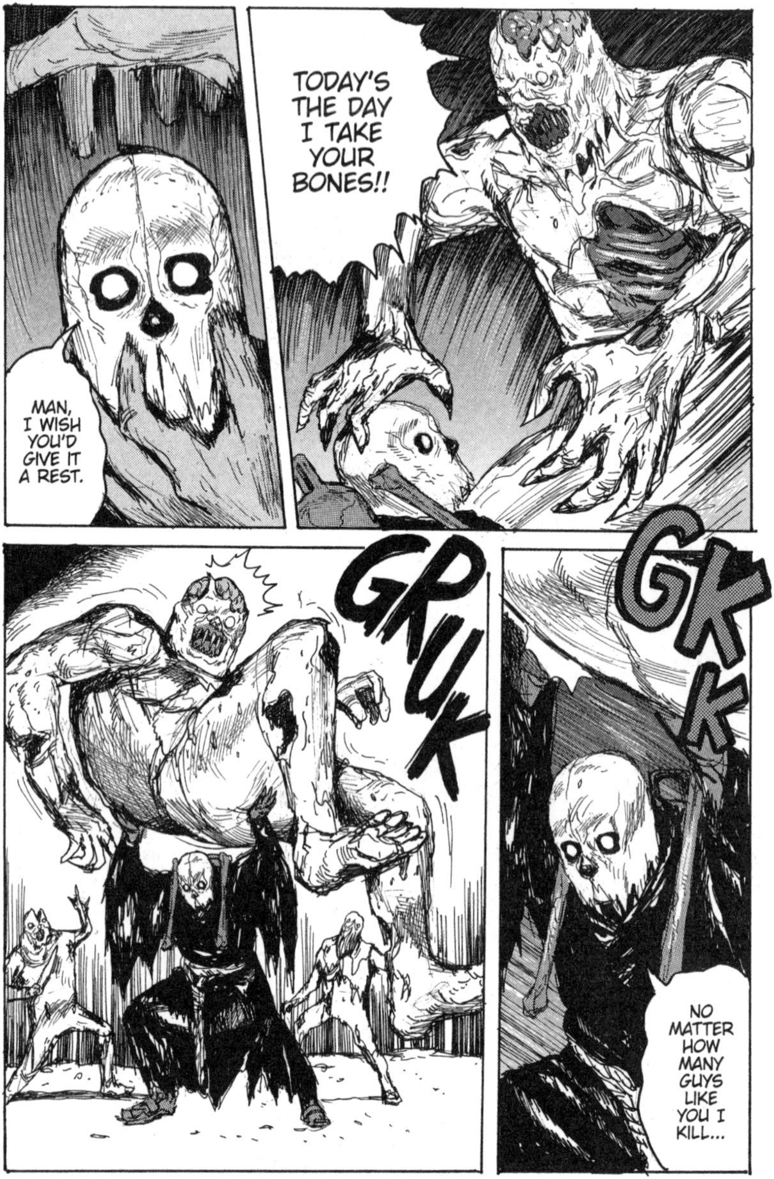
TODAY'S THE DAY I TAKE YOUR BONES!!
MAN, I WISH YOU'D GIVE IT A REST.
GKK
NO MATTER HOW MANY GUYS LIKE YOU I KILL...
GRUK

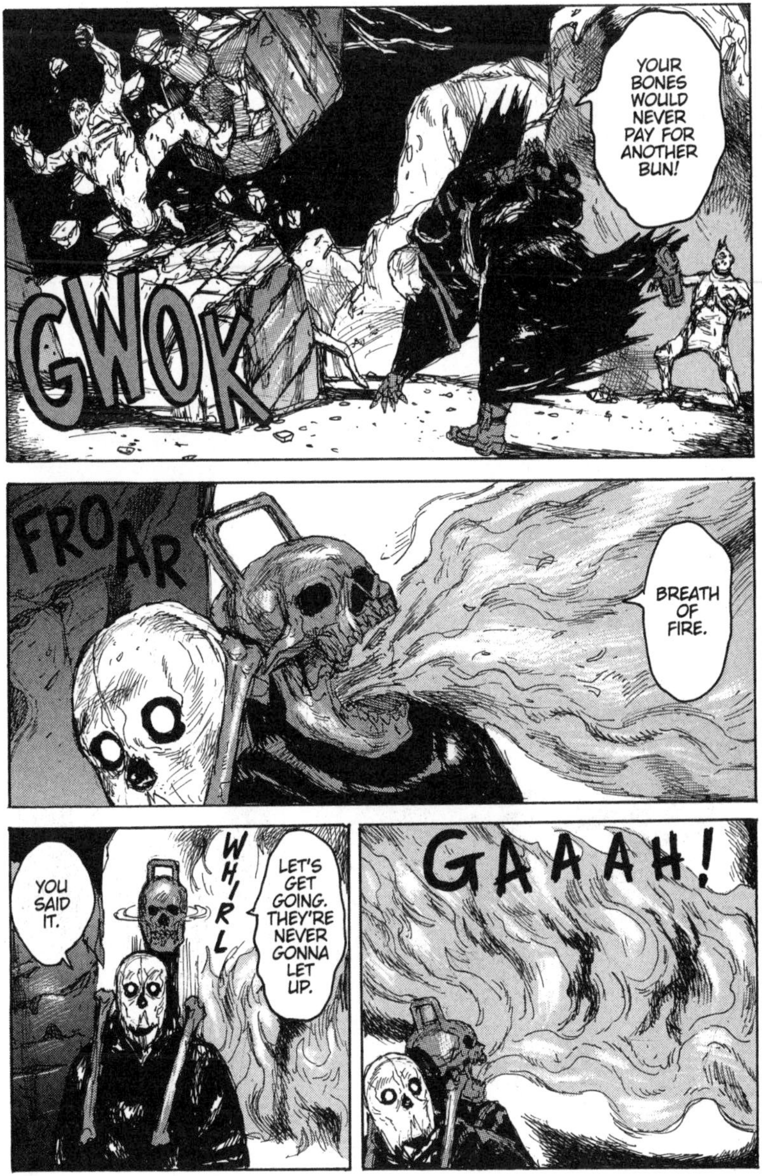
YOUR BONES WOULD NEVER PAY FOR ANOTHER BUN!
GWOK
FROAR
BREATH OF FIRE.
GAAAH!
LET'S GET GOING. THEY'RE NEVER GONNA LET UP.
WHIRL
YOU SAID IT.

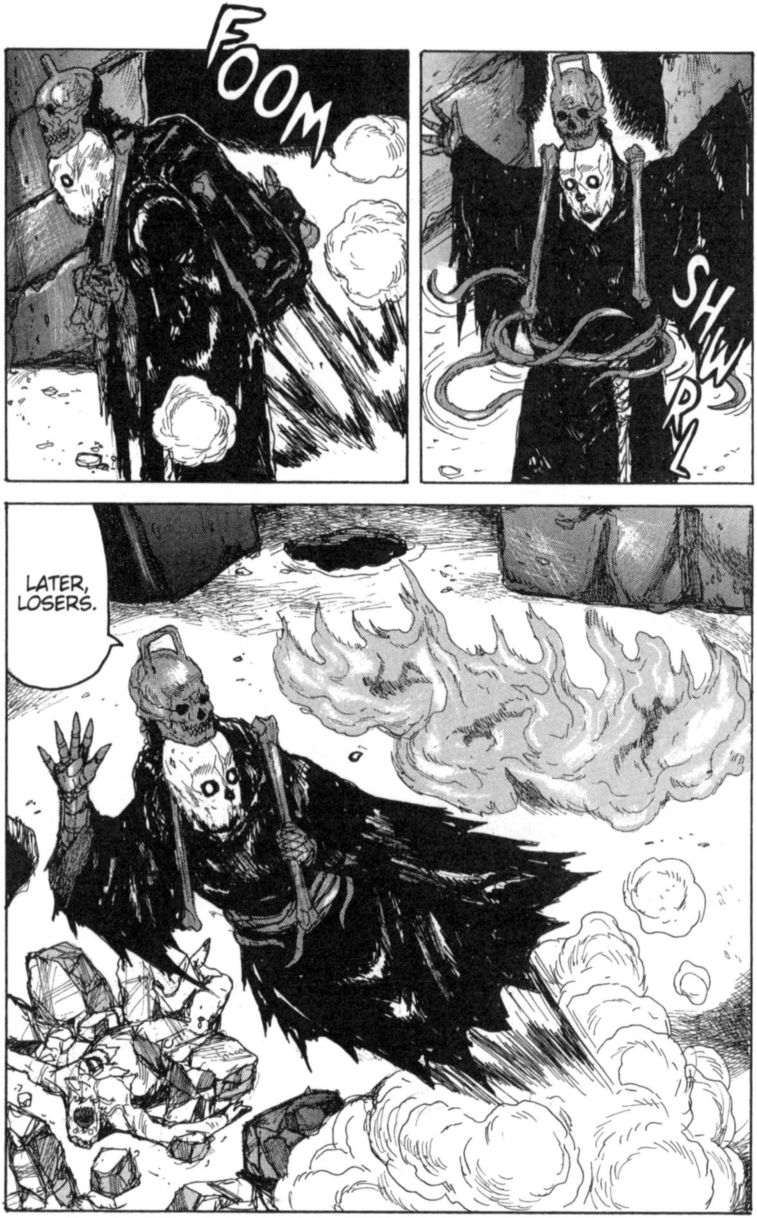
SHWRL
FOOM
LATER, LOSERS.

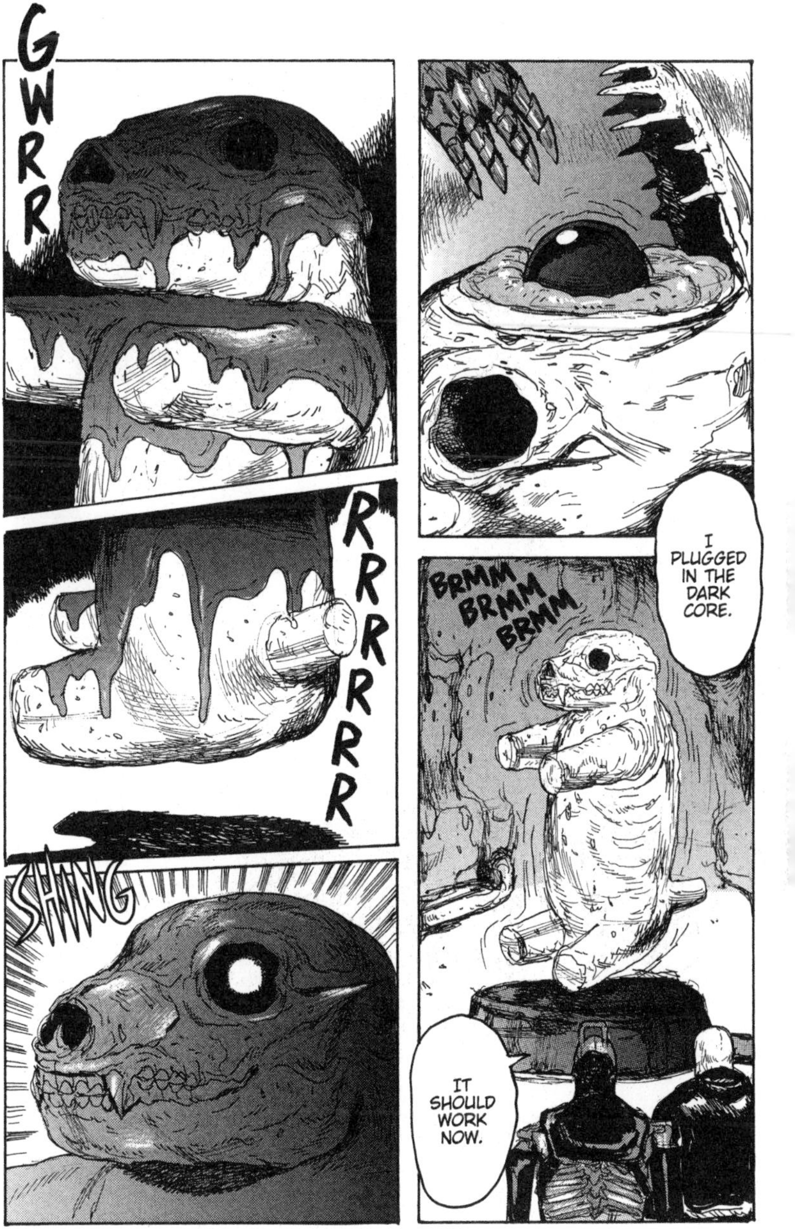
GWRR
RRRRRRR
I PLUGGED IN THE DARK CORE.
BRMM BRMM BRMM
IT SHOULD WORK NOW.
SHING

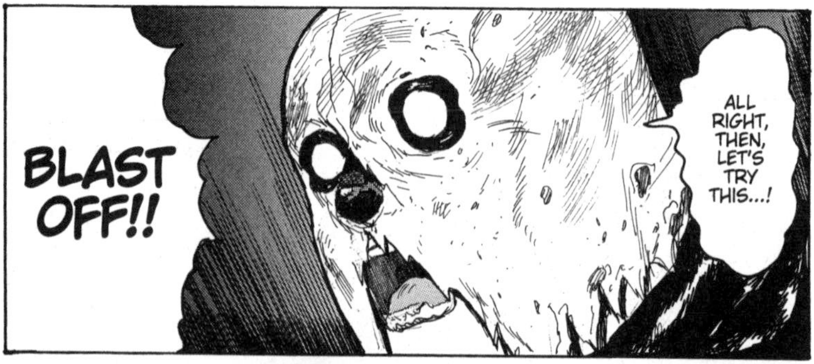
ALL RIGHT, THEN, LET'S TRY THIS...!
BLAST OFF!!
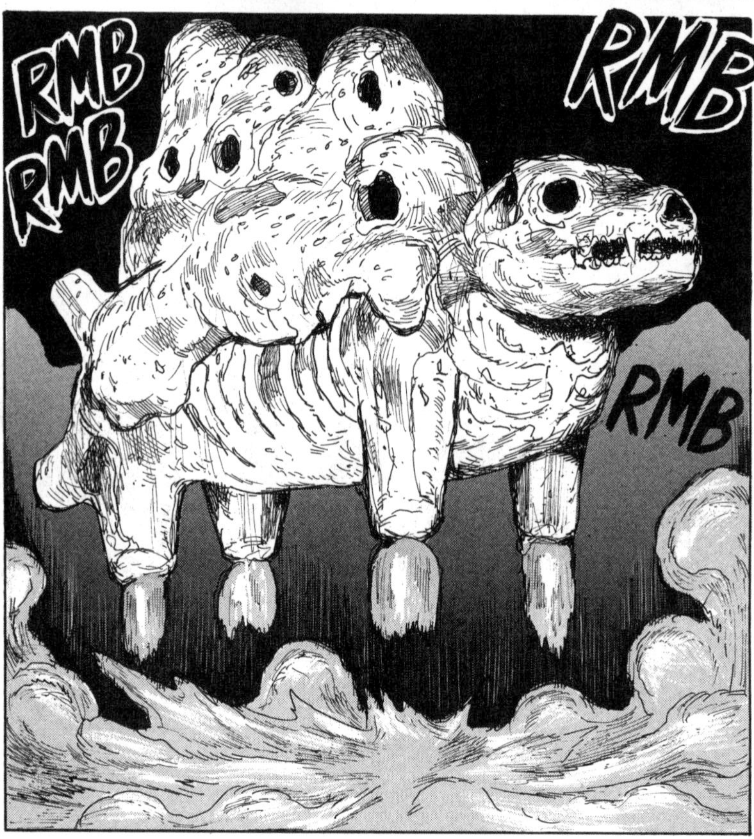
RMB
RMB RMB
RMB

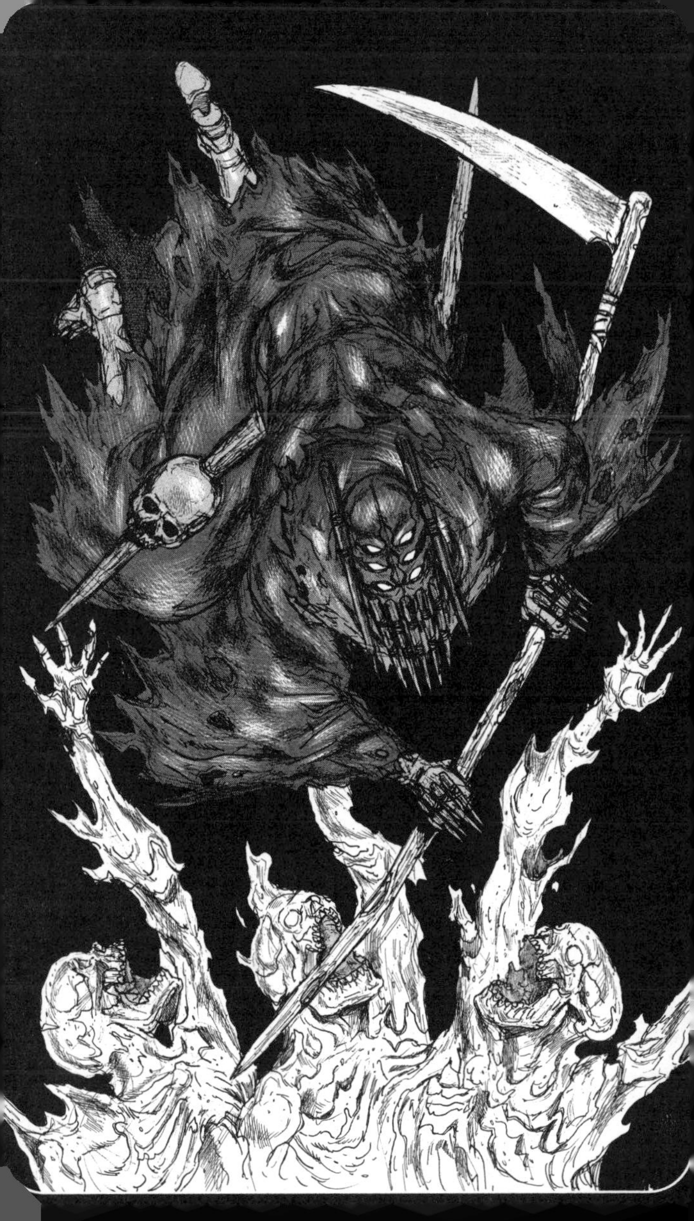

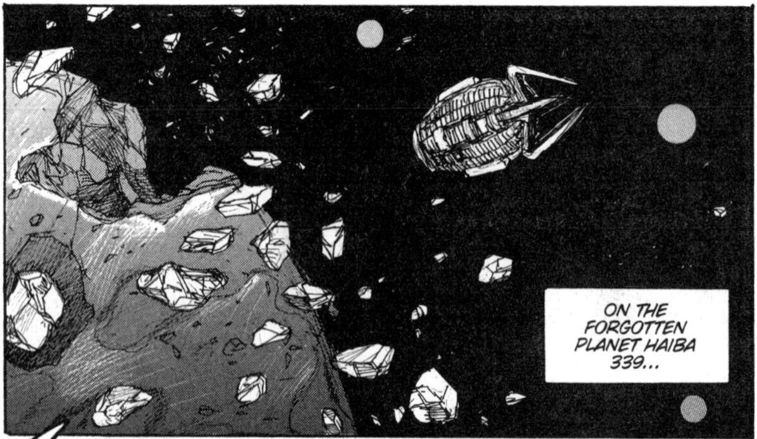
ON THE FORGOTTEN PLANET HAIBA 339...

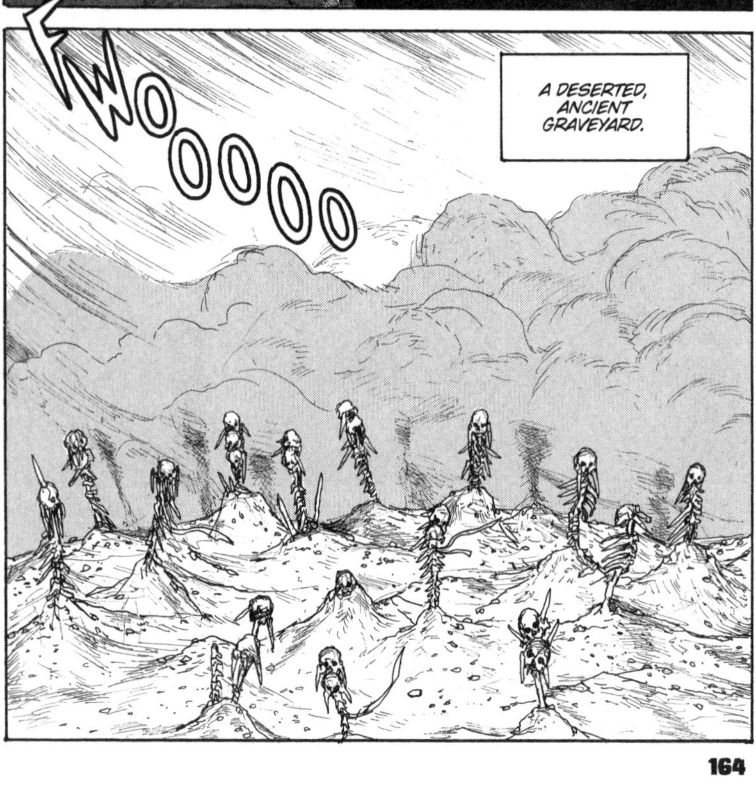
FWOOOOO
A DESERTED, ANCIENT GRAVEYARD.

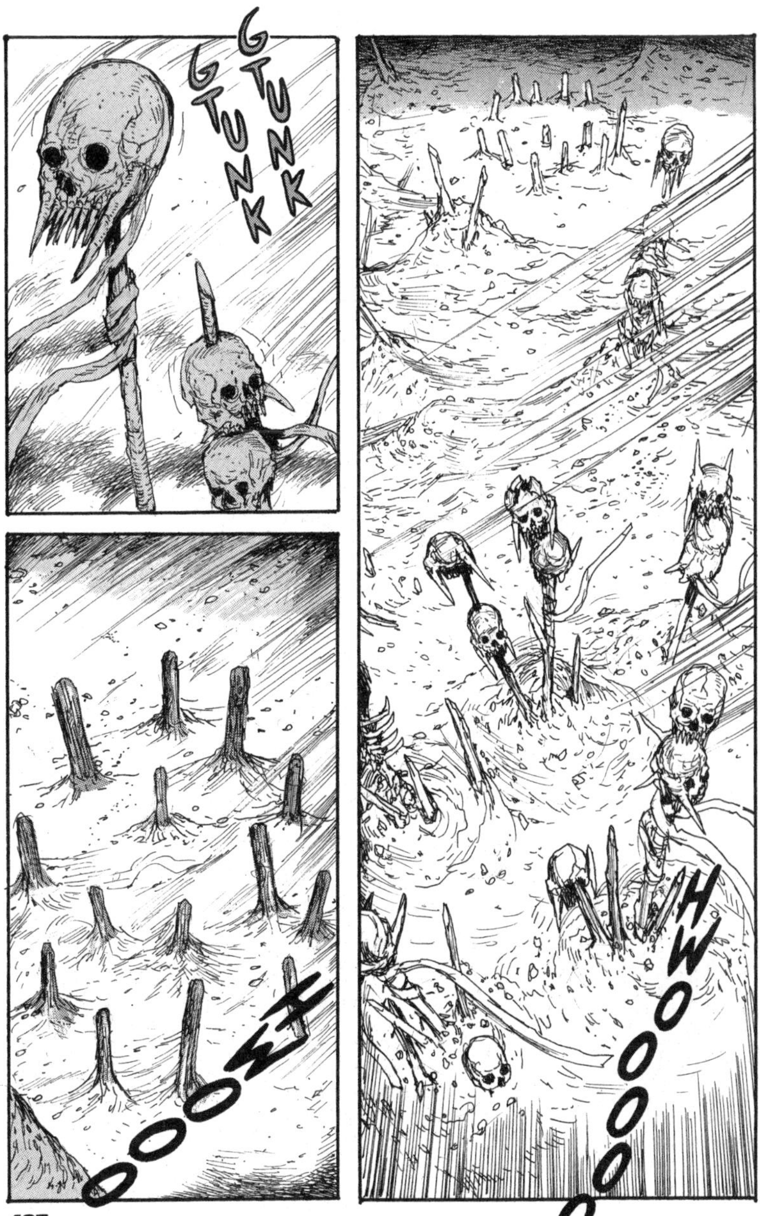
HWOOOOOOOO
GTUNK
GTUNK
HWOOOOOO

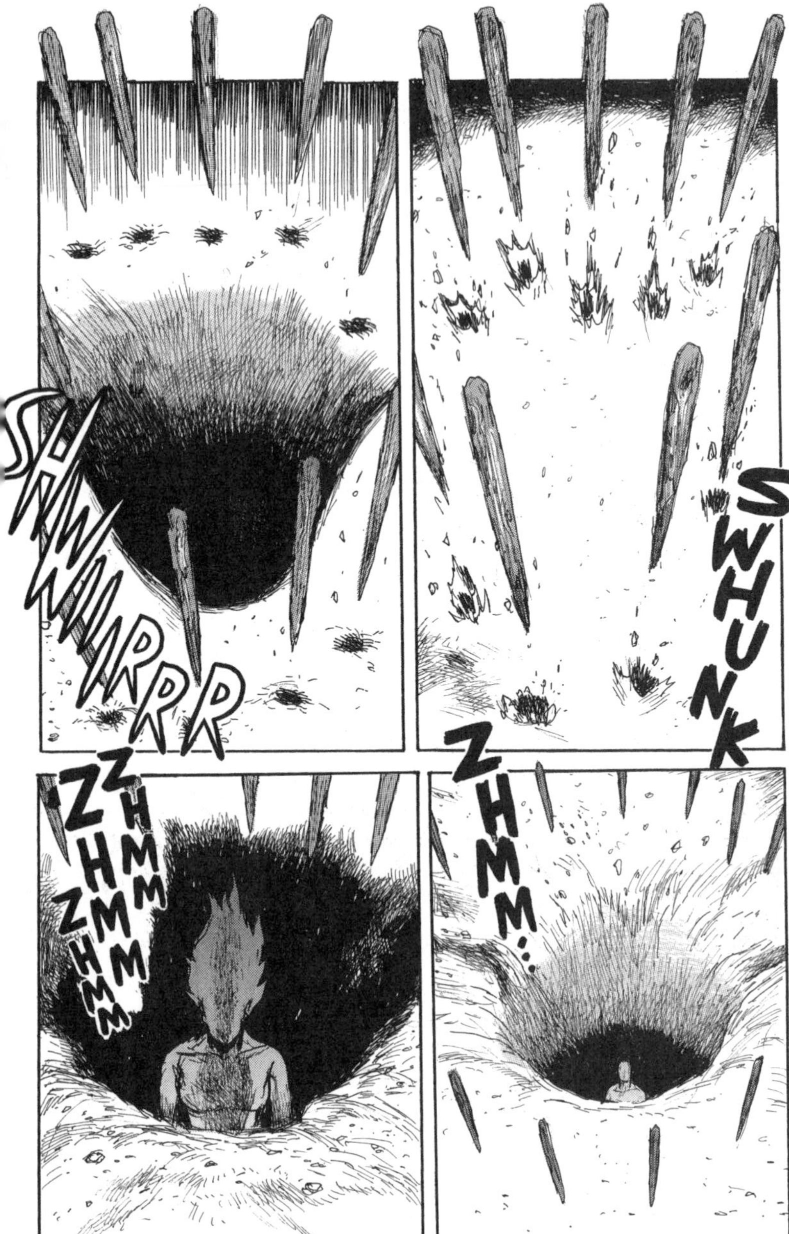
SWHUNK
SHWHIRRR
ZHMM...
ZHMM
ZHMMM
ZHMM

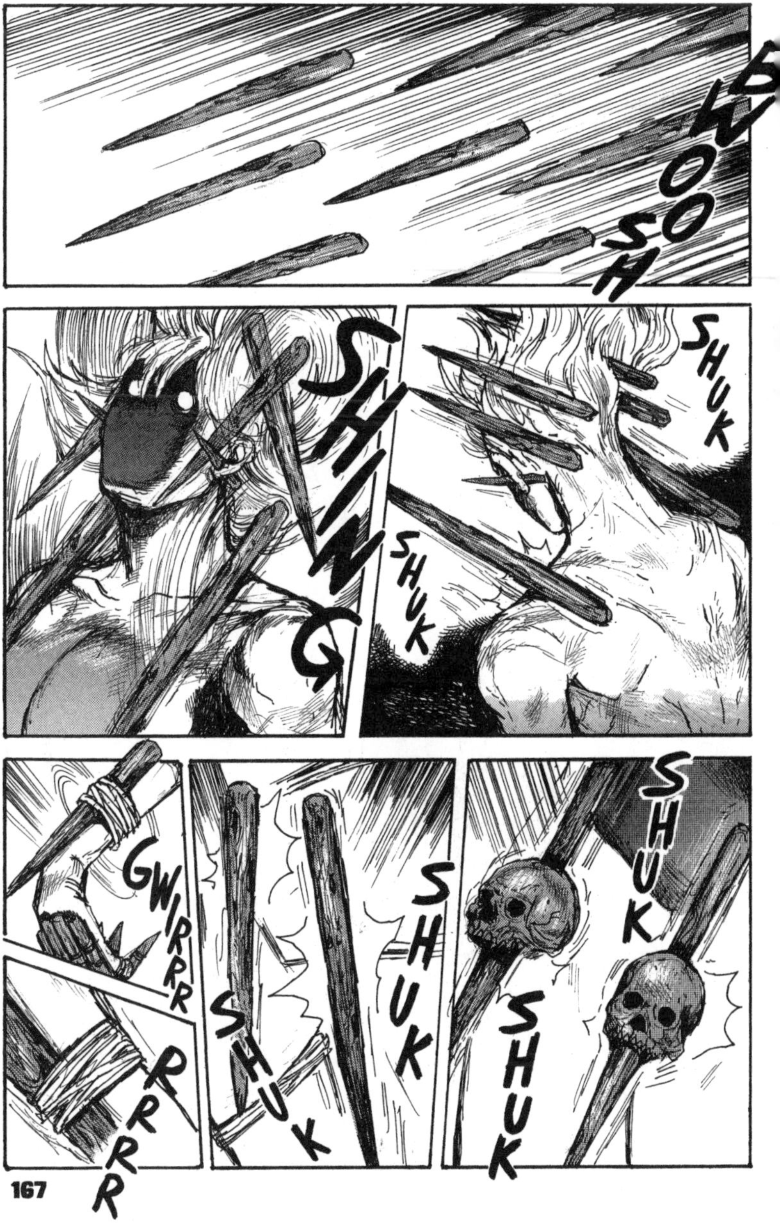
BWOOSH
SHUK
SHUK
SHING
SHUK
SHUK
SHUK
SHUK
GWIRRRR
RRRRR

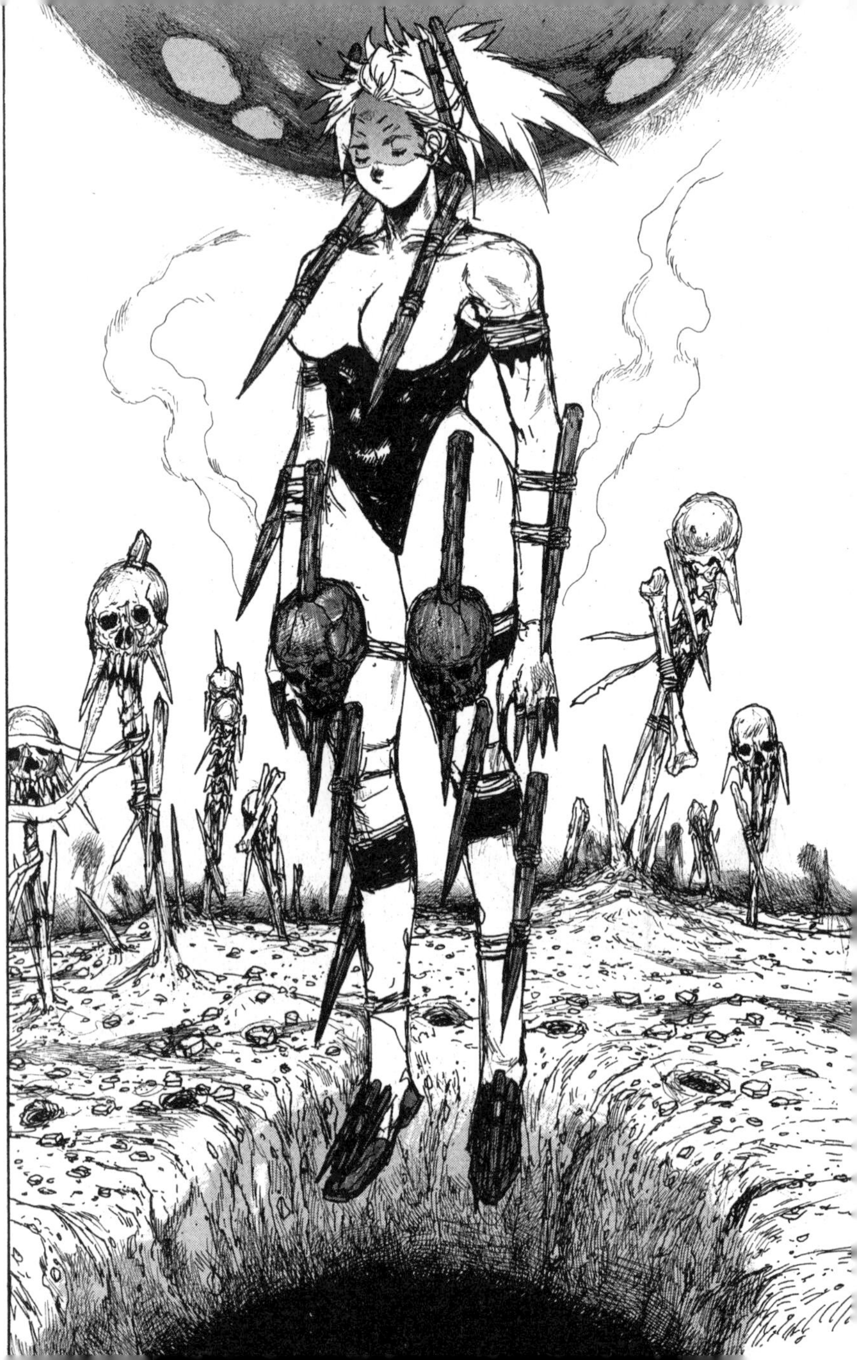

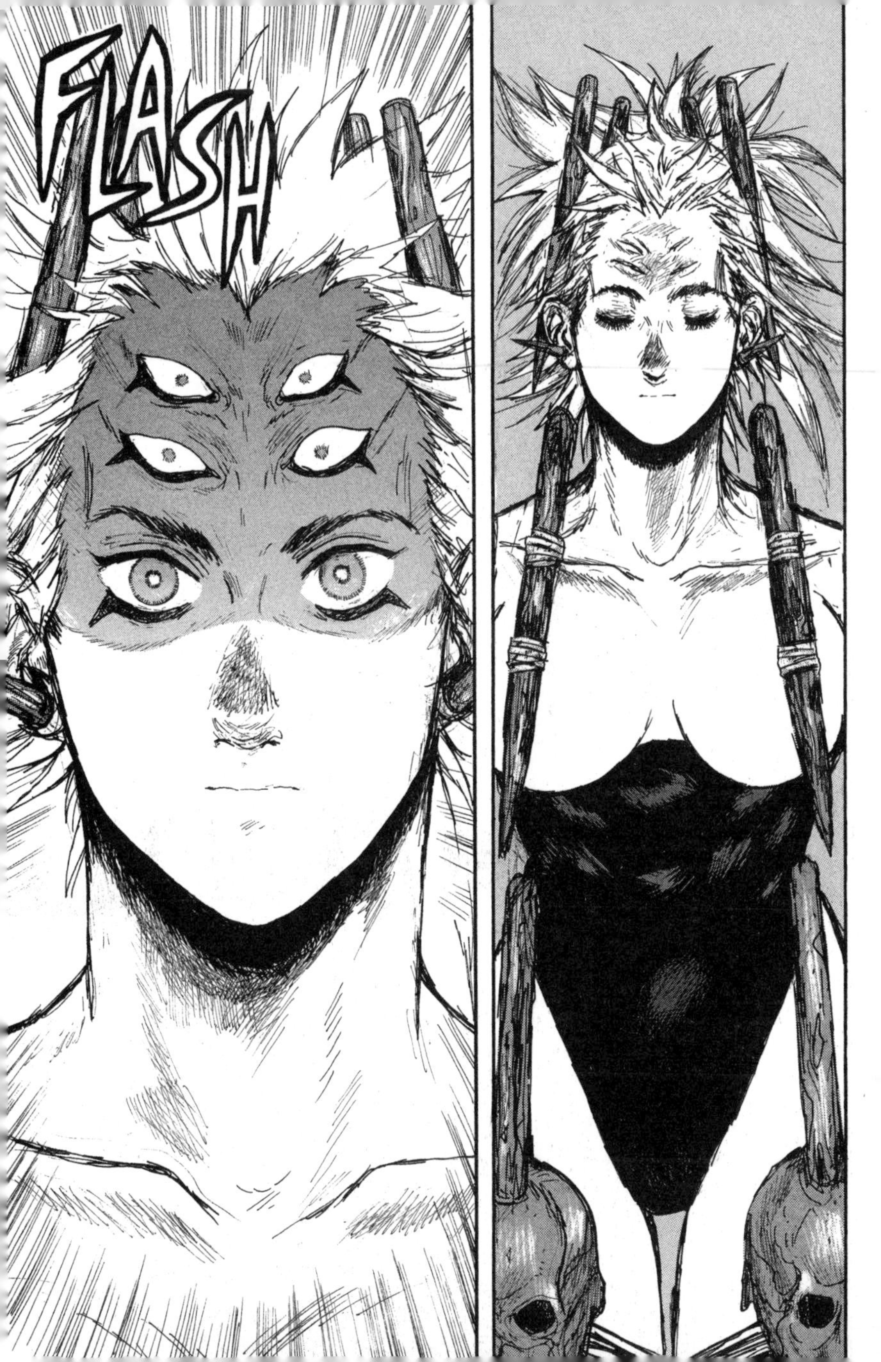
FLASH

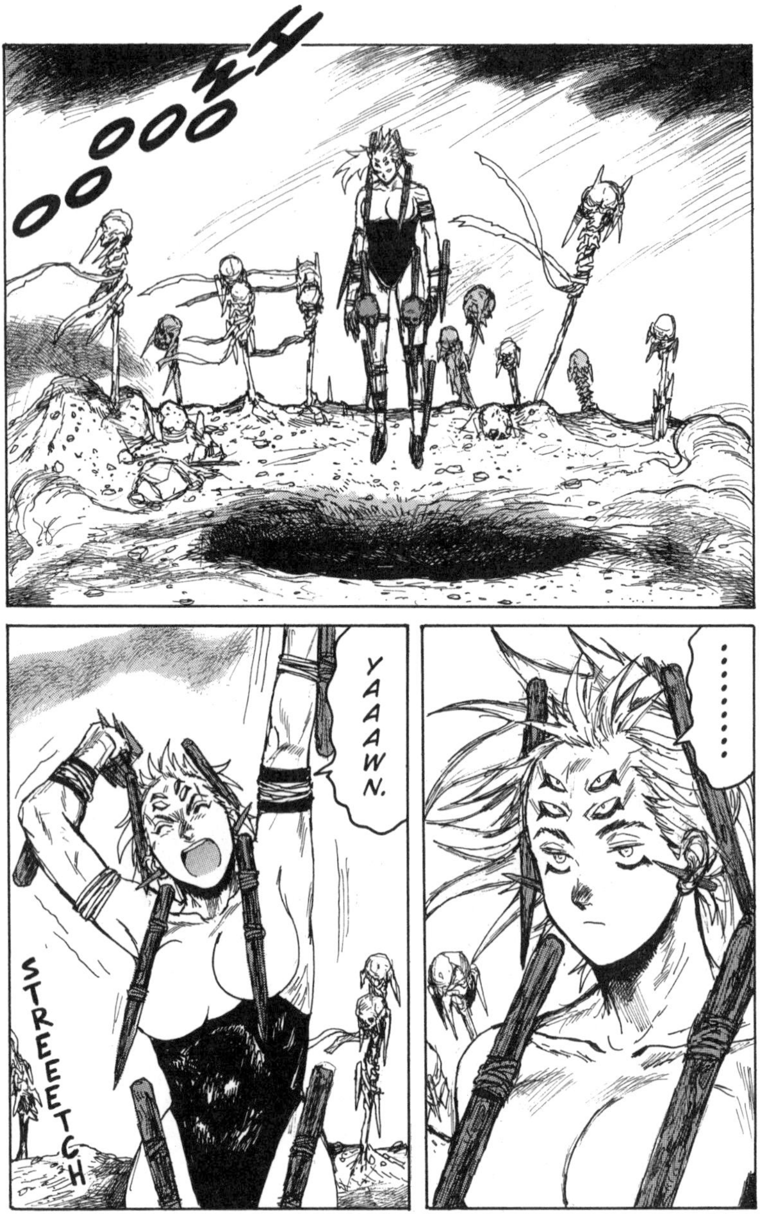
OOOOOSH
....
YAAAWN.
STREEETCH

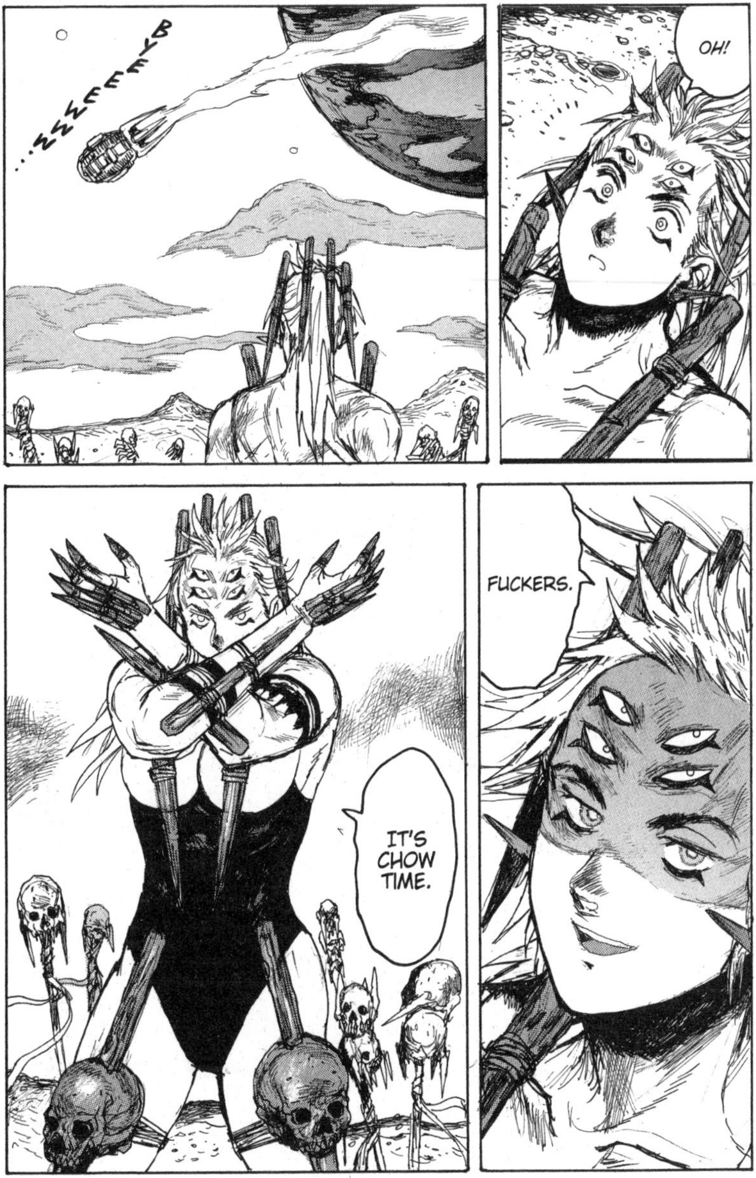
OH!
...ZZWEEEYB
FUCKERS.
IT'S CHOW TIME.

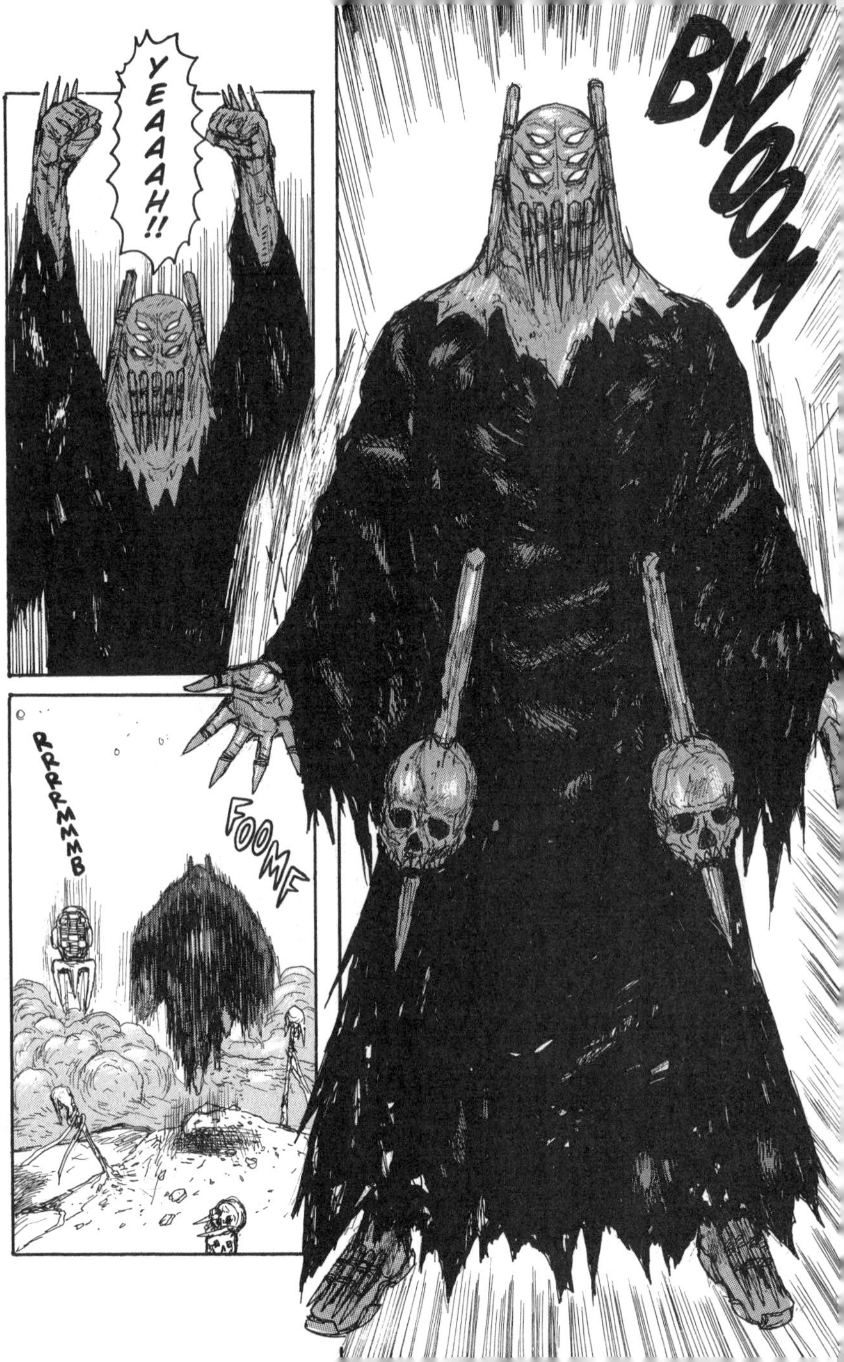
BWOOM
YEAAAAH!!
FOOMF
RRRRMMMB

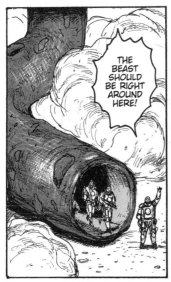

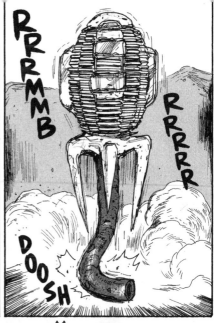

RRRMMB
RRRRR
DOOSH
THE BEAST SHOULD BE RIGHT AROUND HERE!
WHEN YOU SEE IT, KILL IT!
!!
THUP
LOOKING FOR ME, FELLAS?

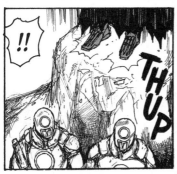

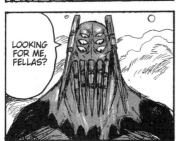

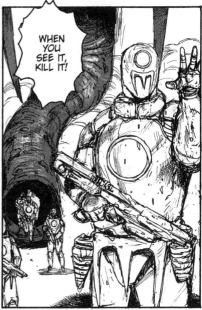

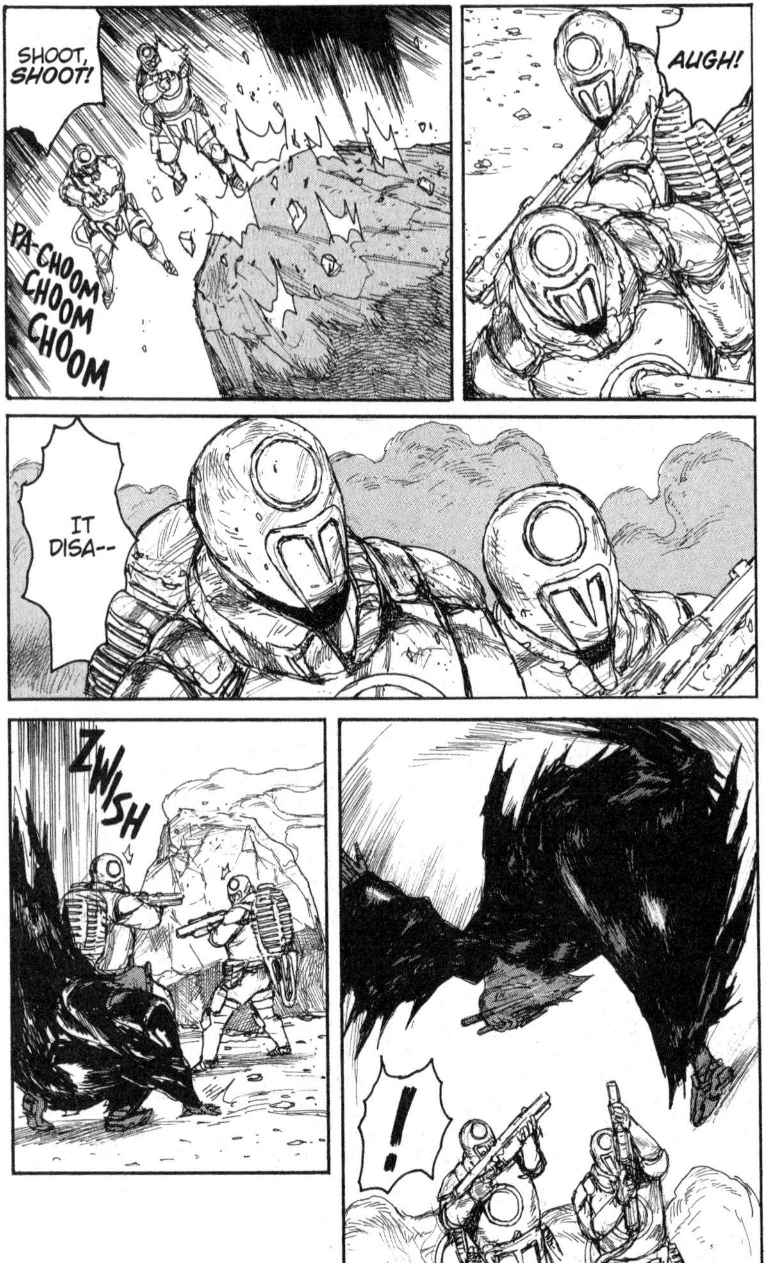
AUGH!
SHOOT, SHOOT!
PA-CHOOM CHOOM CHOOM
IT DISA--
!
ZWISH

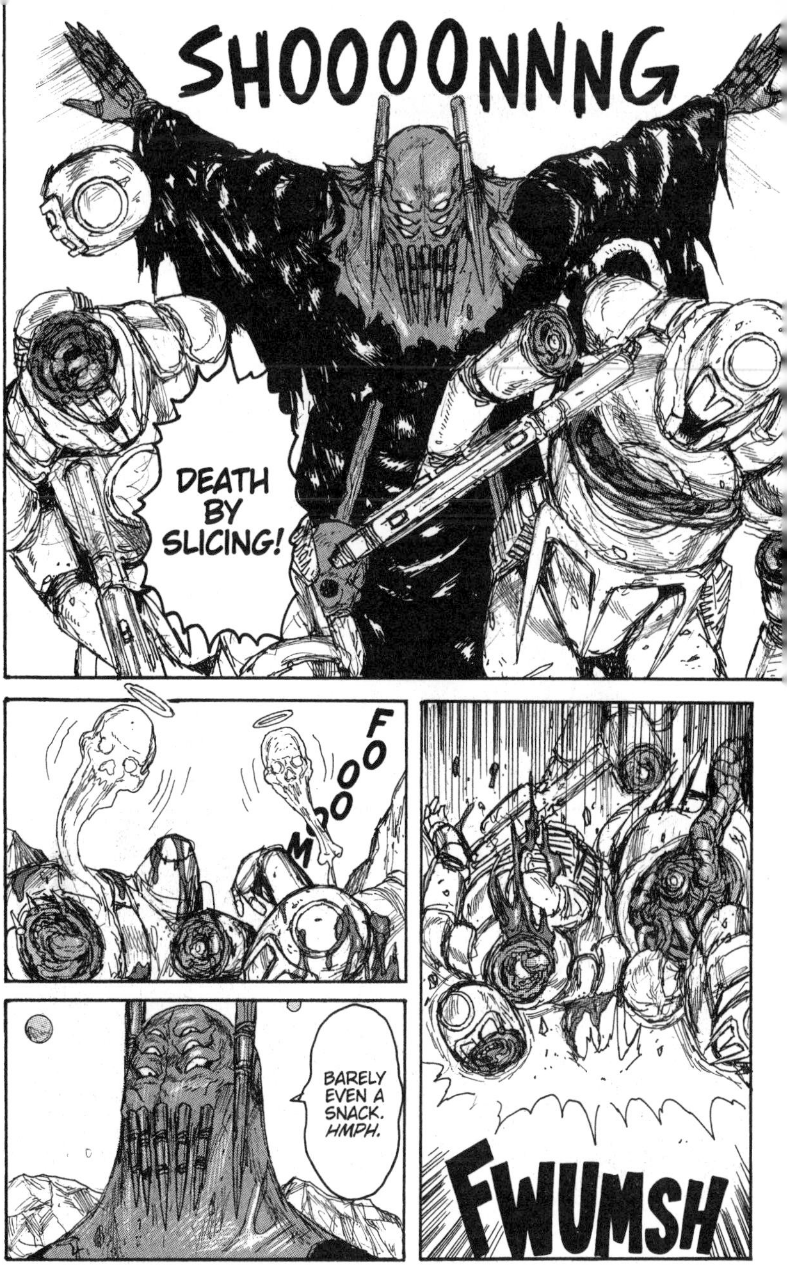
SHOOOONNNG
DEATH BY SLICING!
FWUMSH
FOOOOOM
BARELY EVEN A SNACK. HMPH.

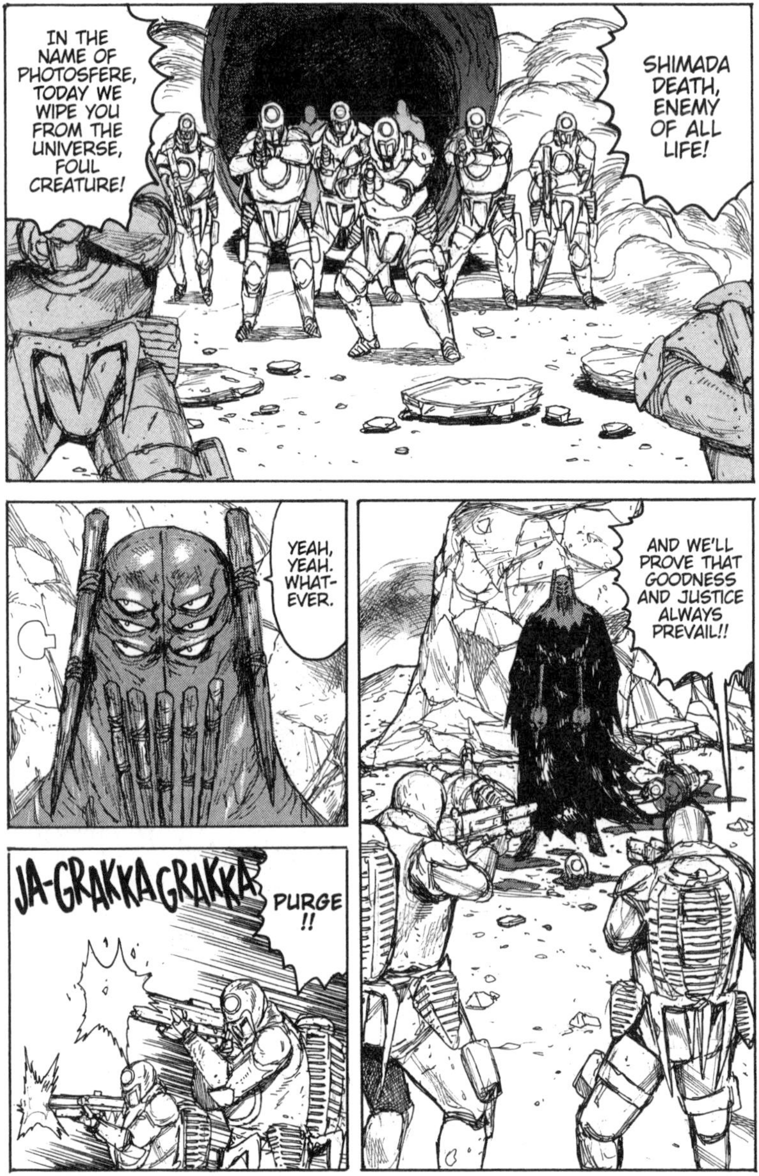
SHIMADA DEATH, ENEMY OF ALL LIFE!
IN THE NAME OF PHOTOSFERE, TODAY WE WIPE YOU FROM THE UNIVERSE, FOUL CREATURE!
AND WE'LL PROVE THAT GOODNESS AND JUSTICE ALWAYS PREVAIL!!
YEAH, YEAH. WHAT-EVER.
PURGE !!
JA-GRAKKAGRAKKA

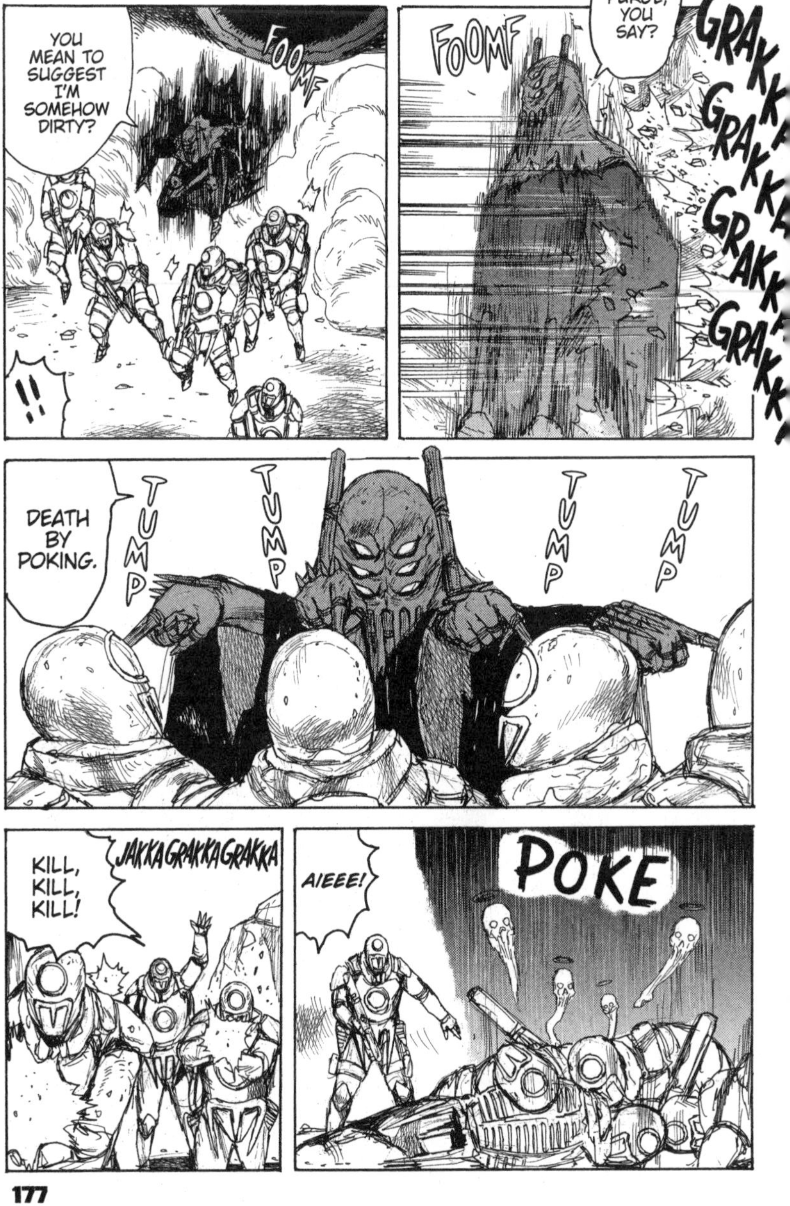
"PURGE," YOU SAY?
GRAKK GRAKK GRAKKA GRAKKA GRAKKA GRAKK
FOOMF
YOU MEAN TO SUGGEST I'M SOMEHOW DIRTY?
FOOMF
!!
TUMP
TUMP
TUMP
TUMP
DEATH BY POKING.
POKE
AIEEE!
JAKKAGRAKKAGRAKKA
KILL, KILL, KILL!

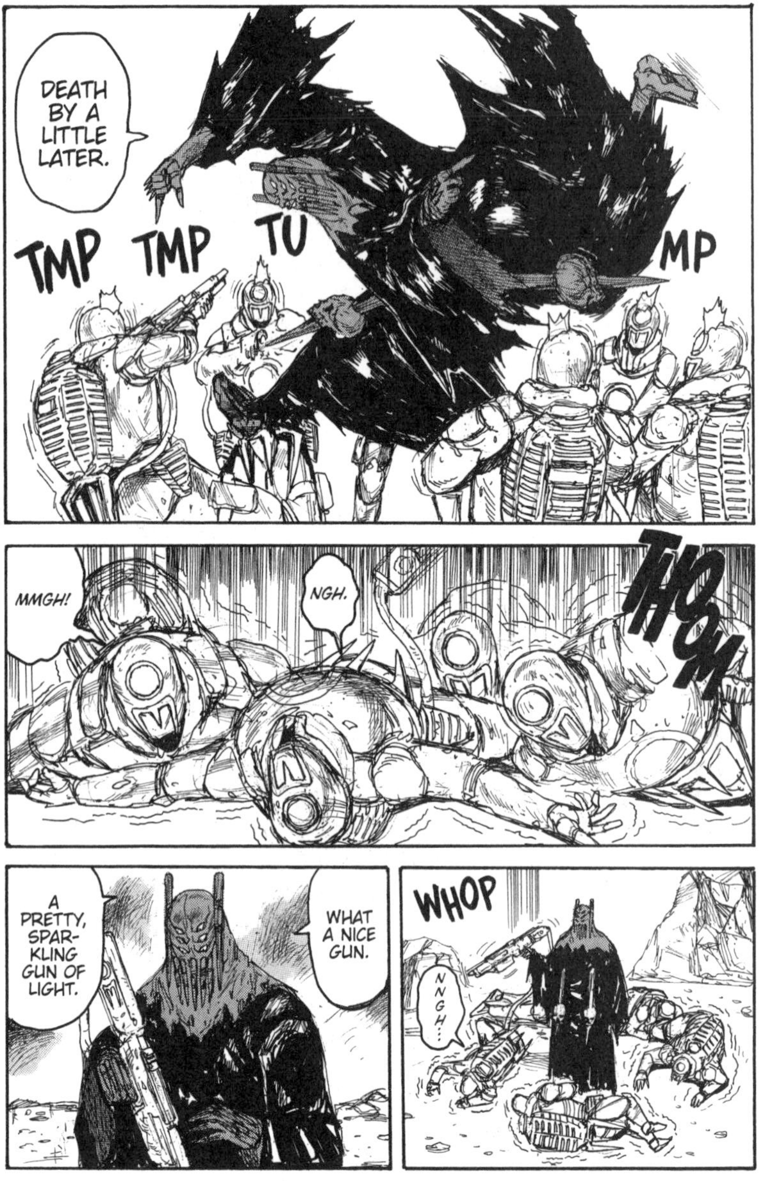
DEATH BY A LITTLE LATER.
TMP TMP TU MP
THOOM
NGH.
MMGH!
WHOP
NNGH...
WHAT A NICE GUN.
A PRETTY, SPAR-KLING GUN OF LIGHT.

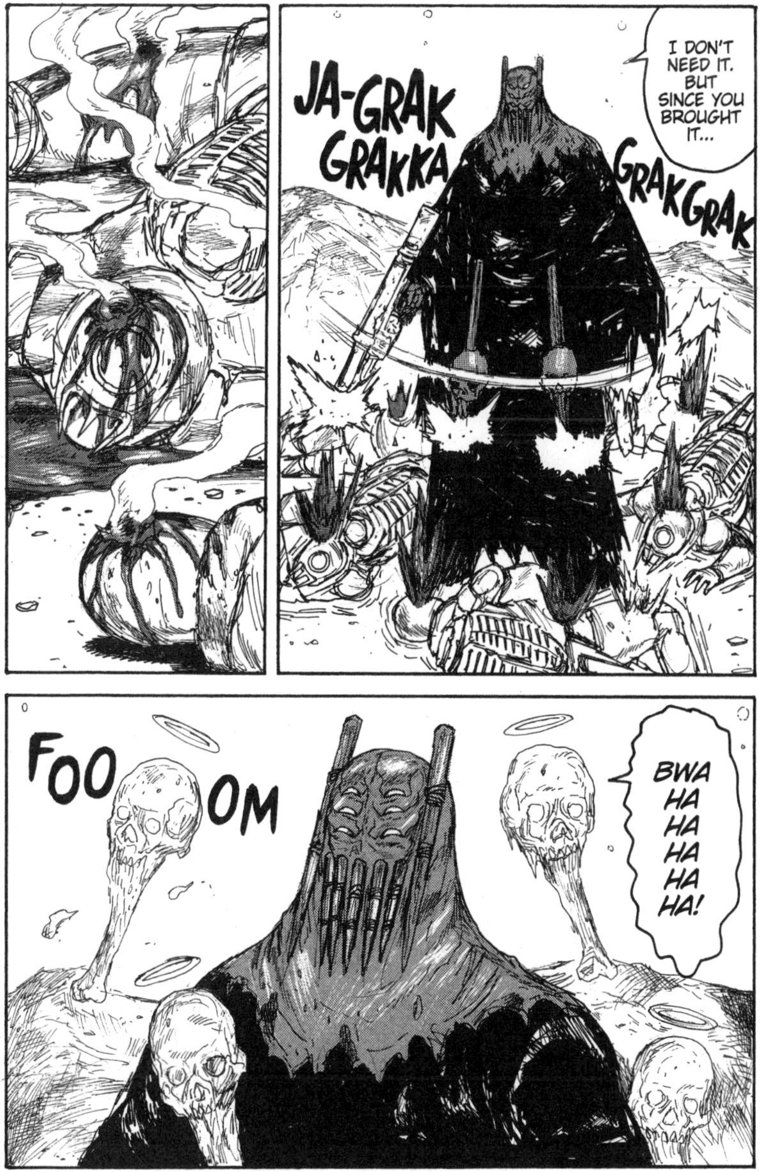
I DON'T NEED IT. BUT SINCE YOU BROUGHT IT...
JA-GRAK GRAKKA
GRAKGRAK
BWA HA HA HA HA HA!
FOO OM

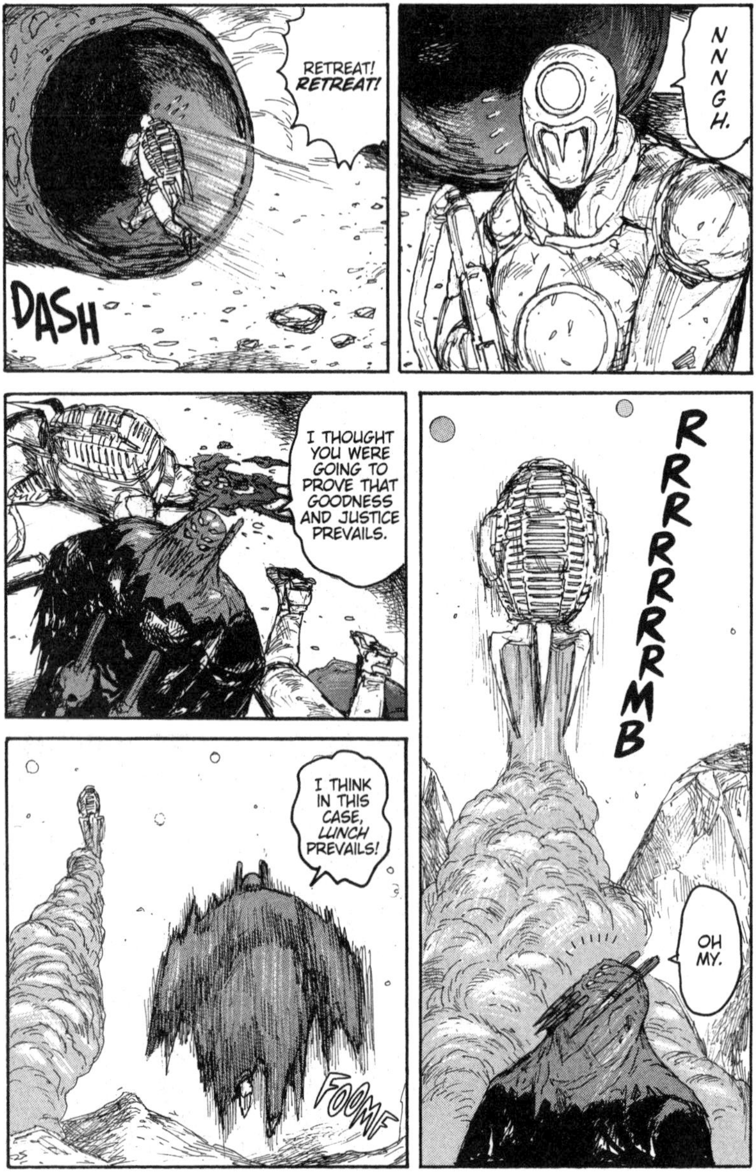
NNNGH.
RETREAT! RETREAT!
DASH
RRRRRRRMB
OH MY.
I THOUGHT YOU WERE GOING TO PROVE THAT GOODNESS AND JUSTICE PREVAILS.
I THINK IN THIS CASE, LUNCH PREVAILS!
FOOMF

RRRRMM
THIS IS SHINE EIGHT.
I'M SORRY. THE MISSION IS A FAILURE.
UNDERSTOOD. RETURN TO HEAD-QUARTERS.
AH!
HERE'S ANOTHER ONE OF MY TALENTS.
I CAN GET IN AND OUT OF ANY-WHERE.
AN EXPLOSIVE DEATH FOR YOU.

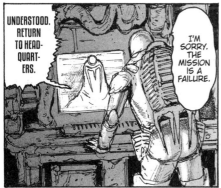

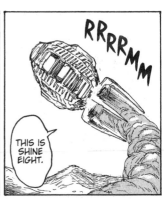

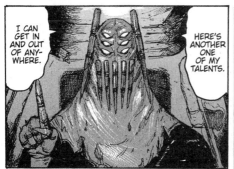

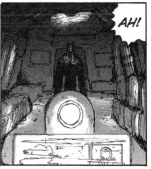

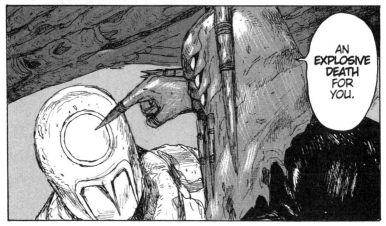

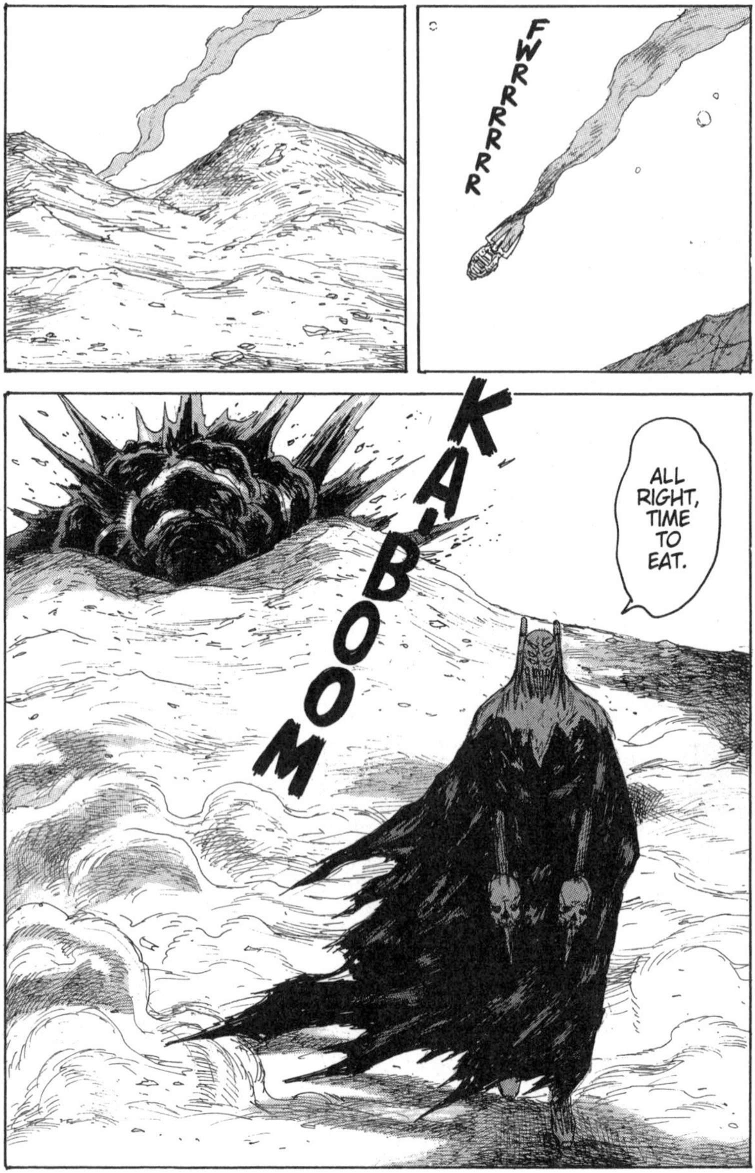
FWRRRRRR
KA-BOOM
ALL RIGHT, TIME TO EAT.

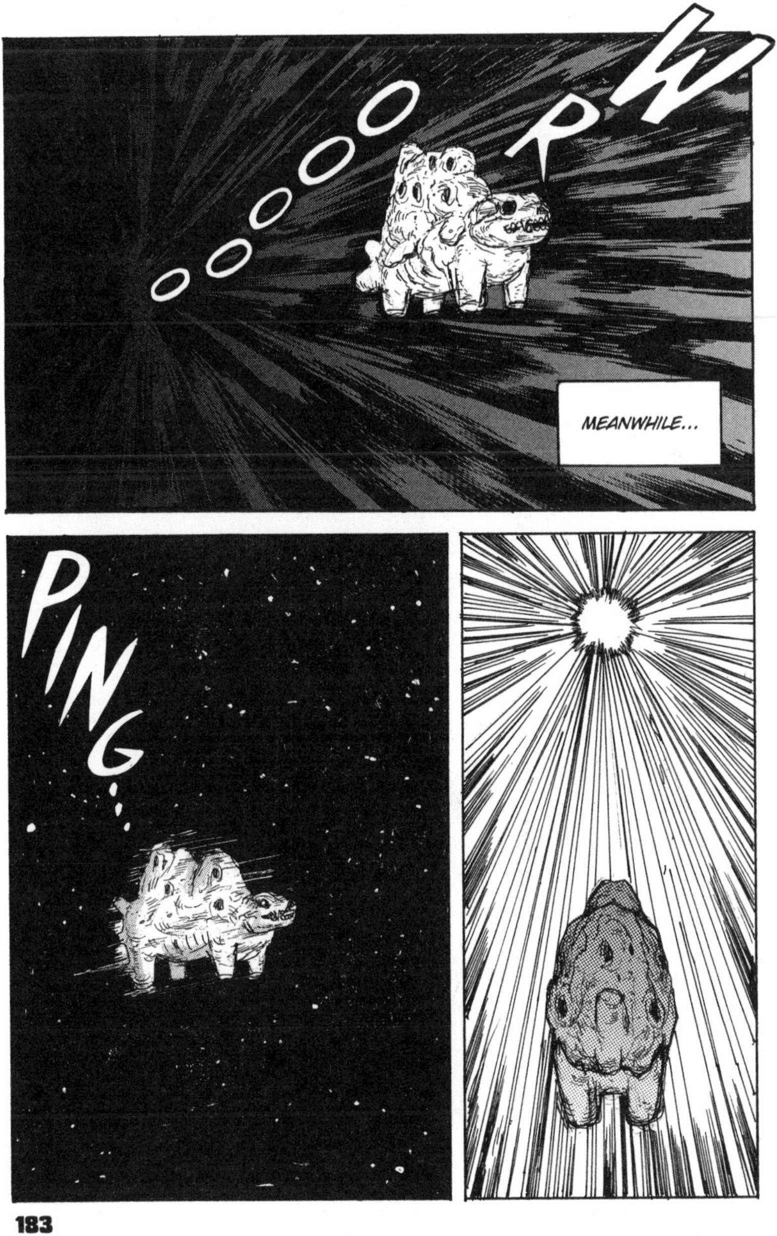
OOOOORW
MEANWHILE...
PING...

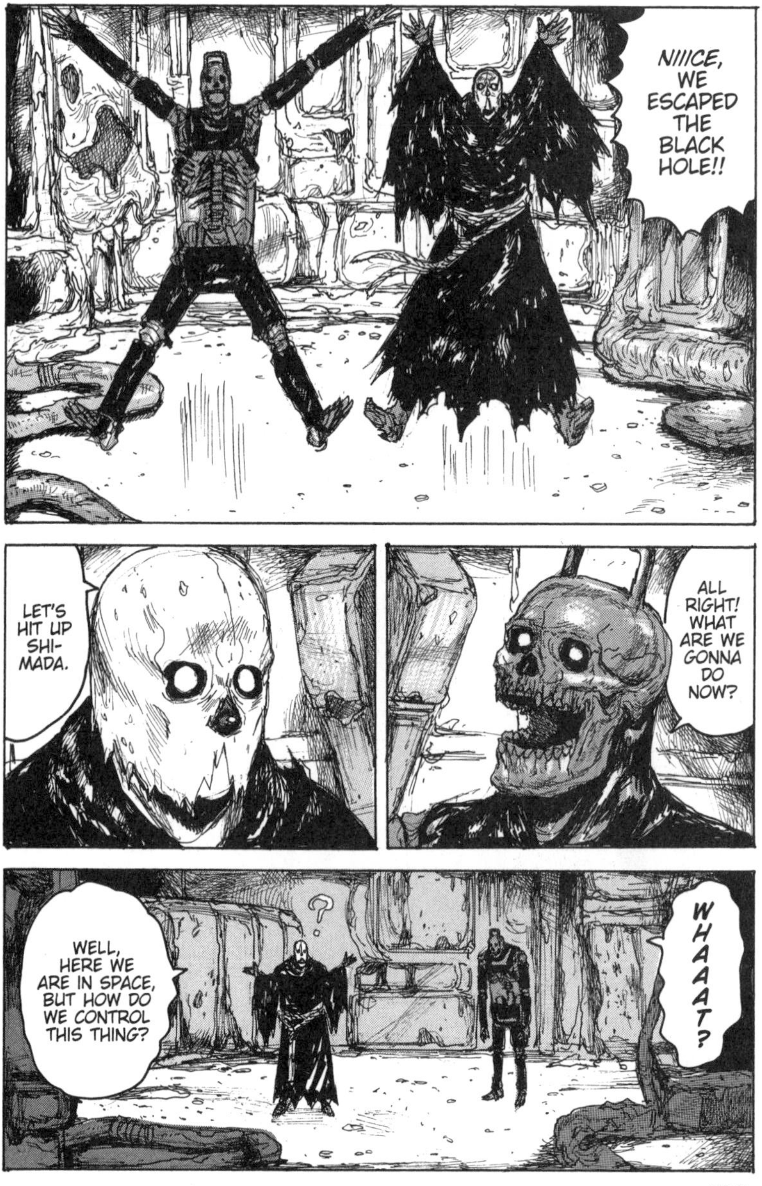
NIIICE, WE ESCAPED THE BLACK HOLE!!
ALL RIGHT! WHAT ARE WE GONNA DO NOW?
LET'S HIT UP SHIMADA.
WHAAAT?
WELL, HERE WE ARE IN SPACE, BUT HOW DO WE CONTROL THIS THING?

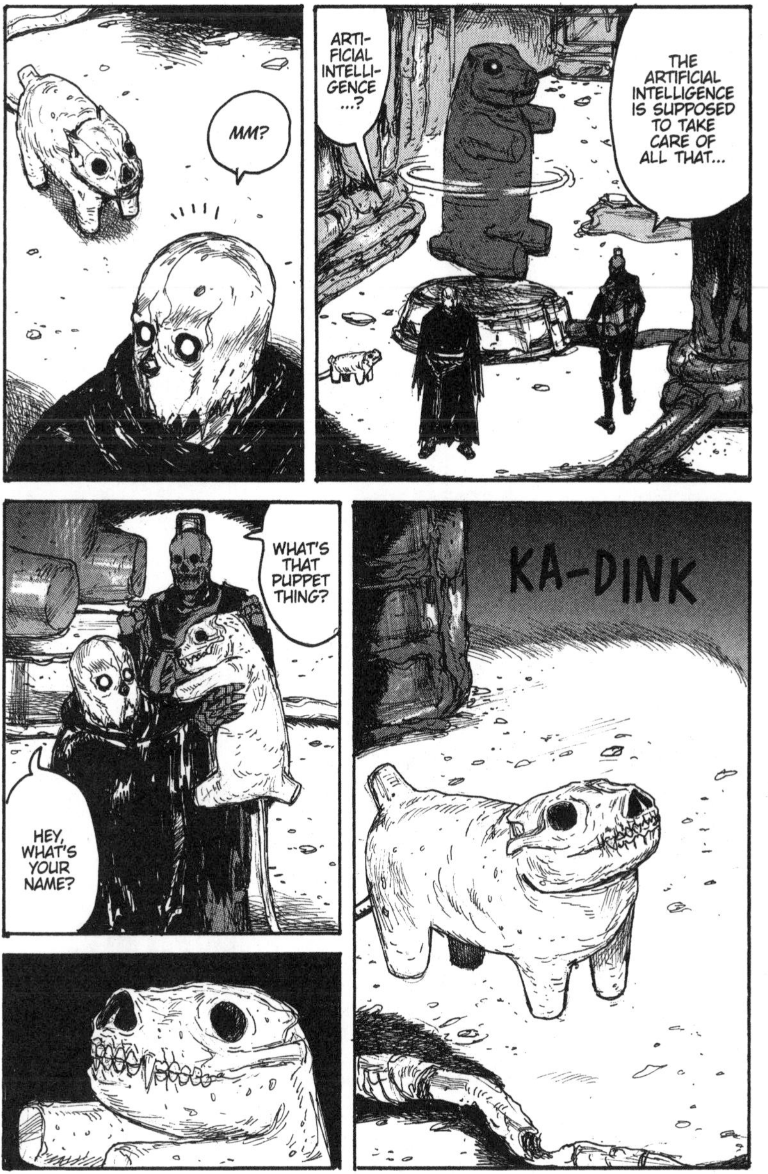
THE ARTIFICIAL INTELLIGENCE IS SUPPOSED TO TAKE CARE OF ALL THAT...
ARTI-FICIAL INTELLI-GENCE ...?
MM?
KA-DINK
WHAT'S THAT PUPPET THING?
HEY, WHAT'S YOUR NAME?

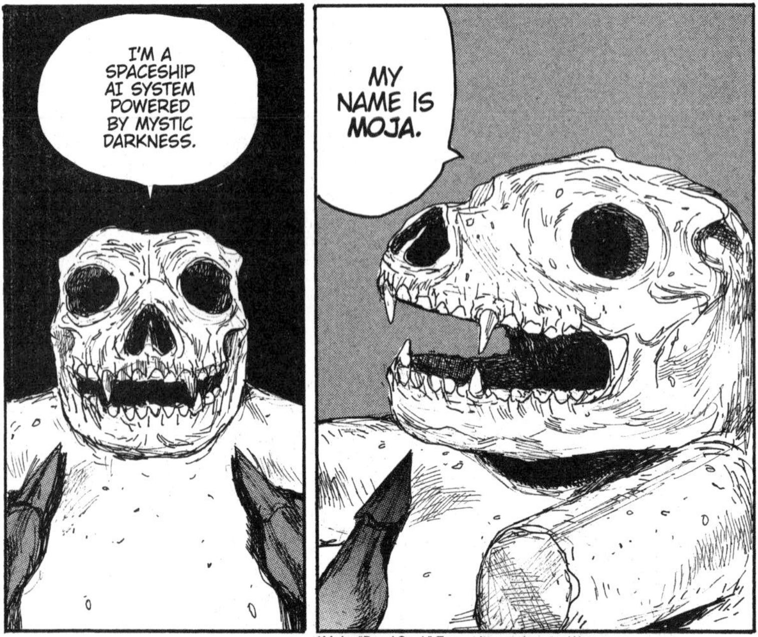
MY NAME IS MOJA.
I'M A SPACESHIP AI SYSTEM POWERED BY MYSTIC DARKNESS.

*Moja: "Dead Soul." Except it sounds cute. We swear.

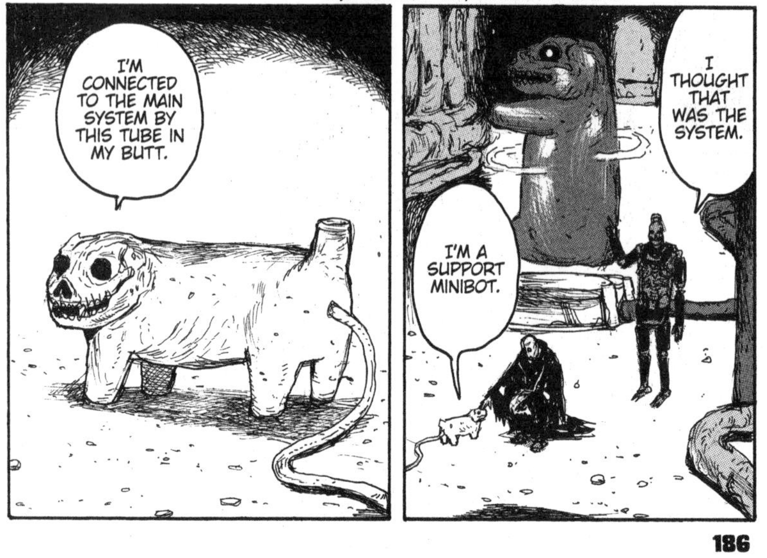
I THOUGHT THAT WAS THE SYSTEM.
I'M A SUPPORT MINIBOT.
I'M CONNECTED TO THE MAIN SYSTEM BY THIS TUBE IN MY BUTT.

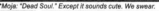

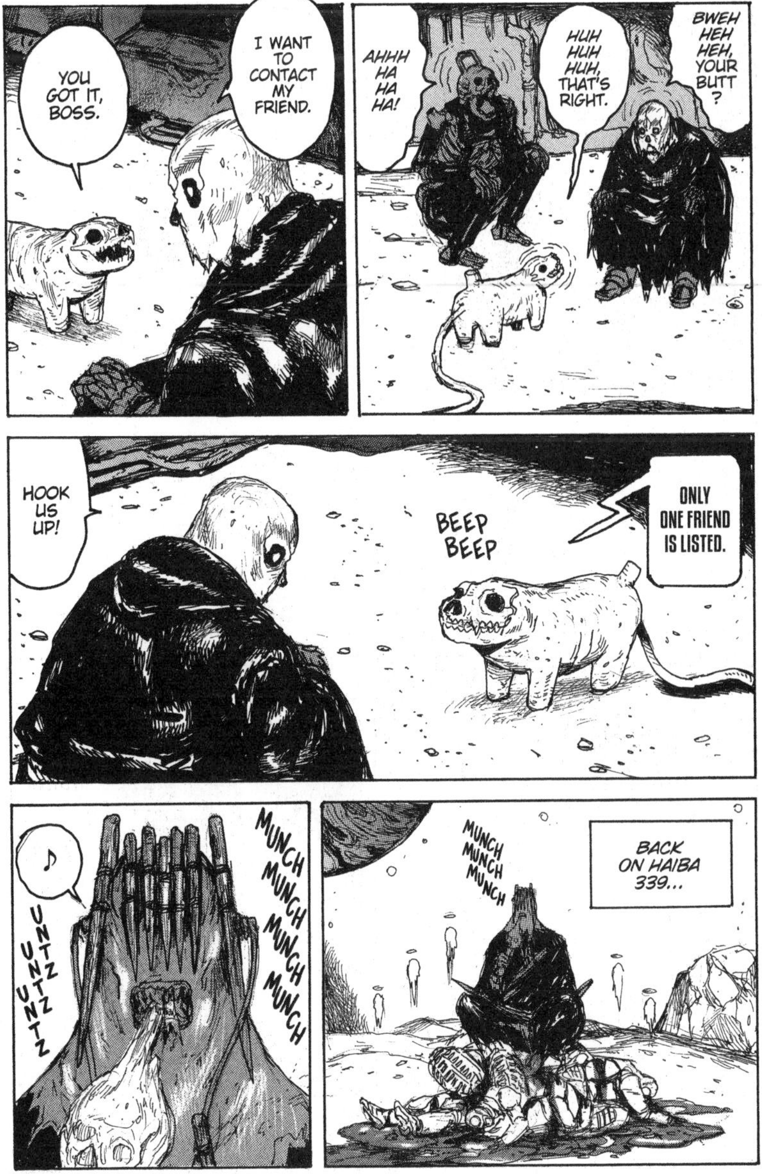
BWEH HEH HEH, YOUR BUTT?
HUH HUH HUH, THAT'S RIGHT.
AHHH HA HA HA!
I WANT TO CONTACT MY FRIEND.
YOU GOT IT, BOSS.
ONLY ONE FRIEND IS LISTED.
BEEP BEEP
HOOK US UP!
BACK ON HAIBA 339...
MUNCH MUNCH MUNCH
MUNCH MUNCH MUNCH MUNCH MUNCH
♪
UNTZ UNTZ UNTZ UNTZ

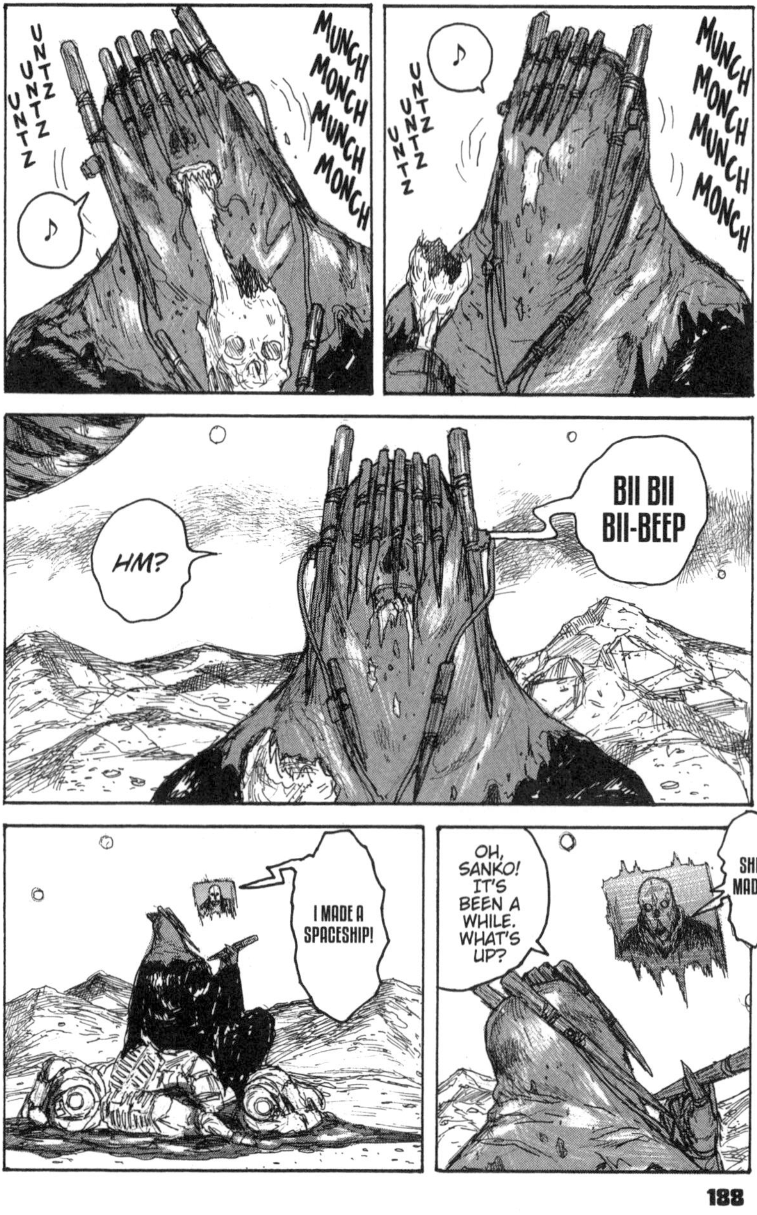
MUNCH MONCH MUNCH MONCH
♪
UNTZ UNTZ UNTZ
MUNCH MONCH MUNCH MONCH
UNTZ UNTZ UNTZ
♪
BII BII BII-BEEP
HM?
SHI-MADA!
OH, SANKO! IT'S BEEN A WHILE. WHAT'S UP?
I MADE A SPACESHIP!

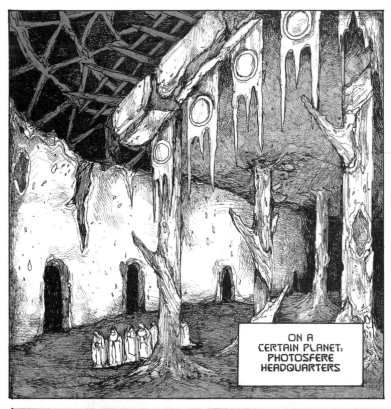

ON A
CERTAIN PLANET:
PHOTOSFERE
HEADQUARTERS

WE HAVE LOST CONTACT WITH SHINE EIGHT.

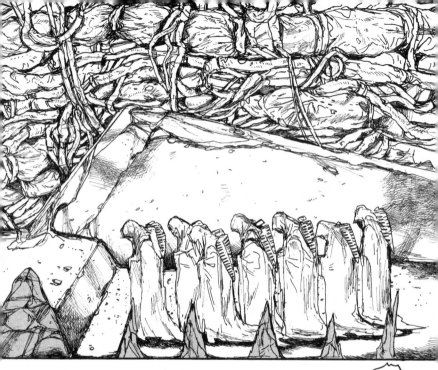

DARK PAGGY AVAKIAN.

ZAHA SANKO.

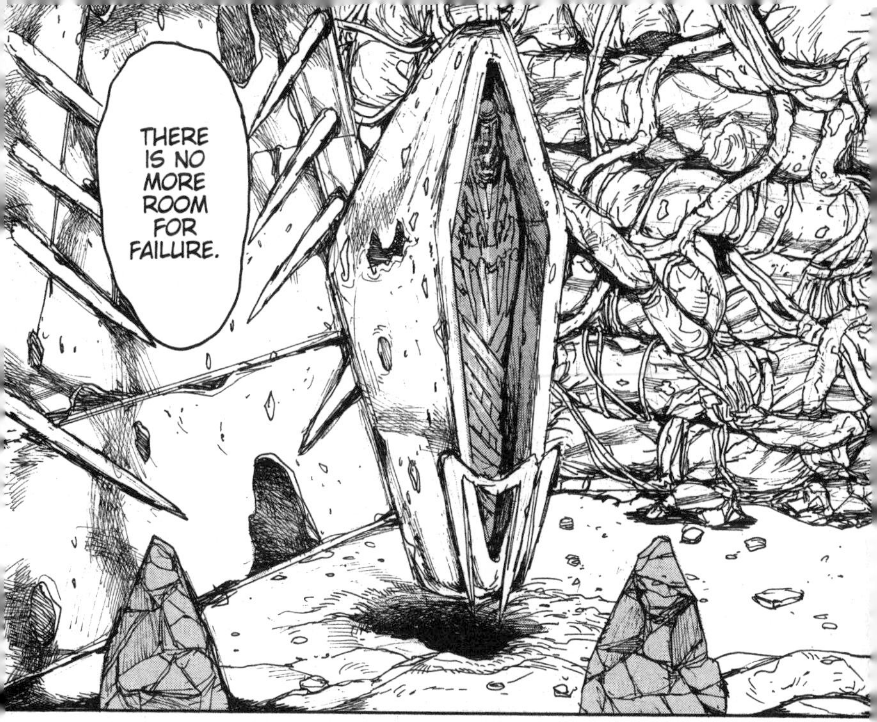
THERE IS NO MORE ROOM FOR FAILURE.

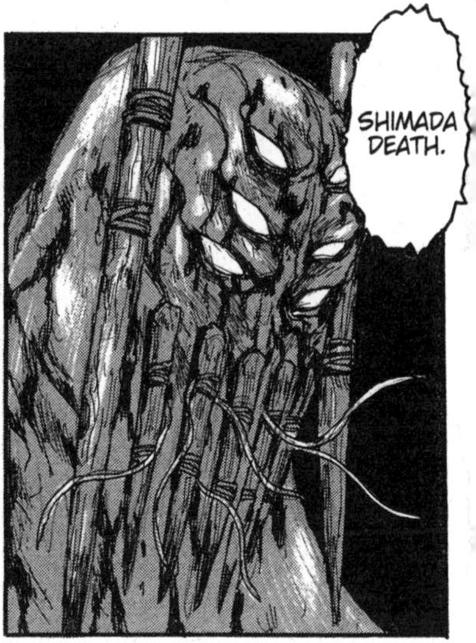
SHIMADA DEATH.

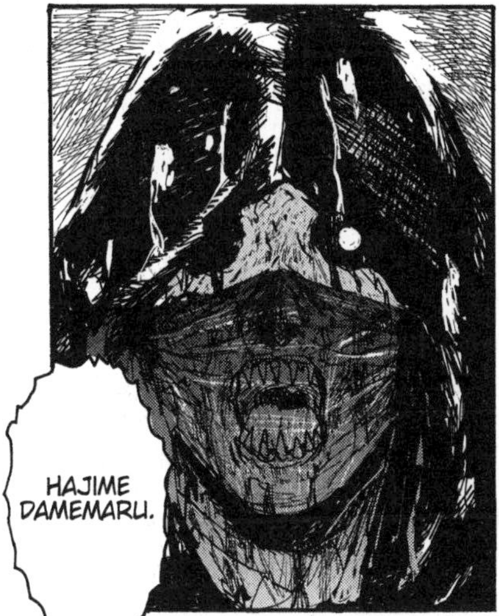
HAJIME DAMEMARU.

*Hajime Damemaru: "First Failureson."

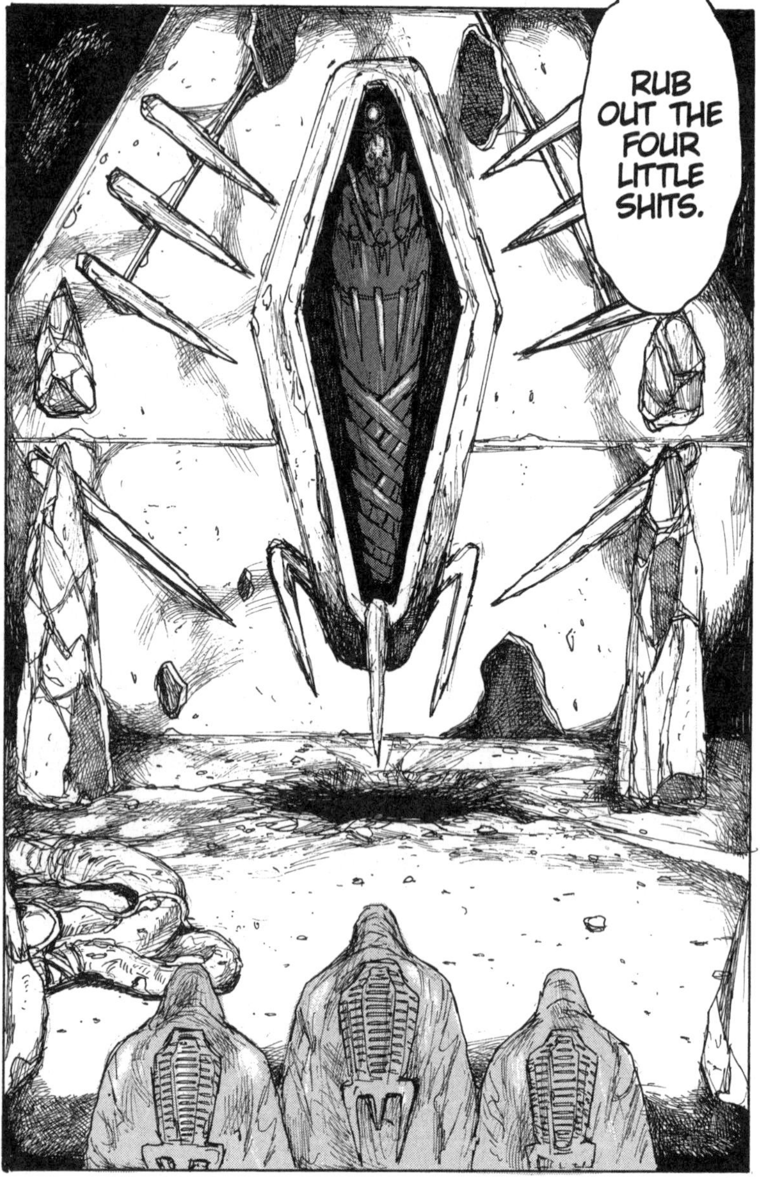
RUB OUT THE FOUR LITTLE SHITS.

End of *Dai Dark 1*

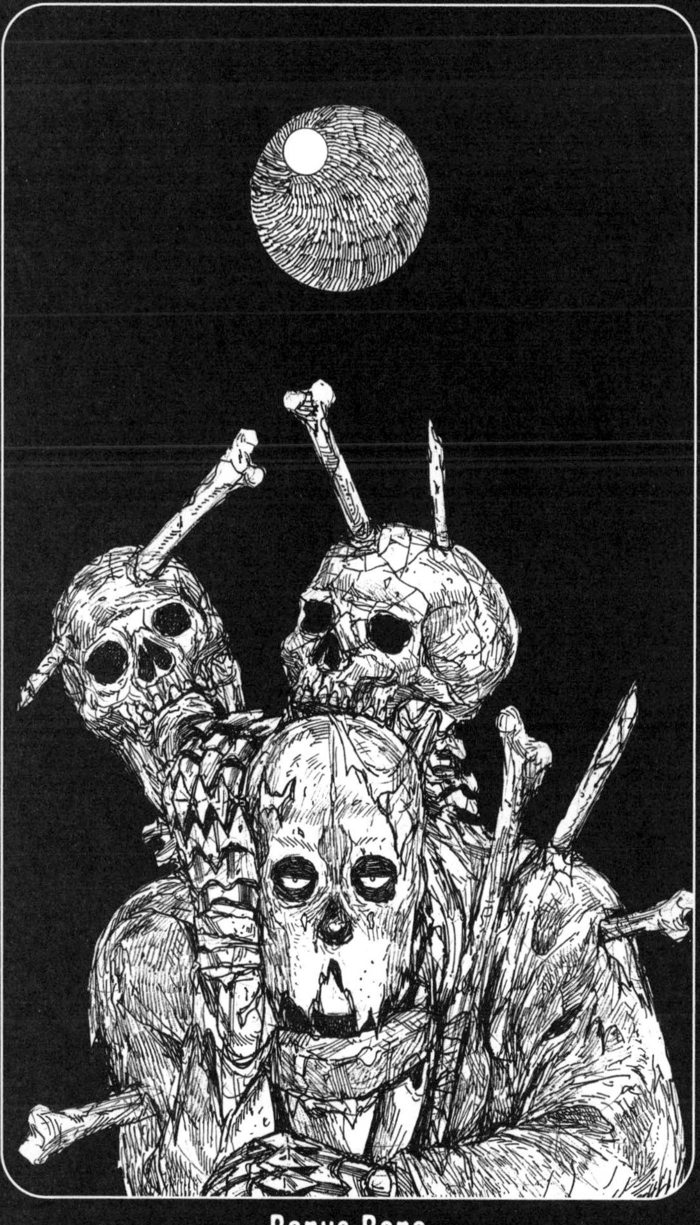

Bonus Bone

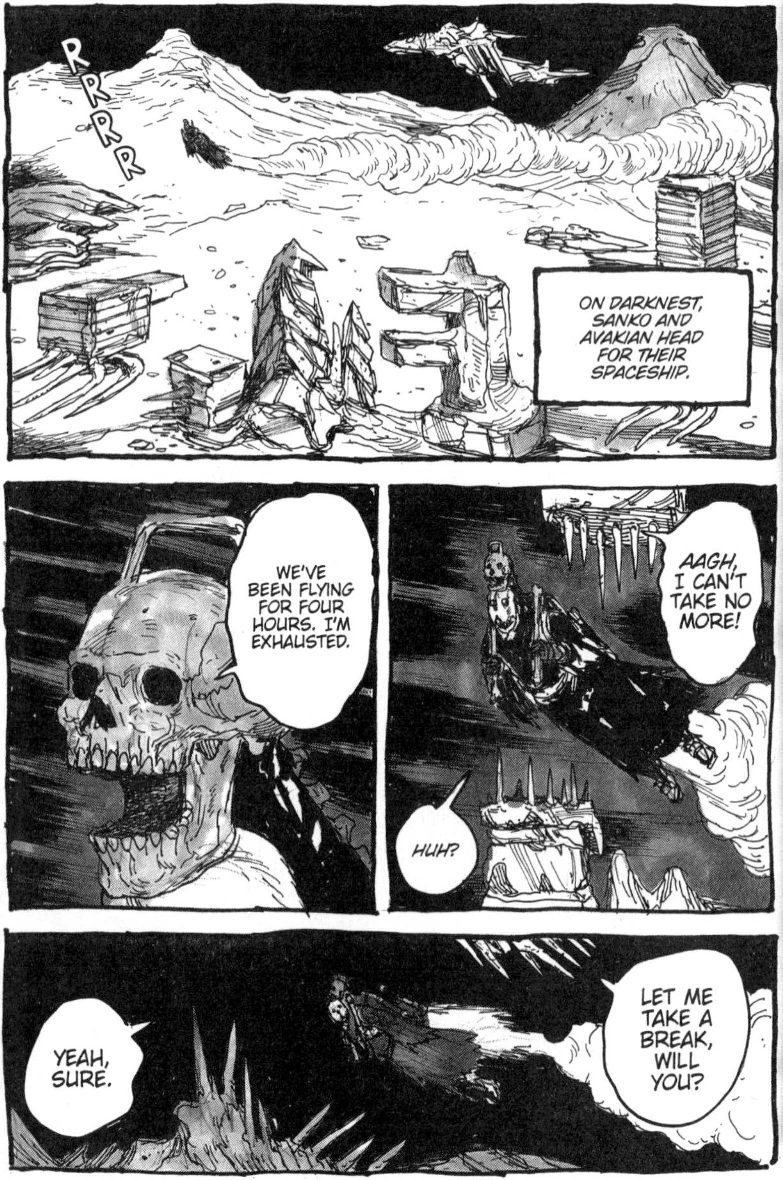
ON DARKNEST, SANKO AND AVAKIAN HEAD FOR THEIR SPACESHIP.
RRRR
AAGH, I CAN'T TAKE NO MORE!
HUH?
WE'VE BEEN FLYING FOR FOUR HOURS. I'M EXHAUSTED.
LET ME TAKE A BREAK, WILL YOU?
YEAH, SURE.

Shit That Happens in Space: You set off casually, then realize it's a hell of a long way.

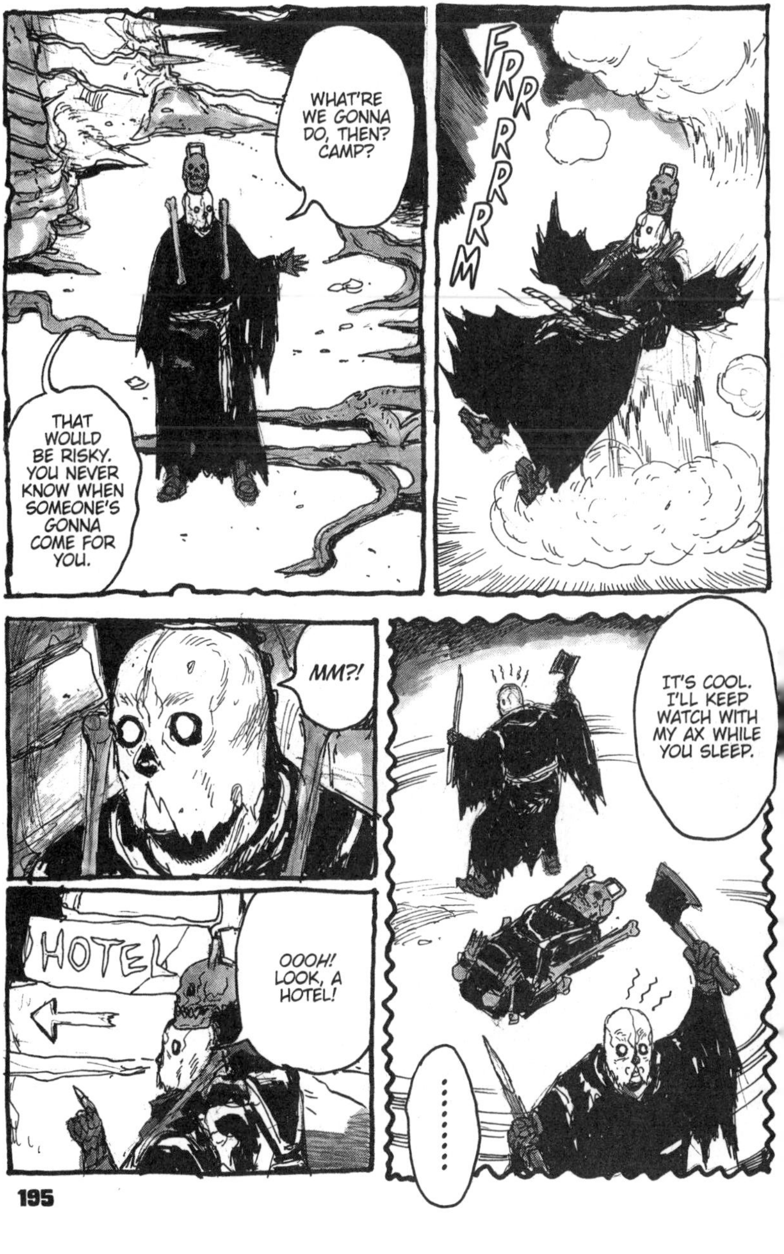
FRRRRRM
WHAT'RE WE GONNA DO, THEN? CAMP?
THAT WOULD BE RISKY. YOU NEVER KNOW WHEN SOMEONE'S GONNA COME FOR YOU.
IT'S COOL. I'LL KEEP WATCH WITH MY AX WHILE YOU SLEEP.
....
MM?!
HOTEL
OOOH! LOOK, A HOTEL!

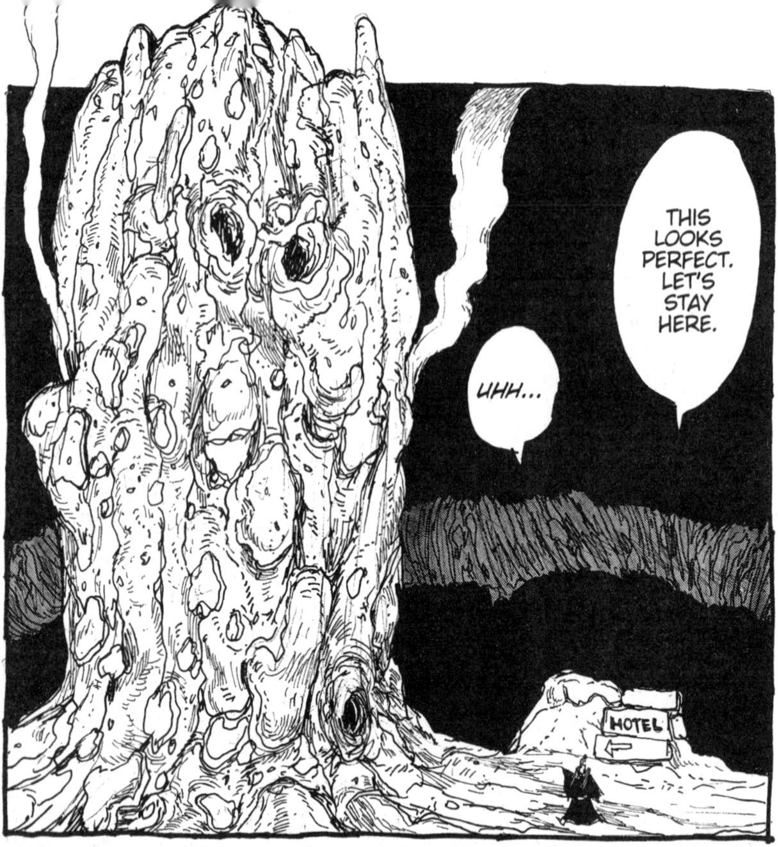
THIS LOOKS PERFECT. LET'S STAY HERE.
UHH...
HOTEL

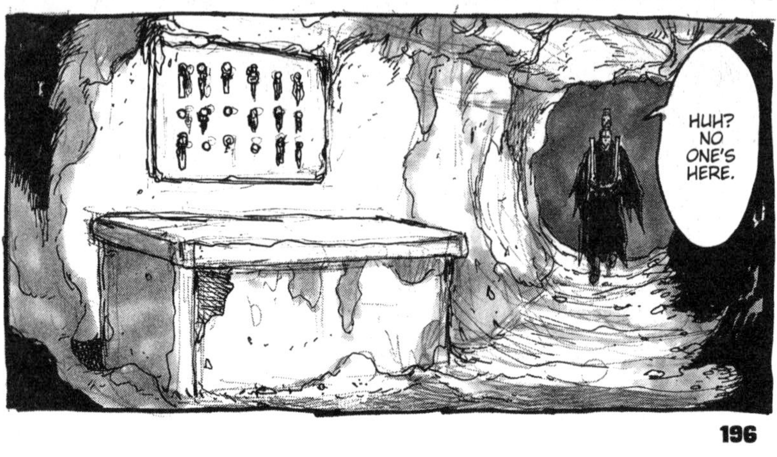
HUH? NO ONE'S HERE.

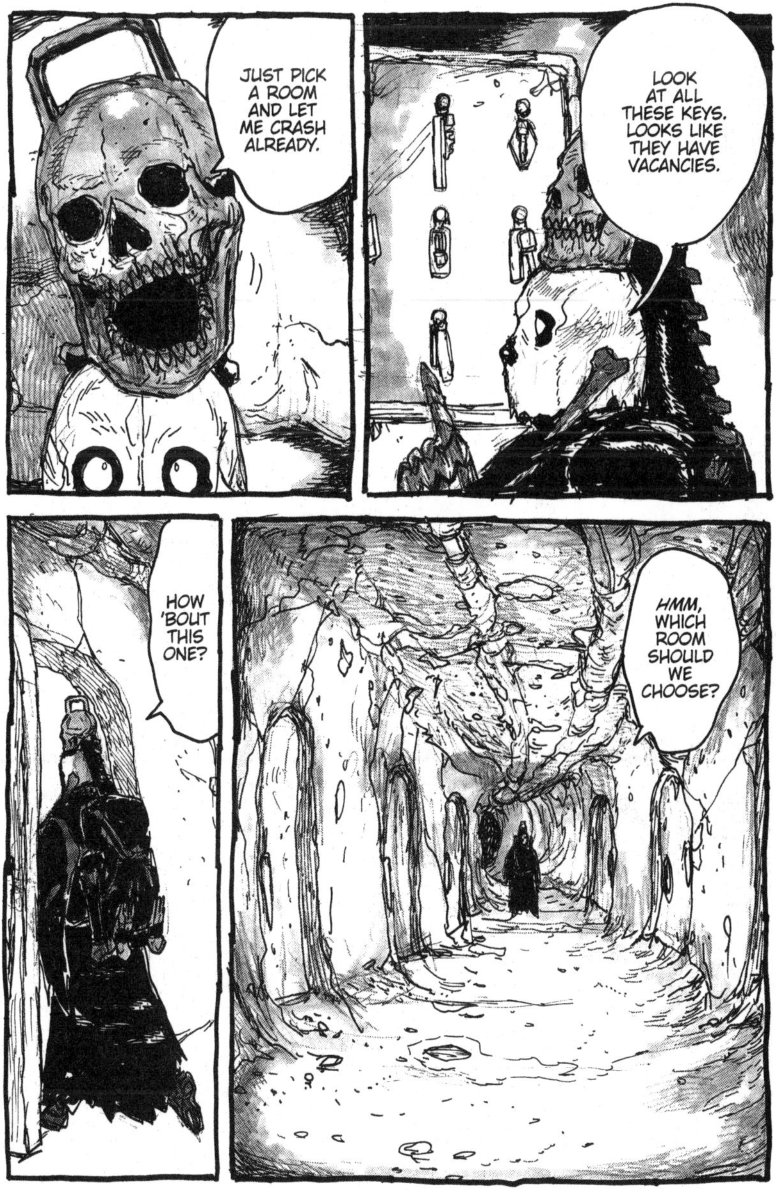
LOOK AT ALL THESE KEYS. LOOKS LIKE THEY HAVE VACANCIES.
JUST PICK A ROOM AND LET ME CRASH ALREADY.
HMM, WHICH ROOM SHOULD WE CHOOSE?
HOW 'BOUT THIS ONE?

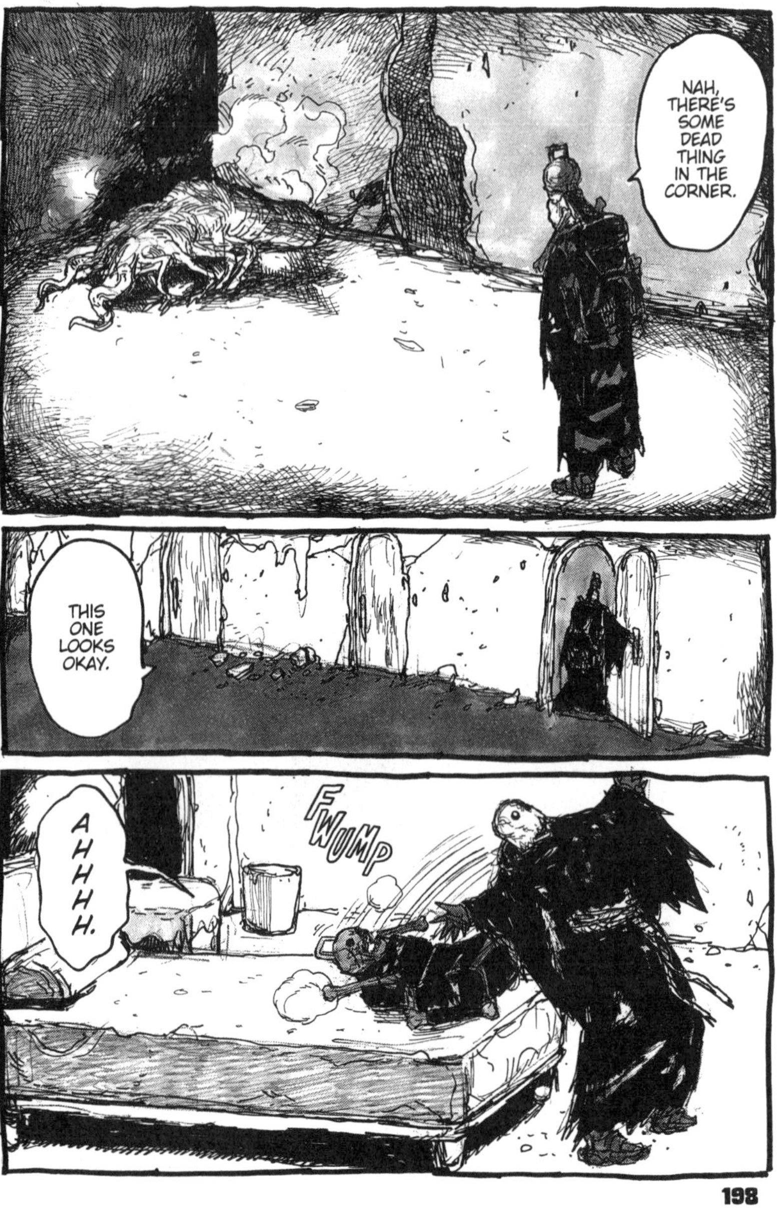
NAH, THERE'S SOME DEAD THING IN THE CORNER.
THIS ONE LOOKS OKAY.
FWUMP
AHHHH.

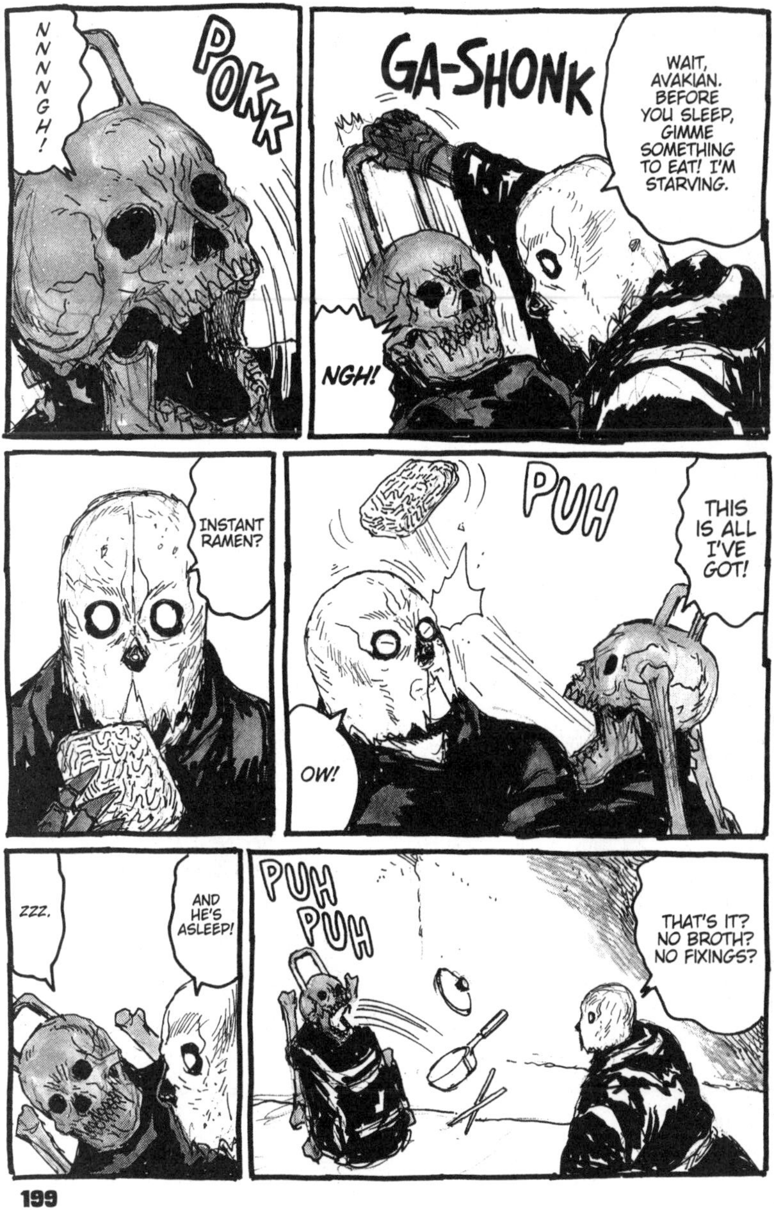
WAIT, AVAKIAN. BEFORE YOU SLEEP, GIMME SOMETHING TO EAT! I'M STARVING.
GA-SHONK
NGH!
POKK
NNNNGH!
THIS IS ALL I'VE GOT!
PUH
OW!
INSTANT RAMEN?
THAT'S IT? NO BROTH? NO FIXINGS?
PUH PUH
AND HE'S ASLEEP!
ZZZ.

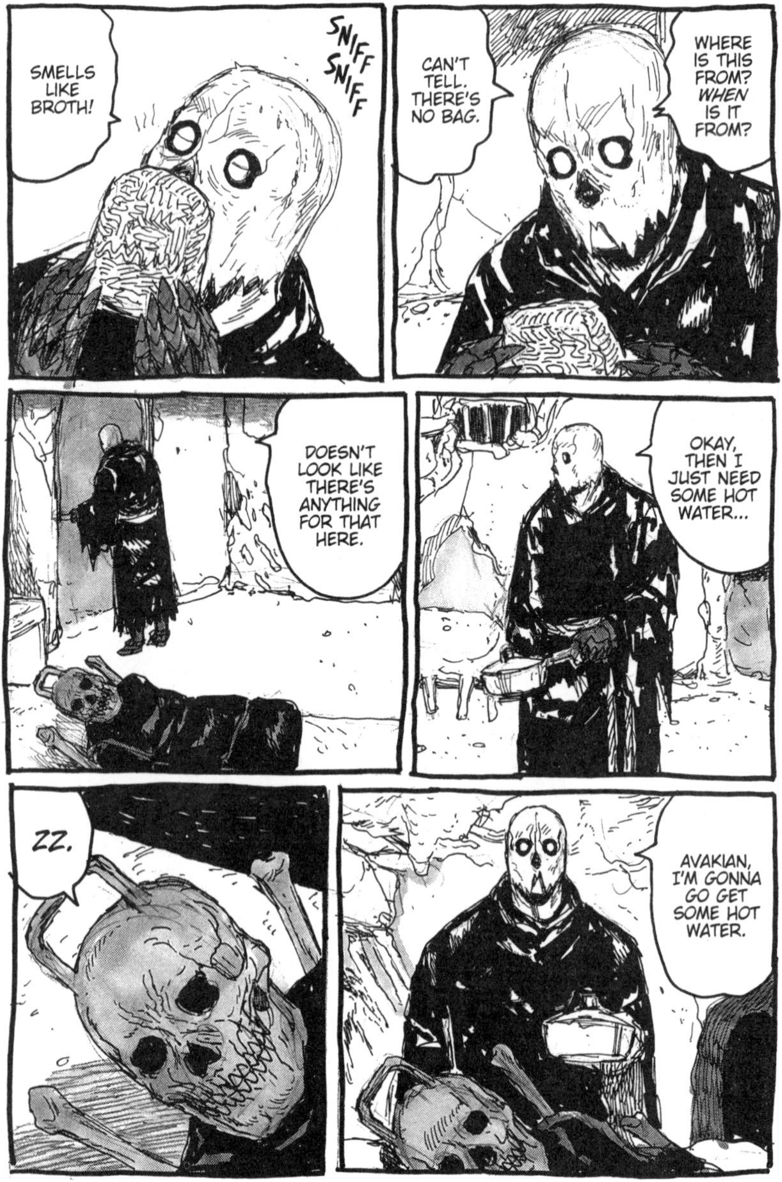
WHERE IS THIS FROM? *WHEN* IS IT FROM?
CAN'T TELL. THERE'S NO BAG.
SNIFF SNIFF
SMELLS LIKE BROTH!
OKAY, THEN I JUST NEED SOME HOT WATER...
DOESN'T LOOK LIKE THERE'S ANYTHING FOR THAT HERE.
AVAKIAN, I'M GONNA GO GET SOME HOT WATER.
ZZ.

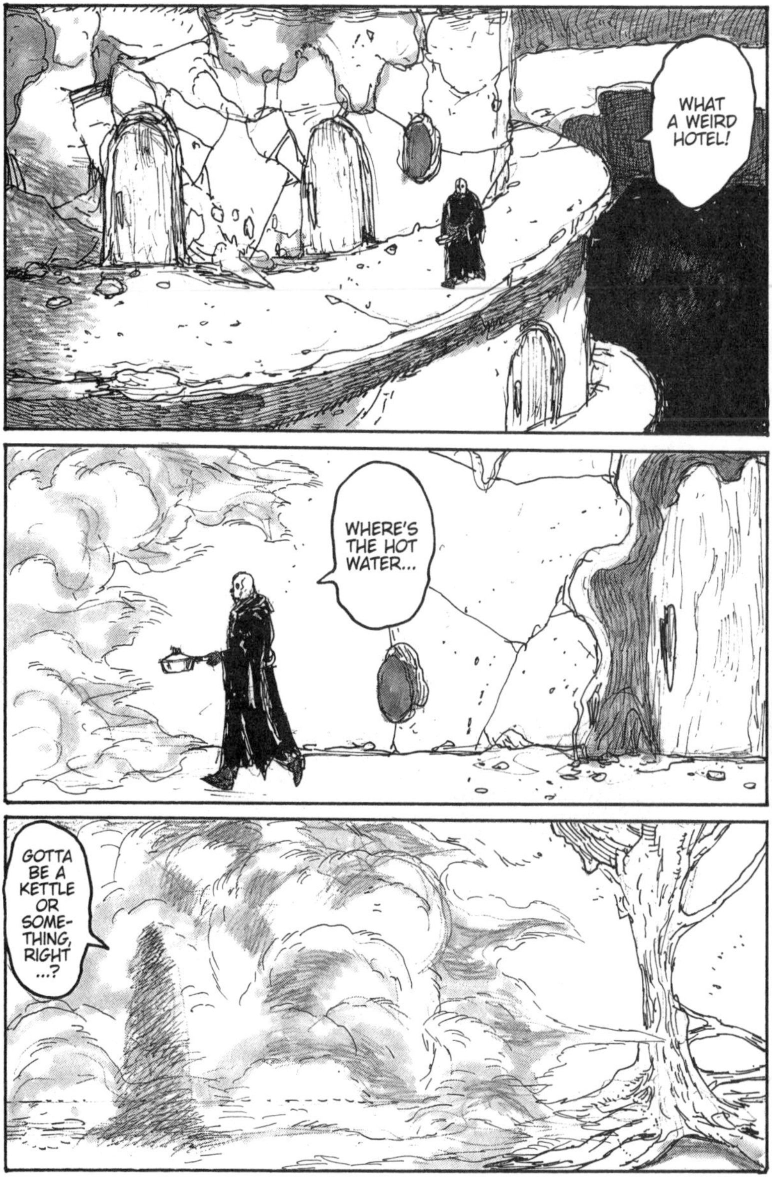
WHAT A WEIRD HOTEL!
WHERE'S THE HOT WATER...
GOTTA BE A KETTLE OR SOME-THING, RIGHT ...?

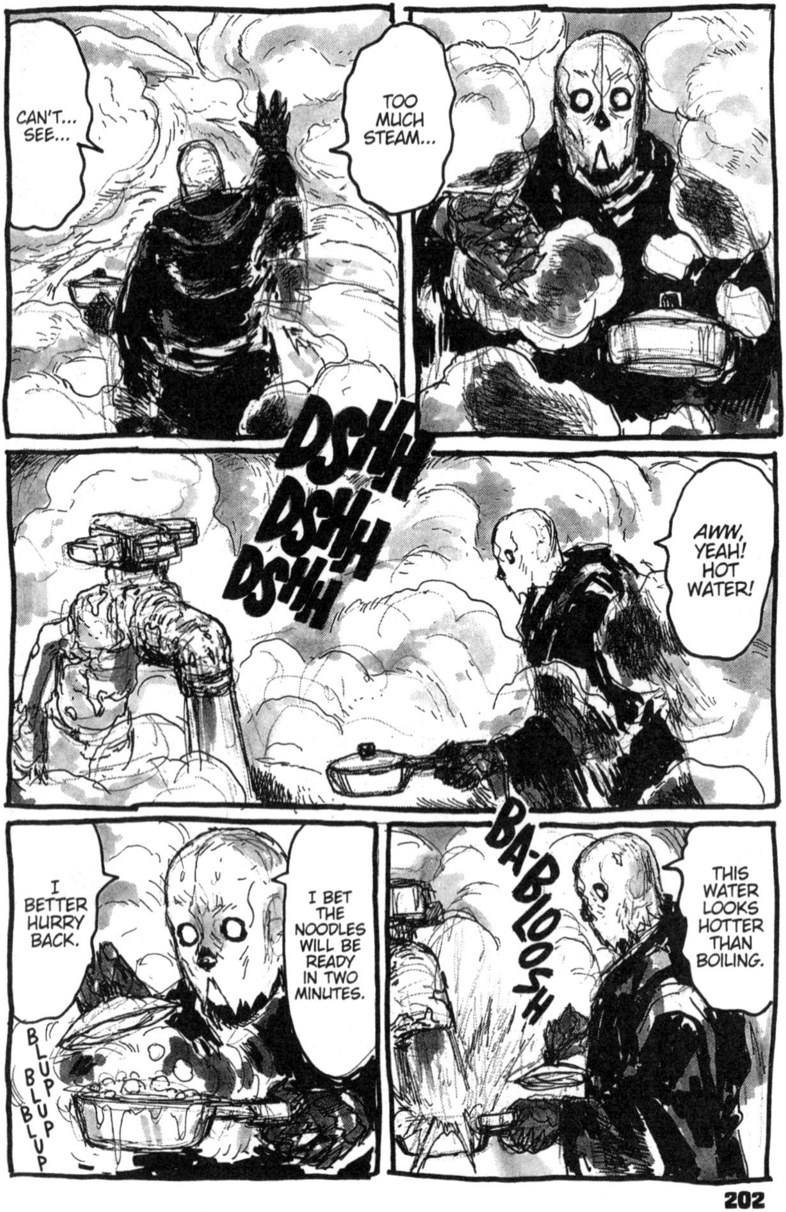
TOO MUCH STEAM...
CAN'T... SEE...
AWW, YEAH! HOT WATER!
DSHH DSHH DSHH
BA-BLOOSH
THIS WATER LOOKS HOTTER THAN BOILING.
I BET THE NOODLES WILL BE READY IN TWO MINUTES.
I BETTER HURRY BACK.
BLUP BLUP BLUP

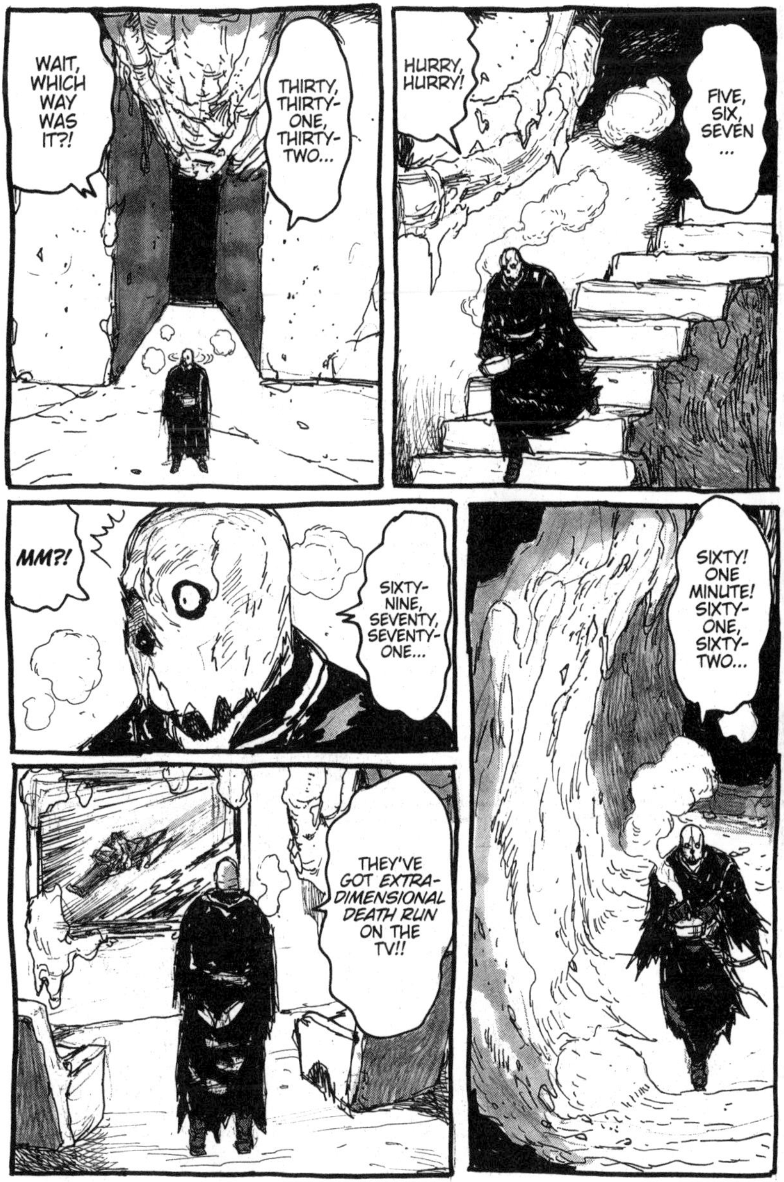
FIVE, SIX, SEVEN...
HURRY, HURRY!
THIRTY, THIRTY-ONE, THIRTY-TWO...
WAIT, WHICH WAY WAS IT?!
SIXTY! ONE MINUTE! SIXTY-ONE, SIXTY-TWO...
SIXTY-NINE, SEVENTY, SEVENTY-ONE...
MM?!
THEY'VE GOT *EXTRA-DIMENSIONAL DEATH RUN* ON THE TV!!

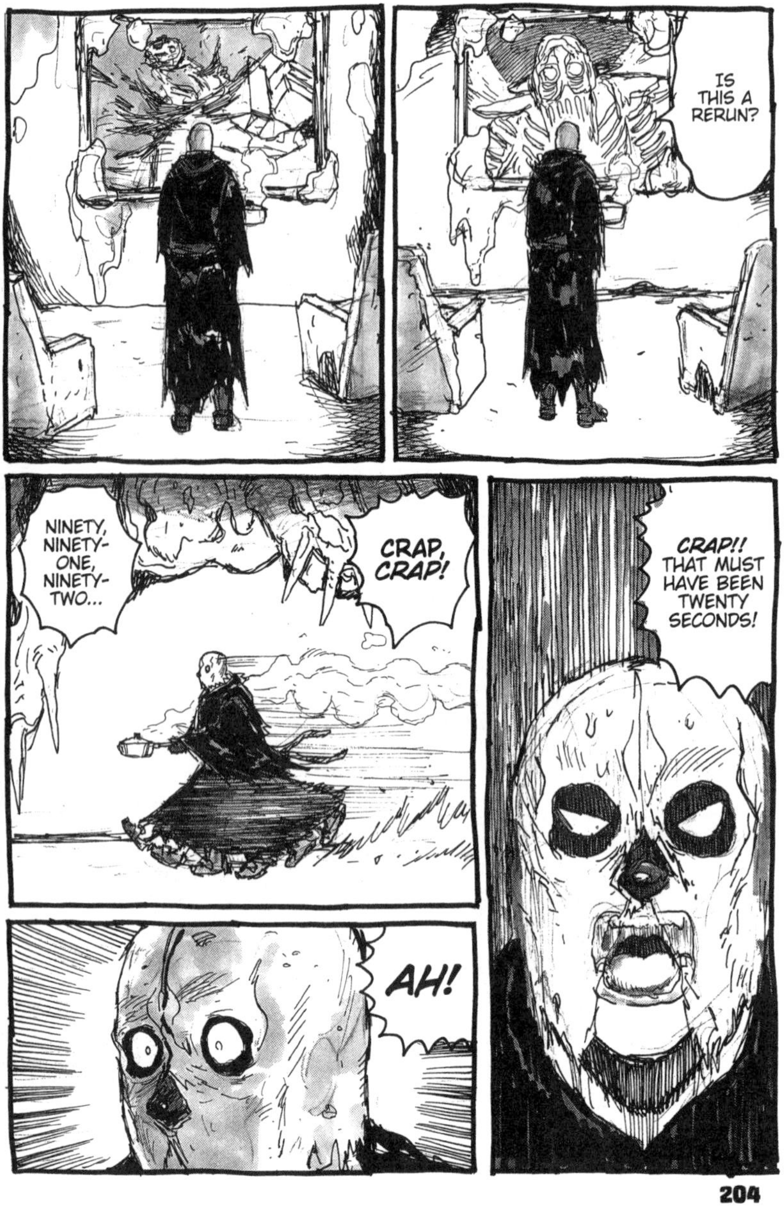
IS THIS A RERUN?
CRAP!! THAT MUST HAVE BEEN TWENTY SECONDS!
CRAP, CRAP!
NINETY, NINETY-ONE, NINETY-TWO...
AH!

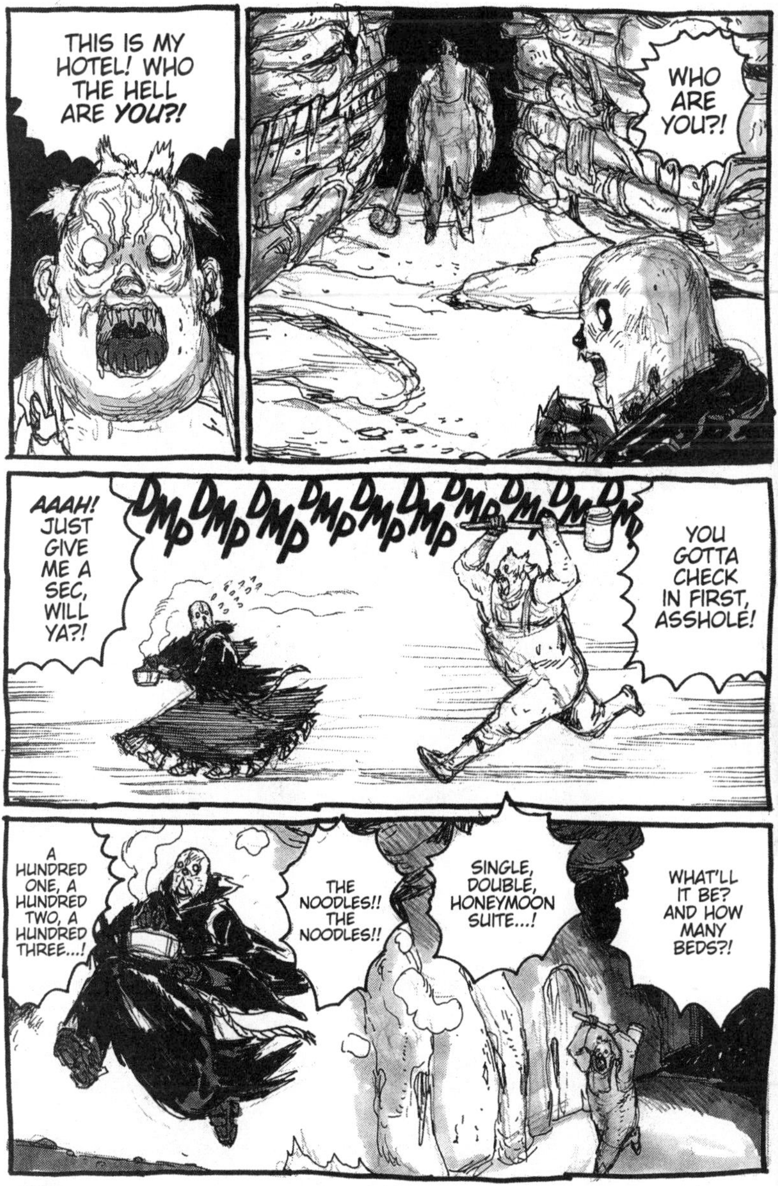
WHO ARE YOU?!
THIS IS MY HOTEL! WHO THE HELL ARE *YOU?!*
YOU GOTTA CHECK IN FIRST, ASSHOLE!
DMP DMP DMP DMP DMP DMP DMP DMP DMP DMP
AAAH! JUST GIVE ME A SEC, WILL YA?!
WHAT'LL IT BE? AND HOW MANY BEDS?!
SINGLE, DOUBLE, HONEYMOON SUITE...!
THE NOODLES!! THE NOODLES!!
A HUNDRED ONE, A HUNDRED TWO, A HUNDRED THREE...!

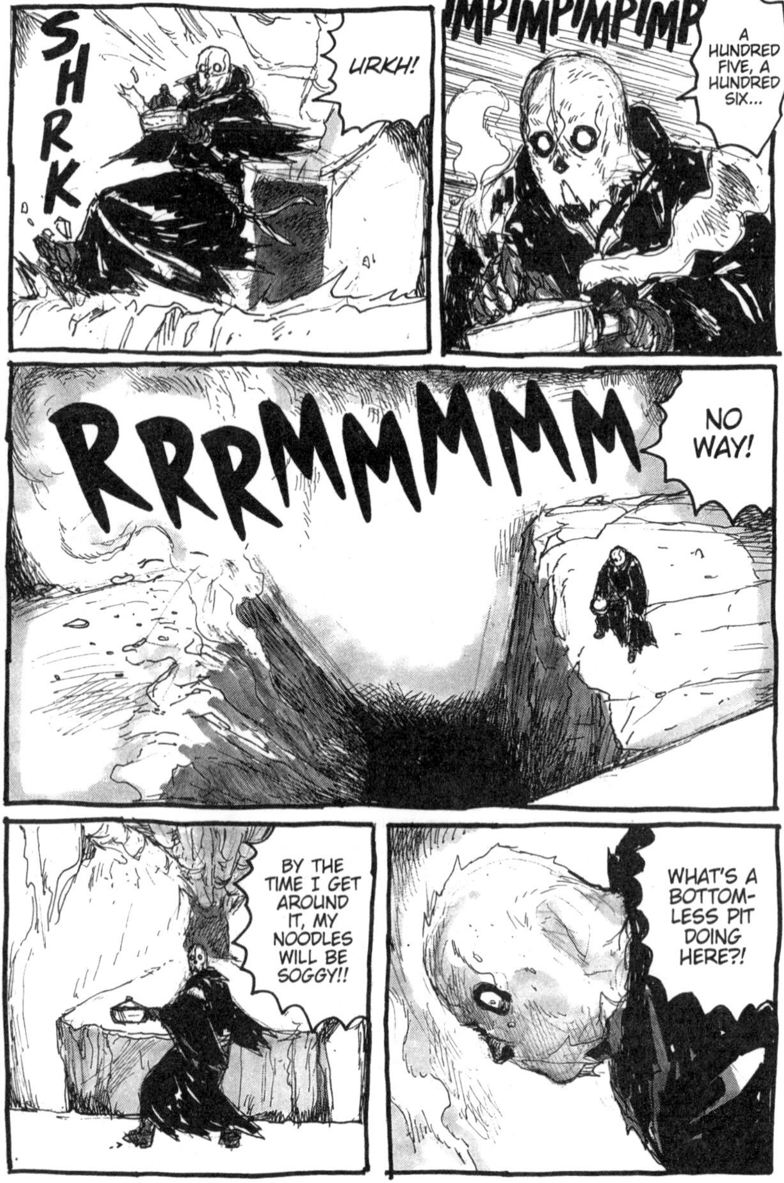
TMPTMPTMPTMP
A HUNDRED FIVE, A HUNDRED SIX...
SHRK
URKH!
RRRMMMMM
NO WAY!
WHAT'S A BOTTOM-LESS PIT DOING HERE?!
BY THE TIME I GET AROUND IT, MY NOODLES WILL BE SOGGY!!

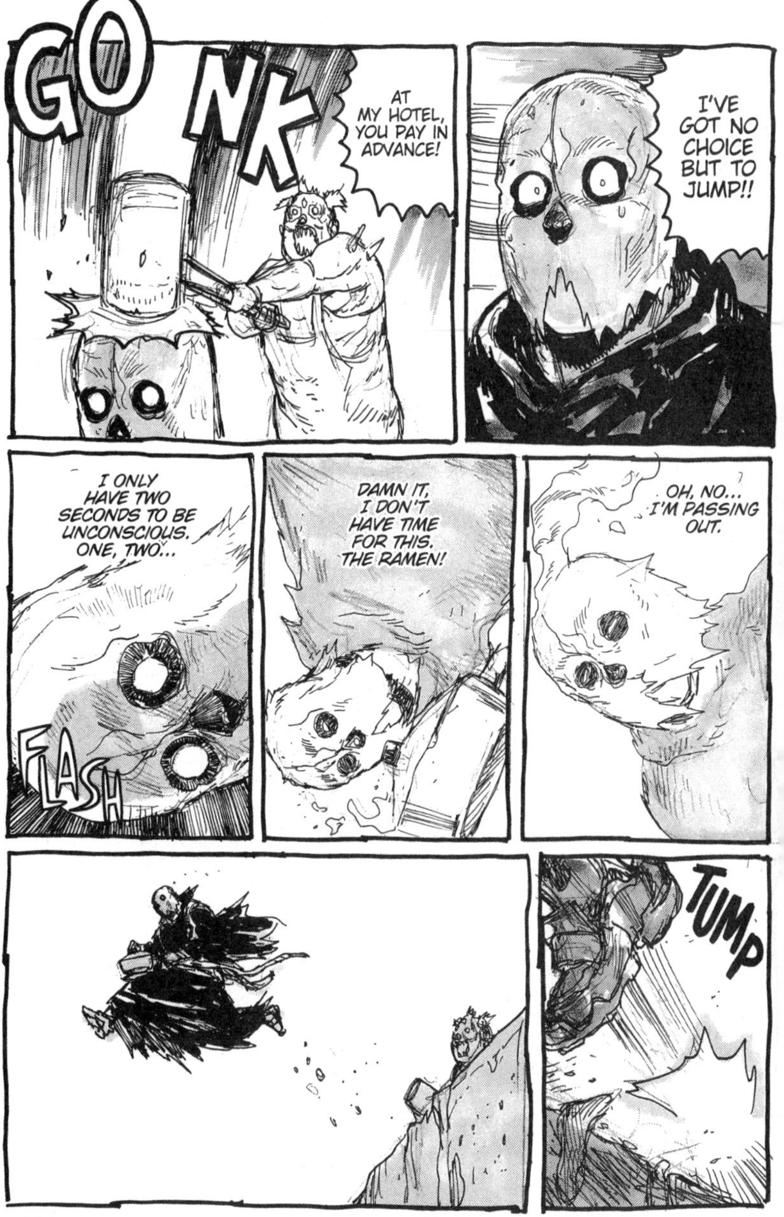
I'VE GOT NO CHOICE BUT TO JUMP!!
AT MY HOTEL, YOU PAY IN ADVANCE!
GONK
OH, NO... I'M PASSING OUT.
DAMN IT, I DON'T HAVE TIME FOR THIS. THE RAMEN!
I ONLY HAVE TWO SECONDS TO BE UNCONSCIOUS. ONE, TWO...
FLASH
TUMP

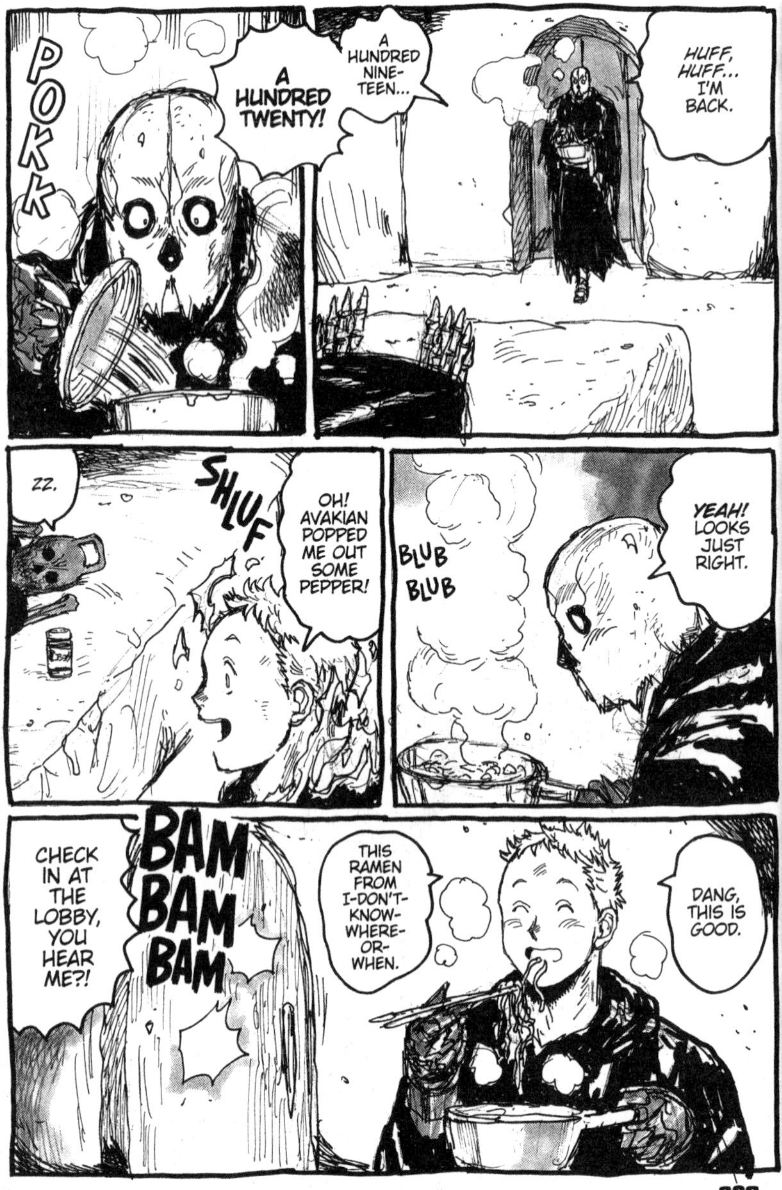
HUFF, HUFF... I'M BACK.
A HUNDRED NINETEEN...
A HUNDRED TWENTY!
POKK
YEAH! LOOKS JUST RIGHT.
BLUB BLUB
OH! AVAKIAN POPPED ME OUT SOME PEPPER!
SHLUF
ZZ.
DANG, THIS IS GOOD.
THIS RAMEN FROM I-DON'T-KNOW-WHERE-OR-WHEN.
BAM BAM BAM BAM
CHECK IN AT THE LOBBY, YOU HEAR ME?!

Dining on unidentified ramen in a hotel of mysterious management in some questionable location: delicious.

★ Design of Shimada Death (2)

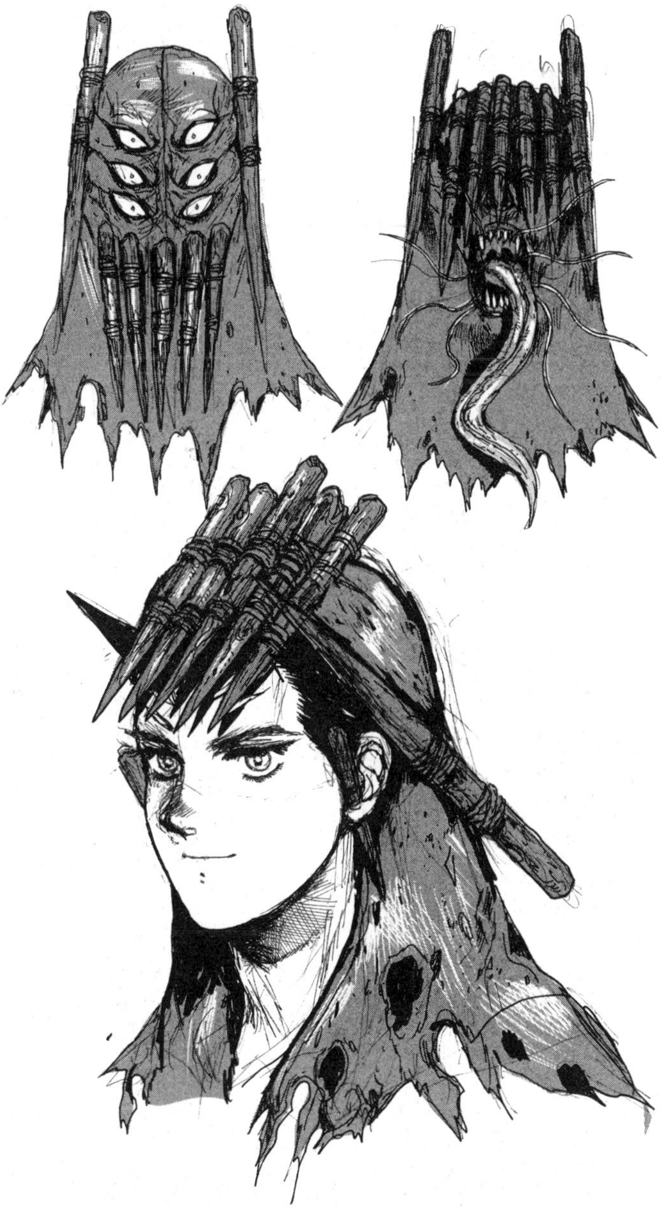

Dai Dark ① EXTRAS

And in volume 2...we're gonna

[A] [B] [C] [D] till we drop!

ACROSS

2. Setting of *Dai Dark*.
4. Cool word for the planet Earth.
7. Where the support minibot of 11 Down is connected to the main system.
9. 2 Across is an endless black _____.
10. The world of darkness inside a black hole.
15. What Sanko collects. Can be used to buy things from Misetani Box.
16. The *Treegun* is Sanko's _____.
18. How to make people hate you.
19. Zaha Sanko's favorite food.
20. Sanko's favorite weapon. Usually used for chopping down trees.

DOWN

1. One of Avakian's special skills. Used for combusting a pile of corpses.
3. What walls, skin, and human relationships develop.
5. Vast numbers of children were killed on the *Treegun* by Mini_____lings.
6. What Photosfere puts in each student on the *Treegun* for control.
8. The only place for tea and soda on 10 Across.
11. Name of Sanko's spaceship means "dead soul." How _____y!
12. Jumbo _____ dumplings.
13. Shimada's favorite food.
14. Poor ship that had its crew massacred to the last man by Sanko.
17. What everyone carries on their backs in this world. Sanko's is special.
18. Organism that can jump 150 times its height. Sucks blood.

SEVEN SEAS ENTERTAINMENT PRESENTS

DAI DARK

story and art by Q HAYASHIDA   VOLUME 1

TRANSLATION
Daniel Komen

ADAPTATION
Casey Lucas

LETTERING
Phil Christie

ORIGINAL COVER DESIGN
Shun SASAKI +
Yoko NAKANISHI(AYOND)

COVER DESIGN
Nicky Lim

PROOFREADER
Kurestin Armada

COPY EDITOR
Dawn Davis

EDITOR
J.P. Sullivan

PREPRESS TECHNICIAN
annon Rasmussen-Silverstein

PRODUCTION ASSISTANT
Christa Miesner

PRODUCTION MANAGER
Lissa Pattillo

MANAGING EDITOR
Julie Davis

ASSOCIATE PUBLISHER
Adam Arnold

PUBLISHER
Jason DeAngelis

DAI DARK Vol. 1
by Q HAYASHIDA
© 2019 Q HAYASHIDA
All rights reserved.
Original Japanese edition published by SHOGAKUKAN.
English translation rights in the United States of America, Canada and the
United Kingdom arranged with SHOGAKUKAN through Tuttle-Mori Agency, Inc.

Seven Seas press and purchase enquiries can be sent to Marketing Manager Lianne
Sentar at press@gomanga.com. Information regarding the distribution and purchase of
digital editions is available from Digital Manager CK Russell at digital@gomanga.com.

Seven Seas and the Seven Seas logo are trademarks of
Seven Seas Entertainment. All rights reserved.

ISBN: 978-1-64827-116-8
Printed in Canada
First Printing: April 2021
10 9 8 7 6 5 4 3 2 1

Crossword Puzzle Hidden Answer: SHOP

//// READING DIRECTIONS ////

This book reads from *right to left*,
Japanese style. If this is your first time
reading manga, you start reading from
the top right panel on each page and
take it from there. If you get lost, just
follow the numbered diagram here.
It may seem backwards at first,
but you'll get the hang of it! Have fun!!

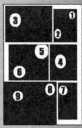